# TENSE AND ASPECT

OXFORD STUDIES IN COMPARATIVE SYNTAX
Richard Kayne, *General Editor*

# TENSE AND ASPECT
## From Semantics to Morphosyntax

*Alessandra Giorgi*
and
*Fabio Pianesi*

New York    Oxford
OXFORD UNIVERSITY PRESS
1997

## Oxford University Press

Oxford   New York

Athens   Auckland   Bangkok   Bogota   Bombay   Buenos Aires
Calcutta   Cape Town   Dar es Salaam   Delhi   Florence   Hong Kong
Istanbul   Karachi   Kuala Lumpur   Madras   Madrid   Melbourne
Mexico City   Nairobi   Paris   Singapore   Taipei   Tokyo   Toronto   Warsaw

and associated companies in
Berlin   Ibadan

Library of Congress Cataloging-in-Publication Data
Giorgi, Alessandra.
Tense and aspect : From semantics to morphosyntax / Alessandra Giorgi, Fabio Pianesi.
p.   cm. — (Oxford studies in comparative syntax)
Includes bibliographical references and index.
ISBN 0-19-509192-2; ISBN 0-19-509193-0 (pbk.)
1. Grammar. Comparative and general—Tense.   2. Grammar, Comparative and
general—Aspect.   3. Semantics.   4. Grammar, Comparative and general—Syntax.
5. Germanic languages—Grammar, Comparative—Romance.   6. Romance langues—
Grammar, Comparative—Germanic.   I. Pianesi, Fabio.   II. Title.   III. Series.
P281.G54   1997
415—dc20   96-29089

P
281
.G54
1997

# Acknowledgments

The elaboration of this book has taken several years during which we discussed the topics studied here with many scholars and students. We are grateful to all of them as their comments and suggestions have been precious for the development of our ideas. It is impossible to properly thank all of them, much to our regret. We can only express our strong feelings that without the help and support of the whole linguistics community we would never have been able to complete this work.

With some scholars, however, our intellectual debts are especially significant. *In primis*, our thanks go to Richard Kayne, for the time he dedicated to discuss our ideas, for his trust (we always thought: *in spite* of our ideas), and for his encouragement. Many thanks also to Guglielmo Cinque and James Higginbotham for their comments and suggestions. Special thanks to the people of the Italian community, who helped us through discussions, and also with their constant friendship and patience: Denis Delfitto, Anna Cardinaletti, Giuliana Giusti, Laura Brugè, Andrea Moro, Maria Teresa Guasti, Massimo Piattelli Palmarini, Maria Rita Manzini, Giorgio Graffi, Pier Marco Bertinetto, Cecilia Poletto, Paola Benincà, Laura Vanelli, Giuseppe Longobardi, Andrea Bonomi, VIeri Samek-Lodovici, Elena Giupponi, Adriana Belletti, Gennaro Chierchia, Luigi Rizzi, and Raffaella Zanuttini. Thanks also to S. Vikner, I. Heim, K. von Fintel, D. Pesetsky, M. Kenstowicz, K. Wexler, T. Taraldsen, M. DeGraff, S. Miyagawa, G. Brugger, A. Holmberg, C. Platzack, H. Sigurdsson, H. Thráinsson, O. Olafsson, J. Guéron, J.Y. Pollock, and I. Roberts for judgments and discussion. Thanks to Achille Varzi for fruitful discussion on the semantics of events. Special thanks to Stephen Trueman for being always available to provide judgments on odd pseudo-English sentences. Our gratitude to Christina Tortora, who rendered our English intelligible to real English speakers, beside providing judgments and comments. Alessandra Giorgi thanks her colleagues of the Faculty of Languages of Bergamo, especially Monica Berretta and Piera Molinelli, for their support and friendship. Fabio Pianesi thanks his colleagues at IRST, and especially Oliviero Stock, for their encouragement. Last but not least, Alessandra heartily thanks her friends Anna, Lorenza, Elsa, Gabriella, and Irene (Grazie!), and dedicates this book to her parents, Wanda and Maurizio. Fabio thanks Guiliana for her constant support, and dedicates this book to her, Marco, and Luca.

# Contents

# Symbols

# Introduction

This book considers the domain of the temporal and aspectual interpretation of sentences from a point of view of the interface between syntax and semantics. The empirical domain of investigation covers the Romance and Germanic languages, with special reference to Italian and English.

One of the reasons we wrote this book stems from the consideration that while it is possible to find a huge amount of important literature on the temporal and aspectual interpretation of utterances (on both the semantic and the morphosyntactic levels), considerably less has been written on the way the two levels are connected. The main questions to be answered in this respect are the following: How are the semantic values expressed by means of *words* or, rather, *morphemes*? What rules govern the interface—that is, the procedures operating between the two levels? Where is language variation in this picture? How do children acquire the temporal and aspectual system of their language; more generally, how do they learn to connect form and meaning with respect to the temporal and aspectual domain? We have only partial answers to these questions. Our aim is to address them and sketch some possible solutions and some lines for future research.

Let us stress again that this is a book on the syntax/semantics interface. We will address questions concerning morphology and word order on the one hand, and questions concerning tense, aspect, and Sequences of Tense (SOT) phenomena on the other. The focus, however, will always be on the relationships between the two levels.

In this book we adopt the minimalist framework recently developed by Chomsky (1995). In particular, we propose a theory of features to account for the crosslinguistic variation existing among Romance and Germanic languages in their temporal and aspectual systems.

From a theoretic and technical point of view, we will present two leading ideas. The first aims at providing an answer to the problem of morphological variation across languages. It can be observed that the same *tense* is realised differently in the various languages. For instance, a particular tense can be realised with or without an auxiliary (chapter 2), or the same tense may exhibit different constraints with respect to compatibility with temporal specifications (chapter 3). To explain these phenomena we develop the notions of *syncretic* and *hybrid* categories, which are typically found in flexive languages. A syncretic category, and similarly a hybrid category, is the structural realisation, in X-bar theoretic terms, of a bundle of features. That is, it is a single structural head projecting several morphological values. The structural realisation of categories is ruled by the Universal Ordering Constraint, which establishes that the features are universally ordered, and by the Feature Scattering Principle, which states that each feature *can*, but does not have to, head a projection. We will also show that this theoretical proposal correctly predicts some apparently unrelated phenomena, such as extraction from subjunctive sentences in Italian and complementiser deletion facts (chapter 5).

We think that the approach emerging from our investigation might also provide some insight on acquisition facts; where possible, we will discuss these questions. In particular, we will propose that the child selects from a universal inventory of features those relevant for his/her language. In this book we argue that the inventory of features from which the child selects, and the general mechanisms which project the structure from the bundles of features (the Universal Ordering Constraint and the Feature Scattering Principle) are universal components of grammar. On the basis of this analysis, we will show that it is not necessary to assume that the structure per se is universally given.

The second idea concerns the interface with semantic interpretation. We will propose some interface conditions which might also have import for a Sequence of Tense theory, even though we will not provide a full theory of SOT phenomena. It is well known that events must be temporally ordered with respect to temporal *anchors* (see Enç 1987). To simplify somewhat, the event of the main clause is anchored to the speech event. The event of an embedded clause is anchored to the event of the superordinate clause. We argue that the events which provide a temporal anchoring are all conceptualised as punctual, as far as their anchoring role is concerned. The punctuality of the anchoring event will be shown to interact with the morphosyntactic properties of languages. We will show that such an analysis explains many phenomena, in both the temporal and the aspectual domains (chapter 4 and chapter 6).

This book is organised as follows. In the first chapter we briefly sketch the theoretical background. We discuss the semantic hypotheses concerning the representation of tenses—namely, the operator hypothesis versus the so-called referential approach—and we briefly review some arguments in favour of the second. Then we summarise the basic concepts of the minimalist approach and illustrate the notions of *syncretic* and *hybrid* category.

In the second chapter we argue in favour of a referential, neo-Reichenbachian theory of tense, and propose some principles in the mapping between semantic representations and morphosyntactic structures. We will show that our proposal correctly accounts for the differences among the systems of Italian, Latin, and Portuguese. The comparison among these languages is particularly interesting because their systems differ minimally from each other, with respect to the way tenses are morphologically expressed. The Portuguese system exhibits intermediate properties with respect to Italian and Latin. In particular, we will show that our theory can predict the presence or the absence of an auxiliary verb, as a consequence of the interface system we are proposing.

In the third chapter we extend our analysis to English and to the other Germanic languages. We further develop the notions of syncretic and hybrid categories, showing that they make the correct predictions setting apart English and the Mainland Scandinavian languages from Romance and the other Germanic languages. Interestingly, this morphosyntactic bipartition is also found when considering the peculiar interpretative properties of the present perfect in Romance and Germanic, a set of phenomena which are often referred to the *present perfect puzzle*. We will propose a theoretical account for these facts, arguing in favour of the existence of temporal *arguments*, as real arguments in the thematic grid of predicates.

In the fourth chapter we apply our theory to the interpretation of the present tense in the Romance/Germanic languages on the one hand, and to the properties of the present-in-the-past interpretation of embedded predicates, on the other. We also propose that anchoring events have the property of being *punctual*. While in the third chapter the interface questions were investigated from the point of view of temporal interpretation, in this chapter the focus will be mainly on aspectual facts.

In the fifth chapter we consider embedded contexts in more detail, analysing the distribution of the subjunctive. Interesting theoretical insights come from the analysis of languages where the subjunctive is missing, or obsolete, and we will show how our interface approach can account for much of the variation found in the Romance/Germanic domain.

In the last chapter, we briefly consider the Double Accessibility Reading, a property of the present tense in embedded contexts. We will show that this phenomenon can be captured by means of our hypotheses without any additional stipulations.

The authors have elaborated every part of this book together. As far as academic requirements are concerned, A. Giorgi takes official responsibility for chapter 1, §1.1; chapter 2 §2.1, §2.2, §2.3, and the appendix; chapter 3 §3.1, §3.2.1, §3.2.2, §3.2.3 and the appendix; chapter 4 §4.1.5.3, § 4.1.5.4, §4.1.5.5, and §4.2; chapter 5 §5.1.10 and §5.2; chapter 6. F. Pianesi takes official responsibility for chapter 1 §1.2 and §1.3; chapter 2 §2.4 and §2.5; chapter 3 §3.2.4, §3.2.5, §3.2.6, §3.3, and §3.4; chapter 4 §4.1.1, §4.1.2, §4.1.3, §4.1.4, §4.1.5.1, and §4.1.5.2; chapter 5 §5.1.1, §5.1.2, §5.1.3, §5.1.4, §5.1.5, §5.1.6, §5.1.7, §5.1.8, and §5.1.9.

# TENSE AND ASPECT

# 1

# The Syntactic and Semantic Background

## 1.1. The syntactic framework

In this book we analyse some phenomena concerning the temporal and aspectual interpretation in Italian and English, extending some of the conclusions to the Romance domain and to some Germanic languages. The level of investigation is the interface between semantics and morphosyntax. We consider some questions concerning the rules and the principles governing the expression of the semantic information concerning tense and aspect by means of temporal and aspectual morphemes realised on the verb.[1]

### 1.1.1. The Split-Infl hypothesis

The analysis of verbal morphemes has become more and more important for linguistic investigation in generative grammar starting from Pollock's (1989; see also Moro 1988) proposals on clausal architecture — that is, the formulation of the so-called Split-Infl hypothesis. According to this hypothesis, the node I, the head of the clause, has to be split in two different projections. One, called AGR, is for agreement features, gender, number, and person, and the other, called T, is for temporal features. Pollock's analysis was mainly based on the distribution of negation and adverbials along the lines originally developed by Emonds (1976). Pollock (see also Guéron 1993) proposed that the head of the clause is the temporal projection T; according to other scholars (Chomsky 1991; Belletti 1990) the head is AGR. In this work we assume that AGR is higher than T, even though we recognise that it might be a rather controversial hypothesis.[2] Pollock's (1989) discussion is based on *distributional* evidence — that is, on the analysis of the distribution in a sentence of the verb, the auxiliary, negation, and various adverbs. The crucial idea is that different linear orders are not due to a different base position of negation or adverbs with respect to the verb and to the auxiliary but are determined by an application of the rule *Move-α*, which raises the verbal head to a different position. Differences in head-movement determine the differences among sentences of the same language and across languages. Such a hypothesis has to be preferred to the alternative one in which the adverb and negation move because it is justified on a morphological basis. The verb in fact raises to incorporate its morphological endings. Moreover, as discussed at length by Pollock (1989), AGR and T can be separated by intervening projections, given that they are two distinct heads. Accordingly, certain distributional facts can be accounted for by hypothesising that the NEG projection occurs between the two. Let us briefly illustrate the relevant evidence:

(1)    John has not seen Mary.

(2)    Jean n'a pas vue Marie.

In this case English and French behave alike in that the auxiliary precedes negation (*not* in English and *pas* in French) in both languages. Consider the following example, however:

(3)    John does not see Mary.

(4)    Jean ne voit pas Marie.

Abstracting away from the presence of the auxiliary *do* in English, the two languages in this case exhibit a contrast, given that the negation precedes the main verb in English but follows it in French. Consider now the distribution of an adverb such as *often* (French *souvent*), which is generated in the *Spec* of the V projection:[3]

(5)    a. Jean a souvent vu Marie.
       b. John has often seen Mary.

(6)    a. Jean voit souvent Marie.
       b. John often sees Mary.

Again, English and French do not differ when there is an auxiliary, compare examples (5a) and (5b), and diverge when there is a simple verbal form, cf. examples (6a) and (6b). These data have been explained by proposing that auxiliaries raise from the basic position to the highest functional projection, which is T according to Pollock (1989) and AGR according to other scholars. Full verbs move in this way in French, but not in English. The raising of the full verb in French through T and AGR (or conversely AGR and T) determines the observed linear order, because it passes over the VP adverbial *souvent* and over the NEG projection to land in the highest functional projection. Full verbs do not move at all in English, and therefore the verb is preceded by negation in (3) and by the adverb in (5b). Italian (see Belletti 1990) is almost like French. Consider the following examples:

(7)    a. Gianni non ha più incontrato Maria.
          Gianni *non*-has NEG met Maria.[4]
       b. Gianni non incontra più Maria.
          Lit.: Gianni *non* meets NEG Maria (G. does not meet M.).

(8)    a.  Gianni ha spesso incontrato Maria.
            Gianni has often met Maria.
      b.  Gianni incontra spesso Maria.
            Lit.: Gianni meets often Maria.
            Gianni often meets Maria.

Both the auxiliary and the full verb precede negation and the VP adverb. Consider
the infinitival forms, however:

(9)    a.  Ne pas recontrer Marie. . .
            Lit.: To not NEG meet Marie
      b.  Rencontrer souvent Marie. . .
            Lit.: To meet Marie often

(10)   a.  Non incontrare più Maria. . .
            Lit.: Not to meet NEG Maria
      b.  Incontrare spesso Maria. . .
            Lit.: To meet often Maria

In French the infinitive does not move past the negation, but it does move past
the VP adverb — that is, it is raised to the intermediate functional projection
(AGR according to Pollock, or T, according to Belletti). In Italian, on the other
hand, there is no difference between infinite and finite verbal forms. The verb
always raises over both the VP adverb and negation.[5]

Summarising, these data show that the Split-Infl hypothesis makes the
correct predictions on linear order in various languages. In fact, the data
illustrated above could not be explained by resorting to a single projection I.
Moreover, this discussion shows that languages can exploit various movement
options, such as no verb-movement at all (English), long and short
verb-movement (French), and long verb-movement (Italian). Finally, the
splitting of I creates an additional *Spec* position, namely, the *Spec* of T. In the
literature there are various speculations on the role of this position. It has been
claimed that the *Spec* of T is the locus for temporal projections, as is the case,
for instance, for Stowell's (1992) ZP (*Zeit Phrase*). It has also been claimed that
it is an A position available for subjects, as, for instance, in Icelandic (see Jonas
& Bobaljik 1993). We will briefly discuss this question in the following
chapter, §2.3.[6]

From a conceptual point of view, Pollock's proposal raises several questions
which deserve further research. On the one hand, the nature and the syntactic
properties of the functional categories, AGR and T (and of the other ones which
have been hypothesised in several recent works) must be rendered more precise.
On the other, the representation of the temporal and aspectual interpretation
which is associated to the category T must be more deeply investigated.[7]

The aim of this work is to connect the morphosyntactic level with the
semantic representation of tense and aspect. Therefore we will briefly illustrate
our assumptions concerning morphosyntax on the one hand and the temporal
representation on the other. Recall that in frameworks preceding the Split-Infl

hypothesis, no explicit mention of a temporal projection was made, and the temporal information was listed together with agreement features. In spite of this, there are several works on the morphosyntax of tense in the generative framework preceding the Split-Infl hypothesis, which we will take into account in the following chapters.[8]

Let us summarise here our starting point. Abstracting away from periphrasis and adverbials, in natural languages tense and aspect are typically expressed by means of verbal morphology. Our hypothesis is that languages (and the various sentences in the same language) convey different temporal and aspectual information because the morphemes expressing tense and aspect exhibit different properties. According to this view, the hypothesis can be formulated as follows: the differences across languages in the temporal and aspectual interpretation are due to, and can be explained by, differences in the morphological system which is employed to express them. In this way the temporal and aspectual system of a given language might become predictable from a theoretical point of view and, most important, it is possible to explain the acquisition process in the tense and aspect domain.

In this work it will be shown that the differences in the morphosyntactic realisation of the temporal and verbal categories between, for example, Italian and English, play a major role in accounting for subtle differences in the interpretive domain. Moreover, in his recent works Chomsky recognises the importance of morphological variation, proposing that morphology is the *locus* of crosslinguistic differences and parametrisation. This idea, that parameters are part of lexical information, is not a new one, having been proposed and argued for in the 1980s by Borer (1984) and by Wexler and Manzini (1988) among others, even if it has never been applied to the domain of temporal and aspectual interpretation before. In this work we argue that such a view is correct and try to reformulate it in the minimalist framework, which seems to us the most appropriate framework with which to capture and express the idea of parameters as morphological variation.

### 1.1.2. Chomsky's minimalist approach

In this section we introduce the minimalist framework, which constitutes the theoretical basis of this work. We will review here only the points which are important to the subsequent analysis.

Chomsky (1994) proposes that the structure $\Sigma$ is built out of an *array*, or better, a *Numeration (N)*, of lexical choices. Given $N$, the computational system ($C_{HL}$) computes until it converges at PF and LF, yielding the pair $(\pi, \lambda)$, where $\pi$ is interpreted at the articulatory-perceptual interface and $\lambda$ at the conceptual-intentional interface. $\pi$ is a PF representation, and $\lambda$ is an LF representation. The derivation is said to converge at a certain level if it yields a representation that is interpretable at that level. It *converges* if it yields representations that are interpretable both at LF and at PF. According to this hypothesis, D-structure and S-structure are no longer needed, and a system is obtained where the only levels of representation are the interfaces LF and PF.

Chomsky (p. 5) also points out that not every pair $(\pi, \lambda)$ formed by a convergent derivation is a linguistic expression of L — namely, of the language in question. To obtain this result, the relevant derivation must also be the *optimal* one. That is, it must satisfy certain natural economy conditions. Less economical derivations are blocked in favour of the most economical one.[9] Finally, Chomsky (1994) points out that economy considerations apply only to alternative derivations starting from *the same* array.[10]

At any step of the derivation, the structure $\Sigma$ is constituted only of the elements already present in $N$, and nothing else can be added by the computation itself. Most important, the elements constituting the initial array which are selected from the lexicon are bundles of features, either lexical, morphological, or phonological.[11]

The operation Spell-Out plays a crucial role in the general structure of the minimalist approach. Its successful application is strongly connected with the morphological properties of lexical items. Spell-Out may apply to the structure $\Sigma$ already formed at any point in the derivation. It *strips away* from $\Sigma$ those elements relevant to PF (that is, the phonological features), leaving those relevant to LF. It then delivers $\Sigma_\pi$ (i.e., the stripped $\Sigma$) to morphology, which builds word-like units. Chomsky calls the subsystem mapping the output of morphology to PF the *phonological component*, whereas the system which continues the computation to LF is called the *covert component*. The derivation does not converge if the initial array has not been entirely consumed. Given that after Spell-Out neither the phonological nor the covert component has any further access to the numeration, the latter must be empty when Spell-Out applies.[12] The Spell-Out operation can take place anywhere. The derivation does not converge — that is, it *crashes* if the wrong choice has been made. Notice also that any distinction between pre- and post-Spell-Out is taken to be a reflex of morphology within the phonological component.

### 1.1.2.1. Phrase structure theory

A phrase marker is formed by two operations — namely, *Merge* and *Move-α*. Merge forms larger units starting from those already constructed. Such larger units are sets so that the result of applying Merge to $\alpha$ and $\beta$ is $\{\alpha, \beta\}$. An independent process of *feature projection* (Project) determines the *label* of this new object, in such a way that, for example, nominal constituents can be distinguished by verbal ones at the interfaces. The label, $\delta$, is a set of features which must be constructed from the two constituents $\alpha$ and $\beta$. Chomsky (1994) shows that $\delta$ is either $\alpha$ or $\beta$, one of the two thus becoming the head. Hence, the result of the complex operation Merge + Project (or Move + Project, see following discussion) as applied to $\alpha$ and $\beta$ is $\gamma = \{\delta, \{\alpha, \beta\}\}$, where $\delta$ is the projecting head. In this sense, the complex operation thus formed (which we may continue to call Merge [Move] for the sake of convenience) is asymmetric since, of the two objects it applies to, only one projects. Finally, Merge is, by definition, a binary operation. Therefore unary projections are disallowed. Such a welcome consequence follows without any further stipulation.

The operation Move can be either a substitution or an adjunction operation. Substitution can be described as follows. Given the phrase markers $\Sigma$, Move selects $K$ and $\alpha$, such that either $K$ dominates or c-commands $\alpha$. It then forms the new constituent $\gamma = \{\delta, \{K, \alpha\}\}$ and the chain $(\alpha_1, \alpha_2)$. Moreover, according to Chomsky, the targeted constituent, $K$, always projects so that the label of $\gamma$ is the head of $K$.

We have been mentioning *phrase markers*. In this system, however, phrase markers do not have a theoretical status anymore, because the only relevant notion is the one of unordered *set*.[13] Left-to-right ordering is a distinctive feature of phrase markers, whereas such a notion is meaningless by definition if applied to unordered sets. Following Chomsky, we will continue to use phrase markers to represent the structure of sentences, because it is a simple and familiar way to visualise linguistic structures, even if the notion has a different meaning in the present framework with respect to the pre-minimalist one.

Adjunction is a movement operation which forms a two-segment category, differing in this respect from the operation substitution which forms a new category; Chomsky (1994, p. 23) also points out that adjunction is a very limited option in the minimalist framework. For the purposes of our work it will not be considered further.

### 1.1.2.2. Movement theory

A crucial contribution of the minimalist approach is the clarification of the notion of movement. We already saw that the repertoire of basic operations contains Move, which does not crucially differ from the Move-$\alpha$ of GB theory (at least according to the formulation given so far, but see following discussion). It is now possible, however, to motivate the existence of such an operation, and of movement tout court, by giving a precise formulation to ideas that have been around in the GB literature for quite a long time. Crucially, movement of a linguistic object $\alpha$ is due to the necessity of satisfying properties of $\alpha$ itself. That is, movement is only admitted if (essentially morphological) properties of $\alpha$ would not be otherwise satisfied in the derivation. Such properties are encoded by the features forming the content of the linguistic object, and the satisfaction process is realised by means of a process (checking) that (1) pairs the relevant feature(s) of $\alpha$ with those of a suitable category (the target), and (2) accepts or rejects the input configuration depending on whether the features match. Furthermore, upon rejection the derivation crashes. It follows, as a natural consequence of this theory, that movement only affects objects having unchecked features (that is, properties not yet satisfied).[14] With these modifications the operation Move has not ordered pairs of linguistic objects in its domain (the mover and the target) anymore but ordered pairs of features $<f_1, f_2>$. In such a pair, $f_1$ is unchecked, and the result of Move is a configuration in which $f_1$ is in a checking relation with $f_2$. Therefore, Move-$\alpha$ (for $\alpha$ a category) is replaced by Move-F (for F a feature).

This view of movement has a number of theoretical and empirical advantages over previous formulations. For instance, as already observed (see fn. 14) there is no need for additional principles restricting movements to self serving cases (therefore preventing a category from moving for the sake of some other constituent). The highly goal-directed behaviour of Move is simply due to the fact that it only sees unchecked features. Such a state of affairs, in its turn, requires that the features of a structure $\Sigma$ be appropriately marked so that the distinction between checked and non-checked ones may be readily available.

### 1.1.2.3. Features

Before addressing the latter question, however, let us see where features originate. As already said, in a sense linguistic objects are nothing but features and feature aggregates. For example, Chomsky (1993) represents a lexical item $l$ as $\{\alpha, \{F_1, F_2, \ldots, F_n\}\}$, where $\alpha$ is a morphological complex and $F_1 \ldots F_n$ are inflectional features (the ones we have been mainly dealing with up to now). We can safely extend those features so as to encode all the relevant properties of $l$, be they semantic or syntactic (or even phonological) ones. Some of these features are intrinsic to the item itself — for example, expressing the fact that *man* is a noun (its categorial features), that it refers to an animate entity, and so on. Other features such as case and $\phi$-features are not intrinsic but are determined by its being a noun, and it can be assumed that they are not listed in the lexicon but are added before the given lexical item is used in an actual derivation. Whether this happens when the item is inserted in the numeration $N$ or at the point in which it is extracted from $N$ to be used in the derivation (by the operation Select) is something that need not concern us here.[15]

Returning to the question of the status of checked features, note that there are two properties a feature may exhibit: (a) that of being available (visible) to $C_{HL}$, which determines its capability of entering checking relations, and (b) the property of being visible (interpretable) at the interface (either LF or PF, though we will mainly consider here the first case). At any stage of a derivation the state of a feature can be exhaustively characterised according to whether it has or does not have the relevant properties. There are four logical possibilities: a given feature may either have both property $a$ and $b$, let us say that it is in the state $(a, b)$; or it may satisfy property $a$ but not $b$, $(a, \neg b)$; property $b$ but not $a$, $(\neg a, b)$, and, finally, none of them $(\neg a, \neg b)$. The third logical possibility can be excluded by requiring interpretable features (those visible to LF) to be always available to $C_{HL}$; therefore $b$ entails $a$ (cf. Chomsky 1995 §5.2) The last possibility corresponds to the case in which the feature is neither interpretable nor available to $C_{HL}$, thus it is absent, either erased after checking or not present in the initial numeration. Finally, the second possibility corresponds to a feature that is not interpretable but continues to play a role in the computation.[16] The

condition of convergence at LF is now that each feature be either *(a, b)* or
*(¬a, ¬b)*.

Returning to Move-F, it takes a pair $<f_1, f_2>$ where $f_1$ is an unchecked feature
producing a configuration in which $f_1$ is in a checking relation with $f_2$. In other
words, $f_1$ is in the domain of Move-F only if its state is *(a, b)* or *(a, ¬b)*.
Checking may affect the state of $f_1$, by changing the *a* property (*b*, being an
intrinsic property, cannot be affected by any operation of $C_{HL}$). Since $C_{HL}$ is
uniform in $N \rightarrow \lambda$, if a feature is to undergo checking it must be visible to $C_{HL}$
from the very beginning. Thus we can exclude transitions of the type $\neg a \rightarrow a$.
Therefore, checking can only affect the state of a feature by making a previously
visible feature invisible — that is, by turning *a* into *¬a*. Now, keeping in mind
that *b* entails *a*, the only possible state transition for a feature is
*(a, ¬b)* → *(¬a, ¬b)*. Finally, observe that economy considerations dictate that
state transitions due to checking be performed whenever possible — that is,
whenever the resulting configuration does not prevent the derivation from
converging. For instance, the transition must be blocked if it were to make
non-visible a strong feature that would otherwise provide a position for an item
selected from the numeration, or if it resulted in the erasure of an entire term
(Chomsky 1995).[17]

In order to exemplify, consider a case in which a feature remains active after
checking. This is the case for the φ-features of the subject of simple adjectival
constructions (Chomsky 1995, ex. 55):

(11)    John is [$_{AGR-P}$  t'  AGR [$_{AP}$  t   intelligent ]]

The φ-features of a DP are interpretable. Hence, at the beginning of the
computation the φ-features of the subject *John* are *(a, b)*. Checking first takes
place in the *Spec* of the embedded AGR-P (by subject raising) to realise
agreement with the adjective. Then the subject moves to the *Spec* of the higher
$AGR_S$ for Case checking. This process independently triggers agreement with the
verb in the $AGR_S$ position. Therefore, φ-features do not disappear, once checked.
This is expected if the φ-features of a DP are always interpretable, so that their
only admissible state is *(a, b)*, throughout the derivation.

The Case feature, on the other hand, provides an instance of the only
admissible state transition *(a, ¬b)* → *(¬a, ¬b)*. Case is a purely formal feature,
being non-interpretable. Thus, once entered into a checking configuration, it
disappears. That is, it becomes invisible to further operations of $C_{HL}$. It is
important to note that formal features must undergo the described transition to
prevent the derivation from crashing at the interface (LF) because of the presence
of non-interpretable features. A similar requirement, imposed by the other
interface (PF), may be used to distinguish an important class of features that can
(and accordingly to what was said above, must) change their state, namely the
so-called *strong* features. They are not interpretable at PF and thus must be made
invisible, hence checked, before Spell-Out.[18]

Finally, let us observe that the state of a feature, when inserted in the
derivation, is determined on a local basis, according to the lexical item that

contains it. Thus, the φ-features of a DP are *(a, b)*, but the φ-features of a verb are *(a, ¬b)* — that is, they are not interpretable. Furthermore, the categorial feature *D* of a DP is not strong, whereas the same feature, when in a category triggering subject movement (EEP), is strong. Therefore, properties like strength and interpretability are not intrinsic to features but to features as belonging to a given feature set (lexical item).

### 1.1.2.4. More on economy

Another important principle in the minimalist framework is *Procrastinate*, which establishes that a syntactic operation must be performed as late as possible. Procrastinate implies that when movement is not required by strong features before Spell-Out, it must be postponed to the covert component. An argument in favour of such a view is the observation that languages vary with respect to the strong/weak status of some features and, accordingly, vary with respect to whether movement applies in the overt or covert component. This is the case, for instance, for languages such as Italian and Japanese, with respect to Wh-movement. Italian has overt Wh-movement, whereas Japanese has Wh-in situ. The difference between the two might be expressed as a difference in feature specification. In Italian the *Wh* feature is strong, thus requiring overt movement of the Wh-phrase. In Japanese it is taken to be weak, and, as such, Procrastinate dictates that movement is covert. It is reasonable to claim that most of the differences in word order among languages are due to the strong/weak specification of the morphological features.

### 1.1.2.5. Word order

Let us add a few words on linear order. Kayne (1994) proposes that the linear order is a reflex of the structural condition of asymmetric c-command by means of the Linear Correspondence Axiom (LCA). Such a principle requires that if a constituent *A* asymmetrically c-commands a constituent *B*, then every terminal dominated by A linearly precedes all the terminals dominated by B. According to Chomsky (1994), the LCA is part of the phonological component and applies to the output of morphology — that is, to $X^0$ terms. Therefore it affects neither the construction of $\Sigma$ nor the checking procedure. As we said above, $C_{HL}$ creates unordered sets which are then delivered to $\pi$. Sentences, however, are constituted by ordered strings; therefore at a certain point in the derivation, the correct linear order must be obtained. The LCA is therefore an interface condition due to the particular format the performance system imposes on its output — that is, the string of words.

Kayne (1994) suggests that the only basic order is VO and that all other orders are derived by means of movement operations. Chomsky's (1995) system embodies these considerations, even if under a slightly different formulation. As a consequence of either proposal, it must be assumed that in languages exhibiting an OV order, the constituents have undergone various movements in order for the object to precede the verb.

### 1.1.3. A few words on phrase structure

Generally speaking, according to Chomsky (1995) the items in the initial array are sets (of sets) of features, and the functional and lexical categories themselves are nothing other than sets of features. In other words, categories are the result of a particular *grouping* of feature values. One task of language acquisition, then, consists in forming the correct groups and associating the sets (of sets) of features with lexical and grammatical morphemes. In the minimalist framework, therefore, the innate components of grammar are the features and the procedure $C_{HL}$. X-bar theory by itself is not a primitive notion of the grammar anymore. According to the minimalist approach, in fact, the only legitimate objects to start with are arrays constituted by sets of features, and a procedure $C_{HL}$ that *builds $\Sigma$.*

Let us briefly consider the development of that part of generative grammar concerning phrase structure. In the 1960s, up to the mid-1970s, the structure attributed to the sentence was, roughly speaking, the following:

(12)   [$_S$ NP VP]

Here S is a binary phrase, consisting of a subject and a predicate. The actual realisation of the subject and the predicate might vary in a limited range, given that the subject can also be a sentential one and the predicate structure might assume various forms. Successive developments of the theory of phrase structure, mainly due to Chomsky (1970) and Jackendoff (1976), permitted the theory to draw important generalisations on the structure of phrases; Jackendoff (1976) formulated the so-called X-bar theory, which establishes that all constituents have the following form:

(13)   [$_{X''}$ Z'' [$_{X'}$ X W'']]

From X-bar theory it follows that every category heads a maximal projection and that, conversely, every maximal projection has a head. According to such considerations, the sentential constituent as given in (12) does not fit into the theory, because it lacks a head. Empirical arguments lead to the conclusion that the head of the clause is the node Inflection (I):

(14)   [$_{I''}$ NP [$_{I'}$ I VP ]]

Such a hypothesis solves the problem raised by (12). The structure in (14), in fact satisfies the requirements imposed by X-bar theory. For a long time the picture in (14) has been taken to hold universally, given that it followed without further stipulation from the assumptions concerning phrase structure which were already present in the theory.

Pollock's (1989) work, as we have seen above, raised the question of a more articulated analysis of I. Starting from his proposal, many hypotheses have been made concerning a richer inventory of functional categories, together with analyses of language variation in this domain (cf. for instance Ouhalla's 1988, 1991 proposal of parametric variation among Semitic languages). Moreover, recently, due to Kayne's (1994) and Chomsky's (1993, 1994) work, the legitimacy of X-bar theory itself has been questioned. The minimalist theory, as we have already said, is based on the notion of *feature*, the operations Merge and Move which build $\Sigma$ plus economy principles. The conclusion which Chomsky (1994) draws, also on the basis of Kayne's discussion, is that the empirical content of X-bar theory can be derived by means of independently needed principles and therefore can be dispensed with in the theory of grammar. If such a conclusion is correct, there is nothing in this system which might lead us to conclude that the clausal architecture per se is universal.

Let us now consider the assumptions needed if one wants to maintain that the clausal architecture is the same across languages. The first obvious consequence, already discussed in the literature, concerns the fact that if in a certain language a functional category X has to be hypothesised in the clausal structure on the basis of empirical evidence, it is also necessary to generalise its existence even in languages where there is no evidence of it whatsoever.[19] Notice that according to such a view, as we stated above, there is no crosslinguistic variation with respect to the clausal architecture and also no variation among the various sentences of the same language. One has to assume, in fact, that the selected array *always* contains *all* the feature specifications for every possible item appearing in $\Sigma$. In other words, the hypothesis of a universal clausal architecture requires a similar assumption of universality on the content of the array. Such a system, though possible in principle, seems to be at least redundant and not in the spirit of the minimalist proposal. Given these considerations, it follows that the idea that clausal architecture is a priori given — that is, universal, can and must be questioned. As an alternative, it might be claimed that the clausal architecture is a derived construal, varying from language to language and from one sentence to another. In the following chapters we show that such a theoretical proposal is at least worth investigating and that it might make interesting predictions on questions concerning language acquisition on the one hand, and language variation on the other.

### 1.1.4. Syncretic categories and the Feature Scattering Principle

In this section we address the problem related to the nature and the acquisition of lexical items and how they affect the building of $\Sigma$. As we said in section 1.1.2, we propose a system strongly embodying Chomsky's (1993) observation that linguistic variation is a function of morphological properties.

Let us rephrase the question we are going to analyse: Which are the universal components of a grammar compatible with the minimalist hypothesis and, obviously, with empirical observations? More specifically, is the richness of the information available in the lexicon sufficient to dispense with the assumption that the clausal architecture is invariant across languages? In this work, an affirmative answer to the last question is argued for by developing some natural hypotheses on the acquisition process, in accordance with economy considerations. Our proposal is that the universal components of grammar are (a) the inventory of features among which a child selects the ones relevant to his/her language, and (b) the order of checking, which can be expressed by means of the following principle:

(15)   **Universal Ordering Constraint**:
       Features are ordered so that given $F_1 > F_2$, the checking of $F_1$ precedes the checking of $F_2$.[20]

The structure by itself is therefore not universal: it can vary across languages, and the same language can instantiate different structures depending upon the specific array to be expressed. Since checking can take place only by means of raising and not lowering, a universal order of checking entails the existence of an ordering on the nodes of the structure.[21] Notice that the universal properties given in (a) and (b) must also be assumed by the scholars proposing a universal clausal architecture. For them, in fact, (a) is a necessary assumption, because it is trivially implied by the universal hypothesis itself. Assumption (b) also seems necessary to meet empirical observations, such as the ones discussed in Cinque (1994) — that is, that the *sequence* of categories does not vary across languages.[22] We are proposing therefore that (a) and (b) are the *only* universal components determining clausal architecture and that the additional stipulation that the clausal architecture is universal can and must be dispensed with.

As we said in the preceding discussion, a child learns a language by associating morphemes to features. The association could be one to one, giving agglutinative or isolating languages, or it could happen that the same morpheme is associated to more features, in this way obtaining the so-called inflected languages, such as Italian. We will call the categories obtained by means of such a multiple association *syncretic* and *hybrid* categories. As an example, consider the following case: in Italian, the same morpheme can express both gender and number. For example, in the word *bella* (beautiful), the morpheme -*a* simultaneously expresses feminine and singular, constituting a typical case of a syncretic category. The languages we consider in this work are in general like Italian — that is, they have syncretic categories. In the traditional literature, it has often been assumed that English is an *isolating* language and not a *inflected* one. We will show that such a classification is not entirely correct, because English exhibits several properties which must be attributed to the existence of syncretic categories. The few inflectional morphemes of the English language in fact play several different roles and functions. For instance, we will show that the past tense morpheme -*ed* has many functions; analogously, the third person ending -*s* implies the existence of temporal values. In chapter 3, in fact, we show that in English the category Tense surfaces together with AGR. The category obtained in this way has some additional properties making it a *hybrid* category and not only a *syncretic* one. The computational system $C_{HL}$, which projects the structure, has only the constraint of consuming all the items selected in the array. We think that some interesting predictions could follow if we introduce the following principle concerning the projection procedure:[23]

(16)   **Feature Scattering Principle**:

Each feature can head a projection.

A (syncretic or hybrid) category, which is nothing other than a set (of sets) of features, must project at least one node. The Feature Scattering Principle states that the upper limit on the number of nodes is given by the number of features selected in the array. That is, each feature can head a projection. The other principles of grammar should not be violated — in particular, the Universal Ordering Constraint, which defines the order in which the nodes are projected, and scattered, if the scattering option is taken. To exemplify these ideas, consider an abstract example: let the array contain a bundle of features $[F_1, F_2, F_3]$; assume that the Universal Ordering Constraint requires the checking of $F_1$ to precede that of $F_2$ (which can be notated as: $F_1 > F_2$) and the checking of $F_2$ to precede that of $F_3$ (notated as: $F_2 > F_3$). Therefore, a structure in which the projections of $F_1$ dominate those of $F_3$ and the projections of $F_3$ dominate those of $F_2$ cannot be built. However, the structure in which $F_3$ is higher than $F_2$, and $F_2$ is higher than $F_1$, is possible. The bundle in question might be projected as a single node, or *scattered*, if necessary, giving two or three projections. For instance, $F_1$ can be projected with $F_2$, and $F_3$ can be scattered — that is, projected separately. As another option, $F_1$ can be projected by itself, and $F_2$ and $F_3$ can be projected together. Finally, each of the three features can be projected by itself. The actual number of projections is defined according to economy considerations. That is, the shortest derivation compatible with the initial array is selected (cf. Chomsky 1994, §3). As a consequence, the option of feature scattering is taken only to project the items contained in the array. A separate head must be projected if something is present in the array that is supposed to appear in its *Spec*. Scattering, however, cannot take place for the sake of movement — that is, to create positions which can license a movement option that would otherwise violate the other principles of grammar. For a discussion see §5.2.[24]

To give a concrete example of how the system works, let us sketch a brief account of Cinque's (1994) data using a *feature scattering* approach (we will again consider this evidence in chapter 3). Cinque takes into account some distributional evidence namely, data showing that across languages *Spec* positions can be filled by the same kind of elements, mostly adverbials, appearing in the same reciprocal order across languages. He also shows that each *Spec* is associated with a head position. Arguments in favour of this conclusion come from a comparative analysis of head movement in various languages. It can be shown, in fact, that the head position associated with the *Spec* is used as a landing site for the verb. Cinque discusses sentences like the following (from Cinque 1994, *handout*, exx. 20-22):

(17)   I bambini non hanno mica più tutti detto tutto bene alla maestra.

Lit.: The children *non* did not anymore all said everything well to the teacher.

In (17) there is a series of specifiers that may be observed: *mica più tutti tutto bene* (lit.: not anymore all everything well). Cinque shows that the intermediate head positions can be occupied by the participle, either obligatorily or optionally, and that if certain positions are not available in Italian they are available in other languages. Cinque's data can follow from our analysis. According to economy considerations, if an adverb, or rather, the bundle of features identifying it in the lexicon, is present in the array, it must be projected. In order to obtain a well-formed structure, the features of the relevant head can be *scattered* and an additional head can be provided. Such a head can be used as a landing site for movement, if required, even if it cannot be created for the sole purpose of adjusting movement.

It seems therefore that our system can account for Cinque's data by means of the Feature Scattering Principle. We would like to stress, however, that our theoretical proposal is not a mere notational variant of the alternative one, given that it makes different predictions in various domains, which we will illustrate in the following chapters.

Let us briefly introduce the empirical and conceptual problems which will be investigated in the following discussion. According to our view, the scattering option is taken only under very special conditions, due to principles of economy. A bundle of features associated with a single morpheme, in fact, can be projected by means of more than one head (i.e., scattered) only if extra *Spec* positions are required to locate other bundles of features contained in the initial array. This implies that if there are no Specifiers to be projected from the initial array, no extra head can be created by scattering.

As is well known, heads also constitute the landing site for movement. As a consequence, our hypothesis interacts with the movement options of a particular structure. If the scattering option has not been taken, no head movement is possible, since a possible landing site is lacking. Furthermore, as we just said, if there is only one head there is only one *Spec* position. That is, given a syncretic head, there is only one *Spec* associated with the bundle of features of the head. If such a *Spec* is filled basically by an XP, it cannot be used again as a landing site for movement. Additional landing sites either for heads or for XPs could be provided by the scattering option, but the scattering is constrained by economy principles and cannot take place just to provide a landing site. In §5.2. we will show that in at least two cases such a hypothesis makes the correct empirical predictions and proves superior to alternative proposals according to which we can have as many projections as possible heads.

Finally, there is another important issue we will not investigate here, because it lies too far away from the central questions of this work. It has to do with typological considerations. According to our proposal, the so-called agglutinative languages typically exhibit a one-to-one relation between features and morphemes. These languages do not have (non trivial) syncretic categories; rather, some of the categories which can be expressed syncretically in a inflected language are not syncretic in an agglutinative one. We predict therefore that in such languages, those phenomena that, according to our hypothesis, are due to the existence of syncretic categories cannot be found. From a typological point of view this might be an interesting perspective worth pursuing. An important problem is constituted by the characterisation of the evidence relevant for the acquisition process. It might happen, in fact, that in a certain language it is possible to find only indirect evidence in favour of the existence of a given feature specification. We think that such evidence is sufficient to hypothesise the existence in that language of the functional category expressing that feature. Let us consider an example. In Italian both the simple past such as *mangiai* (I ate) and the so-called imperfect, such as *mangiavo* (I ate-IMPF) express the temporal value PAST. The forms *mangiai/mangiavo* contrast with each other with respect to their aspectual value: the first is perfective and the second imperfective. In Italian there is no separate morpheme for expressing such an aspectual alternation.[25] The aspectual values, though not expressed by means of a morpheme which can be freely combined with the other ones, are relevant in the system of Italian, given that there is at least one pair in the system whose members differ by virtue of such a distinction (see chapter 4). We suggest that in this case the values concerning perfectivity can be acquired because the evidence exemplified above is sufficient to create a multi-valued system (at least with respect to aspectuality). In this case, therefore, we predict the existence of a syncretic category, collapsing tense and aspectuality. We propose that when even this kind of indirect evidence is lacking, the feature, though present in the innate inventory provided by UG, is not realised in that particular language.

## 1.2. The semantic representation

In this section we illustrate our hypothesis concerning the framework for interpretative issues in the temporal domain. We briefly discuss the approach which is usually referred to as *tense logic* and then compare it to the so-called *referential approach* to tense.

Tense logic represents tenses by means of temporal operators. We will show, however, that such operators do not exhibit the kind of scopal properties of other, non-temporal, operators. Furthermore, we will illustrate that to correctly account for the temporal meaning of a sentence, reference to temporal *entities* and not just temporal operators, is required. Typically, the nature of such temporal entities is fully specified in the referential approach, and not in the tense logic one. We will also provide arguments to conclude that *events* are needed besides, or perhaps instead of, temporal *points* and *intervals*.

### 1.2.1. Tenses as sentential operators

Tense logical approaches to time in natural language (cf. Prior 1967; Montague 1974) consider tenses as sentential operators. Such operators apply to the basic or *untensed* form of a sentence to yield another sentence. Their effect is to shift the evaluation time of a sentence to the past or to the future. In the cases we are going to consider, the evaluation time always coincides with the time of the utterance, which is symbolised by $u$.

Consider the following examples:

(18)  a.  John saw Mary.
      b.  P[see(John, Mary)]

(19)  a.  John will see Mary.
      b.  F[see(John, Mary)]

The logical form for sentence (18a) is (18b), where $P$ is the past operator.
Analogously, in the case of a future tense verb (*will see*), the operator is $F$. Such
a simple tense logic combines propositional logic together with the two
operators $P$ and $F$. A suitable model for this logic is a triple $M = (T, <, V)$
where $T$ is a set of moments of time, $<$ is the binary relation *earlier than* on $T$,
and $V$ is the interpretation function which assigns a truth value $V_t(\phi)$ to each
propositional formula $\phi$ and to a moment of time $t \in T$.[26] The relevant truth
conditions for the operators $P$ and $F$ are given in (20a) and (20b), respectively:

(20)  a.  $V_{M,t}(P\phi) = 1$ iff there is $t'$, $t' < t$ and $V_{M,t'}(\phi) = 1$

      b.  $V_{M,t}(F\phi) = 1$ iff there is $t'$, $t < t'$ and $V_{M,t'}(\phi) = 1$

$P\phi$ is true at a time $t$ with respect to a model $M$ iff there is a time $t'$ which is
*past* with respect to $t$, such that $\phi$ is true at $t'$ with respect to $M$. Analogously,
$F\phi$ is true at a time $t$, with respect to a model $M$ iff there is time $t'$ which is in
the *future* with respect to $t$, such that $\phi$ is true at $t'$ with respect to $M$. Applying
(20) to (18) and (19), we obtain (21):

(21)  a.  $V_{M,t}(P(\text{'John see Mary'})) = 1$ iff there is $t'$, $t' < t$ and $V_{M,t'}(\text{'John see}$
          $\text{Mary'}) = 1$

      b.  $V_{M,t}(F(\text{'John see Mary'})) = 1$ iff there is $t'$, $t < t'$ and $V_{M,t'}(\text{'John see}$
          $\text{Mary'}) = 1$

That is, *John saw Mary* is true at a time $t$ iff there is a time $t'$ which precedes the
time of the utterance and the untensed proposition $p = $ 'John see Mary' is true at
$t'$. On the other hand, *John will see Mary* is true when uttered at a time $t$ iff there
is a future time $t'$ such that $p$ is true at $t'$.

As can be seen from (20), both $F$ and $P$ have an existential flavour, in that
their truth conditions require the *existence* of a time at which the proposition
they apply to is true. Classical Priorean tense logic also includes the
corresponding universal operators $G$ and $H$, where $G\phi$ can be paraphrased as "in
the future it will always be the case that $\phi$," and $H\phi$ as "in the past it has always
been the case that $\phi$".

An important feature of tense operators is that they can be combined with
each other to yield more complex configurations. This possibility has been
exploited to capture the meaning of tenses such as the English pluperfect, which
is represented as the composition of two past operators, $PP$, and of the future
perfect, which can be represented as $PF$.

The tense operator approach has been criticised both from an empirical and a theoretical point of view. We will consider some of these criticisms, namely those discussed by Enç (1986), and others arising from observations originally made by Kamp (1968). An exhaustive review of the literature on the topic is, however, beyond the goals of this work.

Since tenses are operators, we expect them to exhibit scope properties analogous to those of other operators and quantified expressions, such as DPs. Consider (22) (cf. Enç 1986, ex. 3):

(22)    All rich men were poor children.

The meaning of (22) can be paraphrased as in (23):

(23)    All rich men (past and present ones) were at a previous time poor children.

The logical forms for (22) are given in (24):

(24)    a.  $\forall x$ (rich-man$(x) \rightarrow$ P(poor-child$(x)$)))
        b.  P($\forall x$ (rich-man$(x) \rightarrow$ poor-child$(x)$)))

The verb *were* instantiates a past operator $P$. Furthermore, in (22) the universally quantified DP *all rich men* appears. Given that operators manifest scope properties, we expect the temporal operator $P$ to interact with the quantified DP, each taking scope on the other. Consider the case where the universal quantifier has wider scope, thus yielding (24a). The corresponding proposition is true iff for every *present* rich man $x$ there is a *past* time at which $x$ is a poor child. This is not, however, the meaning of (22), according to our intuitions, because it takes into account only *presently* rich men. If the past tense operator takes scope over the universal operator, (24b) is obtained. Such a proposition is true iff there is a *past* time $t$ such that every man who is rich at $t$ is also a poor child at the *same past* time. Again, (24b) is far from the meaning of (22) as expressed by (23). Thus, both scope possibilities fail to capture (23), and it seems that a standard account of the scope interactions of a tense operator with quantified expressions does not suffice to obtain the correct result.

It also has been observed that tense operators introduced by verbal morphology are not sufficient to account for some interpretative facts. Consider, for example, the following sentence (Enç 1986, ex. 13):

(25)    Every fugitive is now in jail.

The operator approach assigns (25) the following meaning:

(26)    Every $x$ who is *now* a fugitive is *presently* in jail.

Example (25), however, is an assertion about *past* fugitives who are *presently* in jail. The correct truth conditions are exemplified by (27):

(27)    $\forall x$ ((P(fugitive$(x)$))) $\rightarrow$ in-jail$(x)$)

To obtain (27) it must be assumed that the past tense operator $P$ is instantiated by the subject DP. Notice in fact that the verbal tense is *present* and therefore cannot be the verb which instantiates the operator. Moreover, the scope of the operator should not include the predicate and should be restricted to the subject. Generally, however, tense operators are introduced by tense morphemes related to the verbs and have the predicate in their scope. In (25) and similar cases, there is no such past tense morpheme — that is, there is no morphosyntactic evidence of its presence and there is no obvious way to constrain the scope of this operator to the DP. In principle, in fact, an operator associated to the DP could take scope over the whole sentence. In this case we would obtain (28):

(28)    $\forall x \ (P(\text{fugitive}(x) \rightarrow \text{in-jail}(x)))$

Example (28) is true iff everyone who was a fugitive at a *past* time was in jail at the *same* time. Again, such a reading is not the correct one. Therefore the hypothesis according to which DPs introduce tense operators does not make the correct predictions, because the scope properties of such operators are anomalous and should be constrained by means of ad hoc conditions. Consider also that if it were correct to hypothesise the presence of an operator taking scope over the DP, we should also investigate the scope relations between two DPs, each bearing its own temporal interpretation (and, consequently, its own tense operator). In particular, when a DP is c-commanded by another one, we would expect the temporal interpretation of the former to depend on the temporal interpretation of the latter. Consider the example in (29) (modelled after Enç 1986, ex. 8):

(29)    Every student will have met a president.

A possible reading of (29), which is the one relevant to our discussion, is the following: let us hypothesise a scenario where every *present* student either *met*, or *is meeting*, or *will meet* at a future time, the president in charge at *that moment*. Sentence (29) is true at the utterance time if there is a later time at which *every student met a president* is true. In this scenario, the DP *every student* is evaluated at the present time, whereas *a president* can be evaluated at a past, present, or future time. That is, the times relevant for the two DPs must be kept separate, so that the temporal interpretation of the DP *a president* does not depend on the interpretation of the DP *every student*, even if *a president* is in the scope of the latter. As a consequence, the expectation that tense operators introduced by DPs exhibit the scope properties of ordinary quantified expressions is not met.

To summarise, tense operators introduced by DP do not take scope over the main predicate, as shown by (27), and they do not interact with each other, as shown by our discussion of (29). If we still want to maintain the hypothesis that a DP can be associated with a tense operator, we should constrain such a tense operator to take only very local scope, because it seems to have only the DP itself in its scope. As we said in the preceding discussion, this move is possible, but requires a rather ad hoc hypothesis.

Another argument against the use of tense operators comes from the analysis of the interactions between tenses in complex sentences. Consider (30):[28]

(30)   a.  A child was born who would be king.
       b.  A child was born who will be king.

(31)   $P(\exists x \, (child(x) \wedge born(x) \wedge F(king(x))))$

The sentences in (30a) and (30b) differ only in the use of two different future forms in the relative clause namely, the auxiliary *would* vs. *will*. The logical form in (31) represents the meaning of (30a). The future tense operator, introduced by the verb of the relative clause, is in the scope of the tense operator of the main verb. Formula (31) is then true iff there is a past time $t$ in which a child was born and there is a time future with respect to $t$ when it is true that the child is king. Thus, (31) correctly captures the meaning of (30a). On the other hand, it is not so easy to account for the meaning of (30b), the version in which the simple future, *will*, appears in the relative clause. Formula (31) does not capture the correct truth conditions for (30b). The latter, in fact, requires the time at which the child is said to be king to be in the future with respect to the utterance *now*, a possibility which is not available on the basis of (31). There is an alternative option — namely, that the future operator takes scope over the matrix clause past operator, yielding (32):

(32)   $FP(\exists x \, (child(x) \wedge born(x) \wedge king(x)))$

Formula (32), however, is not a correct representation for (30b) either, since it requires a future time $t$ and a time $t'$, $t' < t$, such that $born(x)$ and $king(x)$ are both true at $t'$. What is needed for (30b) is the possibility for the two tenses to be independently evaluated with respect to the utterance time. Tense logic, however, cannot represent the two operators as being independent from each other.[27]

The examples in (30) raise a problem very similar to those discussed by Enç. One major inadequacy of the tense operator approach is constituted by the fact that the interactions among the temporal properties of the constituents of a sentence are not the ones expected for tense operators. In other words, an operator based representation is insufficient to account for the temporal interpretation of the sentences considered above. Another problem with the tense logical approach is the possibility of compounding the basic operators $F$ and $P$ to yield more complex ones. On the one hand, languages like English have tenses which seem to be naturally analysable by means of such a property. For instance, the pluperfect and the future perfect could correspond to $PP$ and $FP$, respectively. On the other hand, there are compound tenses which resist a similar treatment. For example, the present perfect cannot be straightforwardly distinguished from the simple past by virtue of operator compositions. Another problem is that there is nothing preventing an unlimited composition of tense operators. Any sequence is a priori possible, such as $FPF$ or $PPP$, $FPFP$ and so on, even if none of them correspond to an observable tense in any language. The composition of operators could be constrained by means of *ad hoc* conditions for instance, by explicitly disallowing combinations of more than two operators. Such a condition, however, would have no explanatory power at all, since the very fact that only a limited number of tenses exist across languages would not be explained, but just stipulated.

### 1.2.2. Temporal entities

Let us now consider a different approach, the so-called *referential approach*, which allows temporal expressions to refer directly to temporal entities. According to such an alternative view there are no tense operators and, consequently, no issues arise concerning scope interactions. Tenses are regarded as relational expressions that directly encode temporal relations between temporal entities. In such a system the inventory of possible tenses is obtained from the interaction between the nature and functioning of the relevant temporal entities with their morphosyntactic realisation.

An argument in favour of the referential approach has been provided by the analysis of temporal anaphora (cf. Kamp & Reyle 1993; Partee 1984). Consider (33) and (34):

(33)    John left the room. He was furious.

(34)    John said that Mary was pregnant.

In (33) the second sentence is understood as holding at the same time as the first. Example (34), on the other hand, can either mean that Mary's pregnancy holds at the time of John's utterance, or that the pregnancy is at an earlier time. Thus, both in (33) and (34) the time of the second clause (*he was furious* and *Mary was pregnant*) is dependent on the time of another sentence, the preceding one and the matrix, respectively. This phenomenon is reminiscent of the behaviour of pronouns (see Partee 1973), which is why this approach has been called the *referential* approach.

The operator approach could not easily account for the facts in (33) and (34). Anaphoric phenomena, in fact, require a context where entities such as times and events (but also ordinary individuals referring to spatial objects) are stored and accessed for later reference. No natural notion of context is possible with tense logic, unless major changes are proposed, undermining the spirit of these logical systems (for a discussion, see Kamp & Reyle 1993). Furthermore, in Priorean tense logic there are no terms referring to temporal entities (cf. the logical forms given above). Rather, the temporal dimension is built in the operators and in their truth conditions. That is, *times* belong not to the object language of tense logic but to its metalanguage. This way of encoding the temporal dimension was motivated by considerations about verbal tenses, given that their intrinsic relational meaning could be captured by means of truth conditions such as those in (20), repeated here for simplicity:

$V_{M,t}(P\phi) = 1$ iff there is $t'$, $t' < t$ and $V_{M,t'}(\phi) = 1$

$V_{M,t}(F\phi) = 1$ iff there is $t'$, $t < t'$ and $V_{M,t'}(\phi) = 1$

Verbal tense, however, is not the only manifestation of time in natural languages, because there are other situations in which direct reference to temporal entities might be needed. This is the case of temporal anaphora as argued above, and presumably also of temporal adverbials such as *at four*, *yesterday*, and so on. There are, therefore, many cases where direct reference to times appears to be necessary. It seems to us that tense logic would hardly be empirically adequate, since it excludes temporal terms from the vocabulary of the theory, and fails to capture an important property of natural languages.

In the previous section we have shown that (a) the temporal properties of sentences cannot be easily accounted for by means of the scopal dependencies among temporal operators; (b) the compositional character of temporal operators does not provide an upper limit to the number of temporal operators which can be combined to yield tenses, failing therefore to explain the limited variety of tenses found in natural languages; and (c) tense logic does not provide an account for temporal anaphora and certain expressions that seem to require the availability of terms directly referring to times. All these considerations seem to favour the referential approach, which allows tenses, temporal adverbials, and the like to directly refer (or contain a direct reference) to temporal entities.

In this section we briefly address the question of the nature of such temporal entities. It has been argued, in fact, that metaphysical assumptions may affect the explanation of linguistic phenomena (cf. Bach 1981) in many domains of the semantic analysis of natural languages, and not only with respect to temporal interpretation.[29] Our purpose, however, is not to give a full picture of what a correct ontology for natural language may look like but simply to clarify and justify a number of assumptions that will then be maintained in the rest of this work and which will often play a crucial role in accounting for empirical facts.

We will first consider temporal entities such as time points and intervals. It will be shown that the semantics based on them exhibit some shortcomings that can be avoided if events (Davidson 1967) are taken to be the primitive notion.

Let us first consider time points. According to the tense logic discussed above, the temporal component of a model is formed by time points. Now let us consider more closely what the truth conditions in (20) require.[30] Example (20) says that for a sentence such as *John ran* to be true at the utterance time $u$, there must be a time $t < u$ such that the proposition *run(John)* is true at $t$. Under what conditions *run(John)* is true at time $t$? Is John moving his left leg, his right leg, or both? What if at $t$ John is pausing between two successive steps? It seems quite difficult to discern what the truth conditions might be. This is not only a problem for theories based on tense operators. Even referential theories having time points as the primitive ontological objects face the same issue, that of specifying what happens at $t$ in order for a proposition to be true. Despite the different logical forms, (35a) for the operator approach and (35b) for the referential one, their truth conditions both require that a proposition be true at a particular time *point*.

(35)    a.  P(run(John))

        b.  $\exists t(\text{run}(\text{John}, t) \wedge t \leq u)$

This problem is not due to some idiosyncratic property of the predicate *run,* for the situation does not improve if we consider a sentence like *Mary wrote a letter*.[31] Again, the operator approach would require that there is a past time *t* at which *Mary writes a letter* is true. Is Mary expected to move her pen in a particular way on a piece of paper? What if she is refilling the pen?

Intuitively, a solution could be to take into account time *intervals* rather than time points. Within a referential approach, one can propose the semantic primitive of *being true at an interval i* (rather than *being true at a time point t* ) and use it to investigate the temporal properties of natural language sentences. The proposition corresponding to the sentence *John ran* is then true iff there is a past interval *i* such that *i* exactly spans (or contains) a state of affairs that involves John running. Both larger and shorter intervals do not work, and the proposition would be false at any such interval. The interval hypothesis, however, might run into troubles. Consider for instance the following sentence:

(36)    John was sick.

Suppose that *i* is a past interval corresponding exactly to the sickness of John. That is, the interval starts when John begins to be sick and ends when the sickness ends.[32] Then, according to the truth condition given above, (36) is true. The problems come when we try to assess the truth at intervals containing *i* or contained within *i*. The main predicate of (36), in fact, is stative. According to a widely accepted view (cf. Dowty 1979), propositions whose main predicate is stative have the property that their truth at an interval *i* entails their being true at any subinterval of *i*. Thus, if *i'* is a subinterval of *i*, it holds that John is sick at *i'*. Suppose now that *j* is an interval containing *i*. Then, there is a part of *j* where John is sick (*i*), and another part where he is not, (*i'*). What is the status of (36) or, more precisely, of the propositions corresponding to (36), with respect to *j* ? Example (36) is not true at *j*, since the subinterval property is not satisfied by *j*, because of *i'*. On the other hand, (36) cannot even be false at *j*. Its negation *John was not sick* is not true at *j*, because there are subintervals where it is not true, at least in a naive interpretation of negation and on the assumption that the negation of a stative predicate still yields a stative one. Thus (36) turns out to be neither true nor false at *j*.[33]

To conclude, both time points and time intervals exhibit similar difficulties. In many cases it is unclear how to tell whether a sentence is true or not at a given time point or interval. More precisely, it is unclear what the conditions holding in the world should be like in order for the truth conditions to be met. If so, it seems that some other entity is needed to base a semantic theory of time on.

## 1.2.3. Events

As an alternative to time points and intervals, we can take seriously the intuition that sentences like (35) and (36) involve reference to *events* of running and *states* of sickness. On this view, (36) would be true iff there is a past state of sickness of John. Analogously, *John ran* is true iff there exists a past event of running by John. If we hypothesise the existence of entities such as events and states, then the problems considered in the previous section do not arise.[34] In fact, the truth conditions for these propositions would be very similar to the ones of a normal existential sentence, such as *there is a table*. In both cases, the crucial factor would be the existence of a suitable individual — an event in the case of *running* and an object in the case of *table*. Suppose, then, that we admit individual events in our basic ontology so that propositions are evaluated with respect to a world including both objects and events, such as a particular running of John, the eating of an apple by Mary, and the like.

If this reasoning is correct, terms referring to events are needed in the logical forms. Following Davidson (1967; see also Higginbotham 1983, 1985, 1989; Parsons 1990) we hypothesise that verbs have an argument for events in their predicate-argument structure. In a Davidsonian perspective, a verb such as *to run* is a two-place predicate, and a sentence like (35) has the logical form in (37):

(37) $\exists e(run(John, e))$[35]

Example (37) is true iff there is a (past) event that is a running of John. Similarly (and assuming that states are on a par with events), the logical form of (36) is (38):

(38) $\exists e(sick(John, e))$

A comparison between (37) and (35b) should make it clear why an event-based-semantics does not exhibit the problem discussed above with respect to point and interval semantics. Examples (37) and (38) simply require the existence of an *event* of running (or of a *state* of sickness), contrasting with (35b), where we had to ascertain whether certain relations between participants and time entities held.

To sum up, the present theory considers simple sentences such as *John ran* as involving an existential quantification over individual events, the eventive variable being contributed by the verb. This view is based on Davidson's work (cf. Davidson 1967, 1970). Davidson, however, had other reasons to assume that individual events are part of the basic ontology of natural language. He was interested in reducing certain patterns of entailments between propositions to a matter of logical form. For example, he aimed at explaining the fact that the truth of (39a) entails the truth of (39b) simply on the basis of the properties of their logical forms:

(39)   a. John buttered the toast slowly.
      b. John buttered the toast.

Davidson showed that if (a) verbal predicates have an event position, (b) (at least certain) adverbials are event predicates, and (c) a hidden existential quantifier binds the eventive variable, then the relevant entailment is obtained by virtue of conjunction reduction, as shown by (40a) and (40b), which are the logical forms of (39a) and (39b), respectively:[36]

(40) a. $\exists e(\text{butter}(\text{John, the-toast}, e) \wedge \text{slow}(e))$
     b. $\exists e(\text{butter}(\text{John, the-toast}, e))$

In a similar vein, it is possible to capture the entailment of (41b) by (41a) by assuming that prepositional modifiers are also event predicates:

(41) a. I flew my spaceship to the morning star.
     b. I flew my spaceship.

Other scholars have provided further evidence in favour of the presence of events in the logical form of sentences. For instance, Higginbotham (1983) and Parsons (1990) discuss perceptual reports. In particular, Higginbotham argues that the naked infinitival of a sentence like (42) should not be considered as a clause, at least from the point of view of interpretation:

(42) a. I saw Mary leave.
     b. $\exists e[\text{leave}(e)](\text{saw}(I, e))$

The naked infinitival behaves as an indefinite description of events so that it could be analysed as in (42b). This treatment, according to Higginbotham, explains by means of a highly restrictive theory a number of otherwise puzzling phenomena: (a) the (quasi) veridicality of perceptual reports, if *Mary saw John leave* is true, then *John left* is true; (b) the transparency of naked infinitival, from *Mary saw Brutus stab the emperor* and *Caesar is the emperor* it is possible to infer that *Mary saw Brutus stab Caesar*. Concerning this point, Parsons (1990) observes that perceptual reports differ from "perceive-that" contexts, such as (43), which are not referentially transparent:

(43) Mary saw that Brutus stabbed the emperor.

From (43) and from the fact that Caesar is the emperor it cannot be inferred that Mary saw Brutus stab Caesar. This difference follows if we take the meaning of the embedded clause in (43) to be propositional-like, thus differing from the event descriptions provided by naked infinitivals.

In conclusion, the (individual) event-based semantics has several advantages and does not exhibit the same shortcomings typical of the semantics based on time points and time intervals. Furthermore, it solves many empirical questions, such as the entailments between propositions and perceptual reports.[37]

## 1.3. A revised Reichenbachian framework

The hypothesis we will develop here is that tenses instantiate relationships between events. According to this proposal, the logical form of a tense contains terms referring to particular events, $e$ and $s$ (the speech event), and a term introducing a relationship of temporal precedence between them. Consider the following case, where a past verbal form appears:

(44)  a.  John ate an apple.
      b.  $\exists e \exists x (\text{eat}(e, \text{John}, x) \wedge \text{apple}(x) \wedge e{<}s)$

This representation can be extended also to present and future tenses.[38] Let us now consider compound tenses:

(45)  a.  John has eaten an apple.
      b.  John had eaten an apple.
      c.  John will have eaten an apple.

To correctly represent the meaning of these tenses, a more complex system seems to be required. The presence of only two points could not distinguish the simple forms from the ones given in (45).

Focusing on this problem, Reichenbach (1947) proposed and discussed a theory of tenses based on three temporal primitive entities: one, denoted by $S$, is an indexical referring to the utterance time — that is, the *speech time*; $E$ denotes the time of the event $e$ instantiated by the predicate of the clause and is, therefore, called the *event time*. Finally, another point, $R$, is introduced, which is called the *reference time*. When he introduced it, Reichenbach developed an idea originally proposed by Jespersen (1924), showing that $R$ is required to account satisfactorily for the semantics of perfect tenses.[39]

Tenses order the three temporal points. For example, the meaning of the present tense could be represented as $S = R = E$, or, as proposed by Reichenbach, $S,R,E$, (where the comma represents temporal overlapping), whereas the meaning of the present perfect can be represented as $E\_R,S$.

The Reichenbachian model has been adopted and revised by several linguists (among others, Comrie 1976, 1985; Vikner 1985; Hornstein 1990; Scorretti 1991; Declerck 1986). As already suggested by Reichenbach and then further discussed by Comrie (1985) and Hornstein (1990), both for empirical and theoretical reasons it has been proposed that the relation among the three points be split into two distinct relations, one between $R$ and $S$, which will be called here T1, and the other between $E$ and $R$, which we will call T2. By means of such a system, a direct relationship between $E$ and $S$ is never realised, but is always mediated by $R$. The possible relations are the following:

(46)  T1:  $S\_R$    future        T2:  $E\_R$    perfect
            $R\_S$    past              $R\_E$    prospective
           $(S,R)$   present           $(E,R)$   neutral

(The coincidence relations, expressed by means of a comma, have a peculiar status, which will be better considered in the following chapter.) We hypothesise that the various tenses are the result of the composition of a relation of type T1 with a relation of type T2. For instance, according to this picture, the representation of the present tense is the result of the combination of $S,R$ with $E,R$, to yield $S,R,E$, as given above, and the representation of the present perfect is the result of the combination of $S,R$ with $E\_R$, to yield $E\_R,S$. From the point of view of the final representation, this proposal exhibits an important empirical difference with respect to the original one developed by Reichenbach. The crucial empirical data, which have already been discussed in the literature (see Comrie 1985 and Hornstein 1990), come from the analysis of the future perfect. The future perfect results from the combination of $S\_R$ and $E\_R$. Comrie points out that in English (and in Italian as well), a sentence such as (47) is ambiguous in three ways:

(47)    John will have finished his manuscript by tomorrow.

That is, we do not know the exact temporal relation holding between the finishing of the manuscript and the $S$ point. In fact, it could be the case that John, at the time in which the sentence is uttered ($S$), has already finished the manuscript; or that he is finishing it exactly at that moment; or that he will finish in a future time lying between the time of the utterance and *tomorrow*. This ambiguity is captured by the representation resulting from the combination of the two temporal relations T1 and T2:

(48)                     S          R

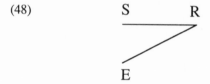

                         E

Given (48), there is no unique way of ordering the three temporal entities, because the relation between $E$ and $S$ is not specified. As pointed out by Comrie and then by Hornstein, this approach presents several advantages besides the one just discussed. In fact, given the picture sketched by Reichenbach, we would in principle expect the existence of languages where for each possible position of $E$, there is a morphologically different realisation. In other words, Reichenbach predicts the existence of languages in which the meanings corresponding to $S\_E\_R$; $S,E\_R$; $E\_S\_R$ are expressed by means of different morphological tenses. Comrie points out that this does not seem to be the case.

The revised Reichenbachian theory accounts in a natural and elegant way for the limited number of morphologised tenses. The system is based on three primitive objects plus binary relations. As such, the possibilities of combining the various forms are a priori very limited. This is not the case with the operator approach, as seen in the preceding discussion. Finally, as pointed out by Hornstein (1990), such a system can be easily acquired, satisfying therefore an important requirement for any theory of tense. The inventory of tenses is the following (see Hornstein 1990, p. 117; the following schemata, however, is not identical, because we have added the distant-future to the list):

(49)    present:            $(S,R) \bullet (R,E) = S,R,E$
        past:               $(R\_S) \bullet (E,R) = E,R\_S$
        future:             $(S\_R) \bullet (R,E) = S\_R,E$
        present perfect:    $(S,R) \bullet (E\_R) = E\_S,R$
        future perfect:     $(S\_R) \bullet (E\_R)$
        past perfect:       $(R\_S) \bullet (E\_R) = E\_R\_S$
        future in past:     $(R\_S) \bullet (R\_E)$
        proximate future:   $(S,R) \bullet (R\_E) = S,R\_E$
        distant-future:     $(S\_R) \bullet (R\_E) = S\_R\_E$

The triple at the right of the equal sign appears in the cases in which the relation between $E$ and $S$ can be inferred without ambiguity; otherwise we have nothing.

By suggesting that the two relations instantiate T1 and T2, we hypothesise a *categorial* distinction between the two. Such a distinction will be motivated showing that the morphemes realising T1 and T2 have different contents, in terms of features, as well as different morphosyntactic behaviours. We will also show in chapters 2 and 3 that on the basis of the morphosyntactic considerations, it is possible to predict the legitimate combination of these two categories.

We also hypothesise that T1 and T2 are *lexical* categories assigning a *T-role* (for a proposal in this direction, though with different empirical and theoretical consequences, see Guéron & Hoekstra 1988; Zagona 1988). The notion of T-role is meant to capture the observation that T must always have a VP complement. More precisely, T-roles are assigned under government to *event* positions in the thematic grids of verbs.[40] A T-criterion can thus be established:

(50)    **T-criterion**: every T-role must be uniquely assigned to an *event* position, and every event position can receive at most one T-role.

That is, a VP-*event* cannot bear more than one T-role, and every T-role must be assigned to an *event* position.[41] Therefore, a T-role, analogously to a θ-role, is a formal device that permits the identification of the *event* argument of a verb, or more generally of a predicate, with an empty argumental place in the *T-grid* of the temporal predicate, this way assigning it a specific temporal interpretation. Furthermore, according to (50) a verb cannot be temporalised twice (or more than twice). From a morphosyntactic point of view this seems to be a correct generalisation. That is, empirically it has been observed that at most one tense morpheme appears on each verb. We will see in the next chapter that the T-criterion plays a major role in predicting the occurrence of auxiliaries in Italian and Latin. In chapter 3 we will show that it also accounts for the presence of *do*-support in English. We also hypothesise that the lexical category T bears temporal features which in the following discussion we will call τ-features.

Let us briefly consider the question concerning the theoretical content of the Reichenbachian entities $E$, $R$, and $S$, which will be discussed in chapter 3 on the basis of empirical evidence. We said at the beginning of this section that tenses instantiate relationships between events, and we represented the semantics of simple verbal forms as a relation between the event identified by the predicate, $e$, and the speech event, $s$. They can be easily taken to correspond to the Reichenbachian entities $E$ and $S$. The question now concerns $R$.

We do not want to hypothesise the existence of a third event, because such a hypothesis would be purely ad hoc and not justified on an empirical basis. Our proposal, which will be better discussed in chapter 3, is that both T1 and T2 instantiate a relationship between two eventive variables. The variable corresponding to $R$ constitutes the *trait d'union* between the event variable and the context. When the relevant context is extrasentential, the connection is established with the speech event; when it is intrasentential, $R$ is provided by the superordinate clause or by a superordinate auxiliary. The empirical arguments in favour of such a view will be discussed at length in chapter 3.[42]

## Notes

1. There are various linguistic devices to express tense and aspect in natural languages: morphemes on verbal forms such as *-s* in *loves* or *-ed* in *loved*; adverbials such as *today*, *at four*; and periphrasis such as *to finish V-ing*, and so on. In this work we focus primarily on the realisation of tense and aspect as morphemes related to the verbal form, even if in the following chapters we will also marginally take into account some properties of temporal adverbs.

2. For a brief discussion on the nature and feature content of AGR, see chapters 3 and 7.

3. There are different proposals with respect to the position of adverbs such as *often*. Pollock (1989) simply assumes that they are in the *Spec* of V. If the subject is generated VP internally, however, it must be hypothesised that *often* occupies a different position, which according to Chomsky (1994) is a *Spec* position lower than the subject in a Larsonian shell configuration.

4. The Italian sentential negation *non* is similar to French *ne* in that it is a clitic. It therefore appears close to the verb. The lexical item *più*, literally *anymore*, is in the *Spec* position of the NEG projection. Therefore when the head cliticises, the Spec *più* marks the basic NEG position, analogously to *pas* in French, even if they are not identical. See Belletti (1990) for a discussion of these cases; see also Zanuttini (1991). The two authors develop different analyses of negation in Italian, which we will not consider further here. Independently of the theory assumed here, the main difference between Italian and French seems to be that *pas* is obligatory, whereas *più* is not.

5. In French the infinitive auxiliaries exhibit a different behaviour, being able to raise more freely than the other infinitives. As we have seen in the examples given in the text, even in English auxiliaries can move higher. For a discussion of the differences between full verbs and auxiliaries, we refer the reader to Pollock (1989), Belletti (1990), and Roberts (1993).

6.   Following Larson (1988), we will propose in chapter 3 that, contrary to what might be claimed at first sight, temporal adverbs such as *yesterday* or *at four* are generated not in the *Spec* of T but in a position internal to the verbal projections.

7.   The literature on these two topics is very rich, and we are not able to give an exhaustive list of all the relevant references. We will mention only some of the recent works — namely, those which have been particularly significant for our work. With respect to the first problem, consider Ouhalla (1988, 1991), Belletti (1990), Zanuttini (1991), Laka (1990), Roberts (1993), Poletto (1992), Holmberg & Platzack (1988), Thráinsson (1994), and Vikner (1995). With respect to the second issue, consider among others Stowell (1992), Zagona (1988), Guéron & Hoekstra (1988), Delfitto & Bertinetto (1995a, 1995b).

8.   See among others Enç (1987) and Zagona (1988). There is very interesting work which has been done on tense and aspect from a typological point of view; again our list cannot be exhaustive. See among others Comrie (1976, 1985) and Dahl (1985).

9.   In Chomsky's (1994) article, however, it is not clear what happens if there are two or more equally economical derivations. Presumably such a situation has to be ruled out by independent considerations.

10.  This means that the initial numeration functions as a *reference set* for economy evaluations. In other words, only derivations starting from the same choices of lexical elements are compared. In Chomsky (1995) this view is extended to stages of a derivation. To see how this works, let us observe that a given stage of a derivation starting from a numeration $N$ can be exhaustively characterised by the pair $(A, \Sigma)$ where $A$ is what remains of $N$ and $\Sigma$ is the structure built so far. Thus a derivation is a sequence $S = ((N_1, \Sigma_1), \ldots, (N_n, \Sigma_n))$ of such pairs, where $N_1 = N$, $\Sigma_1 = \varnothing$, $N_n = \varnothing$ and $\Sigma_n = (\lambda, \pi)$. Now suppose that a derivation has already formed the sequence $S_i = (s_1, \ldots, s_i)$, reaching the stage $s_i = (N_i, \Sigma_i)$. Let us call the set $R(S_i) = \{(s_k, \ldots, s_{k+1}), \ldots, (s_m, \ldots, s_{m+r})\}$ the *convergent extension of* $S_i$ (Chomsky 1995), where $R(S_i)$ is the set of sequences such that the result of concatenating $S_i$ with each of the sequence in $R(S_i)$ is a convergent derivation. Then, application of any operation to $s_i$ yields one of the $s_k, \ldots, s_m$, and ultimately maps $S_i$ onto one of the (partial) derivations in $R(S_i)$ (under the assumption that the chosen operation keeps convergence). Now, given two operations $O_1$ and $O_2$ which are both applicable to $s_i$, the one that yields the more economical derivation will be chosen. It is clear that as the computation proceeds the dimension of the convergent extension set will decrease so that the complexity of evaluating such a *relative* economy will also drastically decrease as well. Notice, furthermore, that it is not the case that such computations need always be performed, for it may often be the case that the choice among candidate operations is forced by different considerations — for instance, because one of them permits a strong feature to be checked. See following discussion.

11.  Let us reproduce here Chomsky's (1994) original formulations. In §2 he assumes that "an item in the lexicon is nothing other than a set of lexical features, or perhaps a further set-theoretic construction from them (e.g. a set of sets of features), and that output conditions allow nothing beyond such elements" and, still in §2 that

"L is then to be understood as a generative system that construct pairs $(\pi, \lambda)$ that are interpreted at the articulatory-perceptual level and conceptual-intentional interfaces, respectively. . . . A linguistic expression of L is at least a pair $(\pi, \lambda)$ of this sort, under minimalist assumptions, at most such a pair, meaning that there are no levels of linguistic structure, apart from the two interface levels PF and LF; specifically no levels of D-structure or S-structure". In §3 he claims that " . . . in a *perfect language* any structure $\Sigma$ should be constituted of elements already present in the lexical elements selected for $N$ and no new objects are added in the course of the computation".

12. This condition may need to be relaxed in view of the possibility of covert merge at the root (see Chomsky 1995).

13. Actually, if we consider the complex operations mentioned above — namely, those resulting from an application of the basic Merge (Move) followed by Project, — then the result, $\gamma$, of applying them to $\alpha$ and $\beta$ can be seen as the ordered pair $<\alpha, \beta>$ where $\gamma = <\alpha, \beta>$ iff $\gamma = \{\alpha, \{\alpha, \beta\}\}$. This formulation highlights the intrinsic asymmetry of the composed operations. Note, however, that the ordering so obtained does not necessarily (or trivially) reflect the left-to-right ordering of normal phrase markers. It would be interesting to speculate on possible connections between the two, a task that we will not pursue here.

14. Thus, a separate stipulation to the effect that constituents only move to satisfy their own requirements is superfluous. The principle ruling the satisfaction of the requirements of the moved item was named *Greed* (cf. Chomsky 1993, 1994) .

15. Chomsky (1995) opts for the first alternative, but we have no reasons for rejecting the other choice, so we remain neutral on this point. Formally, though, the choice is not neutral. In fact, Chomsky (1994, 1995) proposes that a numeration is $N = \{<\mathcal{F}_1 i_1>, \ldots, <\mathcal{F}_n i_n>\}$, where each $\mathcal{F}$ is a lexical item, some arrangement of (set theoretic construction from) features, and each $i_j$ is an integer which refers to the number of times the lexical item has to be used. The operation Select applies to $N$ by extracting a lexical item, handing it over to $C_{HL}$, and decreasing the relevant index by one. Furthermore, no derivation converges unless $N$ has been exhausted — that is, unless each index in $N$ is 0. In other words, each lexical item must be selected so many times as specified by its original index. However, if we take the view that optional features are specified before inserting lexical items in $N$, then it is necessary to formally distinguish in $N$ different instantiations of the same lexical item produced by different choices of optional features. But then the view above cannot be maintained since $<\mathcal{F}_j i_j>$ does not distinguish the $j$th occurrence of $\mathcal{F}$ from the $k$th. Indeed, the simplest solution seems to have $N$ as a mere collection of fully instantiated lexical items, dropping the integers altogether. The procedure Select, now, simply draws objects from $N$ handling them out to $C_{HL}$, and the condition for convergence reduces to $N = \varnothing$.

16. The notions developed in the text do not correspond closely to the operations of deletion and erasure proposed by Chomsky (1995, §5.2). According to him, a checked feature is deleted — that is, made invisible to LF whenever possible. Furthermore, a deleted feature is erased — that is, completely eliminated, again whenever possible. The terminology of the text collapses such a distinction.

Moreover, given that visibility at LF (interpretability) is not affected by $C_{HL}$, the only admissible transition is $(a, x) \rightarrow (\neg a, x)$, where x is $\neg b$.

17. Observe that the behaviour of Move-F and checking is not symmetrical. For if Move-F raises a visible feature $f$, checking can extend to the other features that $f$ carries along (cf. Chomsky's *free-riders*). In general, Move-F and checking (whether the latter is seen as a procedure or simply as a relation) are divorced in the following sense: Move-F is motivated by the need to check a feature, $f$, and only considers such a feature. Checking, on the other hand, applies to a pair of sets of features $(\mathcal{F}_1, \mathcal{F}_2)$ and tries to match all the corresponding visible features of $\mathcal{F}_1$ and $\mathcal{F}_2$ — that is, it is not driven by any particular feature.

18. The extension of the above treatment to account for PF interpretability is straightforward and will not be pursued here. A third component can be added to the state descriptors, and the relevant definitions and operations can then be suitably modified. Let us observe, however, that, as long as Spell-Out can apply anywhere in $N \rightarrow \lambda$, PF non-interpretability entails LF non-interpretability, but not vice versa. Thus strong features are always non-interpretable at LF. It must be observed, however, that the idea itself of extending the interpretability requirement at PF to account for strong features may prove to be too simplistic. If we consider the operation of Spell-Out closely, we see that it acts like a filter that takes a syntactic object $\Sigma$ and strips away from it all the features not relevant to PF (Chomsky 1993, 1994, 1995). Thus, if strong features interfere with PF, it must be the case that they are not stripped away at S-O and therefore *are* relevant for PF, despite the fact that they cause the derivation to crash. It seems, therefore, that something more should be said about strong features to correctly capture their behaviour. The approach proposed in the text, however, has the merit of putting them on a par with the other features. A different proposal is elaborated in Chomsky (1995). He abandons the connection between the notion of strength of a feature and PF requirements and simply stipulates that strong features are something that derivations cannot tolerate. Therefore they are made non-visible by checking as soon as possible.

19. For a discussion, see Iatridou (1990a); Thráinsson (1994); Platzack and Rosengren (1994). All these authors conclude on the basis of considerations concerning different languages that the clausal architecture cannot be taken to be universal per se. Notice also that these authors develop a different view with respect to the parametric perspective discussed by Ouhalla (1988, 1991).

20. Or, more appropriately, the checking of $F_1$ does not follow the checking of $F_2$.

21. Note also that it could be the case that the ordering relation is not a *total* one — that is, not every pair of features is necessarily ordered. This implies that a certain space for parametrisation might still be available in the grammar.

22. Cinque (1994) also shows by means of an analysis of Italian and French that the ordering of the verbal specifiers does not vary, even if the position of the participle might be different. He also cites a number of references on various languages (Navajo, Basque) which seem to have the same ordering of specifiers as Italian and French. We refer the reader to Cinque's work and to the references cited there.

23. See chapter 3 for a discussion of this topic and of English verbal morphology.

24. Essentially, (16) is a consequence of the crucial role that features play in the minimalist approach. On the one hand, it simply says that singleton categories are allowed, a trivial fact. On the other hand, it allows the features of a syncretic category to function in an autonomous way, provided that other principles of the grammar are respected.

25. Significantly, in Italian there is no perfective/imperfective alternation in the future. There is, in fact, no separate morpheme which can be used to give the desired aspectual meaning. On the aspectual value of the future in Italian, see Bertinetto (1991).

26. Here we will only consider a simplified version of propositional tense logic, as predicate tense logic lies outside the scope of our analysis. For a discussion, see Burges (1984). Furthermore, questions concerning the relationships between tense logic and modality will not be addressed. For the sake of completeness, let us say that if modality is considered along with time, the model is $M = (W, T, <, R, V)$ where $W$ is a set of worlds, $T$ is the set of time instants, the same for all worlds, and $<$ and $R$ are, respectively, the *earlier than* relation on moments of time and the *accessibility* relation on worlds. $V$ is the interpretation function which assigns truth values to triples consisting of a propositional letter $p$, a time instant, $t \in T$, and a world, $w \in W$, this way relativising the truth of a proposition to a given world and a time instant. In the text, for simplicity, we disregard worlds and the corresponding accessibility relation.

27. For a discussion, see Kamp (1968).

28. The operator approach could account for (30b) by introducing another operator, $N$, that forces the relative clause predicate to be evaluated with respect to the utterance time (cf. Kamp 1968). The logical form for (30b) would then be (i):

(i)     $P(\exists x \ (\text{child}(x) \wedge \text{born}(x) \wedge NF(\text{king}(x))))$

29. Compare the vast literature on the algebraic approach to the semantics of natural language (Link 1983, 1987), where hypotheses on the structure of the domain of interpretation play a major role in accounting for such phenomena as the mass/count distinction (Link 1983), plurals, aktionsarten (Bach 1986), and so on.

30. For the purpose of discussing the status of temporal entities, we can either consider the operator approach or the referential one, as the issues we are going to address do not depend on a specific approach.

31. This example is modelled after Kamp & Reyle (1993).

32. Assuming that we know how to tell when the sickness starts and when it ends.

33. This deadlock could be circumvented by adopting, for example, a more elaborate logical apparatus capable of dealing with truth value gaps.

34. Bach (1981) coined the term *eventuality*, which encompasses both events (such as the stabbing of Caesar by Brutus) and states (such as the sickness of John). The philosophical literature has considered also things such as actions and happenings. We disregard these distinctions and use the term *event* as a label

encompassing both events as traditionally conceived of (as entities involving change) and states (cf. Vendler 1967).

35. Note that we have implicitly used a language for logical forms with sorted variable, where $e$ ranges on events. Alternatively, we could have written (i) instead of (37):

(i)     $\exists x$ [x is an event](run(John, x))

In this way, the fact that the variable ranges over events is made explicit in the logical form.

36. Davidson constructs his argument starting from the theory of events proposed by Reichenbach (1947). The main point of contact between the two theories is that, according to both Reichenbach and Davidson, the logical form of a sentence like *Brutus stabbed Caesar* contains an existential quantifier. They do differ, however, in the way they analyse events. For Davidson they are *individuals*, whereas Reichenbach explained them as consisting of *facts*.

37. Some scholars, though admitting events, deny that they are primitive objects and that they can be assimilated to ordinary individuals. Rather, they (e.g., Kim 1976; Peterson 1989; Chisolm 1990) regard events as complex entities. According to Kim, events are triples consisting of a *participant*, a *time*, and a *property*. Chisolm, on the other hand, argues that time should be dropped, while maintaining the other two. Finally, Peterson endorses Kim's view but allows events themselves to be parts of complex ones. A crucial issue concerns their identity conditions for events. Such a question has been answered differently also according to the kind of metaphysical status assigned to events. We will not consider this topic here, but only point out that within a Davidsonian view, according to which events are individuals, the question of the identity conditions can be addressed on the basis of the structure assigned to events. For example, if we conceive of events as having parts and posit that the *part-of* relation plays a major role in characterising event domains, then we may reduce identity conditions to the ordinary extensional one — that is, two events are identical iff they have the same parts.

38. In the following chapters we will hypothesise that the morphosyntax of the present tense is crucially different from that of the other tenses. See chapters 2 and 5.

39. The introduction of $R$ is a rather controversial hypothesis. For different proposals see, among others, Bertinetto (1986) and, within the GB framework, Zagona (1988). For a defence of the Reichenbachian point of view, see Hornstein (1990). An argument suggested by Reichenbach (p. 290, fn. 1), who credits Jespersen (1924) for hypothesising the presence of $R$ to distinguish between the simple past and the present perfect, is constituted by the presence of sentences such as:

(i)     Now I have eaten enough.

Reichenbach does not give the full reasoning with respect to this example, which we try to reconstruct as follows. Given that the point $R$ is always realised, the simple past and the present perfect are associated with the following representations respectively: $E,R\_S$ and $E\_R,S$. In the case of the present perfect, therefore, $R$ coincides with $S$. Time adverbials, according to Reichenbach's hypothesis, refer to $R$.

As a consequence, we must assume that the adverbial *now* is a specification of *R*. Given that *S* represents the utterance *now*, the present perfect is the only past form compatible with a context such as the one exemplified in (i).

40. We assume that the process of T-marking is very close to the θ-binding hypothesised by Higginbotham (1985). See chapter 2 for further discussion.

41. The reverse property seems to be too strong, at least in our framework. In fact, it does not seem to be true that every *event* must receive a T-role, at least not directly from T. Notice also that analogously to θ-marking, the T-roles are assigned to syntactic positions (VPs) and not to referential items. In *John loves himself*, for instance, there are two syntactic positions, each receiving an independent θ-marking, but only one referential entity.

42. Another important problem is constituted by the analysis of the relationship between events and time. In chapter 4 we will provide empirical arguments in favour of the idea that times might be reduced to events. Recall, in fact, as we said above in the text, that the events are temporally located with respect to the utterance *now*, which in turn is nothing other than an event — that is, the *speech event*. In the literature there are several proposals showing that such a reduction can be pursued, by construing *time* out of a domain of event individuals (cf. Russell 1914, 1936; Kamp 1979; van Benthem 1983; Pianesi & Varzi 1996a).

# 2

# On the Italian, Latin, and
# Portuguese Temporal Systems

In this chapter we compare the morphosyntactic systems of tense in Italian with that of (classical) Latin, and then we further extend our analysis to Portuguese. The reason for this choice of languages is due to the consideration that Latin on the one hand and Italian and Portuguese on the other are strictly related for historical reasons, although superficially they are very different. A major point of investigation is constituted by the fact that Italian uses auxiliaries to obtain complex verbal forms, whereas this seems not to be the case in (classical) Latin, at least in the active voice. We will show, however, that the main difference between Latin and Italian, and to a certain extent Portuguese, does not lie in the presence or absence of auxiliaries, but rather in a divergent feature specification of the temporal morphemes in the two languages. We will show that, in spite of the differences, the same theoretical apparatus which accounts for Italian can be adopted for Latin; the temporal systems of the two languages, in fact, instantiate similar temporal values by means of items that exhibit different morphological properties. According to the hypothesis sketched in the first chapter, in fact, languages vary morphosyntactically. The inventory of features contained in the adult grammar and the way in which they are organised into categories — that is, the syncretic and hybrid realisations — differ from language to language. We will show that the main property which distinguish Latin and Italian in the domain considered here consists in a different categorial specification of the temporal items — that is, in a difference in the association of the temporal morphemes with the features determining the categorial status. Independent evidence in favour of our ideas will be provided by our analysis of the (European) Portuguese temporal system. We will show that Portuguese exhibits *intermediate* properties with respect to Italian on the one hand and Latin on the other.

## 2.1. The temporal projections

As far as our theory predicts the empirical phenomena of Italian, Latin, and Portuguese, it can be concluded that the general hypothesis sketched in chapter 1 is correct. In particular, the point which will be considered here concerns the double representation of tense inside a clausal structure — that is, T1 and T2.

We hypothesised that T1 and T2 are lexical items requiring a predicate for a process of T-identification, analogous to θ-identification, which has been hypothesised for the internal arguments of a "standard" predicate (cf. Higginbotham 1985). This requirement will play a crucial role in predicting the occurrence of auxiliaries to build complex verbal forms.

Our analysis of Italian, Latin, and Portuguese also provides an argument in favour of the "general philosophy" proposed by Chomsky's minimalist hypothesis (1993, 1994, 1995). As we discussed in the previous chapter, in fact, he claims that the interface-levels are the *only* levels in a simple design of the language faculty and proposes that all parametric variations can be reduced to differences in the morphological systems of various languages. A strong argument in favour of this position is given by learnability considerations. Only what is detectable at PF can be learned, and, accordingly, LFs are different only as a reflex of PFs. We will argue that this idea has important and promising consequences with respect to the general problem of tense interpretation, and, in particular, we will show in this chapter that our proposal can reduce the differences among the temporal representations allowed by the various languages to detectable morphological properties.

Let us illustrate this reasoning by means of an actual structure to be discussed in greater detail in the following chapters. Recall that the goal of this analysis is to provide an empirical argument in favour of the Reichenbachian model we are adopting and of the T-criterion we just illustrated. We introduce, therefore, the minimal structure necessary to this end. As a consequence, the functional projections present in the tree are only the ones relevant to our discussion. We therefore introduce $AGR_S$ (our AGR1); the AGR node closing the projection of the participle (our AGR2); and the projections of T, T1 and T2, whereas we are not taking into account other possible projections, such as the aspectual ones.[1] The following picture represents only a first approximation of the actual structure:[2]

(1) AGR1-P

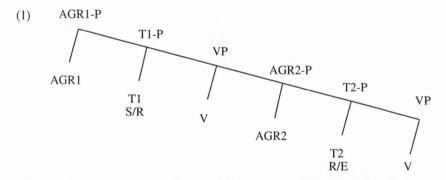

As we will better see in the following sections, this structure is instantiated in Italian for sentences with a verb expressing the past perfect (*ebbi mangiato* = I had eaten) or the future perfect (*avrò mangiato* = I will have eaten). The two temporal projections, T1 and T2, lexicalise the tense relations, *S/R* and *E/R*, respectively, as indicated in the tree. The AGR nodes, AGR1 and AGR2, resemble Chomsky's Agreement subject and Agreement object, respectively, even if in our case their presence is simply justified on the basis of the morphological expression (and consequently, syntactic checking) of the features of person and number (AGR1) and of number and gender (AGR2) when both T1 and T2 are present; see following discussion.

The structure in (1) is very similar to the one proposed by Belletti (1990). The only difference is that she seems to attribute only aspectual values to the past participial morphology, whereas we also attribute it a temporal function. The presence of a temporal value, however, does not imply at all that the participle has no aspectual property. On the contrary, as we will better argue in chapter 3, we propose that the aspectual information is syncretically realised together with the temporal one and can be "scattered" when necessary.

In this chapter we show that the presence of the temporal projection T2 makes some correct predictions with respect to both the interpretative properties and the distribution of auxiliaries. The lower VP is projected by the verb, whereas the higher one is projected by the auxiliary in Italian, either *essere* (be) or *avere* (have); in Latin, only *esse* (be).[3] We will show that auxiliaries don't give any contribution per se to the temporal interpretation of the sentence and that therefore their presence is required only by the syntax. Chomsky (1993) proposes that auxiliaries disappear at LF because they are replaced by the main verb moving in the highest available position. The *replacement* idea presumably cannot be maintained if Kayne (1993) is correct. Kayne in fact argues that *have* and *be* differ in that the former incorporates an abstract preposition whereas the latter does not, and this information should presumably be recoverable at LF. Given these considerations, we can conclude that an approach following Chomsky's (1995) more recent suggestions, according to which covert movement can be thought of as bare feature movement (Move-F), seems more promising. The relevant features of the verb, in fact, could be moved covertly to adjoin to the feature bundle of the auxiliary in order to undergo the checking procedure.

Note that with respect to the question concerning the choice of auxiliary we hypothesise that it is a function of properties other than the temporal ones, perhaps case assignment and θ-marking.[4] For our purposes, we will take auxiliaries to be verbs whose *event* specification is, roughly speaking, inherited by that of the main verb. In chapter 3 we will better consider such an idea while discussing the empirical content of the Reichenbachian points; see also §1.3.

As stated above, AGR1 represents the set of φ-features, in Italian *person* and *number*, that are shared with the subject, i.e. (Spec, AGR1"). We argue that in Italian and Latin only the AGR-bearing person specification is able to assign nominative case.[5] AGR2 is specified for gender and number features.[6] An interesting descriptive generalisation seems to be that φ-features define word boundaries, at least in Latin, Romance, and Germanic.[7]

Observe also that T2 in Italian requires an AGR2 and is not compatible with AGR1. The reason is that T2 is an adjectival category and is therefore incompatible with the feature *person*, typical of verbal categories, which is realised by AGR1; thus feature checking, which in Italian in this case takes place before Spell-Out, would fail. We can say that T2 is a *[+V; +N]* category; AGR2, bearing *gender* and *number* features, is also specified as *[+V; +N]*, and therefore meets the compatibility requirement. If, on the contrary, an AGR1 is present, the final result would be ungrammatical. AGR1, in fact, being specified for person, is characterised by the features *[+V; -N]* and is therefore incompatible with an adjectival form.[8] However, it is not the case that in every language T2 is specified in this way. For instance, we will see that in Latin the T2 morpheme expressing $E\_R$ must be seen as a verbal projection and, as predicted, is compatible with AGR1.[9]

Let us summarise. In Italian, every sentence containing a T2 also has an AGR2. Descriptively, AGR2 bears $\phi$-features and defines word boundaries, identifying an $X^0$ item which the morphological component might be able to deal with. Given, however, that further information is present in the tree, i.e. T1 (at least in some cases, as we will discuss later) and AGR1, a head has to be provided to check the features of such items. In Latin, the T2 morpheme expressing $E\_R$ in active sentences is not adjectival, being characterised by the verbal features *[+V; -N]*. As such, AGR2 cannot appear, whereas the verbal AGR1, also *[+V; -N]*, is compatible with it. In the next section the empirical and theoretical implications of this hypothesis will be considered.[10]

Note finally that in a structure such as the one proposed in (1) for Italian, two factors determine the realisation of an auxiliary. We have just discussed the first one namely, the presence of an AGR category defining word boundaries. The second one is the T-criterion. In (1) both T2 and T1 are lexically realised and must assign a T-role, to satisfy the T-criterion. T2 discharges it on the "real" verb, and consequently T1 needs an auxiliary verb to satisfy the requirement. We will see how these two requirements bear out in Latin, providing empirical evidence in favour of our hypothesis.

## 2.2. The Italian system

Let us begin with the morphosyntactic analysis of the present tense. From an empirical point of view, Italian, as well as many other languages, does not make use of any morpheme to express the present tense in (matrix) clauses. It is very well known that the present tense is the unmarked form. That is, it is the one appearing more often across languages with no specific marker identifying it. The semantics of this tense, as suggested by Reichenbach (1947), is $S,R,E$ — that is, the three points coincide. Compositionally, according to Comrie and Hornstein, it can be represented as $(S,R) \cdot (R,E)$. Our conclusion is the following: in all the cases in which a relation is represented by means of a comma, there is neither a morpheme lexicalising it nor the corresponding category. Our proposal is that the temporal properties of the present tense are specified only at LF.

Observe that in languages which have "nominal sentences" — that is, where it is possible (or obligatory) to dispense with the copula, such as in Latin or Russian, the interpretation given to such predicative constructions is always *present*. As soon as the sentence expresses a different tense, such as past or future, a copula must be inserted. The generalisation is that in order to have the present tense interpretation, no (tense) category has to surface and the copula is, accordingly, not necessary. This is not true for the past or future: T1 must be lexicalised and the support of a verb is required. The difference between the present, on the one hand, and the past and future on the other can be accounted for by our hypothesis on the basis of the following observation: if the case of the subject can be assigned in some other way, there is no need to support the present tense with a copula. We do not discuss here the structure of copular constructions and the reasons a copula is always needed in Italian, English, and several other languages.[11] In §2.2. and §2.3. of this chapter we will give additional arguments in favour of the idea that in Italian the present tense does not have a lexical T. Such a proposal will be shown to play a crucial role in the account of the distribution of auxiliaries in Italian and Latin.

Considering the question from another perspective, we hypothesise that there are no Ø lexical heads — that is, lexical heads devoid of lexical content, and consequently no Ø, T1, or T2 heads. This seems a reasonable claim, given the general philosophy of introducing only items corresponding to features present in the array, as proposed by Chomsky (1995). On the other hand, there might be null AGR, since this category is functional, as opposed to lexical. We can suppose that functional heads are independently required by the principles of grammar and therefore can be represented in the syntax to satisfy other requirements.[12] According to these considerations, the representation of a verbal form such as *mangio* (I eat) is the following:

(2)     Mangio.
        I eat.

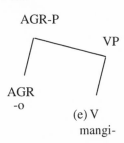

AGR-P

VP

AGR
-o

(e) V
mangi-

The verb must check before Spell-Out the features associated with the agreement morpheme, presumably person and number, and the resulting structure constitutes the input to LF interpretative rules. Present tense in Italian, Latin, and several other languages (for instance, French, English, Japanese, Russian, Greek, Spanish, Portuguese, Catalan, and others) is realised in this way. There might be some apparent counterexamples to such a generalisation, which are easily handled by means of a closer analysis of the temporal system of the language in question. Let us briefly discuss one such case as an exemplification of a possible argument against the view proposed here. In Turkish (see Thomas & Itzkowitz 1967), present tense is formed by adding a morpheme to the verbal root. Such a morpheme can either be $\alpha$,-er, or $\alpha'$, -iyor, which on its turn is followed by agreement. Given such a distribution, one could be led to conclude that the morphemes $\alpha$ or $\alpha'$ realise present tense. However, upon a deeper analysis this hypothesis turns out to be incorrect. In fact, both $\alpha$ and $\alpha'$ can combine with an explicit mark of past tense yielding the form $V + \alpha$ (or $\alpha')+past+agreement$. We also find a simple form for past tense namely, $V+past+agreement$. To describe the whole system correctly, therefore, the morphemes $\alpha$ and $\alpha'$ cannot be considered present tense morphemes, otherwise they would be incompatible with the past tense. On the contrary, they seem to behave as aspectual markers: one for progressive and the other, called *aorist*, to convey the meaning of "general truth" (see Thomas & Itzkowitz 1967, p.75). Consider, for instance, the verb *gitmek* (to go); the verbal stem is *gid*. The simple past has the following form:

(3)    gid-d-im (gittim)

       V+past+agr

       I went

The particle -d- is therefore the past morpheme. Consider now:

(4)    a.  gid-er-im

           V+$\alpha$+agr

           I go (habitually)

       b.  gid-er-d-im

           V+$\alpha$+past+agr

           I used to go

(5)    a.  gid-iyor-um

           V+$\alpha'$+agr

           I am going

       b.  gid-iyor-d-um

           V+$\alpha'$+past+agr

           I was going

The two morphemes,-er- and -iyor- , must therefore be treated as aspectual markers.

Let us now discuss the structure which can be associated with the present perfect, according to these considerations:[13]

(6)     Ho mangiato.
        I have eaten.

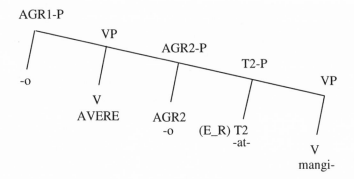

Here, the verb is directly dominated by T2 — that is, by the head expressing the relation between *E* and *R*; T2 assigns its T-role to V, and, being adjectival, requires AGR2 to close the projection. As we stated above, in this case the features corresponding to the ending *-o* are *masculine singular*, which we assume to be the default option. Moreover, an auxiliary must be inserted to lexicalise AGR1. Let us stress that, everything being equal, an auxiliary should appear even for a ∅-agreement. That is, it should appear in languages with no overt agreement features, since a ∅-agreement triggers checking. In the next example we analyse the cases in which both T1 and T2 are realised namely, the future perfect or the past perfect:

(7)     Ebbi mangiato.
        I had eaten.

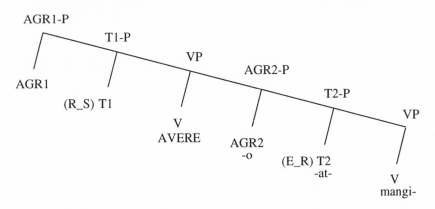

In this example T1 must assign its T-role and therefore requires an auxiliary verb. As we already pointed out in the preceding discussion, in these cases the auxiliary is required in Italian, both because of the presence of AGR2, defining word boundaries, and because of the presence of T1, to satisfy the T-criterion.

The two requirements are independent from each other therefore, we expect them to split in other languages. As we are going to see, Latin provides such a case. Before proceeding further, notice that the simple future and the simple past instantiate the first part of the structure in (7), since only T1 is present, followed by the main verb (instead of an auxiliary). The association of the semantics concerning the *E/R* relation with T2 (in Italian, with the past participle) seems to be able to correctly predict some phenomena. In particular, we predict that in absolute constructions (see Belletti 1990) a temporal interpretation should be available, since, due to the presence of the past participle, a T2 node is present in the tree, and, accordingly, the relation between *E* and *R* is instantiated. Consider the following example:

(8)   Salutati gli amici, Maria partì.
      Having said good-bye to her friends, Mary left.

The past participial clause corresponds to the following structure:

(9)      AGR2-P

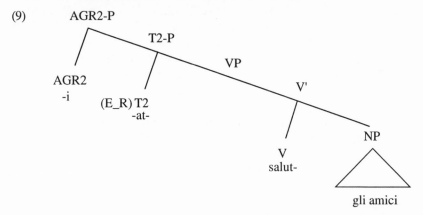

Following Hornstein's view on the combination of tense structures of adverbial and matrix clauses, we propose the following temporal interpretation of (8):

(10)      $E_1, R_1\_S$
               |
          $E_2\_R_2$

That is, the event of leaving $(e_1)$ follows the event of saying good-bye $(e_2)$. We will better discuss the formal system of tense interpretation in the following chapters, but for the purposes of the arguments given here, the notation in (10) is sufficient. Note that it is possible to modify (8) by means of time adverbials, as in the following example:

(11)   Salutati gli amici alle quattro, Maria partì alle cinque.
       Having said good-bye to her friends at four, Mary left at five.

As expected, the opposite is not possible:

(12)    *Salutati gli amici alle cinque, Maria partì alle quattro.
        Having said good-bye to her friends at five, Mary left at four.

These data follow from the presence of T2 in the participial clause. In other words, without a temporal value assigned to the participial construction, the temporal ordering of the two events would be impossible.[14]

## 2.3. The Latin system

In this section we briefly present some data concerning Latin which we have already discussed in greater detail in previous work (cf. Giorgi & Pianesi 1991). Here, we summarise the results already achieved and propose some new generalisations in light of the theory proposed in this work. We discuss examples from classical Latin — that is, when Latin was at the stage of linguistic development in which the periphrastic perfect forms, with auxiliary *habere* (have), were not yet productive.[15]

Notice that Latin is often taken to be a language *without* auxiliaries (in the active system), even if it exhibits an array of morphologically possible tenses as rich as the Italian one, and almost in a one-to-one correspondence with them. Simplifying somewhat, we are assuming that the Latin imperfect is equivalent to the Italian simple past. Such an idea is compatible with the description of the temporal values associated with such a form.[16] For syntactic purposes, therefore, we claim that *laudavi* lexicalises the information $E\_R$ (plus $S,R$, which, however, does not correspond to a morpheme; see preceding discussion), whereas *laudabam* lexicalises $R\_S$ (plus $E,R$ not corresponding to a morpheme either). The point which we are going to discuss concerns the correspondence between the Italian periphrastic form *ho lodato* and the Latin synthetic *laudavi*. More generally, we would like to single out the invariant properties of UG underlying such different realisations. We will compare each Italian form with the corresponding translation in Latin. In Latin, the present tense is like the Italian one (cf. ex. 2):

(13)    Laud-o.
        $[_{\text{AGR1}''} \text{AGR1} \, [_{\text{V}''} \text{V}]]$
        I praise.

In the past, *laudabat* (he praised), and in the future, *laudabit* (he will praise), the verbal theme *lauda-* is followed by a tense morpheme, *-ba-*, or *-bi-*, and then by an agreement morpheme, expressing person and number features.[17] According to our hypotheses, we can say that these forms lexicalise V+T1+AGR1 and express the following semantics: $S\_R$ (plus $R,E$, which, however, does not correspond to a morpheme, as we mentioned in the preceding discussion), for the future, and $R\_S$ (plus $R,E$) for the past. So far, Latin seems identical to Italian, but different properties can be observed in the perfect forms.

Consider the form *laudavit* (he has praised), where we recognise the following components: *laud(a)-*, which is the verbal stem, *-vi-*, which expresses the temporal value of the form, and, finally, -t, which lexicalises the $\phi$-features (third person singular). In our paradigm the morpheme -vi- realises T2 in this case $E\_R$ and -t lexicalises AGR1.[18] As we have discussed, the presence of AGR2 is required for Italian because of the adjectival nature of T2 in this language. However, T2 seems to be verbal in Latin, since AGR1 is perfectly compatible with it. If this description is correct, we immediately have an explanation for the reason the Latin perfect form does not require an auxiliary. AGR2 is not present in Latin; therefore, there is no word boundary. Accordingly, no necessity for inserting a supporting verb to check the $\phi$-features of AGR1 arises. Let us give the structure we hypothesise for the Latin perfect:[19]

(14)   Lauda-vi-t.
       $[_{AGR1''} \text{AGR1} [_{T2''} \text{T2} [_{V''} \text{V}]]]$
       He has praised.

According to our theory, the difference between the verbal systems of Italian and Latin simply follows from the language-specific property concerning the categorial status of T2.

Consider now the past and future perfect, *laudaveram* and *laudavero*, respectively. According to our hypotheses, the form *laudaveram* is analysed in the following way: *lauda-v-er-A-m*.[20] The semantics corresponding to this form are the following: T1 expresses the relation $R\_S$, and T2, the relation $E\_R$. We hypothesise that the form *eram* is an incorporated auxiliary more precisely, the past form (imperfect) of the verb *sum, esse* (be), which realises the past as a long vowel, A. See, for instance, Lindsay (1984) for the hypothesis which analyses -*eram* and -*ero* as forms of the verb "be".[21]

(15)   Lauda-v-er-a-m.
       $[_{AGR1''} \text{AGR1} [_{T1''} \text{T1} [_{Vaux''} \text{V} [_{T2''} \text{T2} [_{V''} \text{V}]]]]]$
       I had praised.

As we discussed above, -vi- is verbal; therefore it is compatible with AGR1. Hence, it does not require AGR2. If T1 is present in the tree ($R\_S$ for the past; $S\_R$ for the future), it needs a verb to discharge its T-role, and the auxiliary *be* must be realised. As a further consequence of the absence of AGR2, in the active form the auxiliary is incorporated, since no functional category intervenes (the only functional category being AGR1).

The last point to be considered concerns the Latin forms with the future participle in -*urus*; in Italian there is no (morphemic) equivalent of this participle.[22] We propose that such a form lexicalises $R\_E$. See Reichenbach (1947) for a similar suggestion. This participle is adjectival and therefore requires AGR2 (-*us*). Moreover, because of the presence of AGR2, incorporation processes will not be able to include the AGR1 morpheme, or the one corresponding to T1. As a consequence, an auxiliary must be inserted. Our theory concerning the nature of T2 predicts the morphological difference between the future corresponding to $S\_R,E$, where only AGR1, T1, and the verb surface, as in *laudabo* (I will praise), and the future corresponding to $S,R\_E$, as in *laudaturus sum* (I will praise, I am going to praise), where the auxiliary "be" must appear to permit the features of AGR1 to surface. The existence of this form is predicted by our approach. In fact, since T2 lexicalises the relations between $R$ and $E$, we expect both $E\_R$ and $R\_E$ to be instantiated across languages: the form lexicalising $E\_R$ corresponds to the perfect forms. $R\_E$ is lexicalised by the future participle. The forms obtained in this way are the present prospective, past prospective, and future prospective respectively:

(16) a. laudaturus sum.
  I am going to praise *(S,R • R_E)*.
 b. laudaturus eram.
  I was going to praise *(R_S • R_E)*
 c. laudaturus ero.
  I will be going to praise *(S_R • R_E)*

Let us summarise the arguments discussed so far. If one supposes that T1 is *always* realised in the tree, even in the present tense, the wrong prediction would obtain with respect to the Latin (active) present perfect. If T1 is in the tree, T-marking *must* take place to satisfy the T-criterion, and as such an auxiliary verb *must* be provided for this purpose. In this way, the occurrence of an auxiliary would be predicted *both* in the Italian *and* in the Latin present perfect, a conclusion which we showed to be contradicted by empirical evidence. On the contrary, our hypothesis that there is no T in these cases makes the correct predictions.

## 2.4. The Portuguese system

In this section we consider the verbal system of (European) Portuguese and compare it with Italian and Latin. Let us start our analysis by considering the semantic value of the Portuguese simple past.

In a footnote, Reichenbach (1947), attributing the observation to Jespersen (1924), points out that the present perfect (in English) is crucially different in its distribution from the simple past, because it has the property of expressing a past situation with current relevance (cf. chapter 1, fn. 39). The example Reichenbach cites is the following:

(17) Now I have eaten enough.

The acceptability of the adverb *now* distinguishes the two past forms — that is, the present perfect from the simple past. The simple past cannot appear in this context:

(18) *Now I ate enough.

The same pattern is found in Italian:

(19) a. Adesso ho mangiato abbastanza.
  Now I have eaten enough.
 b. *Adesso mangiai abbastanza.
  Now I ate enough.

In general, in the languages which have both tenses in their inventory, the compound form can cooccur with *now*, whereas the simple one cannot. In chapter 3 we will propose an explanation for this fact. Here we are only interested in the crosslinguistic distribution of this phenomenon.

In Portuguese, as in English, Italian, Spanish, and Catalan, we find two past forms: a periphrastic one comprised of the auxiliary verb *ter* plus a participle, *tenho comido* (I have eaten), and a simple one, *comi* (I ate). It is rather surprising, therefore, that in Portuguese, the translation of (17) is the following:

(20) Agora já *comi* o suficiente.
Lit.: Now I *ate* enough.
Now I have eaten enough.

The compound form, though possible, conveys a different meaning, which refers to a *habit* of eating enough:

(21) Agora já tem comido o suficiente.
Now I took the habit of eating enough.

In chapter 3 we will consider the semantics and the morphosyntax of (21) in more detail. Here we focus on the fact that the simple form is grammatical with *now*, constituting in some sense an *exceptional* case which requires an explanation. We will show that a crosslinguistic analysis of the verbal system as a whole can provide a possible reason for the distribution of the simple past observed above.

The Portuguese temporal system can be schematised as in (22). We also list the strong verbal forms of the verb *saber* (to know) when they are crucially different from the weak ones of the verb *falar* (to speak):

(22) present: falas (you speak)
It.: parli

imperfect: falavas (you spoke)
It.: parlavi

simple past: falaste (you spoke)
It.: parlasti
saber: soubeste (you knew)
It.: sapesti

present perfect: tenho falado (I have spoken)
It.: ho parlato

pluperfect : tinha falado (I had spoken)
(imperfect + participle) It.: avevo parlato

past perfect : *tive falado (I had spoken)
(past + participle) It.: ebbi parlato

synthetic pluperfect: falara (falaras, falara, faláramos, faláreis, falaram)
It.: avevo parlato, etc.
soubera (souberas, soubera, soubéramos, soubéreis, souberam)
It.: avevo saputo, etc.

This system exhibits two main peculiarities. The first one is the complete unavailability of the so-called past perfect — that is, the periphrastic tense comprised of the simple past of the auxiliary *ter* and the past participle of the main verb. The form *tive falado* does not exist, and the speakers do not even understand its value; it is almost incomprehensible. This fact is rather surprising because in the other Romance languages, with the exception of Romanian, we find such forms: It. *ebbi mangiato* (I had-simple past eaten); Fr. *j'eus parlé* ( I had-simple past spoken); Sp. *hube hablado* (I had-simple past spoken); Cat. *haguí portat* (I had-simple past taken). Notice that the existence of the past perfect in French is especially relevant, because in this language the simple past is obsolete. In the languages listed here, the past perfect does not have a wide distribution. For instance, in Italian it appears only in a very limited numbers of contexts typically in clauses introduced by *quando* (when) or *dopo che* (lit.: after that):

(23)  a.  Quando *ebbe mangiato*, Gianni si sentì meglio.
          When he had eaten, Gianni felt better.
      b.  Dopo che *ebbe mangiato*, Gianni si sentì meglio.
          After he had eaten, Gianni felt better.

In these contexts, however, the past perfect is almost obligatory:

(24)  ??Dopo che mangiò, Gianni si sentì meglio.
      After he ate, Gianni felt better.

(25)  ??Dopo che aveva mangiato, Gianni si sentì meglio.
      After he had-IMPF eaten, Gianni felt better.

Although these sentences are not completely ungrammatical, it must be pointed out that another tense could not convey the meaning of the past perfect. The past perfect signals that the time of the *eating* precedes the time of the *feeling better*: this tense has more or less the same distribution in Spanish, French, and Catalan.[23]

The second peculiarity of the Portuguese system is the existence of a synthetic pluperfect, which is rather obsolete and has practically disappeared in Brazilian Portuguese. This form is comprised of the theme of the past and a peculiar desinence, appearing only in this tense. The hypothesis on the origin of this form is that it is derived from the Latin pluperfect: Lat. *amaveram* > Port. *amara* (cf. Huber 1986; Vázquez Cuesta & Mendes da Luz 1989). Its meaning is identical to that of the periphrastic pluperfect, consisting of the imperfect of the auxiliary *ter* and the past participle.[24] This is an interesting fact, for, with respect to this property, Portuguese resembles Latin, which has the synthetic pluperfect, whereas in Italian such a form does not exist. Notice, finally, that in the schema in (22) above, in addition to the forms of the verb *falar*, we also give the simple past of the verb *saber* (to know) *soubeste* (you knew), which is an irregular, strong, form. The synthetic pluperfect is construed on the theme of the past, and this can be seen only with strong verbs, which have a different theme for past.

Let us try to provide a unified explanation for the two "anomalous" properties of Portuguese, the lack of a past perfect and the presence of a synthetic pluperfect. Our idea is that the Portuguese verbal system is very similar to the Latin one. In particular, the crucial property the two languages have in common concerns the morphosyntactic structure of the simple past form, in our examples *falaste* and *soubeste*. As we have seen in the preceding discussion of the distribution of this tense with *now*, these forms correspond to the Italian present perfect. Consider also the following examples:

(26)  a.  Ho mangiato / mangiai alle quattro.

I have eaten/ I ate at four.

b.  Comi as quatro.

I have eaten/ I ate at four.

c.  Tenho comido as quatro.

I took the habit of eating at four.

The sentence in (26b) corresponds to both of the forms given in (26a). The Portuguese simple past is perfectly adequate in both cases, whereas the periphrastic form, *tenho comido*, is unavailable with the same interpretation. As can be seen by the glosses, in fact, it expresses a completely different meaning (see chapter 3 §3.3.). These data point to the conclusion that the simple past in Portuguese is a T2 — that is, it is the equivalent of the Latin form *laudavit*.[25] The only simple past form in Portuguese, analogously to what we have hypothesised above for Latin, is the imperfect, which, besides being associated with a non-perfective value, conveys a temporal meaning belonging to the T1 class.[26]

This hypothesis predicts the nonexistence of a form such as \**tive comido*. Intuitively, given that the past participle is a T2, we cannot have a sequence composed of two identical forms. This prediction is borne out. As we pointed out above, the periphrastic form *tive comido* is impossible and almost incomprehensible for native speakers. Notice that there is no intuitive reason which determines this property. The corresponding form which has an imperfect auxiliary is acceptable in Portuguese (*tinha comido*), and it has exactly the same meaning as the corresponding Italian, or, more generally, Romance form: *avevo mangiato* (I had-IMPF eaten).[27]

Consider at this point the synthetic pluperfect. The obvious suggestion following from the observations made above is that the Portuguese pluperfect has a morphosyntactic structure analogous to the Latin one. It can be argued that the characteristic desinence of this tense is the imperfect of the Portuguese auxiliary *ser* (be), which is attached to the past theme, exactly like in Latin. Consider the following paradigms:

(27)      era, eras, era, éramos, éreis, eram

(28)   a.   falara, falaras, falara, faláramos, faláreis, falaram
           I had spoken, you had spoken . . .
       b.   soubera, souberas, soubera, soubéramos, soubéreis, souberam
           I had known, you had known . . .

In (27) we have given the imperfect of *ser*, and in (28a) and (28b) we have reproduced the paradigms of the first conjugation verb *falar* (speak) and of the irregular verb *saber* (know). The first vowel of the auxiliary is assimilated with the thematic vowel of the verb, giving the forms listed above. This view thus constitutes an important additional piece of evidence in favour of our analysis. The only forms in our system which can be combined with auxiliaries are T2s, and not T1s. The fact that with strong verbs such as *saber* we have *soubera* and not *sabera* is an argument in favour of this idea.

Let us point out another piece of evidence (from Vázquez Cuesta & Mendes da Luz 1989, p. 526) which seems to go in the same direction, even though its explanation goes beyond the limits of this work. Consider the following example:

(29)   Outro exame mais e terminaste o curso.
       One more examination and you *have done* with the course.

The sentence in (29) does not mean that the finishing of the course is located in the past, but rather, that it is located in the future. It means "one more examination and you will have finished the course". The appropriate translation in the other Romance languages (e.g., French, Spanish, Catalan, and Italian) has the present perfect and not the simple past. Let us consider Italian:

(30)   a.   Un altro esame ancora e *hai finito* il corso.
           One more examination and you *have finished* with your course.
       b.   *Un altro esame ancora e *finisti* il corso.
           One other examination and you *finished* with your course.

The form in (30b) is not interpretable as the future outcome of a certain situation. This is true independently of the usage the language in question makes of the simple past (i.e., independently of the geographic distribution of the present perfect vs. the simple past; see chapter 3, §3.2.).

To summarise: we propose that the Portuguese simple past must be interpreted as a T2 — that is, as morphologically equivalent to the Latin present perfect, and we have discussed various pieces of data pointing to this conclusion. The first piece of evidence is that there is no form such as *tive comido*, as opposed to *tinha comido*. The second one consists of the existence of the synthetic pluperfect, which can be analysed analogously to the Latin form. The third piece of evidence consists of various pieces of data suggesting that the equivalent of the Romance present perfect is the Portuguese simple past, even in those cases where the corresponding Romance sentences would yield an impossible temporal structure (see the data in (20) and (29)). In the following schemata we provide a synopsis of the Portuguese and the Latin systems along the lines suggested above:

(31)

| | Latin<br>laudare (praise) | Portuguese | |
| | | falar (speak) | saber (know) |
|---|---|---|---|
| present | laudas | falas | (sabes) |
| imperfect | laudabas | falavas | (sabias) |
| simple past | laudavisti<br>It.: hai lodato | falaste<br>It.: hai parlato | (soubeste) |
| pluperfect | laudaveras<br>It.: avevi (avesti)<br>lodato | falaras<br>tinha falado<br>It.: avevi (avesti)<br>parlato | (souberas)<br>(tinha sabido) |

Our idea is that the Portuguese system has the property of lexicalising T2 by means of a verbal suffix.[28] Such a suffix is compatible with the verbal features (person and number), exactly as the Latin one is. As a consequence, a form such as *falaste* is the exact analogue of a form such as *laudavisti*, and *falaras* is equivalent to *laudaveras*.[29]

## 2.5. On nominative case assignment

In this section we are going to consider the following question: Is nominative case assigned by AGR or by T?[30] The relevance of this question for our work stems from the fact that we hypothesise that T is not always realised in $\Sigma$. In the present tense, at least in Italian (and Latin, in fact), there is no temporal projection between AGR and the verb. In principle, therefore, our proposal seems incompatible with the idea that T assigns nominative, because, obviously, we want it to be assigned even in present tense clauses.

Chomsky (1994; 1995) claims that nominative is checked by T. Such a view is supported by some interesting facts concerning Icelandic as analysed by Jonas & Bobaljik (1993). Taken literally, such a proposal is not compatible with our idea that a category T is present only when a temporal morpheme is realised on the verbal form. Since we must conclude that there is no T node when the verb is in the present tense, then we must also be able to show how nominative case is checked in these cases. In this section, we review some arguments which show that the presence of the nominative case, at least in Italian, is strongly related to the ϕ-features, and in particular to *person*. To the extent that such a close relationship is correct, it can be argued that it is encoded by means of a functional projection embodying both *NOM*(inative) and *person*, thereby providing evidence in favour of $AGR_S$.

The first piece of evidence comes from the analysis of expletive subjects, along the lines proposed by Cardinaletti (1995) and by Chomsky (1995). Cardinaletti points out that there is a correlation between the direction of agreement and case. That is, if the expletive is unambiguously case marked as a nominative, the verb agrees with it. On the other hand, if the expletive is either a locative, or a nominal item which is not unambiguously nominative, the verb agrees with the postnominal DP. Let us consider some examples (from Cardinaletti 1995, exx. 1; 2a; 2b; 3a):

(32)  a.  Il est / *sont arrivé trois filles.
      b.  pro sono arrivate / *è arrivate tre ragazze.
      c.  There come / *comes three girls.
      d.  Es sind / *ist viele Leute angekommen.
          There are many people arrived.

In French, the verb agrees with the expletive subject, which is unambiguously a nominative form. Let us consider the languages where the verb agrees with the postnominal DP. In English the expletive is a locative, and locatives might be taken to be caseless; in Italian, the subject is null, and, as discussed by Rizzi (1986), *pro* can either appear in subject position or in object position, thus being compatible both with accusative and with nominative case. Finally, German *es* is either nominative or accusative. In all these cases the verb agrees with the postverbal DP. Interestingly, Cardinaletti (1995) points out that in Northern Italian dialects, such as Bellunese, Paduan, Venetian, and Bergamasco, the verb agrees with the null expletive, and, as expected, the latter is unambiguously nominative — that is, there is no object *pro*. The reasons why an expletive, if not unambiguously nominative, does not trigger agreement are not trivial and will not be discussed here.[31] Whatever the solution to this question might be, however, it seems to us that the pattern illustrated above can be an argument in favour of our hypothesis. In all the cases listed in (32), in fact, one cannot easily explain how the temporal projection might determine the direction of agreement. In other words, under the T hypothesis, nominative case assignment and agreement phenomena should be regarded as two unrelated facts. If, on the contrary, we hypothesise that nominative case assignment *is* related to agreement, we can account for the pattern noted above. Agreement and nominative in Italian "go together", and the one triggers the other.[32]

The second piece of evidence comes from the following considerations about the so-called dative subjects in Italian. It has been claimed (see Belletti & Rizzi 1988; Cardinaletti 1994) that the dative experiencer of certain psych-verbs, when occurring preverbally, occupies the (Spec,IP) or (Spec,AGR) position:

(33)  A Gianni piacevano le torte al cioccolato.
      Lit.: To Gianni pleased (3d pers plur) chocolate cakes.
      Gianni liked chocolate cakes.

That the dative experiencer occupies a subject position and not a fronted, topicalised one can be shown, following Belletti and Rizzi (1988), on the basis of systematic contrasts between goal datives and experiencer datives. Consider, for instance, the following cases (from Belletti and Rizzi 1988, exx. 104; 105):

(34)   a.  Tutti sono preoccupati perché ho raccontato questa storia a Gianni.
           Everybody is worried because I told this story to Gianni.
       b.  ?? Tutti sono preoccupati perché a Gianni ho raccontato questa storia.
           Everybody is worried because to Gianni I told this story.

(35)       Tutti sono preoccupati perché a Gianni piace la linguistica.
           Lit.: Everybody is worried because to Gianni pleases linguistics.
           Everybody is worried because Gianni likes linguistics.

We will not discuss here the evidence concerning the position of the dative, and we refer the reader to the cited references. Let us consider now case and agreement. As can be seen in (36), the verb agrees with the non-dative DP, which is nominative:

(36)   A Gianni piacevo io.
       Lit.: to Gianni pleased I.
       Gianni liked me.

The question is then: Why are nominative case and agreement "assigned" to the same DP, even if such a DP is neither in subject position nor thematically prominent? Our answer again is that nominative and agreement "go together". Notice that there are some interesting cases where neither argument is nominative, and, accordingly, the verb does not agree with either of them:[33]

(37)   a.  A Gianni importava di questo.
           Lit.: To Gianni cared (3d pers sing) of this.
       b.  A Gianni e a Mario importava di questo e di quello.
           Lit.: To Gianni and to Mario cared (3d pers sing) of this and of that.

The verb appears in both examples in the third person singular, even if in (37b) both arguments are coordinate structures. Notice that a coordinate subject triggers plural on the verb in "normal" cases:

(38)   Gianni e Mario hanno mangiato la torta.
       Gianni and Mario ate (3d pers plur) the cake.

From these examples we can conclude that the verb in (37a) and (37b) is not in an agreement configuration with either argument and that the third person features constitute a "default" agreement.[34] Furthermore, as we already pointed out with respect to the previous example, the simultaneous disappearance of both agreement and case should be considered an epiphenomenon.

Let us consider a third argument. As discussed in Giorgi (1990), in certain constructions an anaphor appears where we usually find, or at least expect to find, a nominative subject:

(39)    Passando davanti allo specchio, le apparve se stessa.
        Passing by the mirror, to her appeared herself.

It can easily be shown that the third person singular agreement appearing on the verb is a *default* agreement, and in fact it does not vary for person:[35]

(40)    a.  Passando davanti allo specchio, mi apparve me stesso.
            Passing by the mirror, to me appeared (3d pers sing) myself.
        b.  Passando davanti allo specchio, ti apparve te stesso.
            Passing by the mirror, to you appeared (3d pers sing) yourself.

To fully explain the data in (40), one should say which case is assigned to the anaphor.[36] For the purposes of this section, however, let us only observe that it is not nominative, given that *me* and *te* are the accusative forms; the verb, however, is an unaccusative; therefore the question concerning the case assigned here remains open. Notice, furthermore, that the verbal form must be singular and cannot be plural. Consider for instance:

(41)    *Passando davanti allo specchio, ci apparvero noi stessi.
        Passing by the mirror, to us appeared (3d pers plur) ourselves.

(42) ?*Passando davanti allo specchio, ci apparve noi stessi.
        Passing by the mirror, to us appeared (3d pers sing) ourselves.

These sentences constitute an argument in favour of our analysis, because, whatever the reason for the ungrammaticality of (41) and (42), they clearly show that the verb does not agree with the anaphor. The possible generalisation is that on the one hand the *default* agreement has singular features and not plural ones and that, on the other, a sort of *compatibility* requirement must be met. The post-verbal argument, which could be the grammatical subject (when nominative), must agree in number with the verb. Consider also that, perhaps more marginally, the following sentences are still acceptable:[37]

(43)    a.  ?Passando davanti allo specchio, le apparve me.
            Passing by the mirror, to her appeared (3d pers sing) me.
        b.  ?Passando davanti allo specchio, le apparve te.
            Passing by the mirror, to her appeared (3d pers sing) you.

Again, in these cases the verb appears in the third person singular and the two pronouns are dative (*le*) and accusative (*me* and *te*), respectively. As soon as an unambiguously nominative form appears, the default agreement is no longer possible:

(44)    a.  *Passando davanti allo specchio le apparve io / io stesso.
            Passing by the mirror, to her appeared (3d pers sing) I / I self.
        b.  Passando davanti allo specchio, le apparvi io / io stesso.
            Passing by the mirror, to her appeared (1st pers sing) I / I self.

Example (44a) clearly contrasts with the examples in (43). These cases are similar to the ones concerning the distribution of the expletives illustrated above. Nominative always correlates with "real" — that is, non default, agreement. Moreover, as in the *importare* (to care) cases, the presence of a tense by itself does not obligatorily trigger nominative case. In (40) and (41), in fact, there is no nominative around. Notice that with respect to the contrast given in (41) and (42), it cannot be concluded that agreement is in general related with nominative case assignment; instead, *person* is.[38]

As a final consideration, let us point out that infinitival verbs, as soon as they have an agreement morpheme, assign nominative, as is well known on the basis of the analysis of Portuguese (see Raposo 1987).

To conclude, we might say that in Italian the relation holding between *person* agreement and nominative case in finite clauses can be expressed as biconditional. In other words, whenever a DP agrees in person with the verb, such a DP is nominative and vice versa. In non-finite clauses the situation might be different, as, for instance, in Aux-to-Comp constructions where we find a non-finite form, without (overt) $\phi$-features, triggering nominative on the subject. Our proposal in terms of syncretic categories is the following. Let us hypothesise that there is a feature *NOM*, and that its checking must not follow the checking of AGR ($\phi$-features), $NOM \geq \phi$, and must not precede the checking of temporal features, $\tau \geq NOM$. *NOM* is not a strong feature in Italian, and it is acquired by the child as syncretic with agreement. That is, $AGR_S$ is $[NOM;\ \phi]$.[39] As expected, the feature might also be scattered, as discussed in chapter 1. We will see in chapter 5 that the scattering option will be needed to account for the distribution of overt and non-overt subjects in complementiser deletion constructions. Finally, according to our hypothesis, Universal Grammar allows *NOM* to be syncretic with $\tau$-features. This might be the case for Icelandic — that is, T might be $[\tau;\ NOM]$ in this language.

The generalisation that agreement and nominative case are correlated would be challenged if a case such as the following could be found: *Ai ragazzi piacciono tu* (to the boys like-3rd pers plur you-NOM). In other words, the verb agrees with an argument (the boys) not receiving nominative case and the other argument has nominative case. However, the sentence is sharply ungrammatical in Italian. Inasmuch as examples of this kind are not found, our proposal makes the correct predictions. The question is obviously an empirical one and remains open for further investigation.

## Appendix: On the Etymology of the Latin Pluperfect and Future Perfect

Let us say something more about the etymological problems connected with our interpretation of the Latin verbal system. With respect to our analysis here, the most important point we have to argue for is the interpretation of *laudaveram* and *laudavero* as incorporating an auxiliary. One might wonder whether such an analysis can be extended to the infinitival form *laudavisse*, since it corresponds to Italian *avere lodato*, analogously to the forms discussed above, and to the subjunctive *laudavissem* and *laudaverim* as well, corresponding to *avesse lodato* and *abbia lodato*. The extension of our analysis to these other forms rests on some controversial hypotheses. Let us briefly address the question, illustrating possible solutions compatible with our hypothesis.[40]

It has to be recalled first that the form *laudaveram* is an innovation of the Latin system with respect to the Indo-European (henceforth ie.) one (cf. Ambrosini 1987, p. 17). Therefore its morphological form and semantic value must be reconstructed starting from the elements composing it, because they cannot be historically derived. The crucial point in our analysis is constituted by the interpretation of *laudaveram* as the result of the incorporation of the imperfect of the auxiliary *esse* in the verb. This interpretation, though considered correct by some scholars (cf. among others Lindsay, German ed. 1984), is rather controversial and is by no means the usual one. We will provide several arguments in favour of it, even if some problems will remain open; let us consider first the various proposals in the literature. Pisani (1971, 1974) analyses *laudaveram* as the perfect theme plus the element *-er*, where, according to his analysis, *-er* is the exitum of *-es* in front of a vowel. Pisani claims that *-es* is an aoristic morpheme, also appearing in forms such as *laudavero*, in the subjunctives *laudaverim*, *laudavissem*, and in the infinitive *laudavisse* (1971 §528; 1974 §150). Pisani suggests that the fact that the morpheme appearing in the subjunctive and in the infinitive is *-is*, and not *-es*, is due to an analogy process on the basis of the following equivalence: *es estis: esse = -isti -istis: isse* (1971 §151; 1974 §528). In favour of this proposal he points out that such a form in fact must be considered as a more recent formation. Other authors (cf. among others Vineis 1993, p. 337) argue that the suffix *-eram* is an exitum of *\*-isam*, where *-is* is again taken to be an aoristic suffix. Consider that under this perspective *-er* must be derived from *-is*: $s > r$ and $e > i$ in front of *r*. This process is a plausible one according to the diachronic laws of phonological change. The derivation we have to propose on the basis of the claim that *eram* is the imperfect form of the verb *be* is also a trivial one: *-es > -er* in front of a vowel, as far as the pluperfect and the future perfect are concerned. Deriving the past infinitive and the pluperfect subjunctive, however, would constitute a problem for our approach because the derivation of *-is* from *-es* does not seem to be as simple. In order to explain the presence of *-is* instead of *-es* in the contexts in question (e.g., we do not find *\*laudavesse*), we could follow Pisani (cf. preceding discussion), who proposed that *laudavisse* is formed by analogy with the *-i* appearing in *laudav-isti*, *laudav-istis*. Alternatively, it could be claimed that *laudavisse* is construed by means of *s-*, the theme of the verb *be*, preceded by an epenthetic vowel *-i*. Ernout (1953 §304), in fact, discussing the desinence *-imus* of the perfect (*laudavimus*), points out that the origin of such a vowel is very unclear and that it can be considered a suffixal element introduced between the theme and the desinence. We could therefore simply extend his proposal to the forms under discussion, proposing that *-i* can be introduced between the verbal theme and the zero degree theme of *be*. In this work, however, this problem will remain open, even if it seems to be solvable. Notice also that Ernout (1953 §301) claims that *-is* cannot be analysed as an aoristic suffix.[41] Such a consideration is an argument in favour of our proposal, since our proposal provides an alternative explanation to the "traditional" analysis, even if neither author proposes that *-es/(-i)s* is the theme of the verb *be*. They simply argue that it is a way of identifying the theme more clearly, distinguishing it from the desinence.

Consider now the Latin form of the verb in the imperfect and in the future, which will constitute an argument in favour of our hypothesis. Many scholars suggest that forms such as *laudabam* and *laudabo* are derived via incorporation of the indoeuropean auxiliary *\*bhu-* (to be, to become; from which forms like *fui* are derived) with the verbal theme. There are various hypotheses concerning the verbal form to which the verb *bhu* has been attached; Vineis (1993) proposes, that it is attached to the verbal theme, while other authors suggest that the form it is attached to is a nominal form of the verb.[42] The relevant point here is the fact that this analysis suggests that Latin already knew a process of derivation of tenses by means of the incorporation of the theme of *be*.[43] The imperfect would therefore be constituted by *lauda-b-A-m*, and the future by *lauda-b-O*. The vowel A of the imperfect is a mark of past, and the O is presumably derived from an ancient subjunctive, which, as often happened, acquired the function of future. Therefore, the semantic value of the imperfect could be the following: *I was in the praising*, as a periphrastic form; analogously, the value of the future could be something like *I will be in the praising*. It can easily be hypothesised that at a certain point, the morpheme representing the verb *be* was analysed as a desinence. That is, a process of "morphologisation" occurred. Such a process is rather common across languages, and in fact we must assume that it had an important role in the development from Latin to Italian. For instance, Italian *loderò* and *loderei*, future and conditional, respectively, are the result of the incorporation of the auxiliary have (*habeo*) in the infinitive form of the verb (*laudare habeo*; *laudare habui*). Synchronically, however, the periphrastic nature of these verbal forms is completely lost, and speakers certainly cannot naively reconstruct them, starting from the current Italian forms. Our conclusion is that, if this analysis is correct, an analogous process can be hypothesised for *laudaveram* and *laudavero*.

Consider now the internal structure of a form like *laudaveram*, or *dixeram*. In both cases we can recognise the perfect theme *laudav-* and *dix-*, respectively. Such themes are clearly perfect ones, with no possible ambiguity, and their semantic values are well defined. Notice that a theme like *dix-* can be traced back to *dic-* plus the aoristic suffix *-s*. According to one of the hypotheses mentioned in the preceding discussion, *-er-* is to be interpreted as an aoristic suffix; however, we would then have to say that it was added to a form which already included an aoristic affix, *dix-*, at a time in which the weak forms of perfect in *-v-*, as in *laudav-*, were already productive. Moreover, the semantics of this supposedly aoristic form are not clear at all. In Latin the aorist is not distinct anymore from the perfect, and therefore the aoristic suffix should not be perceived as a meaningful item to a Latin ear, precisely because *dixit* has the same temporal and aspectual value as *laudavit*. Let us suppose for the sake of the argument that the value of the morpheme in question can be generically *past*. However, notice first that it also appears in future forms such as *laudavero,* and secondly that in *laudaverAm* we find another element signalling such a temporal value, -*A*- (see preceding discussion). Therefore on the one hand we should explain the future value of *laudavero*, and on the other we are left with the problem of clarifying the semantics of *laudaveram*, which is redundantly marked for past. If, following Ernout (1953), we reject the hypothesis that such a morpheme is an aoristic one, we still must characterise it. Our proposal offers a tentative solution to this question.

Let us summarise the arguments in favour of our hypothesis. As discussed in the text, the first and most important advantage is constituted by the possibility of providing an analysis which relates the Italian system to the Latin one in particular, *avevo lodato* to *laudaveram* and *avrò lodato* to *laudavero*. According to our suggestion such a relation is quite close and can account for the various similarities in the semantic values attributed to the verbal forms in the two languages. Moreover, such an analysis would simply be the consequence of general principles, such as the T-marking principle ruling the presence of auxiliary verbs, which is not an *ad hoc* hypothesis, as we will also see in the following chapters. The other advantage is given by the possibility of relating this process of tense formation to other analogous processes, which took place at earlier stages of the language. In other words, the process of auxiliary incorporation which we assume gave rise to *laudaveram* and *laudavero* is not an innovation but is a process which already took place in the language in the derivation of *laudabam* and *laudabo,* and which took place again in the evolution from Latin to Italian. We could even say that it can be seen as the "normal" way Latin and Romance have for deriving new tenses.[44] The other point is that the *aoristic* hypothesis on the origin of the -*er* suffix does not clarify its value enough. In particular, its specification as an aoristic morpheme seems to be quite redundant and not well motivated on the basis of the general economy of the Latin temporal and aspectual system.

## Notes

1.  On the properties of agreement and the structure of the participle, see Chomsky (1993), Kayne (1993), Cinque (1994), and den Dikken (1994). In this chapter we will not discuss several important questions having to do with the participial projections in particular, we are not going to analyse the consequences of the various assumptions on case assignment inside the participle. We are also neglecting here a discussion of the aspectual properties of the participle. To this end see chapter 3.

2.  Kayne (1993) proposes that in participial constructions $AGR_{object}$ is lower than T and that there is an extra $AGR_{subject}$ projection above T: $AGR_{subject}$ T $AGR_O$. In

this work we are not taking any position with respect to an $AGR_{subject}$ head in the participial clause.

3. With respect to this point, we differ from Poletto (1992), who inserts the auxiliary directly in a functional head for instance, in ASP, without projecting a node V. We think that the question is largely an empirical one: the presence of an extra-head, in fact, according to our discussion (see chapter 1 and chapter 5), provides an extra *Spec* position. Evidence should be found therefore to clarify whether such a position is available or not.

4. For an extensive discussion of auxiliary selection, see among others Guéron & Hoekstra (1988), Kayne (1994).

5. For a discussion of other possible strategies for nominative case assignment, see Rizzi (1982, chapter 2) and Belletti (1990, chapter 2). Chomsky (1993) suggests that T, and not $AGR_S$, as we are proposing, is responsible for nominative case assignment. Our suggestion seems to be coherent with a possible analysis of infinitival constructions. For a brief discussion of some properties of nominative case assignment, see §2.3.

6. In Italian, as noted by Belletti (1990), the features normally expressed by the past participle are default features — that is, masculine singular. The situation is different when there is a clitic, since the past participle then agrees with the clitic. We will not discuss these facts here; see Kayne (1989).

7. The problems connected with the identification of the crucial properties that make of a certain form a *word* are very important ones, and in principle they might be related to our analysis of the morphosyntactic properties of the verb. For our hypothesis to go through, however, we only need the generalisation given above. Both weak and strong φ-features define word boundaries. *Absence* of φ-features, on the other hand, might have no such effect. This consideration is relevant with respect to the role of $AGR_O$, which, though always present for case assignment reasons (see Chomsky 1993, 1994, 1995), does not block movement if it has no *gender/number* features. There might be a principled reason for this, but we will not further investigate this question here. Notice, however, that our observation holds only in one direction: φ-features define word boundaries, but word boundaries could in principle be defined also in other ways. This must be the case with infinitivals, where AGR1 (i.e., $AGR_S$) has no features (in Italian), but nevertheless defines a well-formed word.

8. An argument in favour of the idea that T2 in Italian is an adjectival category might be the following. In Italian several adjectives are derived by means of the suffix *-ato* or *-uto*, such as *fortun-ato* (lucky), *disgrazi-ato* (unfortunate), *barb-uto* (bearded), *capell-uto* (hairy). Such forms are highly productive. Since *fortuna* (luck), *disgrazia* (misfortune), *barba* (beard), *capello* (hair) are nouns, one is led to conclude that *-at-(o)*, *-ut-(o)* attach to a verbal or nominal stem to give a category specified as *[+V; +N]*. The suffix which appears in these derivations has the same form as the past participle morpheme — that is, *-t-*. Notice that at a more 'intuitive' level of description such adjectives identify a *resultant state* of the subject, analogously to what Parsons (1990) claims to be true for perfect tenses — that is, tenses with participles. See also chapter 3. It might be interesting as a further development to

analyse the lexical processes of word formation bearing in mind such a possibility. Consider also that such a proposal might be extended to the English past participle as well, even if we do not see in that language an overtly realised agreement morpheme.

9. Chomsky (1981, pp. 54–55) points out that participles and the so-called unpassives (*taught, untaught* respectively) do not exhibit the same properties. He attributes this fact to a different feature specification. Participles are specified only as *[+V]*; unpassives as *[+V; +N]*. In our opinion, however, the phenomena in question are quite complex and go beyond a simple categorisation problem. We therefore prefer to maintain the hypothesis suggested in the text, with the proviso that it is insufficient to explain *all* the related data. Chomsky (1995) proposes that categories such as T and AGR have a morphological feature *affix*, controlling head-movement. Our system can be easily made compatible with Chomsky's proposal.

10. The reciprocal ordering of AGR and temporal projections has been argued to be subject to parametric variations. See Ouhalla (1988, 1991), Iatridou (1990a), and Rivero (1990) for interesting suggestions in various directions.

11. See Roberts (1993) for arguments in favour of the idea that tense projections do not provide a position where nominative case can be assigned. This implies that AGR must always be present to satisfy the requirements of case theory, even if not overtly realised. See Chomsky (1995) for a discussion pointing to the opposite conclusion. See also §2.3. for further discussion.

12. This proposal fits with the idea that the presence of functional categories is determined by the principles of UG mainly for the purposes of feature checking.

13. For an analysis along the same lines, see Scorretti (1991) and Bouchard (1984). On the semantic properties of the present perfect in Romance, see chapter 3.

14. On the interpretation and distribution of temporal adverbials, see chapter 3 §3.2.

15. There is a vast literature on phenomena concerning the development of periphrastic constructions. See, among others, Harris & Ramat (1987) and references cited there. We will not discuss the syntactic details of the Latin constructions. On word order phenomena see, among others, Marouzeau (1953). It is often hypothesised that Latin is an OV language more generally, a head final language. On the basis of Kayne's (1993) hypothesis, however, one has to exclude the existence of such languages. Kayne in fact proposes that the OV order is always a derived one. We will not consider the question here, because it lies outside the scope of this work. Our hypotheses in fact remain the same under both assumptions.

16. We give here the paradigm of tenses for a weak (*regular*) verb in Latin:

**Active system** (first conjugation): *laudo* (I praise); *laudabam* (I praised-IMPF); *laudabo* (I will praise-FUT); *laudavi* (I praised-perfect); *laudaveram* (I had praised-pluperfect); *laudavero* (I will have praised); *laudaturus* (future participle); *laudare* (to praise); *laudavisse* (to have praised); *laudaturum esse* (future infinitive); *laudem* (I praise-SUBJ); *laudarem* (I praised-SUBJ); *laudaverim* (I have praised-SUBJ); *laudavissem* (I had praised-SUBJ); *laudaturus sim* (future subjunctive); *laudaturus essem* (future subjunctive); *lauda* (imperative-2d sing); *laudate* (imperative-2nd plur); *laudatum* (supine); *laudans* (who is praising); *laudandi; laudando* . . . (gerund).

**Passive system**: *laudor* (I am praised); *laudabar* (I was praised-IMPF); *laudabor* (I will be praised); *laudatus sum* (I have been praised-perfect); *laudatus eram* (I had been-IMPF praised); *laudatus ero* (I will be praised); *lauder* (I am praised-SUBJ); *laudarer* (I was praised-SUBJ); *laudatus sim* (I have been praised-SUBJ); *laudatus essem* (I had been praised-SUBJ); *laudare, laudamini* (imperative-2d sing and plur); *laudatus -a -um* (participle); *laudari* (pres infinitive); *laudatum esse* (past infinitive); *laudatum iri* (future infinitive); *laudandus -a -um* (gerundive); *laudatu* (supine).

Notice that in Latin the imperfect, contrary to Italian, does not appear in subordinate contexts as an alternative to the subjunctive (see chapter 4 and chapter 5). Therefore, it seems that syntactically the Latin imperfect plays a role similar to the Italian simple past. This is presumably not the case with respect to the aspectual properties, since the Italian and the Latin imperfect seem to be alike with respect to the property of being both imperfective and continuous.

17. For a discussion of the semantic value of Latin tenses, see Palmer (Italian ed. 1977); Väänänen (Italian ed. 1982); Ernout & Thomas (1989); Leuman, Hofman, & Szantyr (1977). For a detailed morphological analysis, see Ernout (1953), Safarewicz (1969), and Lindsay (German edition, 1984). For an analysis of the future in Latin and Romance, see Fleischman (1982) and Roberts (1992).

18. In descriptive grammars of Latin, the *perfectum* is also glossed as a simple past. However, in Ernout (1953, p. 186) this is considered a "secondary interpretation". We will ignore the double value of the perfect, given that it seems to us to be more related to aspectual characteristics than to purely temporal ones.

19. Verbs partition into several classes with respect to the perfect. In the text we ignore these differences, but it is important to keep in mind, especially for those who consider the problem from the morphophonologic point of view, that T2 in Latin might have several different realisations, depending on the verb in question, even if the form *-vi-* is probably the most common (cf. Palmer 1977, p. 333; Ernout 1953, pp. 204 ff.).

20. Upper case vowels stand for long vowels. We will note length only if it is crucial for the purposes of the discussion.

21. See also the appendix to this chapter for a brief discussion.

22. Aronoff (1994, chapter 2) convincingly argues that the Latin future participle can neither be taken to derive from the perfect (passive) participle, nor from the supine form. He proposes that what is common to all these forms is what he calls the *third stem*. According to his analysis, the third stem appears in past and future participle, in the supine, in three derived noun suffixes (the agentive suffix *-or*, and the two abstract nominal suffixes, *-io(n)*, and *-ur*), and in three verb types (the desiderative *-ur-i-*, the intensive, and the iterative *-it-*). In the third stem usually we see the suffix *-t-*, sometimes accompanied by lengthening.

23. On the past perfect, see also Bertinetto (1991).

24. In Romanian there is a similar synthetic form, which is, however, much more productive than in Portuguese in that it is the form normally used, even though a periphrastic construction is also available:

(i)     Jurásem
        I had sworn
(ii)    Aveám jurát
        I had-IMP sworn

We will not consider the data of Romanian in detail. Let us only add that etymologically the synthetic form is derived not from the indicative pluperfect but from the subjunctive pluperfect — that is, from the equivalent of a form such as *laudavisse* (cf. among others Lombard 1974, p. 253; Fisher 1985, p. 111; Rosetti (ed.) 1969, p. 265). The strong verbs build their pluperfect starting from the form of the simple past. The reason for the choice of the subjunctive, instead of the indicative, according to the literature on the topic (cf. for instance, Fisher 1985, p. 115), has to do with the fact that the indicative form had lost, for phonological reasons, the explicit marking of past — that is, it was not recognisable as such by speakers. However, the corresponding morpheme of the subjunctive maintained the anteriority, past, value. On the etymology of the third person plural *-ra* form, which presumably has different origins, see Graur (1935).

The Romanian present perfect is compatible with the adverb *now*:

(iii)   Acum am mâncat destul.
        Now I have eaten enough.

With respect to this fact, Romanian differs from Portuguese, suggesting therefore that the analysis to be provided for the two languages cannot be the same.

Consider, finally, that the Romanian simple past can appear in contexts where in the other Romance languages only the imperfect indicative can appear:

(iv)    a.  A *fost* odata
            Lit.: there was-simple past a time
        b.  French: il *était* une fois
            Lit.: there was-IMP a time
            There was once upon a time

The Romanian data have to be considered more carefully, and further work is required. We heartily thank Teresa Ferro for having brought the relevant literature on Romanian to our attention and for fruitful discussions on these topics; all shortcomings are obviously ours.

25. Notice that this property is clearly recognised in the diachronic literature on Portuguese. Note, for instance, the following consideration by Vázquez Cuesta & Mendes da Luz (1989, p. 406): "The conservative character of Portuguese . . . manifests itself especially in the verb, whose configuration is much more similar to the Latin one than all the other Romance languages. Portuguese, in fact, maintained the perfect value of the Latin indicative past in its indicative simple past . . . ". We think that similar conclusions also hold for Romanian.

26. On the distribution of the imperfect and its aspectual and temporal value, see chapter 4.

27. The corresponding Romanian form is ungrammatical as well:

(i)      *Avui mâncat.
         I had eaten.

Native speakers of Romanian give the same judgement as the native speakers of Portuguese — that is, the form is almost incomprehensible.

28. We will show in chapter 3 §3.2. that a verbal T2 lacks a *consequent state*. This fact has interesting consequences for the semantics of the sentence, which will be covered in the following discussion.

29. The synthetic forms of Latin and Portuguese can be considered equivalent, whereas the periphrastic form is the equivalent of the Italian one, along the following schemata:

(i)      a.  laud-av-er-a-s (falaras; souberas)
             $V + T2(E\_R) + V_{aux} + T1(R\_S) + AGR1$ (T2 = verbal)
         b.  avevo parlato (tinha falado)
             $V_{aux} + T1(R\_S) + AGR1$   $V + T2 + AGR2$ (T2 = a djectival, i.e., cons. state)

30. We will not consider the problems related to case "transmission" to the postverbal subject in pro-drop languages, even though they might be related.

31. See Chomsky (1995) for an explanation. Chomsky argues that French-type expletives, which trigger verb agreement, have both case and $\phi$-features (beside the $D$ feature), whereas Italian and English-like expletives lack both features. For these reasons the latter do not trigger verb agreement. It is the *associate*, for instance, *tre ragazze*, in (32b) which agrees with the verb by covert F-movement to $AGR_S$, driven by the necessity of checking the case feature of $AGR_S$.

32. An exception to such a generalisation is constituted by Aux-to-Comp phenomena (see Rizzi 1982 and chapter 5 below), where a nominative appears with a non-finite form, which does not show any agreement:

(i)      a.  Essendo io partita all'alba . . .
             Having I left at dawn . . .
         b.  Avendo io mangiato una mela . . .
             Having I eaten an apple . . .

We conclude that the relation between nominative and agreement holds only in one direction — that is, agreement implies nominative, but not vice versa.

33. Note that assuming the presence of an expletive *pro* in (Spec,TP) or a lower (Spec, AGR) in sentences like (37) and in the other ones previously analysed would not (trivially) solve the problem. Such a nonreferential *pro* cannot be the one usually hypothesised in Italian — that is, a case-less one. The Italian nonreferential *pro* in fact has no nominative and must therefore be replaced at LF by a nominative argument. In (37), therefore, a French-like null expletive should be hypothesised, which, however, should be ruled out in the other contexts.

34. See also Giorgi (1990), chapter 4.

35. That *3d pers sing* is a default agreement can also be shown on the basis of the observation that it is the form appearing with clausal subjects, even with a coordination:

(i)     Che Mario è partito è vero.

       That Mario left is (3d pers sing) true.

(ii)    Che Mario è partito e che Luisa è tornata è vero.

       That Mario left and that Luisa came back is (3rd pers sing) true.

See also the *importare* (to care) examples above.

36. In Giorgi (1990) it was claimed that the case was partitive, following Belletti (1988). Notice, in fact, that *apparire* is an unaccusative verb and that these phenomena are possible only with this kind of verb. In this work we will not consider these questions further, because they lie outside the scope of this book.

37. Consider the contrast with unergative verbs:

(i)     *Le telefonò me.

       To her called (3d pers sing) me.

(ii)    *Le telefonò te.

       To her called (3d pers sing) you.

It is possible to find the same pattern of *apparire* with verbs in the passive form. Compare, for instance, the following cases:

(iii)   Le venne presentata me.

       To her was (3d pers sing) introduced me.

(iv)   Le venni presentata io.

       To her was introduced I.

Sentence (iii) is slightly more marginal than (iv), but much better than the cases in (i) and (ii).

38. Also Holmberg & Platzack (1988) point out that the feature *person* has a more prominent role in the agreement process with respect to the feature *number*. Kayne (1993, fn. 41) points out that the agreement forms are not to be distinguished on the basis of person *and* number, but on person only. So, the plural forms should more appropriately be seen as fourth, fifth, and sixth persons. The data we are discussing, however, seem to show that such persons are to be considered *similar*, and that for some reasons, they behave differently from the first, second, and third. That is, the notion of plurality might still play a role.

39. Non-pronominal noun phrases in Italian, in fact, do not overtly exhibit case marking.

As Holmberg (1994) observes, the correlation between the strength of the case features and the richness of case morphology is not biconditional. Strong case entails rich morphology, but the reverse entailment does not hold. The direction of the implication is the one relevant for Italian. It cannot happen that a language with no case morphology has strong case features.

40. Notice that in principle one could also propose not to extend our analysis for the indicative to the infinitive and the subjunctive. We think that it might be interesting in any case to consider all the possible consequences of such an extension.

41. Ernout (1953 §301) cites Meillet (BSL, XXXIV, p. 127).

42. Pisani (1974 §538) suggests that the -*b*- appearing in Latin is the exitum of an original -*sw*. Concerning this hypothesis we do not have anything to say. If he is correct, the argument we are going to draw in the following lines of the text in favour of our analysis of the pluperfect and future perfect becomes irrelevant, even if the general view might still be maintained.

43. Fleischman (1982) proposes that the creation of the future is anterior to the creation of the imperfect, whereas Ernout (1953) proposes the opposite.

44. It must be added that (classical) Latin only has auxiliary *be* and that only later auxiliary *have* came to play a relevant role in the system of tense formation. We will not discuss this topic here, and we refer the reader to the relevant literature we already cited.

# 3

# The Present Perfect in Germanic and Romance

In this chapter we consider the properties and the distribution of the present perfect in some Germanic and Romance languages. The reason the phenomena concerning the present perfect are especially interesting is that this tense raises an interesting problem, the so-called *present perfect puzzle,* discussed at length in the literature. Such a problem cannot be trivially explained by means of either a semantic theory or a pragmatic one, and it has never been addressed from a morphosyntactic perspective. As we will see better in §3.1.5., the present perfect puzzle consists of the impossibility, in certain languages, for a present perfect to cooccur with certain temporal adverbials: *John has left (\* at four).* We will show that a morphosyntactic account of the verbal systems of the languages in question is the necessary starting point for any semantic (or pragmatic) theory of the present perfect. In particular, we will see that our application of the minimalist approach, which we have sketched in the previous chapters, to the verbal domain will be especially fruitful, in that it will provide the technical background for the crosslinguistic analysis we are going to develop here.

This chapter consists of four sections. In the first, we consider the morphosyntactic properties of the verbal systems of some Romance languages (namely, Italian, French, Spanish, Catalan, and Portuguese) as well as some Germanic languages (English, Norwegian, Danish, Swedish, Icelandic, German, and Dutch). We will argue that the notion of hybrid category illustrated in chapter 1 plays a crucial role in accounting for the relevant phenomena.

In the second section we consider the semantic properties of the present perfect in Germanic and Romance and show that such properties systematically correlate with the morphosyntactic ones in a way that cannot be considered as a mere effect of chance. On the basis of such a consideration, we will propose a morphosyntactic account of the present perfect puzzle which seems to be satisfactory from an explanatory point of view and which successfully predicts the crosslinguistic differences.

In the third section, we consider in more detail certain phenomena concerning the interpretation of the present perfect in languages that pattern with Italian – namely, Icelandic, Spanish, Catalan, and Portuguese. We will show that they are determined by the specific morphosyntactic properties of the languages in question.

In the fourth section, we provide additional arguments in favour of the characterisation of the past participle argued for in §3.1. and §3.2. – namely, the fact that it simultaneously expresses both a temporal and an aspectual value.

Finally, in the appendix we contrastively analyse the distribution of the simple past and the present perfect in two Italian dialects – namely, Vicentino, a northern Italian dialect, and Catanese, a southern Italian dialect, and will show how the same abstract properties can account for apparently very different systems.

## 3.1. The morphosyntactic properties of the Germanic verbal systems

In this section, we compare the Italian inflectional and temporal systems with the English ones and extend the analysis to other Germanic languages — in particular, to Danish, Norwegian, Swedish, Icelandic, German, and Dutch. We do not analyse the morphosyntactic structure of each language in detail, since our aim is not to provide an exhaustive description of Romance vs. Germanic but only to test the explanatory adequacy of the theoretical proposals we are arguing for in this work.

We will see that Germanic languages are not uniform with respect to the morphosyntactic properties of verbs: Icelandic, German, and Dutch pattern together, as opposed to English and Mainland Scandinavian (henceforth MSc). The languages in the first group have characteristics which make them similar to the Romance languages. We will show that they also share with Romance the interpretative properties of the present perfect and that this fact follows from the morphosyntactic characteristics of the verbal forms.

### 3.1.1. The morphosyntax of the English verbal system

#### 3.1.1.1. AGR/T

A first trivial observation is that English verbal morphology is very poor. The present situation is the result of a diachronic evolution from a much richer system; a similar process also affected MSc.[1] In English the verbal root is followed by (at most) one suffix — that is, the only existing morpheme for tense cannot be followed by the morpheme for person. Consider the following examples:[2]

(1)     a.  He loves/loved.
        b.  *He loveds.
        c.  *He wills love.

These examples contrast with the corresponding ones in Italian, and, more generally, in Romance, and in several Germanic languages such as Icelandic, German, and Dutch. Consider the following Italian and German forms:[3]

(2)  a.  am-o  (Italian)
         love-1t pers sing
     b.  am-av-o
         love-past-1t pers sing

(3)  a.  Du lieb-st  (German)
         You love-2d pers sing
     b.  Du lieb-te-st
         You love-past-2d pers sing

In (2) and (3) the temporal morpheme is followed by an agreement affix. Current accounts based on the Split-Infl hypothesis consider AGR and T as separate heads. Thus, according to this framework, it is predicted that in English, as in Italian and German, there are two distinct head positions which can in principle be filled by one morpheme each.[4] However, in English this never happens, as shown by the ungrammaticality of (1b) and (1c), whereas this is the case for Italian and German, as shown by (2b) and (3b). Assuming the Split-Infl hypothesis as originally proposed by Pollock (1989) and Chomsky (1991), a descriptively adequate grammar dealing with English morphosyntax should also include a rule inhibiting the appearance of the agreement morpheme when tense is lexically realised and, conversely, of the tense morpheme when the agreement position is filled. Moreover, such a theory should also explain why such a rule exists in English but not in Italian or German. It seems to us that a theory dispensing with these additional stipulations should in principle be preferable. We will propose an alternative view which accounts for this fact, as well as for independent observations both in the syntactic and in the semantic domains.

To summarise the observations above, the morphosyntactic system of Italian has the following abstract form:

(4)  Verb (+Tense) +Agreement

The system in (4) has to be generalised to the other Romance languages. In English, on the other hand, we observe the following form:

(5)  Verb+(Tense **or** Agreement)

The descriptive generalisation is, therefore, that in English only one affixal head can be realised. Our theoretical proposal concerning the existence of syncretic and hybrid categories, discussed in chapter 1, permits an alternative analysis of the English system, on the basis of the consideration that the structure $\Sigma$ is not necessarily the same for every language and for every sentence in a language. We have already seen in chapter 2 that the hypothesis according to which different tenses can instantiate different structures makes the correct predictions with respect to Italian, Latin, and Portuguese. We now extend this theory to cover crosslinguistic variation, and propose that in English the structure $\Sigma$ is different from that of Italian and German. We assume a special version of the Split-Infl hypothesis according to which separate $AGR_S$ and T categories are projected only when there is positive evidence in the morphosyntax. Otherwise, a single category is projected, provided that the other requirements of UG can be satisfied — in particular, the Universal Ordering Constraint.

We propose, therefore, that in English the features of AGR, the so-called φ-features, and the features of T, the τ-features, belong to the same bundle in the initial array. Consequently, they project a single category which we call AGR/T. AGR/T is not an ordinary syncretic category, since in this case the value of one of the features affects the value of the other one. That is, a value of the agreement features implies a value of the temporal feature τ (but not vice versa). Concretely, the values *[±3d person]* of the AGR features imply the unmarked value of the temporal τ-feature (i.e., *[- past]*), whereas the presence of the marked temporal value (i.e., *[+ past]*) has no implication on the agreement values. In line with the proposal in chapter 1, the features might also be scattered and an agreement head might be projected, structurally distinct from T. In such a case, an additional *Spec* position becomes available. Finally, due to the Universal Ordering Constraint (cf. chapter 1, §1.1.4.) the φ-features are ordered with respect to the temporal ones so that $τ > φ$. That is, the τ-feature must be checked no later than the φ-features. The scattered ordering in English, therefore, is the one we find in Italian when both the AGR and the T categories are realised in the syntax — that is, the projections of the φ-features dominate those of the τ-features in $Σ$. We call categories such as AGR/T *hybrid*.

In Italian, according to our hypotheses, the structure projected from the array corresponding to (2a) is (6), and the one corresponding to (2b) is (7) (see also chapter 2):

(6)

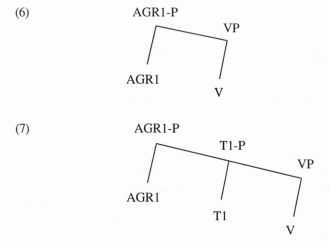

(7)

That is, in the case of the present tense, no τ-feature appears in the array, and therefore no T projection appears in $Σ$. On the other hand, since both φ and τ-features appear in (2b) as two distinct bundles in the array, two distinct projections appear in $Σ$.

In English, according to the hybrid category hypothesis, in the non-scattered option there is only one possible structure, which is instantiated in the present tense, as well as in the past or future:

(8)         AGR/T1-P

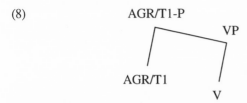

In other words, we propose that in English AGR/T is the only head which appears in $\Sigma$ for any value of $\phi$ and $\tau$-features. Such a head has both the properties of T, in that it bears $\tau$-features and assigns a T-role, and the properties of AGR, since it expresses $\phi$-features and checks nominative case (see chapter 1 §1.6.). As already stated above, the $\phi$-features and the $\tau$-features can also be scattered. In our system such an option is available when it turns out to be the most economical way for the derivation to converge consuming the given array. In particular, scattering obtains if the corresponding *Spec* positions are needed for some item contained in the numeration.

### 3.1.1.2. An excursus on V-to-I movement: auxiliary movement in English

In order to show that our approach is empirically adequate, we must consider some questions concerning word order phenomena in Germanic and Romance. Notice that our proposal concerning the structure of English differs in an important way from the analyses present in the literature. We are arguing, in fact, that in English AGR and T are not usually realised as two different projections.[5] As we briefly discussed in chapter 1, the most important evidence in favour of the Split-Infl hypothesis comes from linear order phenomena. In particular, we are referring to the distribution of VP adverbials such as *often,* and negation. Any morphosyntactic account concerning verbs and their projections should cope with these facts, which since the beginning of the studies on the topic (Emonds 1978; Pollock 1989) have been shown to play a crucial role in this domain. In this section we briefly consider V-to-I movement. We will argue that the position of VP adverbials *is* a diagnostic for verb movement in English, whereas the position of negation is not. We will also show that our theory can explain the phenomena in question.

We start our analysis by considering the trigger of V-to-I movement in general. With respect to this phenomenon, the question to be answered is *why*, observationally, overt movement of the verb correlates with rich verbal morphology and, vice versa, why poor inflectional morphology correlates with the impossibility of such a movement. Several proposals can be found in the literature. In this work we follow Vikner's suggestions (1994, 1995) concerning verb movement in Germanic languages.[6] He points out that V2 and V-to-I movement are two distinct phenomena, since verb movement is driven by different morphological and syntactic properties in the two cases. We agree with this view, and we will not motivate it further here.

Vikner's (1995) generalisation concerning V-to-I movement is the following:

(9)     (From Vikner 1995, §5)
        An SVO-language has V-to-I movement if person morphology is found in all tenses.

In this section we show that this hypothesis is essentially correct, but we also argue that it has to be applied to the empirical domain in a slightly different way than that proposed by Vikner. We claim in fact that (9) does not hold for the *verbs* of a certain language considered as a homogeneous class, but must be taken to hold for *every single verb* of a language. Let us hypothesise, as is usually assumed, that the choice between movement before or after Spell-Out is related to the richness of verbal morphology. There are two possible ways of looking at the problem. On the one hand, it could be supposed that the richness of morphology is a parametrisation holding uniformly for a given language taken as a whole. According to this view, given that English verbal morphology is poor in the relevant sense, there is no V-to-I movement. In Italian we find rich morphology, and, consequently, all verbs overtly move to I. The exceptions, if any, to the presence or lack of V-movement in a certain language must therefore be attributed to independent intervening factors. For instance, in English, whereas "normal" verbs do not move, the exceptional movement of auxiliaries before Spell-Out has been explained by resorting to their θ-properties (Pollock 1989; Chomsky 1993; Roberts 1993).

The other proposal can be formulated as follows. One could expect verb movement to vary not only crosslinguistically but also intralinguistically, according to the presence or absence of a "paradigm" for a certain verb or class of verbs. A theoretical perspective relating the existence of a paradigm to movement before Spell-Out predicts for each verb a behaviour which depends upon the richness of its morphological endings. In other words, if a certain verb has the relevant properties with respect to morphology, it moves before Spell-Out, independently of what happens to the other verbs in the same language. This hypothesis predicts that even in English a verb moves overtly if it exhibits a paradigm.[7]

The two hypotheses can be distinguished on an empirical basis by looking more closely at the behaviour of English auxiliaries. Let us consider some examples. We give the judgements with the first person, but the same also holds with the second and the third person, as well as with both the singular and the plural:[8]

(10)    a.  I am never /often happy here.
        b.  *I never/often am happy here.
        c.  I am not happy here.
        d.  *I not am happy here.

(11)   a.  (At five,) I am often/never running.
      b.  *(At five,) I often/never am running.
      c.  (At five,) I am not running.
      d.  *(At five,) I not am running.

(12)   a.  I have never/often slept well here.
      b.  I never/often have slept well here.
      c.  *I not have slept well here.
      d.  I have not slept well here.

Auxiliary *be* must precede adverbials such as *often* and *never*, whereas *have* can either follow or precede them.[9] With respect to the negation *not*, both *have* and *be* must precede it. We thus observe a difference between the so-called VP-adverbs and the negation. Contrary to negation, the position of VP-adverbs differentiates between the two auxiliaries, given the impossibility for *be* to appear after *often* (or *never*).[10] This fact, under the hypothesis originally suggested by Pollock (1989), and then further pursued by Chomsky (1993), is unexpected. According to their view, in fact, auxiliaries differ from "normal" verbs because they do not θ-mark the external argument, and non-θ-marking verbs move before Spell-Out. If these are the properties which determine the linear order, no difference should arise between *have* and *be*. Therefore, we must conclude that such an account is unsatisfactory, even though it presumably might still be adjusted in some way to cope with the facts given above.

The data in (10) to (12) can be accounted for by resorting to the alternative hypothesis on the relevance of verbal morphology for V-to-I movement. As already said, we assume Vikner's (1995) proposal (cf. (9) above), which correctly predicts a wide range of data in the Germanic languages, both synchronically and diachronically. Observe first that Vikner's generalisation is satisfied by *be*, because it distinguishes person morphology both in the present tense (I *am*, you *are*, he/she *is*, etc.) and in the past (I *was*, you *were*, etc.). Consequently, *be* is correctly predicted to move overtly to I. In fact, we have seen in (10) that it necessarily passes over *often* and *never*. *Have* does not satisfy (9) because in the past tense it does not distinguish any person (I *had*, you *had*, he/she *had*, etc.), and as such it should not move. However, contrary to the other verbs, both the present third person singular, *has*, and the past form, *had,* are not derived from the infinitive *have* by means of a simple suffixation process. *Haves* and *haved* are not included in the English lexicon, and the actual forms must be encoded in the system as *exceptions*. Our proposal is that the more complex morphological process which differentiates the infinitive *have* from *has* and *had* can be sufficient to define the φ-features as strong — that is, as features which must be checked before Spell-Out, requiring overt raising of the verb (cf. (12a)). However, the affixation process of *have* can also be assimilated to a regular one, thus not triggering verb movement before Spell-Out (cf. (12b)).[11] For some varieties of English — for example, British — *have* overtly moves to I. In American English it requires *do*-support. Such properties are also to be extended to non-auxiliary *have* (see Pollock (1989) for a discussion).[12] We therefore conclude that the notion of *morphological paradigm* concerns *each* word of the lexicon. Such a consideration constitutes a further argument in favour of the idea that *all* language variation can be treated as derived from properties of the lexicon.[13]

Notice that the position of negation must still be accounted for. In fact, the distribution of negation does not follow in a trivial way from the hypothesis we have sketched here. As we briefly discussed in chapter 1, the ordering of negation with respect to V has been taken as a test for verb-movement. According to this view, both auxiliaries must have moved because they appear to the left of negation in (10c), (11c) and (12d). However, notice that if this were the case, the position of the VP-adverb would remain rather mysterious, because to move past the negation, a verb should also skip *often* or *never*, which are contained inside the verbal projections. In §3.1.3. in the following discussion, we propose a slightly different analysis. In particular we will object to the idea that the appearance of the negation to the right of the verb is always the effect of verb movement. Notice also that, *a fortiori*, it cannot be hypothesised that negation occurs between AGR and T in English, given the fact that the two categories constitute a single hybrid projection (see §3.3.).[14]

### 3.1.1.3. On the morphosyntax of English modals

Let us now consider another important case in which verb-like items — namely, English modals — behave in some anomalous way. They do not have a morphological paradigm, because they do not distinguish either person or number. Therefore, we expect them not to move, according to the account illustrated above. Consider the following examples:

(13)    a.  John cannot sleep here.
        b.  John must not sleep here.

(14)    a.  *John can often not sleep here.
        b.  John often cannot sleep here.

(15)    a.  *John must often not sleep here.
        b.  John often must not sleep here.[15]

Modals appear before negation but follow adverbials such as *often*. Note also that this ordering is obligatory, as shown by the ungrammaticality of (14a) and (15a). As opposed to *have* and *be,* modals never precede VP-adverbs.[16]

Let us provide an explanation for the data in (13) to (15). As already noticed in the literature (cf. among others Roberts 1993), modals such as *can, must,* and *may,* and the quasi-modals used to mark future tense, *shall* and *will,* are in complementary distribution with tense and agreement morphemes. No modal, in fact, can be combined with the *-s* morpheme (*musts, *cans, *mays, *wills), and forms such as *might, could, should,* and *would* are not "real" past forms, because their meaning is highly idiosyncratic and in several cases cannot be decomposed into the two components MODAL+PAST (see also §3.1.4. following for a more detailed analysis). Interestingly, the modal *must* lacks a

past form *tout court*. Finally, a modal verb can never appear in a perfect form —
that is, it can never be analysed as a participle: *\*I have must/can/could*, etc.
Notice also that no modal in English appears in non-finite forms (*\*to must, \*to
can, \*to may*), contrasting with auxiliary verbs. This evidence can be interpreted
by hypothesising that modals in English are not normal verbs. That is, the
bundle of features they lexicalise projects not a category V but a category which
is in complementary distribution with the agreement and temporal features.[17] We
suggest, therefore, that modals are inserted under the AGR/T projection — that
is, that they project a hybrid category of the type of AGR/T. The features they
lexicalise, however, are neither $\phi$ nor $\tau$-features, but rather *modal* ones. We thus
will call this category MOD/T. In the AGR/T category a value for the $\phi$-features
entails the unmarked value for the $\tau$-ones — that is, *[- past]*. Analogously, a
value for the modal feature, which we call *internal-modality, i-mod*, implies a
present tense interpretation, *[- past]*. Conversely, the marked value of the
$\tau$-feature *[+ past]* does not imply any value of *i-mod*, again in a way completely
parallel to AGR.[18]

According to the Feature Scattering Principle discussed in chapter 1, the
*i-mod* feature and the $\tau$-feature can be scattered, giving rise to a structure where
MOD is distinct from T, analogously to what might happen with AGR and T.
When scattering takes place, an extra *Spec* position is made available and can,
actually must (see chapter 1), be filled by a specifier. We propose that this is the
position occupied by the adverb *often* in examples (14b) and (15b) — that is,
(Spec, T). With respect to the Universal Ordering Constraint, *i-mod* is ordered as
the $\phi$-features are — that is, the checking of $\tau$ precedes the checking of *i-mod:
$\tau$ > i-mod*. Finally, *i-mod* is weak. Therefore, when scattering occurs, it cannot
trigger overt movement of the modal in the corresponding head (cf. examples
(14a) and (15a)).[19] For a discussion of the position of negation we refer the
reader to §3.3.

A similar hypothesis for modal verbs is discussed by Roberts (1993, ch. 3),
who claims that they must be categorised as Ts. Roberts also suggests that even
the supporting verb *do* is inserted in T. However, observe that, contrary to
modals, *do* can combine with the third person morpheme *(does)*, and has a past
form *(did)* which does not exhibit the same semantic irregularities as modals —
that is, it is always only a past tense. With respect to word order, *do* has the
same distribution as modals:

(16)   a.   *I do often not sleep here.
       b.   I often do not sleep here.

As shown by example (16), *do* cannot move past the adverb *often*. However, it
patterns with "normal" verbs as far as other properties are concerned. When it
does not function as a supporting verb, *do* has a non-finite form, *to do*, and a
perfect form, *have done*, and it requires *do*-support (e.g. *how do you do that?*). A
possibility worth exploring is that supporting *do* and the "real" verb *do* belong
to the same category V. When used as a support, *do* is simply devoid of
semantic content and might be used for purely *functional* purposes. Therefore,

we propose that *do* should not be categorised with modals, as proposed by Roberts (1993, ch. 3), but that it has to be considered as a sort of expletive verb, projecting a verbal node lower than AGR/T, as is the case with other verbs. Finally, adverbials such as *often* can appear in its *Spec* (cf. (16)).[20] Notice that, contrary to what is often assumed, the ungrammaticality of (16a) shows that *do* does not move. This is expected given our generalisation concerning the existence of morphological paradigms: *do* has no paradigm and therefore does not move before Spell-Out.[21]

### 3.1.2. Other Germanic languages

The languages that pattern with English in having the hybrid category AGR/T are Norwegian, Danish, and Swedish, whereas Icelandic, German, and Dutch pattern with Italian (and Romance). Let us consider these languages in more detail.[22]

In Norwegian, the present tense is formed by adding *-er* to the verbal stem (i.e., the infinitive minus the final *-e*) and, analogously, the past tense is formed by adding the suffix *-et* (or variants: *-te*; *-ed*; *-dde*). These forms do not vary for gender and number: take, for example, *kaste* (to throw); pres. *kaster*, past *kastet*.[23] Swedish attaches to the verb the suffix *-er* in the present tense and the suffix *-de* in the past tense, for all persons and numbers: *arbeta* (to work); pres. *arbetar*, past *arbetade*. Finally, the Danish present tense is formed by adding the suffix *-er* and the past tense is formed by suffixing *-te* or *-ede*, for all persons and numbers; *leve* (to live); pres. *lever*, past *levede*.

The following generalisations seem to hold in these languages: (a) MSc languages have only two verbal affixes for finite forms — that is, the morphemes *-er* and *-de*, which are in complementary distribution; (b) contrary to English *-s*, the morpheme occurring in the present tense, MSc *-er* appears in all persons and numbers; (c) the past tense morpheme *-de* appears, like English *-ed*, in all persons and numbers.

In the current literature, it has been concluded from these observations that *-er* is a temporal morpheme, just like *-de*. According to the Split-Infl hypothesis, the phrase structure of MSc languages should include an AGR node which is always empty, and a T node containing either *-er* or *-de* (see Vikner 1994, Roberts 1993). Such a proposal has the shortcoming of positing the existence of an AGR node which can never be "seen", either morphologically or syntactically. That is, it is not filled by a lexical item, and it is never used as a landing site for head movement.

MSc languages are V2 only in main clauses (see Vikner 1994 and references cited there). In subordinate clauses the verb is taken to move to T, but not to AGR. In other words, it is taken to undergo *short movement*, yielding the following order of V, auxiliary and negation:

(17)    Subordinate: . . . NEG (AUX) VERB

         . . . *VERB/AUX NEG

In these languages NEG is not a head but a maximal projection appearing in a *Spec* position (Roberts 1993; Vikner 1994).[24] The short-movement hypothesis does not account for the position of adverbs such as *often, never, always*, and the like, which are usually considered VP-adverbials. In MSc, in fact, such elements *precede* the verb in subordinate (non V2) clauses, as negation does. Under the short verb-movement hypothesis, we would expect a contrast in MSc between negation and VP-adverbials. That is, negation should precede, and VP adverbs, follow. However, they both precede the verb. Consider the following examples:

(18) a. Min venn sier at han ikke/aldri har forsøkt. (Norwegian)
Lit.: My friend says that he not/never has tried.
b. . . . da han ikke/aldrig ville komme. (Danish)
Lit.: . . . that he not/never will come.
c. Jag vet, att de inte/alltid måste jobba över. (Swedish)
Lit.: I know that they not/always have to work overtime.

Short movement of the verb to T should in fact leave the adverb to the right of the verb. Consider the English examples:

(19) a. He has never tried.
b. He will never come.
c. They have always worked overtime.

In English, when the auxiliary moves to a higher projection, the VP-adverb occurs to its right. Let us point out that our theory makes the correct prediction with respect to the distribution of VP-adverbials in MSc. We hypothesise that *-er* and *-de* are members of the AGR/T hybrid category. In English, the ordering *Subject-adverbial-Verb+suffix* (e.g., *John often sleeps*) is obtained by hypothesising that $\phi$-feature checking takes place after Spell-Out. We claim that the same phenomenon is found in MSc. In other words, we argue that there is no verb-movement at all (beside V2) and that the ordering of the verb with respect to negation has to be accounted for in some other way. For a more detailed analysis of the position of negation, see the following section.

Summarising, our analysis is that *-er* is not a pure tense morpheme and that in MSc, as in English, there is a category realising the properties of both tense and agreement. Roberts (1993, ch. 3) observes that diachronically the affix *-er* was an agreement marker and proposes that, at a certain point of the evolution of the language, it was reanalysed as T. Under our approach, reanalysis is not necessary, given that AGR and T are collapsed into a single head. Let us propose the following diachronic explanation: MSc *-er* is similar to English *-s*, and the verbal functional systems of both these languages were subject to the same diachronic evolution. That is, both systems became impoverished, and only the agreement morpheme in question survived. However, Scandinavian verbs can be considered to be bound morphemes, $X^{-1}$ in Roberts's terms, and not free morphemes — that is, $X^0$ — as in English. An $X^{-1}$ is not a well-formed word, and therefore cannot be analysed by the morphological component (see Chomsky 1995). In order for it to become a word, it has to be combined with another morpheme to yield an $X^0$. As such, the residual agreement morpheme *-er* had to be generalised to *all* persons and numbers, to satisfy the well-formedness requirements for word formation. This is not necessary for English verbs, which are perfectly well formed words even without any affix. *Eat, read, write*, and the like exist together with *eats, reads*, and *writes*. We therefore hypothesise the following structure for MSc, identical to the English one:

(20)                     AGR/T1-P

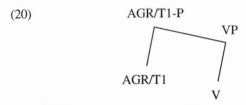

             AGR/T1              |
                                 V

On the contrary, in Icelandic, German, and Dutch, verbal morphology is analogous to the Italian (Romance) one. That is, the affixes corresponding to tense morphemes are combined with the agreement morphemes:

(21)   V+(T)+AGR

Consider the following examples:

(22)   a. pu taladir                                        (Icelandic)
          you speak+past+agr
       b. du lobtest                                        (German)
          you praise+past+agr
       c. jullie speelden                                   (Dutch)
          you (plur) play+past+agr

Recall that in the Italian-like system, T (the τ-feature) is not always realised. This fact introduces a difference among the languages considered here. In some of them — namely English, Danish, Swedish, and Norwegian — τ-features are always present in the tree, as part of the hybrid category AGR/T. Let us call this group of languages Group A. On the other hand, in languages such as Icelandic, German, Dutch, and Italian/Romance, T1 does not appear in the present and the present perfect. We will call this group Group B.

In §3.2. we analyse the consequences of this observation from a semantic point of view. In particular, we will show that our theory helps explain some long-standing puzzles concerning the contrast between the English (and MSc) present perfect and the Romance-like one. The following schemata summarise this discussion:

(23)   a. present; group A (*loves*)
          Verb+AGR/T1
       b. present; group B (*ama*)
          Verb+AGR1

(24)    a.  present perfect; group A (*has loved*)
            Vaux+AGR/T1+ Past Participle
        b.  present perfect; group B (*ha amato*)
            Vaux+AGR1+ Past Participle

We argue that the Romance and Germanic languages group with respect to the morphosyntactic properties of the verbal form. Languages of Group A, English and MSc, have a hybrid category AGR/T. Therefore the $\tau$-feature is always present. In languages of Group B, $\phi$- and $\tau$-features always project different categories — AGR$_S$ and T, respectively. Furthermore, the present tense in Group B lacks the $\tau$-feature and thus T altogether. We will show in the following sections that this property corresponds to a semantic difference. In particular, we will argue that in Group A the presence of T in the syntax determines the relation $S = R$ (i.e., coextension). In Group B, on the contrary, given that no T appears, the default interpretation $S \subseteq R$ (i.e., the reference time is included in the speech time) is directly supplied at LF. In other words, we provide empirical arguments in favour of the idea that the presence of the $\tau$-feature with the value *[- past]* is interpreted as an identity relation between the two temporal variables. The absence of any temporal specification whatsoever is interpreted as an inclusion relation.

### 3.1.3. *The position of negation*

The aim of this section is not to provide an exhaustive syntactic analysis of negation, for which we refer the reader to the existing literature (cf. among others Belletti 1990; Roberts 1993; Laka 1990; Moritz 1989; Vikner 1994; Zanuttini 1991; Kearns 1991), but simply to explain how the ideas illustrated above can account for the phenomena concerning the linear order of negation with respect to other heads. In fact, according to our theory, in English-like languages negation cannot be located between AGR and T, as in Pollock's (1989) original analysis, given that, trivially, the two projections are no longer distinct.[25] We think, however, that our theory can account for negation facts without special stipulations and that many data can follow as a consequence of the T-criterion and of the general mechanisms we hypothesised in the preceding chapters.

In §3.1.1. we pointed out that the linear order of negation and VP-adverbials are instances of two different phenomena. The position of VP-adverbials can be taken as a cue for verb-movement, but the same cannot be said with respect to negation. In this section we argue that the position of negation in English and MSc does not tell us anything concerning verb movement; it only tells us something about the structure projected from the initial numeration $N$.

Let us consider the various cases, beginning with *do*-constructions:

(25)    John did not leave.

Following our proposals, the syntactic structure for (25), when Spell-Out applies, is (26):

(26)    AGR/T1-P

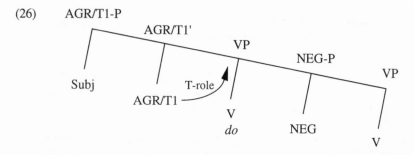

According to current analyses, English *not* is a head which projects a NEG-P. According to the T-criterion, the T-role of AGR/T must be assigned under government to a projection which is the canonical realisation of an event denoting category, essentially VP; NEG does not satisfy such a requirement. *Do* must therefore be inserted for this purpose. We can say that from a purely formal point of view *do* satisfies the syntactic requirements concerning T-role assignment. However, it cannot satisfy the interpretative ones. Its temporal specification must be inherited by the main predicate. Technically, we can say that at LF *Attract-F* is applied and the eventive features of the "real" verb move to the position of *do*.[26] *Do*-insertion is also required in interrogatives. In this case its presence might be due to the impossibility for the English verb to move to C.

An analogous representation can be given for the structures involving auxiliaries:

(27) AGR/T1-P

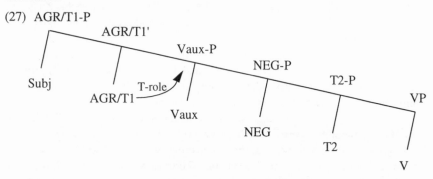

In this case the T-role is assigned to the auxiliary verb, which can then move to AGR/T. In the case of modals, we hypothesise that the T-role is assigned to the modal itself. In an intuitive sense, in fact, in a sentence like (28) the *eventuality* we are talking about is an event not concerning *going* but rather concerning an *obligation* of going.[27] Therefore the representation we propose is the following:

(28)    John must not go.

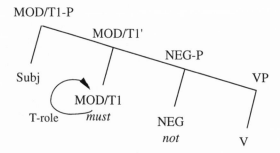

Let us now consider the structure of Mainland Scandinavian. In MSc languages, negation is not a head but an XP. As we stated above, in Vikner (1995) negation is located in (Spec,TP). Furthermore, it occupies a Spec position lower than that of the subject. The only possibility according to our theory is that AGR/T is *scattered* and an additional Spec position is provided — namely, the Spec of T, which can be occupied by negation:

(29)    AGR-P

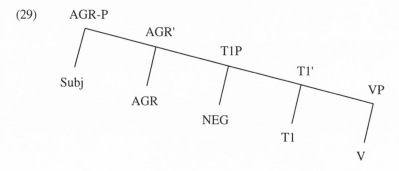

Finally, in Italian-like languages, where two distinct heads are hypothesised for AGR and T, negation intervenes between them. The T-criterion is satisfied given that T always governs the verb. If the T projection is not realised, negation intervenes between AGR and V. The intervention of NEG between AGR and V has no consequence on the structure because no T-role has to be assigned. Recall that, on the contrary, in English *do* insertion is required, given that T is always present and hence assigns a T-role. The basic structure for Italian-like languages is therefore the following (where T is not always realised, as, for instance, in the present tense):[28]

(30)    AGR-P

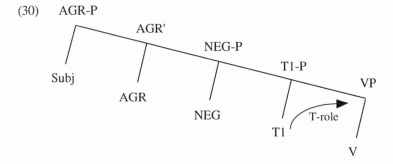

Let us now consider the infinitive in English. Our claim is that *to* is a head —
namely, T (cf. Roberts 1993). Given the existence of sentences such as (31), we
hypothesise the structure in (32):

(31)    For John not to leave is difficult.

(32)    AGR-P

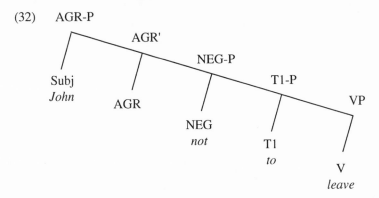

The infinitive, therefore, is a case in which AGR and T do not constitute a
hybrid category; rather, they head two separate projections, analogously to what
happens in Italian-like languages. In Italian, for instance, the infinitival suffix
*-vowel+re* has to be categorised as a T. The structure in (32) is thus not an
instance of scattering but rather is the only structure available once the feature
bundle corresponding to *to* is selected.

Let us add a few words on the relationship between the position of negation
and the Universal Ordering Constraint proposed in chapter 1. As we have shown,
there are reasons to suppose that negation does not occur in the same position in
all languages. The hypothesis concerning different structural locations of
negation across languages has been discussed in the literature — for example, by
Zanuttini (1991) for Romance languages and dialects and by Laka (1990) for
Basque, English, and Romance. These authors propose that NEG occupies
different positions in $\Sigma$. Laka (1990) claims that in Basque it lies above AGR$_S$.
Zanuttini (1991) suggests that in Italian there are two positions for NEG — one
between TP and VP, and another one beyond AGR$_S$, analogously to Laka

(1990). The empirical evidence they discuss seems rather convincing. As a consequence of our and their analyses something must be said about the reasons negation apparently differs from other heads in not being invariably ordered. Our idea is that the Universal Ordering Constraint has no effect on negation, because the latter is not a *functional* category but rather a *lexical* one — that is, it has semantic content. Therefore, we do not expect its distribution to be ruled by the Universal Ordering Constraint, which presumably only affects the position of functional categories. A weaker position could be to say that the feature *neg*, analogously to other features, *is* ruled by the Universal Ordering Constraint. However, the ordering imposed by this principle is not a total one. In particular, NEG and its projections would not be ordered with respect to AGR and T. The possibility of having a weak version of the UOC was briefly discussed in chapter 1. It might have interesting implications from a theoretical point of view, which, however, lie outside the scope of this work and therefore will not be considered further here.

### 3.1.4. English modals again

At LF, modals must take scope over the whole sentence. Modals are quantifiers on possible worlds, or situations, and at LF appear in configurations similar to those of other quantifiers (see also chapter 5). In other words, we hypothesise that a modal moves at LF to a higher head external to AGR/T — call it OP — and ends up in a Spec-head configuration with an operator.[29] We proposed in §3.1.1.3. that the projection MOD/T in English is analogous to AGR/T. The presence of one of the two values *[± i-mod]* implies the unmarked value of T, *[- past]*, analogously to the values of AGR *[±3d pers sing]*. If a morpheme with the marked temporal value *[+ past]* is present, then there is no implication either for the φ-features, as already discussed, or for the *i-mod* ones. Let us illustrate the facts concerning modals.

In a sentence such as *John could leave*, the meaning of the modal — that is, the possibility expressed by the verb — can be understood as a present conditional. (On the availability of a past interpretation of *could*, see discussion following). The appropriate context for such a form is given, for example, by a conditional construction:

(33)    If he had enough money, John could buy a car.

In this case, the modal expresses both a semantic value — that is, possibility, as happens with other modals, such as *must* (obligation), *can* (possibility), *may* (permission), and the like — and a conditional value, common to forms such as *might, would, should*. We suggest that the conditional value is due to the morphologically marked form, *can+ED* — that is, *[+ i-mod]*. The presence of *[+ i-mod]* implies the unmarked value of $\tau$ — that is, *[- past]*. At LF the modal raises to the head of OP to obtain the correct configuration. Let us now consider some other examples where the modal *could* appears:

(34)    a.  On that occasion, John couldn't buy the car he wanted.

        b.  Even if he had enough money, John couldn't buy that car.

(35)        My grandmother could be very unpleasant at times.

In (34a), the modal *could* is ambiguous. In this sentence, beside the conditional interpretation we find in example (34b), it can also have a purely past meaning, as illustrated also by the example in (35), where the sentence is understood as concerning a *past* behaviour of the grandmother.

Our proposal is that in these cases the form *could* is actually interpreted as the past of *can*. That is, T is specified by means of the feature *[+ past]*. Consequently, there is no implication with respect to the value of the feature *i-mod*. After Spell-Out the modal is raised to OP, as in all the other cases. We can say, therefore, that, because of the poverty of English verbal morphology, the morpheme *-ed* can be interpreted either as a past or as a conditional. In other words, it can realise either the temporal value *[+ past]*, or the internal-modality value *[+ i-mod]*. Notice that this reasoning can also be easily extended to the other modals, such as *would* or *should*. In chapter 5, this idea will be shown to make the correct predictions with respect to the analysis of the English forms appearing in contexts where in (some) Romance languages we find the subjunctive.

To conclude, we propose that forms such as *could* check either a feature *[+ past]* or a feature *[+ i-mod]* in the head they occupy at Spell-Out — namely, MOD/T. At LF they are moved to a higher modal position where they receive their modal interpretation. Simple modals such as *can, may, must*, and the like. have the feature specification *[- i-mod]*, implying therefore *[- past]*. After Spell-Out they too raise to the external OP position.[30]

### 3.1.5. On the present perfect puzzle

Let us now consider the semantic properties of the present perfect in Romance and Germanic. In particular, we focus on the very limited cooccurrence of the English present perfect with punctual adverbials such as *yesterday*. We will refer to this phenomenon as the *present perfect puzzle* (Klein 1992).[31] Most of the accounts found in the literature consider the present perfect puzzle to be either a semantic or a pragmatic phenomenon. In §3.2.1. through §3.2.4. we discuss some theories, such as the *extended now* approach (Dowty 1979), a solution based on Parsons's (1990) notion of consequent state and Klein's (1992) pragmatic *P-definiteness constraint*. We will observe that all these accounts have some empirical shortcomings. Importantly, they can barely generalise their conclusions to languages other than English. It can be observed, in fact, that the present perfect puzzle splits the Romance and Germanic languages in two groups. On the one hand we find languages exhibiting a severe limitation on the concurrence of present perfect forms with punctual adverbials — that is, English and MSc. On the other, there are languages such as Italian, German, and Dutch, where the same phenomenon does not occur. Here we will argue in favour of a syntactic explanation for the present perfect puzzle, showing that it holds also for the other languages of the Romance and Germanic domain. In particular, we will propose that the previously discussed partition between languages correlates with the presence or absence of the relevant phenomena. Recall that our hypothesis is that in Group A languages T appears in the syntax as part of the hybrid category AGR/T, and T-marks the verb it governs. As seen in §3.1.1.1., in this case the temporal feature of T is spelled out at LF as $S = R$. In Group B languages, present tense forms do not exhibit any T morpheme. That is, according to our hypothesis, there is no T category in the syntax. In this case, the present tense form is assigned a default interpretation, which corresponds to a looser value as compared to the one found in Group A languages — that is, $S \subseteq R$.

Let us now consider the relevant data more closely:

(36)  a.  John left at four.
      b.  John has left.
      c.  *John has left at four.


(37)  a.  Gianni partì alle quattro.
          Gianni left at four.
      b.  Gianni è partito.
          Gianni has left.
      c.  Gianni è partito alle quattro.
          Gianni has left at four.

A punctual temporal adverbial such as *at four/alle quattro* is compatible with the simple past both in English and Italian (cf. (36a) and (37a)), whereas this is not the case with the present perfect, as shown by the contrast between (36c) and (37c).[32]

In the literature (cf. among others Comrie 1976, 1985), adverbs such as *yesterday, on Thursday, at four o'clock, in 1947,* and *before the war* are given as ungrammatical when cooccurring with the present perfect in all analyses and by all speakers. Adverbs such as *recently, today,* or *just* are usually considered compatible with the present perfect. Deictic adverbs such as *this morning, this week, this year* seem to have an intermediate status. For some speakers they are clearly ungrammatical, while for others they are acceptable, provided that the time span identified by the adverb includes the moment of the utterance.[33]

It is important to notice that the effect in question is not found with other perfect tenses:

(38)  past perfect:   Sam had finished his paper *yesterday*. (Heny 1982, 141)
      modals:         Bill may have been in Berlin *before the war.* (from Comrie 1976, 55)
      infinitives:    The security officer believes Bill to have been in Berlin *before the war.* (ibid, 55)
      gerunds:        Having been in Berlin *before the war*, Bill is surprised at the many changes. (ibid, 55)

The role of the present tense on the auxiliary has been stressed by many scholars who considered the present perfect as being primarily a semantic *present* — that is, a tense that mainly does not report about some past event but attributes to the speech time/event properties that somehow depend on what happened in the past. The data in (36) can then be explained as a mismatch between the "past" meaning of an adverb such as *at four* and the present-like interpretation of the tense. A very influential proposal pursuing such a hypothesis is the so-called *extended now* account (cf. among others McCoard 1978 and Dowty 1979), according to which a present perfect denotes an interval that includes the event time and extends up to the speech time. Dowty (1979), for instance, introduces the predicate *XN* (*extended now*), the truth conditions of which are given (in a simplified form) in (39):

(39)  $XN(t)$ is true at a time $t'$ iff $t'$ is a final subinterval of the interval denoted by $t$.

(For our purposes, the time $t'$ at which the predicate *XN* is evaluated can be taken to be the speech time.) Assuming that these adverbials modify the *extended now*, the latter ends up being identified with "at four" (cf. (40a) and its interpretation in (40b)). Given that the time of the utterance cannot be contained within "four o'clock", a contradiction arises, and (40a) is ruled out:

(40)  a.  *John has left at four
       b.  $(\exists t_1)(XN(t_1) \wedge \text{four-o'clock}(t_1) \wedge (\forall t_2\ (t_2 \subseteq t \wedge XN(t_2)) \rightarrow (XN(t_2) \wedge AT(t_2, \text{leave'}))))$

In fact, according to the third conjunct of (40b), the time of *leaving* is contained in an extended now, $t_2$, which, in turn, is contained in the *extended now* "four o'clock". In order for "four o'clock" to be an *extended now* at $S$, (39) requires its denotation to contain $S$. However, this is impossible; hence, (40a) is illicit.

Dowty's approach has been discussed by a number of scholars, including Richards (1982) and Heny (1982). Let us observe, for the moment, that a major role in the explanation of (40a) is played by the assumption that adverbials such as *yesterday* and *at four* modify the extended now. This hypothesis, however, cannot be maintained for languages belonging to group B, where the sentences corresponding to (40a) are perfectly acceptable (cf. (37c)). In Italian, the definite time adverbial *ieri* (yesterday) modifies the time of the event, and the extended now theory cannot prevent this from happening in English too. A possible way out is to argue that the present perfect in languages such as Italian differs interpretatively from the English present perfect because this tense in Italian-like languages is actually a simple past. We will show in §3.1.6. that such a stipulation is empirically incorrect and that a theory can be developed which accounts for the crosslinguistic variation.

The incompatibility illustrated in (36) also exists in MSc languages, whereas German, Dutch, and Icelandic pattern like Italian. Consider the following examples:

(41)  a.  Jon dro klokken fire.                       (Norwegian)
           John left at four.

         b.  *Jon har dratt klokken fire.
            John has left at four.

         c.  John gik klokken fire.                     (Danish)
            John left at four.

         d.  *John er gaaet klokken fire.
            John has left at four.

         e.  Johan slutade klockan fyra.             (Swedish)
            John finished at four.

         f.  *Johan har slutat klockan fyra.
            John has finished at four.

(42)  a.  Ich bin um vier abgefahren.              (German)
            I have left at four.

         b.  Jon is om vier uur weggegaan.         (Dutch)
            John has left at four.

         c.  Jon hefur faridh klukkan fjögur.     (Icelandic)
            John has left at four.

Descriptively, the divide between languages where the present perfect freely combines with punctual adverbials and languages where this is not the case corresponds to the morphosyntactic division of Romance and Germanic languages we argued for in §3.1. Thus, the present perfect puzzle arises only in those languages which have the hybrid category AGR/T, and not in those which, like Italian, have a Split-Infl and no T category in the present. We will show that this correlation is more than a mere coincidence and that it can be fruitfully exploited to give a crosslinguistically adequate characterisation of the present perfect puzzle.

As stated, the explanations provided in the literature have usually considered as paradigmatic the English situation, often treating the Italian-like present perfect as a "false" one — that is, a variant of the simple past.[34] On the contrary, we propose that even in the languages which belong to Group B there is a semantic distinction between the present perfect and the simple past, despite the fact that they exhibit largely overlapping semantics. Moreover, the English present perfect is very similar from a morphosyntactic point of view to the present perfect in Italian and French. In the following section we present some evidence which points in this direction, mainly considering data from standard Italian and Italian dialects.

### 3.1.6. The simple past and the present perfect in Italian

It has sometimes been claimed in the literature (cf., for instance, Hornstein 1990) that the Italian (and French) simple past (in the examples, SP) and present perfect (in the examples, PrPerf) are actually free variants. According to this view, the choice of the one with respect to the other depends only on stylistic factors. These factors in our opinion do not constitute a satisfactory explanation for the distribution of the two tenses. It seems to us, in fact, that they might still be distinguished as having two different values in Italian, and to a certain extent in (literary) French. In some Italian varieties — for instance, in central Italy — they express different meanings, even if in several contexts they might be non-distinguishable, because their semantic values are overlapping. In the appendix to this chapter we compare northern and southern varieties of Italian, in which only one of the two forms, the present perfect and the simple past, respectively, seems to be productive.[35] The authors of this work, speaking two central Italian varieties, have a temporal system where both tenses are productively used. In this section we analyse such a system, which is also the literary variety of standard Italian.

As observed by Jespersen (1924; see also Reichenbach 1947), the English present perfect is compatible with time adverbials such as *now*, which identify the present moment, whereas the simple past is not (cf. chapter 2 §2.4. and chapter 1 fn. 39). The same pattern obtains in those Italian varieties where both temporal forms can be found:

(43)  a.  Now I have eaten enough.
      b.  Adesso ho mangiato abbastanza.

(44)  a.  *Now I ate enough.
      b.  *Adesso mangiai abbastanza.

Even speakers accepting sentences such as *In quell'occasione mangiai troppo* (On that occasion I ate-SP too much) find (44a) and (44b) ungrammatical. An explanation can easily be given in a Reichenbachian framework. Under the hypothesis that *adesso* (now) modifies $R$, it is predicted that the adverb is compatible with the present perfect (where $R$ coincides with or contains $S$: $E\_R,S$), but not with the simple past (where $R$ precedes $S$: $E,R\_S$).[36]

Notice that, interestingly, the following example is ungrammatical, if pronounced with flat intonation — that is, if *adesso* (now) is not right dislocated:

(45)  *Ho mangiato abbastanza adesso.
      (I) have eaten enough now.

The ungrammaticality of (45) shows that *adesso* (now) is actually the temporal specification of $R$ and not of $E$. As we argue in §3.2.4., in fact, sentence final temporal adverbs can only modify $E$, and not $R$ (see also Bianchi et al. (1995)).

Another case in which the two tenses clearly do not have the same distribution is constituted by some contexts where the present perfect receives a *futurate* interpretation. The simple past cannot express this interpretation (from Bertinetto 1991, 96, exx. 167a and 167b):

(46)  a.  Ti raggiungerò quando ho finito/*finii
           I'll reach you when I have finished-PrPerf/ *SP
      b.  Vengo dopo che ho mangiato/ *mangiai
           I come after I have eaten-PrPerf/*SP

We will not discuss from a theoretical point of view the reasons for these contrasts. Presumably, it has to be connected with the possibility of the present tense to express a (near) future, as in the following case:

(47)  Parto domani.
      I leave tomorrow.

In addition to this evidence we can find other contexts in which the two temporal forms are clearly not in free variation. Consider the following paradigm:

(48)  a.  Gianni è emigrato negli Stati Uniti, ma poi è tornato.
           Gianni has emigrated(PrPerf) to the States, but then he has come(PrPerf) back.
      b.  Gianni emigrò negli Stati Uniti, ma poi tornò.
           Gianni emigrated(SP) to the States, but then he came(SP) back.
      c.  Gianni emigrò negli Stati Uniti, ma poi è tornato.
           Gianni emigrated(SP) to the States, but then he has come(PrPerf) back.
      d.  *Gianni è emigrato negli Stati Uniti, ma poi tornò.
           Gianni has emigrated(PrPerf) to the States, but then he came(SP) back.

The sentence in (48d) is very marginal in the varieties where both tenses are productive. Interestingly, even for the speakers who do not have a productive simple past in their temporal system, typically northern Italian speakers, (48d) is considerably worse than (48c). Notice that the same judgements are obtained in English. This is expected, given that everybody agrees that in this language the two tenses in question are different ones. Furthermore, the pattern in (48) seems to obtain even in French, where on the contrary the simple past is a rather obsolete form. This means that, at least as *passive competence*, a difference between the simple past and the present perfect is encoded in the temporal systems of the various languages. In §3.2.5. we will sketch an informal account of these facts.[37]

Another interesting piece of data which distinguishes the present perfect from the simple past is given in (49) and (50). Suppose that Mario poured a poison in Carlo's tea, and that there is no antidote for this poison. After drinking the tea, Carlo realises that he has been poisoned. He can then utter (49) to Mario but, crucially, not (50):

(49)  a.  Mi hai ucciso.
      b.  You have killed me.

(50)    a.  *Mi uccidesti
        b.  *You killed me

That is, despite their apparently similar meaning, it is not possible to use the simple past in the given scenario, the reason probably having to do with the fact that Carlo's death has not yet occurred. Interestingly, this pattern also obtains in English, as shown by the contrast between (49b) and (50b). A tentative account for these facts will be proposed in §3.2.1.

## 3.2. The semantics of the present perfect

In §3.1.5. we discussed Dowty's version of the extended now theory. In the following section we will introduce Parsons's (1990) *consequent states* and consider how such a theory can account for the present perfect puzzle. Both explanations will be shown to have similar shortcomings — most notably the fact that they do not predict the crosslinguistic variation illustrated in §3.1. We will then discuss a different approach to the present perfect puzzle — namely, that of Klein (1992). Despite the fact that Klein's proposal does not address the problem of crosslinguistic variation either, the crucial intuition it is based on constitutes an interesting generalisation that any adequate theory must take into account. Given this state of affairs, we will show that Klein's generalisation can be expressed in a more direct way by means of (a modified version of) Parsons's consequent state. Eventually, we will develop a syntactic explanation which both predicts Klein's generalisation and explains the crosslinguistic variation. Our theory is based on the hypotheses that (a) (at least certain) temporal adverbials behave like arguments; evidence in favour of this idea will be provided in §3.2.5., and (b) temporal arguments obey Diesing's (1992) Mapping Hypothesis (MH). Thus, definite temporal arguments must move to occupy a VP external position at LF, and the present perfect puzzle arises when the conditions licensing such a movement fail to apply.

### 3.2.1. On the notion of consequent state

Dowty's (1979) extended now theory is couched in terms of interval semantics. More precisely, the extended now is a predicate of time $XN(t)$ which is true at a time $t'$ iff a given temporal relationship holds between $t$ and $t'$:

(51)    $XN(t)$ is true at a time $t'$ iff $t'$ is a final subinterval of the interval denoted by $t$.

We are now going to discuss an approach to the semantics of perfect tenses developed by Parsons (1990), where the crucial notion is an eventuality he calls *consequent* (or *resultant*) *state*. After introducing the basic concepts, we consider how this theory can account for the present perfect puzzle, and we conclude that it has the same shortcomings as the extended now approach — that is, it is not easily generalisable to languages other than English. In order to provide a more adequate account, we will then critically examine some aspects of Parsons's notion of consequent state, and we will propose a revised version of his theory, see §3.2.3.

Working in a (neo)Davidsonian framework, Parsons assigns the logical form in (52b) to (52a):[38]

(52)  a.  John has eaten an apple.
      b.  $\exists e \exists x$ (eat($e$) $\land$ Agent($e$, John) $\land$ Theme($e$, $x$) $\land$ apple($x$) $\land$ hold(CS($e$), $S$))[39]

*CS* is a partial function from eventualities to eventualities which assigns each event $e$ its consequent state. The meaning of (52) is that there is an event of *eating* whose agent is *John* and whose theme is *an apple* and the consequent state of the event holds at the utterance time $S$. Consequent states are defined only for *culminated* events so that the consequent state of an event can be spelled out as "the state of $e$'s having culminated". Furthermore, Parsons's consequent states hold forever after the culmination. This property distinguishes the consequent state of a (culminated) event from the *target state* of the same event. For instance, the target state of *John threw the ball over the roof* is the state of the ball being over the roof. This state is, obviously, momentary. On the contrary, the consequent state of "John's having eaten an apple" will never cease to hold. Parsons extends the notion of consequent states to stative sentences:

(53) John has loved Mary.

Example (53) refers to the consequent state of the state of loving Mary by John. It can be spelled out as "the state of John loving Mary having terminated".

Parsons does not explicitly address the present perfect puzzle. However, in a footnote (1990, fn. 10, p. 313) he assigns (54a) the logical form in (54b):

(54)  a.  Mary has eaten an apple yesterday:
      b.  $\exists I \exists e$ ($I = now \land I \subseteq yesterday \land$ eat($e$) $\land$ Agent($e$, Mary) $\land$ Theme($e$, apple) $\land$ holds(CS($e$), $I$))

The adverbial *yesterday* fixes the time (interval) $I$ at which the consequent state of the event holds. Furthermore, by virtue of the present tense on the auxiliary, this time interval coincides with the speech time *now*. Thus $I$ is subject to conflicting constraints: it must both coincide with *now* and be contained within *yesterday*. We can thus conclude that the unacceptability of (54a) is due to such conflicting requirements which produce the *false* logical form (54b).

Aside from the differences in terminology, this account of the unacceptability of (54a) is very similar to that of the extended now theory. In both cases there is a time interval ($I$ in Parsons's theory and an extended now in Dowty's one) that both contains the speech time and is contained within the interval denoted by *yesterday*. The unacceptability of (54a) is then traced back to such contradictory requirements so that (54a) is logically false. These theories disallow the possibility of having temporal adverbials fixing the time of the event without modifying the extended now or Parsons's $I$. However, we claim that this is what happens in languages like Italian, where the sentence corresponding to (54a) is perfectly acceptable. Moreover, such a possibility is not precluded to English speakers. When asked about the meaning of (54a), were such a sentence acceptable, they provide a meaning very close to the one for the Italian case — that is, one in which the adverbial fixes the time of the event. This fact is not explained by Parsons's theory. Only the consequent state is modified by the adverbial and the time of the event is left unspecified (cf. (54b)).[40] In the extended now theory, the event is correctly understood to take place within *yesterday*, but only because it occurs within the extended now, and the latter is included within *yesterday*. Thus, it is impossible to avoid the contradiction that rules out (54a).[41]

On the basis of this discussion, we conclude that both theories are not empirically adequate. They cannot be extended to cover the Italian case, and they do not capture the intuitions of English speakers on the possible meaning of (54a). Were the unacceptability of (54a) really a matter of logical contradiction (falsity), then the possibility for English speakers to reconstruct the Italian-like meaning would be unaccounted for. An adequate theory must allow the temporal adverbial to directly fix the time of the event without the mediation of other entities, so as to account for the Italian cases.

We now turn to a discussion of some problems for Parsons's notion of consequent state. In particular we will ask whether it is correct to assume that a consequent state holds forever, and we conclude that there is empirical evidence for questioning such an assumption. In the next section we will propose a view according to which consequent states do not necessarily hold forever. Furthermore, instead of having them introduced by means of a function, as in Parsons, we will use the relation *CS(e', e)* between eventualities which holds of two events *e* and *e'* iff *e'* is a consequent state of *e*. This modification will allow for a more compositional treatment of the semantics of the perfect construction, a theme which will be considered in §3.2.4.

As a starting point, consider (55), (Parsons's (2), p. 234):

(55)    *e*'s Consequent State holds at *t* iff *e* culminates at some time at or before *t*.

According to this principle, the consequent state of a culminated event *e* holds forever after *e*'s culmination. However, there are cases in which, apparently, the consequent state of an event may cease to hold. Consider the following scenario. On Wednesday John wins a race. On Friday he is disqualified, because he tests positive on a drug test. Given this scenario, it is possible to assert both (56a) and (56b):

(56)    a.  On Thursday, John had won the race.
            $\exists e \, (\text{win}(e) \wedge \text{Agent}(e, \text{John}) \wedge \text{hold}(\text{CS}(e), \text{Thursday}))$
        b.  (As for today) John has not won the race.
            $\neg(\exists e) \, (\text{win}(e) \wedge \text{Agent}(e, \text{John}) \wedge \text{hold}(\text{CS}(e), \text{today}))$

That is, it is possible to assert that John was in the consequent state of having won the race on Wednesday and that the same consequent state does not hold of

John on Friday. The truth of the first sentence should entail the falsity of the second, on the assumption that consequent states hold forever after an event culmination:[42]

(57)  $\forall e \forall t \, (\text{culm}(e) \wedge e \leq t \rightarrow \text{holds}(\text{CS}(e), t))$

Notice, furthermore, that the present perfect and the simple past have different implications in the above scenario. Consider the discourses in (58) and (59) as a report of what happened. (58iii) is odd as a conclusion, whereas (59iii) is acceptable:

(58)  i.  Mario vinse la gara.
          Mario won the race.
      ii. Mario venne (poi) squalificato.
          Mario was (then) disqualified.
      iii. #Mario non vinse la gara.
          Mario did not win the race.

(59)  i.  Mario ha vinto/vinse la gara.
          Mario has won/won the race.
      ii. Mario è stato (poi) squalificato.
          Mario has been (then) disqualified.
      iii. Mario non ha vinto la gara.
          Mario has not won the race.

Thus, it is not possible to use (58iii) to deny that Mario was the winner of the race, whereas it is possible to use (59iii). In other words, once an event has culminated, it is possible to use a perfect tense both to assert that the relevant consequent state holds at a later moment (cf. (56a)), as well as to assert that it does not (cf. (56b) and (59iii)). However, it is not possible to directly deny that the subject performed the action previously described by means of a simple past (cf. (58) and (59)).

We consider these facts to be evidence for the hypothesis that the connection between (culminated) events and consequent states should not be realised by means of a function, as in Parsons, but by means of a binary relation $CS(e', e)$ which holds of its argument iff $e'$ is a consequent state of $e$.

### 3.2.2. Some tentative speculations on the semantics of the present perfect and the simple past

Let us speculate on the reasons for the existence of these phenomena, although we will not be able to pursue the question in depth here.

We could account for the contrast in (58) and (59) by assuming that the simple past merely asserts the existence of a certain kind of event where the subject plays the role determined by the θ-relation defined by the verb. The present perfect, on the other hand, asserts that a certain property holds of the subject at a given time (the reference time $R$) by virtue of his/her having been a

participant in that event. Such a property, in turn, is crucially determined by the
θ-relation holding between the subject and the verb. The importance of the role
played by $R$ can be better understood by considering (60a) and (60b):

(60)    a.  Martedì Carlo vinse la gara; mercoledì Carlo venne squalificato.
            #Quindi martedì/oggi Carlo non vinse la gara.
            On Tuesday, Carlo won the race; on Wednesday Carlo was
            disqualified. #Therefore, Tuesday/today Carlo did not win the race.

        b.  Martedì Carlo ha vinto la gara; mercoledì Carlo è stato squalificato.
            Quindi oggi Carlo non ha vinto la gara.
            On Tuesday, Carlo has won the race; on Wednesday Carlo has been
            disqualified. Therefore, today Carlo has not won the race.

Sentence initial adverbs such as *martedì* in (60) may fix either $R$ or $E$ (cf.
§3.2.5.). Since in the simple past $E$ coincides with $R$, the last sentence of (60a)
directly contradicts the first sentence. On the other hand, the sentence initial
adverb is fine in the last sentence of (60b), since *oggi* (today) modifies $R$,
asserting that as far as today is concerned, Carlo is not the winner. Thus, the
(present) perfect asserts that at $R$, and hence at the speech time, the subject has a
certain property by virtue of (a) what happened in the past (this being contributed
by T2) and (b) the role he/she played in a past event.

It has been argued (Bianchi et al. 1995) that $R$ acts as a *perspective time*. That
is, it acts as a time (or, more generally, an eventuality) from which the event is
considered. For example, an event is a progressive if it is seen as going on at the
perspective time, and it is a perfective if at that time it is conceived of as
completed (cf. Bianchi et al. 1995, p. 314). Other authors (e.g., Klein 1992)
have stressed that $R$ behaves as a *topic* time; that is, it is the time about which a
particular claim is made. Concerning the latter view, we suggest that (at least
part of) the claim made about $R$ is that the relevant θ-relation holds (or is said to
hold) of the subject at $R$. When $R$ and $E$ do not coincide, as with the perfect
tenses, the assertions concerning the kind of event at stake (which are made
relative to $E$) can be separated from assertions concerning the subject (which can
be made relative to either $E$ or $R$). With the simple tenses, $R$ coincides (or
contains) the time of the event, so that the participation of the subject in the
event is viewed together with the event itself.

According to this view, the meaning of (61a) is that there is a past event of
eating an apple and *as far as the event is concerned* its agent is John:

(61)    a.  John ate an apple.
        b.  John has eaten an apple.

On the other hand, (61b) means that there is a past event of eating an apple and
*as far as the present situation* is concerned the agent of that event is John.
Concerning (56), this approach would predict the following meaning for (56a):
*as far as Thursday is concerned, the agent of the winning is John*. Example (56b)

would instead mean *as far as today is concerned, the agent of the winning is not John*. Both seem to be (intuitively) correct.

There are at least two possibilities for working out these ideas. We may take θ-relations to be time/situation sensitive; for example, by introducing an extra time/situation variable and using *Agent(x, e, e')* instead of the more familiar *Agent(x, e)*, meaning that *x* is the agent of *e* as far as the eventuality *e'* is concerned. This approach would yield the above mentioned reading for (56b). Or we may adopt the proposal by Chierchia (1995a) and Higginbotham (1989, 1994) that even nouns have event/situation variables, in addition to objectual ones. Given this approach, a predicate takes not simply objects as arguments but pairs consisting of an object and an eventuality. This would yield the following reading of (59a): *it is Mario-as-in-the-present-situation that has the property of being the agent of the given event*. Arguments in favour of this view can be found in Raposo & Uriagereka (1995) and in Moltmann (1996).

Let us go back to (49) and (50), repeated here for simplicity:

(49)    a.  Mi hai ucciso.
         b.  You have killed me.

(50)    a.  *Mi uccidesti.
         b.  *You killed me.

Here, due to the lexical meaning of *kill* (cause to die), the separation of assertions about participation in the event and the event itself is particularly clear.[43] In §3.1.6. we pointed out that, given the appropriate scenario, (49) is true and (50) false. The falsity of (50) seems to be due to the fact that Carlo has not yet died. However, Mario has already poisoned him, and, given the absence of any antidote, he has already caused Carlo's death. Thus, (49) asserts that Mario, at the reference time, is the agent of an event that will eventually cause Carlo's death. On the other hand, (50) is false since it asserts that the whole killing (the causing event and the death) have already taken place. That is, (50) does not permit one to separate the two components of the event. This pattern is expected under the account developed here. Only perfect tenses, which separate the reference time from the event time, permit assertions about the involvement of the subject to be separated from those about the event itself. Furthermore, (49) and (50) show that only part of a complex event, such as a killing, is temporalised by perfect tenses. Adopting the view of Hale & Kayser (1993) and of Chomsky (1995) we can say that T2 only affects the upper light verb in the VP shell (corresponding to agency and/or causation), and not the lower verb. T1, on the other hand, affects both.

We will not develop a semantic account of these ideas. For our purposes it suffices to suggest that (at least part of) the contribution of perfect tenses to the meaning of a sentence consists in making available a reference time (or eventuality) distinct from the event time. This makes it possible to relativise assertions about event participants (in the form of θ-relations) to the reference time/eventuality.

An important question about Parsons's consequent states is whether it is correct to regard them as true states. Parsons gives no justification for his choice, and it is not clear what evidence should be considered to this end. For instance, the usual tests for stativity (see Dowty 1979) give dubious results. Consider the one based on the cooccurrence with *for*-adverbials, according to which the verbal predicate that the adverbial modifies cannot be an achievement or an accomplishment. Suppose that (62b) is the logical form for (62a), where the adverbial modifies the main predicate:

(62)   a.  John has run for three hours.
       b.  $\exists e$ (run($e$) $\wedge$ Agent($e$, John) $\wedge$ hold(CS($e$), $S$) $\wedge$ for-three-hours($e$))
       c.  $\exists e$ (run($e$) $\wedge$ Agent($e$, John) $\wedge$ hold(CS($e$), $S$) $\wedge$ for-three-hours(CS($e$)))

Then, the test applies successfully if we find a sentence having the logical form (62c) — that is, a sentence where the adverbial modifies the consequent state. Consider the sentences in (63):

(63)   a.  For three hours John has run.
       b.  John has run for three hours.
       c.  *John has for three hours run.
       d.  *John for three hours has run.

These sentences exhaust all the possible ways of placing the *for*-adverbial. In (63a) and (63b) the adverbial modifies the main event, and their logical form is essentially (62b). Example (63c) and (63d) are ungrammatical; however, it is not clear that the ungrammaticality is due to the fact that the adverbial modifies the consequent state (in this case, we should conclude that consequent states do not pattern together with stative predicates). More probably, the ungrammaticality of (63c) and (63d) is due to syntactic reasons — namely, to the fact that temporal adverbials can only occupy sentence initial or sentence final positions.

Alternatively, it could be that consequent states cannot be modified by *for*-adverbials because of some intrinsic semantic property. For instance, it may be the case that participial clauses yield individual level predicates. If this is so, the failure of the *for*-adverbial test would follow:

(64)   a.  *John knew the answer for three weeks.
       b.  *John descended from a noble family for twenty years.

In (64) it can be seen that the individual level predicates *know* and *descend from a noble family* do not admit *for*-adverbials. Furthermore, Kratzer (1995) shows that the distinction between stage and individual level predicates affects the interpretation of absolutive clauses (Kratzer 1995, exx. 3a and 3b, citing Stump 1985, p.41 – 43):

(65)   a.  Standing on a chair, John can touch the ceiling.
       b.  If John stands on a chair he can touch the ceiling.

(66)   a.  Having unusually long arms, John can touch the ceiling.
       b.  *If John has unusually long arms, he can touch the ceiling.

Example (65a), which has a stage level predicate in the absolutive clause, can be paraphrased by means of an *if*-clause. This is not the case with (66a), which contains an individual level predicate, as shown by the unacceptability of (66b). Now consider (67):

(67)    a.  Having read the book, John passed the examination.
        b.  *If John (had) read the book he (had) passed the examination.

The absolutive clause in (67a) patterns together with the individual level predicate example in (66a), providing an argument in favour of our claim.

If the ideas developed in the preceding discussion are on the right track, the individual level predicate of participial clauses can be seen as the θ-relation holding between the event and the subject. Ultimately, perfect tenses provide individual level predicates that are, in Higginbotham's (1995b) terms, *essential*, no matter how brief or long.

### 3.2.3. A revision of the notion of consequent state

A final point that deserves some discussion is whether consequent states are primitive eventualities, on a par with events and states. If so, we must assume the underlying ontology to be formed by events, states, and consequent states. On the other hand, they could be derived entities, built starting from events and states, which are the primitives. We do not see any reason for assuming consequent states to be primitives. Rather, we take the latter option of assuming that in a domain of eventualities consequent states are derivative.

The simplest approach would be to assume that the consequent state of a culminated event $e$ is the *generalised sum* ($\sigma$) of all the events that follow $e$:

(68)    $CS(e) =_{df} \sigma x(e < x)$

The generalised sum operator applies to a variable $x$ and a predicate $\phi(x)$, yielding the sum of all the entities which satisfy the predicate. See chapter 4, fn. 6, for the notion of generalised sum in a mereological setting. According to (68), the relationship between events and consequent states is a function, and the consequent state holds forever. As we already stated, however, we want consequent states to be introduced by means of binary relations, and we avoid committing ourselves to the view that they last forever. The definition in (68) has another shortcoming: it collapses the notion of consequent states with that of the future of an event (cf. Pianesi & Varzi 1996a), so that every two events culminating at the same time would have the same consequent state. There are intuitive reasons, however, for assuming that two distinct events do not have the same consequent state.[44] Therefore, we conclude that (68) is not the definition we need.

We propose to associate a (culminated) event $e$ not with a single entity (a consequent state) but with a collection (a set) of eventualities playing the role of consequent states. Such entities are construed as events which have the culmination of $e$ as their left temporal boundary. Formally, let $\mathcal{E} = \langle \mathcal{C}, \delta \rangle$ be an eventive structure, and let $e$ be a closed event of $\mathcal{E}$. In chapter 4, §4.1.4. we will argue that culminated events contain their boundaries — that is, they are *topologically closed* entities. A consequent state of such an event $e$ is any connected event the left temporal boundary of which coincides with the right temporal boundary (culmination) of $e$:

(69)    $x$ is a *consequent state* of $e$, where $e$ is topologically closed $\equiv_{df}$
        $lb(x) = rb(e)$.

Where the right and left temporal boundaries of an event are the functions defined in (70):

(70) a.      $lb(e) = \sigma z(B(z, e) \wedge (\forall y, PP(y, i(e)))) \rightarrow z < y)$

     b.      $rb(e) = \sigma z(B(z, e) \wedge (\forall y, PP(y, i(e)))) \rightarrow z > y)$

Here, $i(e)$ is a function which removes the boundaries from $e$. The value of such a function is called the *internal part* of $e$. The relation $B(x, y)$ is true of two events $x$ and $y$ iff $x$ is part of the boundary of $y$ (see chapter 4, §4.1.2. and §4.1.4. for more details on such notions.) The left (right) temporal boundary of an event $e$ is the maximal portion of the boundary of $e$ such that each proper part of the interior of $e$ temporally follows (precedes) it. The requirement that the left boundary of a consequent state be the same entity as the right boundary of the event allows us to incorporate the observation made in the preceding discussion about the impossibility for different events to have the same consequent state. In fact, given two disconnected and culminated events $e$ and $e'$, no consequent state of $e$ will be equal to any consequent state of $e'$, since they differ at least on their left boundary.[45]

We hypothesise that (a) the semantic contribution of the past participle consists in a relation $CS(e', e)$ holding between two events $e$ and $e'$, iff $e'$ is a consequent state of $e$, according to (69); (b) auxiliaries have eventive variables and, when participial clauses combine with them, their eventive variables enter a relation $\rho$ with $e'$ — that is, $\rho(e_{aux}, e')$. We will return to the meaning of such a relation in §3.2.6. In (71) we give the derivation of the logical form for *John has run*:

(71)   a.   $[_{VP} run]$                  $\lambda ex.(run(e) \wedge Agent(e, x))$
       b.   $[_{T2P} run]$                 $\lambda e'ex.(run(e) \wedge Agent(e, x) \wedge CS(e', e))$
       c.   $[_{VP} AUX [_{D/P\text{-}P} \ldots run]$   $\lambda e_{aux}e'ex.(run(e) \wedge Agent(e, x) \wedge CS(e', e)$
                                           $\wedge \rho(e_{aux}, e'))$
       d.   $[_{T1P} \ldots has run]$       $\lambda e'ex.(run(e) \wedge Agent(e, x) \wedge CS(e', e) \wedge$
                                           $\rho(s, e'))$
       e.   $[_{AGRs\text{-}P} John has run]$  $\lambda e'e.(run(e) \wedge Agent(e, John) \wedge CS(e', e) \wedge$
                                           $\rho(s, e'))$
       f.   final existential closure:    $\exists e'e(run(e) \wedge Agent(e, x) \wedge CS(e', e) \wedge \rho(s,$
                                           $e'))$

The contribution of the participial morphology consists in (a) making the event denoted by the VP into a culminated (topologically closed) one and (b) introducing another event in the logical form — namely, the consequent state (cf. (71b)). When the participial clause combines with the auxiliary, the eventive variable of the latter enters the $\rho$ relation with the consequent state (cf. (71c)). Notice that we have adopted Kayne's (1993) analysis of participial clauses. The present tense in T1 makes the eventive variable of the auxiliary coextensive with the speech event $s$ (cf. (71d)). Finally existentially closure applies and binds the main eventive variable and the one of the consequent state.

It is now possible to account for sentences (56a) and (56b), repeated here, by assigning them the logical forms in (72a) and (72b), respectively:

(56)   a.   On Thursday, John had won the race.
       b.   (As for today) John has not won the race.

(72)   a.   $\exists e' \exists e(\text{win}(e) \wedge \text{Agent}(e, x) \wedge CS(e', e) \wedge \rho(\text{Thursday}, e') \wedge$
            Thursday$<s$)
       b.   $\neg\exists e \exists e'(\text{win}(e) \wedge \text{Agent}(e, x) \wedge CS(e', e) \wedge \rho(s, e'))$

That is, in the case of (56a) there is an event of winning and a consequent state $e'$ such that $e'$ is in the $\rho$ relation with *Thursday*. As for (56b), for no relevant event there is a consequent state — that is in the $\rho$ relation with the speech event $s$.

To sum up, in this section we have proposed a view of consequent state — that is slightly different from Parsons's. More precisely, consequent states are events, and their left boundary is the right boundary (culmination) of the relevant event. We have also proposed that past participle forms contribute a relation between eventualities, *CS(e', e)*, where $e'$ is a consequent state of $e$. We have also shown how it is possible to account for the problematic sentences in (56a) and (56b). Furthermore, we have suggested that in sentences with a perfect tense the eventive variable of the auxiliary enters a relationship $\rho$ with the variable of the consequent state. In §3.2.6. we will clarify what $\rho$ amounts to. In the following section we generalise the notion of consequent state to capture the semantics not only of the past participle but also of the future participle. Furthermore, we briefly discuss the difference between analytic and synthetic perfects, exemplified by languages such as Latin and Portuguese (see chapter 2).

### 3.2.4. A compositional semantics for synthetic and analytic perfects

We proposed that participial clauses contain a T2 head projecting a T2P. In this section we suggest that (at least part of) the semantic contribution of T2 is a temporal relation between the T-marked main event and a free temporal variable, $x$, yielding $e \leq x$. Such a purely temporal meaning, which we argue constitutes the core meaning of T2, is found in the synthetic perfect forms of languages such as Latin — take, for instance, *laudavi* (I have praised), *laudaveram* (I had praised) — and Portuguese, with forms such as *tive* (I have had), *tiveram* (I had had). We will propose an account in which the semantics of the analytic perfect stems from the interaction between an independent notion of U(*ndefined*)-*state* and the temporal relation associated with T2. This approach, which separates the purely temporal contribution of the τ-features of T2 from the meaning of the consequent state, will enable us to account for forms such as the Latin future participle in *-urus*, briefly discussed in chapter 2, §2.2.

Let us propose that future participles introduce *prospective states*, entities that are the mirror image of consequent states. As we saw above, the left temporal boundary of a consequent state is the right boundary (culmination) of the relevant event. Therefore, a prospective state of an event $e$ is any event the temporal right boundary of which is the temporal right boundary of $e$:

(73)  $x$ is a prospective state of $e$, where $e$ is culminated $\equiv_{df} rb(x) = rb(e)$.

The only difference between consequent states and prospective states is that the former require their *left* boundary to coincide with the culmination (right boundary) of the event, whereas the latter imposes the same requirement on their *right* boundary. Now, recall the definition of left/right temporal boundaries in (70), and notice that left boundaries only differ from right boundaries because of the temporal relation in the second conjunct of (70a) and (70b). We suggest that such a temporal relation, which distinguishes past participle forms (i.e., consequent states) from future participle forms (i.e., prospective states) is contributed by the category T2, or, rather, by the τ-features of T2. Separating the temporal relation from both prospective and consequent states, we obtain an entity that can be called the *U(ndefined)-state* of an event, defined as follows:

(74)  The *U-state* of an event — written U-state$(e, P)$ — is a relation between an event $e$ and an event type (set) $P$ where $P = \lambda Ke'.(\text{cn}(e') \wedge rb(e) = \sigma z(B(z, e') \wedge (\forall y \, PP(y, i(e')) \rightarrow K(z, y))))$

$PP(x, y)$ is the relation of *proper part* holding of two events $x$ and $y$ iff $x$ is part of $y$ and $x$ is not identical to $y$, see chapter 4, §4.1.2. $K$ is a variable ranging on the set $\{<, >\}$. When $K$ is "$<$" we obtain the relation *CS* introduced above for consequent states (cf. (69) and (70a)). When $K$ is "$>$", we obtain a relation that may be called *PS*, which introduces prospective states. We propose that in the Latin future participle — take, for example, *laudaturus* (praise-fut-part) — the morpheme *-tur-* is responsible for both the temporal meaning (future) and the U-state meaning. More precisely, the temporal contribution is associated with the τ-features of T2; the U-state meaning is associated with an aspectual feature, which we will call *asp*. The two are part of the same category, and as such this category is syncretic; let us call it ASP/T2.[46] Similarly, the Italian suffix *-t-* appearing in the past participle represents both the past meaning and the U-state. Thus, it, too, is a syncretic category, ASP/T2. In the first case the resulting meaning is the relation *PS(e', e)* which holds iff *e'* is a prospective state of *e*. In the case of the past participle we obtain *CS(e', e)*. Recall that we hypothesised in chapter 2 that the categories T1 and T2 assign a T-role to their VP complement. When there is a syncretic category ASP/T2, containing both τ-features and *asp*, the T-marking property is inherited by the syncretic category, and the eventive variable of the VP enters into the relation *CS* or *PS*, depending on the meaning of the participial form.

This approach can be extended to the analytic perfect constructions. Thus, in the case of English, German, French, and the like, we recognise a temporal contribution, due to the feature $\tau$ of T2, and the one responsible for the introduction of a U-state, due to the feature *asp*. We also hypothesised that in the synthetic perfects both of Latin (*laudavi*, I praised) and Portuguese (*tive*, I had) T2 lacks the feature *asp* so that only the temporal contribution is present (cf. the discussion in chapter 2).

### 3.2.5. On the argumental status of temporal adverbials

In this section we consider the behaviour of punctual temporal adverbials. Specifically, we are referring to those adverbials that locate the event of the main verb at a certain time, as in *Mario è arrivato alle tre* (Mario has arrived at three o'clock). In particular, we provide evidence in favour of the idea that they should be analysed as arguments inside the VP-shell, and not as adjoined projections. Here we follow Larson (1988), who hypothesises that these adverbials are the lowest complements in the VP shell (see also Stroyk 1990).[47] We will show that temporal adverbials exhibit the same pattern of head movement that Longobardi (1994) discusses with respect to DP arguments (subjects and objects). In particular, he shows that when proper names are arguments, the nominal head raises to $D^0$. We will reproduce the relevant evidence mainly by considering temporal adverbials that can appear without a determiner (see Larson 1985), as in examples (75a) and (75b), and we will try to show that their behaviour is similar to that of proper names.

(75)  a.  Mario è arrivato ieri.
          Mario has arrived yesterday.
      b.  Mario è arrivato giovedì.
          Mario has arrived Thursday.

Longobardi (1994) observes that in Italian, nominal arguments must be introduced by a category D:

(76)  a.  La madre di Maria è partita.
          The mother of Maria has left.
      b.  *Madre di Maria è partita.
          Mother of Maria has left.
      c.  E' venuto Camaresi vecchio.          (Longobardi's ex. (29c))
          Has came Camaresi old.
      d.  *E' venuto vecchio Camaresi.          (Longobardi's ex. (29b))
          Has came old Camaresi.
      e.  Bevo sempre vino.                      (Longobardi's ex. (12a))
          I always drink wine.

This position can be occupied by an overt determiner (cf. (76a) and (76b)), by the raised nominal head, as in (76c), or by an empty determiner, as in (76e), where a mass noun appears.

Longobardi explains this pattern of data, and, in particular, the fact that proper nouns occupy the $D^0$ position in syntax, by assuming that the functional category D has a feature *[± ref]* which must be checked by a corresponding feature on the noun. *ref* is strong in Romance and weak in Germanic, which explains the contrast between (76c) and (76d) on the one hand and (77a) and (77b) on the other:

(77)  a.  Old John came.
      b.  *John old came.

The feature *ref* is connected to the referential properties of the whole DP. Proper names (and pronouns) have *[+ ref]* since they directly refer to objects. Given that *ref* is strong in Romance, Italian proper names must overtly raise to $D^0$ from their base position (cf. (76c)). Therefore, adjectives cannot precede proper nouns (cf. (76d)). On the other hand, *ref* is weak in Germanic, so that English proper nouns raise covertly, thus explaining the pattern in (77). Finally, common nouns, such as *madre* (mother) in (76a) and (76b) are not object referring, and as such are not endowed with the *ref* feature. As a consequence, the overt article is needed (cf. (76a) and (76b)).[48]

Longobardi observes that names of days also exhibit a similar behaviour. Consider the data in (78):

(78)  a.  Ho passato (il) giovedì scorso al mare.
          Lit.: I have spent (the) Thursday last at the seaside.
      b.  Ho passato *(lo) scorso giovedì al mare.
          Lit.: I have spent *(the) last Thursday at the seaside.
          I spent last Thursday at the seaside.

(79)  a.  (Il) Giovedì scorso è passato velocemente.
          Lit.: (The) Thursday last has passed quickly.
      b.  *(Lo) scorso giovedì è passato velocemente.
          Lit.: *(The) last Thursday has passed quickly.
          Last Thursday passed quickly.

(80)      Ho passato giovedì al mare.
          I have spent Thursday at the seaside.

(81)  a.  Mario ha passato domenica sola al mare.[49]
          Lit.: Mario has spent Sunday only(fem) at the seaside.
      b.  *Mario ha passato sola domenica al mare.
          Lit.: Mario has spent only(fem) Sunday at the seaside.
          Mario spent only Sunday at the seaside.

These examples reproduce the pattern in (76) and can be taken as evidence that the noun *giovedì* (Thursday) can overtly raise to $D^0$, as proper names do in

Longobardi's theory. Thus, in (78a) and (79a), with the postnominal adjective, the definite article may be dropped, showing that the noun has raised in the $D^0$ position.[50] When the adjective is prenominal, however, the article must be present, as in (78b) and (79b). Finally, (81a) and (81b) reproduce the same pattern with a nontemporal adjective, *solo* (only).

The contrast between (78) to (81) and (82) deserves some discussion:

(82)    a.  Ho passato *(il) giovedì prima/precedente al mare.
             Lit.: I have spent *(the) Thursday before at the seaside.
             I spent the Thursday before at the seaside.
        b.  *(Il) Giovedì prima/precedente era passato velocemente.
             Lit.: *(The) Thursday before passed quickly.

Concerning proper nouns, Longobardi notes that the adjectives which tolerate the raising of the nominal head are those which can have a restrictive interpretation, both in prenominal and postnominal position:

(83)    a.  ?Mario alto è venuto a trovarmi.
             Mario tall came to visit me.
        b.  Il Mario alto è venuto a trovarmi.
             The Mario tall came to visit me.

With a restrictive interpretation of the adjective *alto* (tall), (83a) is marginal, whereas an appositive reading is completely unavailable. The sentence improves with an article, as in (83b). If this reasoning is on the right track, one may extend it to the sentences in (82), observing that they contain restrictive phrases which are obligatorily postnominal.

Proper nouns yield better results with postnominal restrictive adjectives, such as *bello* (handsome) than with postnominal (restrictive) adverbials, such as *prima* (before):

(84)     Ci sono due Mari: uno bello e l'altro brutto. ?Mario bello è venuto a
         trovarmi.
         There are two Marios: one is handsome and the other is ugly. Mario
         handsome came to visit me.

(85)     C'erano due Mari in fila: uno prima di me ed un altro dopo di me.
         There were two Marios in the queue: one was before me and the other
         after me.
     i.  Il Mario prima di me è venuto a trovarmi.
         The Mario before me came to visit me.
     ii. *Mario prima di me è venuto a trovarmi.
         Mario before me came to visit me.

The quasi-acceptability of (84) contrasts with the strong unacceptability of (85ii).

   Given this evidence, we suggest an explanation of the contrasts between (78) to (81) and (82), and between (84) and (85ii) whereby we assume that the modifier can endow the nominal head with object referring capabilities. More precisely, adjectives such as *scorso* (last) in (78), being indexical, allow the nominal head to become an object referring item — that is, *[+ ref]*. Therefore, the nominal head can raise overtly to the $D^0$ position. Similar considerations can be extended to *bello* (handsome) in (84) and *alto* (tall) in (83), provided that a suitable context is given. Adverbs such as *prima* (before) both when modifying a calendric unit, as in (82), and when modifying a proper noun, as in (85), do not have this possibility, and in both cases the nominal head cannot raise to $D^0$.[51]

Returning to the main point of our discussion, note that the same pattern presented in (78) is reproduced when the relevant calendric units are used as temporal adverbials:

(86)   a.  Ho incontrato Mario (il) giovedì scorso.
           Lit.: (I) have met Mario (the) Thursday last.
           I met Mario last Thursday.
       b.  Ho incontrato Mario *(lo) scorso giovedì.
           Lit.: (I) have met Mario the last Thursday.
           I met Mario last Thursday.
       c.  Ho incontrato Mario giovedì.
           Lit.: (I) Have met Mario Thursday.
           I met Mario on Thursday.

(87)   a.  (Il) giovedì scorso ho telefonato a Mario.
           Lit.: (the) Thursday last I have telephoned to Mario.
       b.  *(Lo) scorso giovedì ho telefonato a Mario.
           Lit.: (The) last Thursday I have telephoned to Mario.
           Last Thursday I telephoned Mario.
       c.  Giovedì ho telefonato a Mario.
           Thursday I have telephoned Mario.

(88)   a.  ?Mario è venuto a trovarmi domenica sola.
           Lit.: Mario came to visit me Sunday only(fem).
       b.  *Mario è venuto a trovarmi sola domenica.
           Lit.: Mario came to visit me only(fem) Sunday.
           Mario came to visit me only on Sunday.

The article can be dropped in (86a) and (86c), where the adjective is in the prenominal position, showing that the nominal head has raised in (86a) and (86c). The article cannot be omitted in (86b), as the order *adjective-noun* shows, since the nominal head has not raised. Furthermore, these observations can be reproduced when the adverbial is in sentence initial position (cf. (87a) and (87c)). Finally, (88) shows that, as in (81), the relevant behaviour can be obtained not only with temporal adjectives such as *scorso* (last) but also with other ones, such as *solo* (only).

The data in (86) to (88) constitute evidence in favour of the hypothesis that temporal adverbs have argument status. More precisely, they are the lowest arguments in the VP shell, cf. Larson (1988). In particular, (86b), (87b), and (88b) show that these phrases require a filled $D^0$, a behaviour which is typical of arguments. To confirm this conclusion, note that the constraints seen above do not arise in non-argument position — that is, in predicative contexts:

(89)   a.  Sono discorsi da scorsa domenica.
         Lit.: These are talks from last Sunday.
         These talks are typical of last Sunday.
     b.  Sono discorsi da domenica scorsa.
         Lit.: These are talks from Sunday last.
         These talks are typical of last Sunday.
     c.  Ho dichiarato questo giorno (la) sola domenica dell'anno in cui si possa mangiare carne.
         I have declared this day as the only Sunday of the year in which it is possible to eat meat.

In argument position, the lack of the determiner is due to the overt raising of the nominal head to $D^0$. Therefore, adjectives such as *scorso* (last) and *solo* (only) cannot appear in prenominal position (cf. (87b) and (88b)). On the other hand, predicative positions do not require DPs, and bare NPs are allowed. Hence, prenominal adjectives are possible without a determiner:

(90)    Mario si è mascherato da vecchio spartano.
       Mario disguised himself as an old Spartan.

Temporal adverbials manifest the same pattern in predicative contexts:

(91)    Il giorno dell'esame era (il) venerdì prima.
       The day before the examination was (the) Friday before.

Example (91), where *venerdì prima* (Friday before) is an NP, contrasts with (82).

So far we have only considered temporal adverbials exhibiting the same pattern as proper nouns. The data just discussed support the hypothesis that *lo scorso giovedì* (the last Thursday), *il giovedì prima* (the Thursday before), and the like are arguments (when fixing the time of the event). We might hypothesise, therefore, that such a conclusion has to be extended to all the phrases which specify the time of the event, even if expressions such as *alle tre* (at three o'clock), and *in Marzo* (in March), due to the obligatory presence of a preposition, cannot pattern with proper nouns.[52]

There is additional evidence which suggests that this conclusion is on the right track. It is very well known, in fact, that arguments contrast with adjuncts with respect to extraction phenomena: adjuncts are sensitive both to weak and strong islands, whereas arguments are only sensitive to strong islands. Consider the following data:

(92)    a.   *In quale giorno / A quale ora / In quale mese hai trovato qualcuno che voleva partire?
         In which day / At which hour / In which month did you find somebody who wanted to leave?

       b.   *In quale giorno / A quale ora / In quale mese sei partito senza chiudere il negozio?
         In which day / At which hour / In which month did you leave without closing the shop?

(93)    a.   (?) In quale giorno / A che ora / In che mese non sai se partire?
         In which day / At which hour / In which month don't you know whether to leave?

       b.   (?) Quale giorno / A che ora / In quale mese non hai mangiato?
         In which day / At which hour / In which month didn't you eat?

       c.   (?) In quale giorno / A che ora / In quale mese ti dispiace che Mario sia partito?
         In which day / At which hour / In which month are you sorry that Mario left?

(94)    a.   *Come non sai se partire?
         How don't you know whether to leave?

       b.   *Come non hai mangiato?
         How didn't you eat?

       c.   *Come ti dispiace che Mario sia partito?
         How are you sorry that Mario left?

Extraction of temporal phrases fixing the event time from strong islands is ungrammatical (cf. (92)). However, their extraction from weak islands yields better results (cf. (93)) and contrasts with the extraction of adjuncts (cf. in (94)). In conclusion, punctual adverbials fixing the event time pattern with arguments.

    We already noted that preposed adverbials, as in (87), pattern with post-verbal ones (cf. (86)). Thus, we extend the conclusion of this section to these adverbs, too, and we hypothesise that they have been moved from their basic VP internal position to a pre-AGR$_S$ one.[53]

    Until now we have considered only temporal adverbials which fix the event time. We will now extend our account to temporal adverbials which fix the reference time $R$; we will start from the analysis by Bianchi et al. (1995). They note that there are three different positions where temporal locating adverbs may appear: sentence initial position, as in (95a), and two sentence final positions, as in (95b) and (95c):

(95)    a.   Giovedì, Gianni partì.
         On Thursday, Gianni left.

       b.   Gianni partì, giovedì.
         Gianni left, on Thursday.

       c.   Gianni partì giovedì.
         Gianni left on Thursday.

Examples (95b) and (95c) differ according to the intonation they receive. The position in (95b) patterns with the one in (95a) in that it displays the typical intonation of dislocated elements. On the contrary, the adverbial in (95c) is pronounced with a flat intonation. The authors note that in sentences with a pluperfect, the following pattern arises: left and right dislocated adverbials can refer both to the time of the event $E$ and to the reference time $R$. Thus, both (96a) and (96b) can mean either that *on Thursday (R) Mario had already left* or that *Mario left on Thursday (E)*. On the other hand, right internal adverbials can only refer to $E$. Therefore, (96c) can only mean that *Mario left on Thursday*:

(96) a. Giovedì, Mario era partito.
　　　　On Thursday, Mario had left.
　　 b. Mario era partito, giovedì.
　　　　Mario had left, on Thursday.
　　 c. Mario era partito giovedì.
　　　　Mario left on Thursday.

Bianchi et al. extend this analysis to the future perfect and the simple past, noting that the same pattern found with the pluperfect holds for the future perfect. With the simple past, however, the adverbials can only refer to $E$, independently of their position.

As already stated, we propose that left peripheral adverbials which fix the event time $E$ are arguments moved from their basic VP-shell internal position. Concerning the adverbials that fix the reference time $R$, note that they appear only with perfect tenses. That is, they appear only with those tenses where, according to the neo-Reichenbachian framework introduced in chapter 1, $R$ differs both from $E$ and from $S$. Suppose, now, that $R$-adverbials, too, are generated in the VP shell of the main verb, as in (97):

(97)

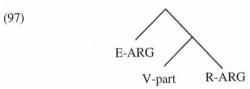

From this position they can be moved to the left peripheral position, as $E$-arguments can.

Kayne (1994) proposes that right dislocated arguments remain in their base position in the syntax and move covertly to the position occupied by left dislocated arguments. Dislocation is due to some feature that is interpreted at PF which determines the typical intonational contour of dislocated phrases. At LF this feature undergoes Move-F. Thus, the only difference between left and right dislocation is that the former involves overt movement, whereas in the latter the phrase moves covertly. We propose to extend this proposal to dislocated temporal arguments. As a consequence, the ambiguity in (96a) and (96b) is a matter of which argument, the $E$ one or the $R$ one, has been left or right dislocated. For instance, in (96a) the interpretation where *giovedì* (Thursday) fixes the event time is obtained when *giovedì* is the *E*-argument moved to the left peripheral position. Conversely, the interpretation where it fixes the reference time is obtained when *giovedì* is the *R*-modifier moved to the left peripheral position. The same holds for (96b), the only difference being that the argument is subject to covert movement. As for (96c), *giovedì* unambiguously fixes the event time.[54] Let us stress that *R*-modifiers are always lower than *E* ones. The evidence for this claim is constituted by the following facts:

(98)  a.  Mario aveva già telefonato venerdì, sabato.
          Mario had already phoned Friday (*E*), on Saturday (*R*).
      b.  *Mario aveva già telefonato, sabato, venerdì.
          Mario had already phoned, on Saturday (*R*), Friday (*E*).

As we stated, right dislocated *R*-arguments stay in their basic position in the syntax. This is demonstrated by the ungrammaticality of (98b), which shows that the (non-dislocated) *E*-argument *venerdì* (Friday) cannot follow the (dislocated) *R*-argument *sabato* (Saturday).

There is an important difference between *E*- and *R*-modifiers: while the former have been shown to behave like arguments of the main verb, the latter fail the relevant tests. For instance, they do not pattern with arguments with respect to extraction from weak islands:[55]

(99)  a.  *A che ora ti dispiaceva che Gianni fosse già partito (da due ore) t?
          At which hour did you regret that Gianni had already left (since two hours) t?
      b.  *A che ora non sapevi se Gianni fosse già partito t?
          At which hour didn't you know whether Gianni had already left t?

Example (99) shows that their extraction over a weak island is impossible. Furthermore, they do not seem to obey the constraint according to which nominal arguments must always be introduced by a determiner:

(100) a.  (Giovedì prima,) Mario era già partito (, giovedì prima).
          (Thursday before,) Mario had already left (, Thursday before).
      b.  *Ho passato giovedì prima al mare.
          I spent Thursday before at the seaside.
      c.  *Giovedì prima, Mario è partito.
          Thursday before, Mario has left.

The *R*-argument in (100a) is not introduced by an overt determiner. It is not the case that $D^0$ is occupied by the existential null determiner, since, according to Longobardi's (1994) theory, it only appears with plurals and mass nouns. Furthermore, the ungrammaticality of (100b) shows that the nominal head has not raised to $D^0$ and that *giovedì prima* is an NP. Now consider (100c). Here the adverbial fixes the reference time and occupies the left peripheral position. According to the theory developed in the preceding discussion, the ungrammaticality of (100c) is expected, given the argumental status of these adverbials. Therefore, (100a) is similar to (91), in that the adverbial does not occupy an argumental position, nor has been moved therefrom.

The fact that $R$-adverbials differ from $E$-arguments is not unexpected, though. Indeed, it is conceivable that phrases fixing $E$ can be licensed by the main verb by means of a temporal θ-role: $R$-adverbials, on the other hand, cannot, since each verb has only one temporal θ-role — namely, the one corresponding to the time of the event. We can conjecture that $R$-adverbials need to enter into some relationship with a higher projection — for example, that of the auxiliary, or of T1, and that dislocation plays a major role in establishing such a relationship.

Our proposal concerning the place where temporal arguments are generated may also explain another piece of data considered by Bianchi et al. (1995). They point out that in nineteenth-century Portuguese the synthetic form in (101a) does not allow the adverbial to fix the reference of $R$, but only that of $E$. This restriction does not hold of the analytic form in (101b) (cf. chapter 2, §2.3.):[56]

(101)  a.  Já eu *chegara* quando elle entrou .
       b.  Já *tinha chegado* quando elle entrou.
           I had already arrived when he entered.

This pattern follows if the overt incorporation of the main verb in the auxiliary, which we have proposed to account for synthetic perfects, prevents the $R$-argument from being licensed by a higher projection (e.g., by suppressing the additional temporal θ-role).

Let us now consider what happens if the temporal arguments are not overtly expressed. We have shown that in a sentence such as *Gianni è partito alle quattro* (Gianni has left at four), *alle quattro* expresses the temporal argument of V, and precisely, the temporal location of $E$. However, the sentence *Gianni è partito*, where no temporal location appears, is also grammatical. One might wonder whether it is simply the case that there is no temporal argument *tout court*, or whether there is an implicit temporal argument receiving a special interpretation.

It has been noted that in the case of indirect arguments, such as the dative of an unergative verb such as *telefonare* (to phone), the omitted dative receives a indexical interpretation (Moro 1992):

(102)  Gianni ha telefonato.
       Gianni called.

In absence of any linguistic or extralinguistic context, (102) means that Gianni called *here*, or *me* — that is, something referring to, or including, the speaker. Consider the following case:

(103)  Ho letto un articolo di Chomsky.
       I have read a paper by Chomsky.

Analogously to what we just stated concerning indirect objects, (103) does not mean that there is a generic past tense in which I read a paper by Chomsky, or that once in my life I did it. In absence of any context, this sentence means that *recently* — that is, in a (short) interval which includes the present moment — I read a paper by Chomsky. In other words, it seems that when not expressed, the temporal argument is interpreted indexically, in a way similar to *real* (locative / dative) arguments, as in (102) above, strengthening, therefore, the view according to which temporal locations *are* arguments in the VP shell. In some sense, this is what in the literature has often been called (Dowty 1979) the *current relevance* expressed by the present perfect.

Such considerations might be extended to other tenses, such as the future:

(104)  Leggerò un articolo di Chomsky.
        I will read a paper by Chomsky.

In absence of any context, (104) does not mean that from now until my death, I will read a paper by Chomsky, but that in the near future, in a (short) interval including the present moment, this will happen.

Finally, the simple past seems to obligatorily require an overt temporal argument. That is, *Lessi un articolo di Chomsky* (I read-SP a paper by Chomsky) is not acceptable if there is no temporal specification available in linguistic or extralinguistic context, such as *nel 1963* (in 1963).

Let us go back to example (48). We will sketch an intuitive explanation for the paradigm on the basis of the considerations given here. Consider again the ungrammatical sentence in the paradigm:

(105)  *Gianni è emigrato negli Stati Uniti, ma poi tornò.
        Gianni has emigrated(PrPerf) to the States, but then he came(SP) back.

In absence of a context providing a temporal reference for the present perfect, (105) instantiates a situation in which the unexpressed temporal argument of the verb *to emigrate* is interpreted indexically. Accordingly, the emigration is considered as happening (almost) at the present time. However, the simple past cannot receive this kind of interpretation and must be interpreted as locating an event in the past, *before* the present moment. Given that the coming back must follow, and not precede, the emigration, the sentence cannot be interpreted coherently. Notice finally that, as predicted by our analysis, if a temporal location for the present perfect is supplied by the context, the sentence is acceptable:

(106)  Gianni è emigrato nel 1923, ma poi tornò nel 1932.
        Gianni emigrated (PrPerf) in 1923, but then came (SP) back in 1932.

To conclude, in this section we have presented evidence in favour of the view that punctual temporal adverbials fixing the event time are arguments of the verb. The evidence is constituted by data concerning N-to-D raising of heads such as *giovedì* (Thursday), and by their behaviour under extraction. In particular, it was shown that temporal adverbials headed by a calendric noun may pattern together with direct objects and subjects headed by proper nouns. Finally, we extended our proposal to adverbials fixing the reference time $R$, proposing that they too are generated within the VP shell. However, they differ from

*E*-adverbials in that they do not behave like arguments but rather need to be licensed by some higher projection, probably for θ-theoretic reasons.

### 3.2.6. The present perfect in English and MSc and temporal localisations

An interesting fact about the English present perfect that was overlooked in the previous discussion is that the ban against *E*-arguments is not absolute. In fact, it disappears if the temporal argument is in the scope of an adverb of quantification (Lewis 1975):

(107)  a.  John has often left at four.
      b.  John has never left at four.
      c.  John has always left at four.

Consider also (108) (from Klein 1992, ex. 57):

(108)  Why is Chris in jail? He has worked on Sunday and working on Sunday is strictly forbidden in this country.

The sentence *He has worked on Sunday* is fine, given the context. However, note that the adverbial *Sunday* does not refer to any particular Sunday.[57] Similarly, (109b) is acceptable as a continuation of (109a) (the auxiliary is stressed) (see also Heny 1982 and Comrie 1985 for similar observations):

(109)  a.  John has never eaten an apple at five.
      b.  No, you are wrong, John has eaten an apple at five.

Thus, it seems that in English there is a prohibition against *specific* temporal arguments. On the basis of this evidence, Klein (1992) proposes that the facts concerning the present perfect puzzle could be explained by assuming what he calls the *P-Definiteness Constraint*. Klein's system is based on three temporal entities which are very similar to the Reichenbachian ones. He observes that temporal expressions can either refer to precise temporal positions or not. He calls the first kind of expression *P(osition)-definite*, and the second kind *P(osition)-indefinite*. According to him, the English present tense is P-definite in that it constrains every temporal entity it attaches to include the speech time. On the other hand, the simple past is not P-definite, since it only requires the time of the event to precede the speech time. A similar distinction holds with respect to the boundaries of temporal entities (Klein considers them as time intervals). Some expressions do not specify the boundaries of the entities they denote. He calls these *B(oundary)-indefinite* expressions. Other expressions fix such boundaries, and are thus called *B-definite*. The present tense is B-indefinite, since the boundaries of the time it refers to are undefined. The English simple past, on the other hand, is both P-indefinite and B-indefinite. Klein accounts for the present perfect puzzle by means of what he calls the P-Definiteness Constraint:

(110)  **P-Definiteness Constraint**: In an utterance the expression of $R$ and the expression of $E$ cannot both be independently P-definite.

By means of (110), sentences such as *John has left at four* are ruled out. $R$, in fact, is P-definite because of the present tense of the auxiliary, and so is $E$, because of the temporal adverbial. Therefore, Klein crucially acknowledges that the adverbial can fix the event time, and he provides an explanation that explicitly addresses this fact. However, (110), as it stands, is more of a generalisation than an explanatory principle. Why should a constraint such as the one in (110) hold? How is it acquired?

Concerning the first question, Klein reduces (110) to a pragmatic constraint. In his system, the reference time $R$ is the *topic time* — that is, the time about which a specific claim is made. In a present perfect sentence the topic time is identified with the speech time, because of the present tense on the auxiliary. Thus, the meaning of *John has left at four* is that there is a past event which is a leaving of John at four, and the topic time ( = the speech time) is in the post-time of John's leaving (this is contributed by the past participle; the post-time of a time $t$ is simply the time after $t$). However, any time after John's leaving time ( = four o'clock) is in the post-time of four o'clock, by definition. Therefore, Klein argues, it is pointless and uninformative to single out a specific time, the speech time (by means of the topic time $R$), rather than another one. This explains the oddity of the sentence in question. On the other hand, a sentence such as (111) does not violate the pragmatic constraint:

(111)  At seven Chris had left.

In fact, the time of leaving is not specified and therefore it makes sense to single out some topic time (here, seven o'clock) rather than another one.

We think, however, that the acceptability of sentences corresponding to *John has left at four* in languages such as Italian and German constitutes a serious problem for Klein's account. The same elements that lead to a violation of the pragmatic constraint in English, according to Klein, *are* present in Italian and German. According to the pragmatic perspective, there is no way to elaborate a theory distinguishing among languages, unless the distinction is simply stipulated by claiming that in these languages there is no *real* present perfect, which, however, is an unsatisfactory solution, as illustrated in the preceding discussion (cf. §3.1.6.).

Concerning the question of how (110) is learnt, there is no way in which the P-Definiteness Constraint could be acquired, as there is a lack of positive evidence. Thus, it should be taken to be a universal principle. One could resort to conversational principles, assume that the latter are innate, and therefore simply reject that there is a learning problem. Such a solution, however, is still subject to the same criticism as above: Why do languages differ with respect to this principle?

We believe that the problems with Klein's account are due to the fact that the P-Definiteness Constraint cannot be taken as a primitive principle but rather as the consequence of morphosyntactic properties that have different crosslinguistic realisations. In particular, we think that Klein is correct in emphasising the role of the simultaneous definiteness of both the event time and of the reference time as a step toward the solution of the present perfect puzzle. We will show how Klein's generalisation can be modified in order to cope with the crosslinguistic data discussed thus far. Finally, in §3.2.7. we propose a syntactic account which derives Klein's generalisation from more general constraints which rule the distribution of definite arguments. In order to generalise Klein's proposal, let us discuss the interpretative properties of auxiliary-participle constructions and whether consequent states can be limited on both sides.

In §3.2.3. we proposed that consequent states are events which are bounded on one side by the culmination of the event. We also suggested that a relation $\rho$ be established between the consequent state variable and the eventive variable of the auxiliary. We can now specify the meaning of $\rho$. First of all, let us rephrase Klein's generalisation as follows:

(112)   A consequent state cannot be definite.

A consequent state is definite whenever both its boundaries are definite. We now define $\rho$ in such a way that $\rho(e', e)$ holds iff $e'$ is a final portion of $e$. Formally:

(113)   For any two events $e$ and $e'$, $e'$ is a final portion of $e$ , $\rho(e', e)$, $\equiv_{df} P(e', e)$
$\land \forall z(e' < z \rightarrow e < z)$.

Thus, $e'$ is a final portion of the event $e$ iff $e'$ is part of $e$ and every event that follows $e'$ also follows $e$.[58]

Recall now that we proposed in §3.1. that in English (and MSc) the $\phi$-features and the $\tau$-features constitute a hybrid category that we have called AGR/T. On the other hand, languages such as Italian realise the $\phi$-features and the $\tau$-features on independent categories (AGR and T, respectively). We argued that a consequence of this fact is that in English the temporal feature is always present, even with the present tense, where it is interpreted as a predicate of (temporal) identity. In Italian-like languages, on the other hand, there is no temporal feature in the present tense and it receives a default (inclusive) interpretation — that is, $S \subseteq R$. Consider the following example:

(114)   a.   Gianni ha telefonato alle quattro.
        b.   *Gianni has telephoned at four.

In Italian, in a sentence such as (114a) the adverbial fixes the time of the arrival. That is, it fixes one of the boundaries (the left boundary) of the consequent state. Let us hypothesise that $R$ fixes the time of $e_{aux}$, and as such fixes the other temporal boundary of the consequent state. In English $R = S$, where $S$ is definite, in the sense of Klein (1992). This way, the consequent state has definite boundaries, so that (114b) is ruled out by (112). On the other hand, the default interpretation of the Italian present does not make $R$ definite, and (112) is not violated.[59]

Despite the fact that it accounts for crosslinguistic variation, this theory is not completely satisfactory, because (112) is simply a stipulation. Both here and in Klein (1992) it is not clear what motivates the constraints in (112) or (110). The restriction on consequent states imposed by (112) requires us to explain why they cannot be definite. To the extent that consequent states can be assimilated to real *states* (cf. §3.2.2.), the impossibility of *John has left at four* could be connected to the contrast in (115):

(115)  a.  Amo Maria da ieri.
       b.  *I love Mary since yesterday.

In English, it is not possible to use an adverbial introduced by *since* to fix the beginning of a state reported by means of the present tense (cf. (115b)). In Italian, on the other hand, this is possible (cf. (115a)). This pattern follows if, in the general case, states can never be specific, in the sense of having specific boundaries.

In the next section we will show that both (112) and (110) follow from a syntactic account.[60]

### 3.2.7. Towards an account of the present perfect puzzle

According to the so called Mapping Hypothesis (MH; Diesing 1992), specific and definite objects must move out of the VP in such a way that they are placed in the restrictive portion of the clause at LF :

(116)  Material in the IP area of a clause external to the VP maps onto the restrictive clause and material in the VP maps onto the nuclear scope (from Borer 1993, p. 36).

Evidence in favour of the hypothesis that definite DPs (and familiar ones) are moved out of the VP is provided by the phenomena of scrambling and object shift in Germanic (Diesing 1992), object agreement, clitic placement (Uriagereka 1994), as well as other phenomena. Although the MH is widely accepted, there is no consensus as to what drives movement of the definite/familiar DP. Some authors have argued that the MH suffices to motivate movement (Borer 1993). Others (Runner 1993) have proposed that objects move to the $AGR_O$ position not for case reasons but as a result of the MH. According to these authors the MH is a principle of the grammar, and any violation of the MH at LF (for instance, when a definite DP remains in the VP) results in ungrammaticality. Such an account, however, does not easily fit with the minimalist approach. In this framework, movement is motivated only by the need to check features. Therefore, movement of a definite DP to the restrictive portion of the clause should be due to the necessity of checking some features that would not be otherwise checked.[61] Consequently, the MH does not play an independent role in the mapping $N \rightarrow (\pi, \lambda)$. Rather, it is a post-LF principle, or, probably, the spelling-out of a set of instructions according to which interpretative procedures assign a meaning to syntactic objects. If this account is correct, violations of the MH do not cause the derivation to crash (provided that the other principles of the grammar are satisfied) but produce interface representations that receive a deviant interpretation, or no interpretation at all.

In this section we propose to extend this approach to temporal arguments, assuming that definite and specific temporal arguments must be outside the VP at LF. We propose that movement is motivated by the need to check an interpretable weak feature T-DEF (temporal definiteness) on definite temporal arguments. The generalisations (110) and (112) of the previous section follow from the combination of the checking of the T-DEF feature and the post-LF requirement of the MH. Let us assume first that there are two functional categories that can be endowed with T-DEF: T1 (AGR/T1 in English-like languages) and the D/P that, according to Kayne (1993), heads participial projections. Consider the English present perfect:

(117)      $AGR/T1_{T-DEF}$      AUX      D/P T2   [$_{VP}$ V . . . ]
           J.                    has      left

The English present tense always has the T-DEF feature in AGR/T1, as a consequence of the fact that it is interpreted as an indexical predicate.[62] In (117), this feature is checked by the empty $R$-argument (which is interpreted as $S$).[63] The illicit cases are reproduced in (118):

(118)  a.  $AGR/T1_{T-DEF}$              D/P      T2  [$_{VP}$ V    $T\text{-}Arg_{T-DEF}$]
           *J.               has                 left          at four
       b.  $AGR/T1_{T-DEF}$              $D/P_{T-DEF}$  T2  [$_{VP}$ V    $T\text{-}Arg_{T-DEF}$]
           *J.               has                 left          at four

In (118a) the empty $R$-argument checks the T-DEF feature on AGR/T1; as in Chomsky (1995), we take features on functional categories to be noninterpretable. Therefore, once checked, the T-DEF on AGR/T1 is erased and there is no reason for the definite $E$-temporal argument to move out of the VP. In this way, however, the MH is violated at the post-LF level. In (118b), D/P has the feature T-DEF. Consider, now, the derivation at the point in which the participial clause has been formed:

(119) [$D/P_{T-DEF}$    T2   [$_{VP}$ V    $T\text{-}Arg_{T-DEF}$]]

The next step consists of an application of Merge that adds the auxiliary:

(120) [BE [$D/P_{T-DEF}$    T2   [$_{VP}$ V    $T\text{-}Arg_{T-DEF}$]]]

Then, D/P incorporates into the auxiliary (cf. Kayne 1993), yielding *have*. The auxiliary thus inherits the T-DEF feature. Further V-to-I movement of the auxiliary ultimately results in a checking configuration between the T-DEF feature of the auxiliary and that of AGR/T1. Checking has the consequence that both features are erased, both being noninterpretable. Thus, the $E$-temporal argument is not forced to move, and the resulting LF configuration receives a deviant interpretation.[64]

Let us now consider the Italian case:

(121)  AGR    D/P$_{\text{T-DEF}}$        T2         [$_{\text{VP}}$ V      T-Arg$_{\text{T-DEF}}$]
        G. è                          partito                alle quattro

In (121) D/P has the optional T-DEF feature. Contrary to English, there is no similar feature either on AGR$_S$ or in T1, given that there is no temporal projection in the Italian present. Thus the definite $E$-temporal argument can covertly raise to check the feature on D/P, thus satisfying the MH. Therefore, it turns out that the main differences between the Italian-like present perfect and the English-like present perfect are explained by their morphosyntactic properties: English present tense always has an AGR/T1 category which, in turn, has both τ-features (interpreted as $S = R$) and a T-DEF feature. Italian present tense forms, on the other hand, have neither a τ-feature nor a T-DEF one. Such differences affect the availability of definite temporal adverbials, complying with the MH at a post-LF level by determining their positions at LF: inside the VP in the case of English, and outside of it, in the case of Italian.

Our account does not rule out (122):

(122)  *Last Thursday, John has left.

The specific $E$-argument *last Thursday* has moved to a left peripheral position for reasons that probably do not depend on T-DEF — that is, to check a TOP feature. What is important is that at LF it is out of the VP, so that it complies with the MH. Therefore we are predicting that (122) is acceptable. Note, however, that, as observed by Klein (1992) and by Bianchi et al. (1995), English left peripheral temporal adverbials cannot fix the event time in pluperfect sentences:

(123)  a.  At five, John had arrived.
        b.  At five, John will have arrived.

Example (123a) can only mean that "at five John had already arrived", whereas the reading (possible in Italian) in which *at five* fixes the time of the arrival is excluded. The same property holds of the future perfect (cf. (123b)). We propose to generalise these observations to the present perfect, too, concluding that it is a general property of English perfect tenses that left peripheral temporal adverbials cannot fix the event time. In (122), *last Thursday* can only fix the event time, because the reference time is equal to $S$. As such, the sentence is ungrammatical.

Now consider (124):

(124)  a.  *Giovedì Maria era partita mercoledì.
        b.  *Thursday Maria had left Wednesday.
        c.  AGR  T1  D/P$_{\text{T-DEF}}$     T2     [$_{\text{VP}}$ V   T-Arg1$_{\text{T-DEF}}$    T-Arg2$_{\text{T-DEF}}$]

In both the Italian and the English examples, the $R$-adverbial *Thursday* has overtly moved to a left peripheral position, which we take to be a topic position. Suppose, then, that *Thursday* in (124) has a Topic feature that is attracted by the corresponding feature in a position higher than AGR$_S$ (cf. Uriagereka 1994; Raposo & Uriagereka 1995; Delfitto & Bertinetto 1995b). If the optional T-DEF

feature is present on D/P, as in (124c), then it should be possible for the definite
$E$-temporal argument to raise covertly and check it, ending up in a position
where it does satisfy the MH. Then we would predict that (124) is acceptable in
both languages, contrary to the facts. However, we have hypothesised that in
(124) *Thursday* occupies the *Spec* of a TOP category. If the auxiliary (covertly)
raises to such a position, then its (inherited) T-DEF feature is checked there, in a
Spec-Head configuration with the raised temporal argument.[65] As in the other
cases seen above, there would be nothing attracting the $E$-temporal argument
outside the VP, and an MH violation would arise. If this account is correct, we
would expect that sentences like (124) improve when the $E$-temporal argument is
forced to move outside the VP for independent reasons. This seems to be the
case, at least in Italian, when an adverb such as *già* (already) is present:

(125)  a.  Martedì Mario aveva *(già) telefonato a Maria tutti i venerdì.
           Tuesday Mario had *(already) telephoned to Maria every Friday.
       b.  Giovedì Mario aveva *(già) telefonato a Maria mercoledì (e lo avrebbe
           rifatto venerdì).
           Thursday Mario had *(already) telephoned to Maria Wednesday (and he
           would do it again on Friday).

The sentences in (125) with *già* are considerably better than those in (124). Note,
furthermore, the following contrasts:

(126)  a.  Martedì, Mario ha telefonato a Maria.
           On Tuesday Mario has called Maria.
       b.  Mario ha già telefonato a Maria martedì.
           Mario has already called Maria on Tuesday.
       c.  *Martedì, Mario ha già telefonato a Maria.
           On Tuesday, Mario has already called Maria.

(127)  a.  Mario aveva già telefonato martedì.
           Mario had already called Tuesday.
       b.  Martedì, Mario aveva già telefonato.
           On Tuesday, Mario had already called

In both (126c) and (127b) the preposed *martedì* cannot refer to the time of the
telephone call. In other words, the $E$-temporal argument cannot be higher than
*già*. This pattern could be explained by hypothesising that adverbs such as *già*
require the $E$-temporal argument to be in a checking configuration with them at
LF. That is, *già* could head a projection higher than VP and have (weak) features
able to attract an $E$-temporal argument.[66] Then, the unacceptability of (126c) and
(127b) in the relevant reading would follow.[67] The same hypothesis about *già*
explains why the sentences in (125) improve when this adverb is present. *Già*
causes the $E$-temporal argument to move and occupy a position outside the VP,
at LF, complying with the MH.[68]

Let us briefly discuss the simple tenses. We hypothesise that T1 in Italian-like languages and AGR/T1 in English-like ones can have the feature *T-DEF*, which attracts the definite temporal argument:

(128)   Mary left yesterday
          . . . . . AGR/T1$_{T-DEF}$ . . . . .

We therefore conclude that the behaviour of the English-like present perfect with definite temporal arguments can be explained on the basis of (a) the morphological properties of the English present tense (i.e., the fact that it always has a $\tau$-feature and a T-DEF feature), and (b) the view that the MH is a constraint applying to a post-LF level, so that independent reasons must be provided for a definite DP to move outside VP. Furthermore, this theory explains why ungrammaticality does not arise in cases such as (107) and (108), repeated here:

(107)   a.   John has often left at four.
        b.   John has never left at four.
        c.   John has always left at four.
(108)        Why is Chris in jail ? He has worked on Sunday and working on Sunday is strictly forbidden in this country.

In (108) the temporal adverbial behaves as an indefinite. Therefore, it does not bear the feature T-DEF and does not need to move outside the VP. Similar considerations apply to the sentences in (107).[69]

Before concluding this section, let us observe that if the above account is correct, it partially agrees with previous theories of the present perfect puzzle in situating the locus of the problem at a non-syntactic level. Note that we argued here that it is a non-syntactic level where the MH applies. At the same time, however, the present explanation differs significantly from those previously discussed because it does not reduce the problem to a violation of the truth conditions of a sentence, as in the extended now approach (Dowty 1979), nor does it resort to pragmatic constraints, as in Klein (1992). Rather, the present perfect puzzle is explained as the impossibility of correctly applying the interpretative procedures to the interface representations produced by the syntax. Furthermore, we propose that the reason for movement is the necessity of checking the weak T-DEF feature. In this sense, therefore, the phenomenon is determined by the syntax, although it essentially arises at the interpretative level.

### 3.3. More on the present perfect in Italian-like languages

In the preceding sections we have proposed a morphosyntactic and semantic analysis of the present perfect. We have seen that English and Mainland Scandinavian are systematically different from Romance and from Germanic languages such as Icelandic, German, and Dutch. These two groups pattern differently with respect to the distribution of definite temporal adverbs. We have shown that this fact cooccurs with, and is explained by, morphosyntactic properties of the languages in question. In English and MSc sentences, the relation between $S$ and $R$ — that is, $S = R$, is incompatible with the presence of a definite time adverbial such as *at four* in the present tense (which is part of the temporal semantics of the present perfect). This is not the case with the languages of the other group, where in the present tense an inclusion relation between $S$ and $R$ holds — that is, $S \subseteq R$. We have argued that such semantic properties of the present (perfect) are due to the presence of a hybrid category in English and MSc, which we have called AGR/T. AGR/T is responsible for the identity relation between the temporal variables $S$ and $R$.

However, it must be observed that the languages belonging to the Italian-like group do not behave uniformly, in the sense that they exhibit different properties with respect to the peculiar interpretation they assign to the present perfect and the constraints they place on it. On the other hand, the other group of languages is quite uniform. If a sentence with a present perfect is grammatical or ungrammatical in English, it exhibits the same status in MSc languages, too.

In this section we deal with some "anomalous" present perfect facts in Italian-like languages, and we will see that, although the phenomena which are found across languages might be very different, our theoretical proposal can still make interesting predictions. Given our framework, we expect the English-like system, in which a strict identity relation holds between $S$ and $R$, to be much more constrained than the Italian-like one. In other words, the exceptional facts, if any, are expected to appear in Italian-like languages, given the looser semantic specification of the present.

In particular, we will briefly illustrate the properties of the present perfect in Icelandic, where under certain circumstances we find a modal interpretation of this tense not found in other languages. We will then consider the interpretation of the present perfect in Spanish and Catalan, where a special constraint holds, the so-called 24-hours rule. Finally we will illustrate the properties of the periphrastic present perfect in Portuguese, which can only express a habitual meaning of a certain type.

### 3.3.1. A note on Icelandic

The facts in Icelandic are the following: the present perfect is formed by an auxiliary plus an uninflected supine. When it cooccurs with a definite time adverbial, it has a modal reading with an epistemic value:

(129)   Jòn hefur fari∂ klukkan fjögur.
         John has left at four (epistemic).

This sentence actually means "According to the available evidence, John *probably* left at four", or "*According to what I know,* John left at four". It is the equivalent of the Romance epistemic forms, usually containing a modal or a future:

(130)   Gianni deve essere partito.
         Gianni must have left (epistemic).

(131)   Gianni sarà partito.
         Gianni will have left (epistemic).

Such an epistemic reading is not found if the temporal adverbial is missing:

(132)   Jòn hefur fari∂.
         John has left.

Nor is it available if the tense is the simple past rather than the present perfect, even in the presence of the temporal adverb:

(133)   Jòn fòr klukkan fjögur.
         John left at four.

Thus, in Icelandic, the definite time adverbial determines a special reading of the whole sentence. However, note that, in spite of this, Icelandic still differs from English and MSc. In these languages a sentence with a present perfect and a definite temporal specification is always impossible. It is never the case that such a sentence is interpreted epistemically.[70]

A satisfactory account of these phenomena lies beyond the scope of this work. Here we will only sketch a possible direction for further investigation.

Let us propose that the epistemic interpretation corresponds to a feature in the array and to a projection in $\Sigma$. As we have seen in §3.1.1.3. and §3.1.4. with respect to English, there are two projections in $\Sigma$ where modal features are checked: the MOD/T position, where the feature *[+ i-mod]* is checked, and the external OP position, where the modal covertly moves to create a Spec-head configuration with the appropriate operator. We will not reproduce here the arguments discussed for English, but simply propose to extend our hypothesis to Icelandic. As we have just seen, Icelandic differs from English in that it does not have a hybrid category collapsing AGR and T together; consequently, it does not have the hybrid category MOD/T, either. Icelandic in fact belongs to the Group B languages which exhibit compositional verbal morphology. In the present tense (and in the present perfect), Icelandic has no $\tau$-feature in the array. Therefore, there is no T node in the tree. In a sentence with a present tense, or a present perfect, the projections of AGR dominate those of the (auxiliary) verb. In a modalised (present or present perfect) sentence, AGR dominates the projections of the modal verb, as in Italian (cf. 3.1.1.1). As in English, modals must be interpreted in two positions: one internal to the sentence, where what we called the *internal modality* is checked (i.e., the MOD projection), and an external one above AGR (i.e., OP), where the modal must raise to have the correct scope. Our hypothesis is that in Icelandic the verb *have* can, under certain circumstances, play the role of a modal. This fact is not exceptional, because even in Italian and English this happens in some cases, as in the following sentences:

(134)  a.  Mario *ha* da arrivare in orario, altrimenti lo licenziano.
       b.  Mario *has* to arrive on time (deontic), otherwise they will fire him.

(135)  a.  Mario *ha* da essere arrivato.
       b.  Mario has to have arrived (epistemic).

In (134), the (deontic) modality is expressed by means of *avere* (have) plus an infinitive verb (preceded by the preposition *da*, lit. "from"). In (135) the epistemic modality is expressed by *avere* and a perfect infinitival. In Icelandic *have* is simply followed by the supine, but we might think of the constructions in (129) and (134) and (135) as essentially similar with respect to what is at issue here.

Notice, finally, that in many languages an overt marker for tense can be given a modal value. For instance, in Italian the future can express epistemic modality, and, to a certain extent, even the imperfect indicative can:

(136)  Gianni sarà uscito.
       Lit.: Gianni will have left.
       Gianni has left (epistemic).

(137)  Stasera cantava Pavarotti.
       Lit.: Tonight sang-IMPF Pavarotti.
       Pavarotti is going to sing tonight (epistemic).

In these sentences the future and the imperfect do not convey a future or past meaning, respectively, but are used to express different nuances of epistemicity. Even if we will not give here a formal account for these facts, let us simply note that the relation between tense and (epistemic) modality is very close, and that in several cases they seem to be in complementary distribution.

To account for the facts of Icelandic let us suggest the following hypothesis. We have seen in §3.2.7. that a definite temporal argument such as *at four* bears a T-DEF feature which must be checked in order to obtain a grammatical sentence. In Italian this feature is checked in D/P. For reasons that are not clear to us, and which we will not attempt to discuss, in Icelandic D/P cannot satisfy this requirement of the definite temporal argument. As we argued in §3.2.7., T-DEF can also be checked in T. This is what normally happens in sentences such as *John left at four*, or its equivalent in Icelandic (133), which is grammatical. In the present perfect there is no T1 because of the present tense of the auxiliary; however, we hypothesise that Icelandic has an additional way out: the T-DEF feature of the temporal argument can be checked in the MOD position. In this case, the verb *have* must be interpreted as a modal to satisfy such a requirement. This is in principle possible for two reasons: (a) *have* in Icelandic, like in other languages, can express a modal value, and (b) in general it seems that MOD and T play a very similar role in the morphosyntax of the verbal system, as we tried to argue in the preceding discussion. Therefore MOD can satisfy the requirements usually satisfied by T.[71]

As a final consideration let us point out that given our framework, the situation we found in Icelandic does not occur in languages belonging to the other group. Here, in fact, in the present perfect the category AGR/T always has the T-DEF feature. If for whatever reason D/P cannot check the features T-DEF of a temporal argument, AGR/T is always able to do it, without resulting in a modal interpretation of the auxiliary.

### 3.3.2. The interpretation of the present perfect in Spanish and Catalan

In Spanish and Catalan, as well as in seventeenth-century French and Limouzi (an Occitanian dialect; see Comrie 1985, p. 93), there is a constraint called the *24-hours rule* on the temporal distance between the event described by the sentence and *now*. This interval cannot exceed 24 hours. In other words, the sentences in (138) are grammatical, but those in (139) are not:[72]

(138)  a.  Juan ha salido a las cinco.                              (Spanish)
      b.  En Joan ha sortit a les cinc.                        (Catalan)
        Lit.: John has left at five.

(139)  a.  *Juan ha salido ayer.                                   (Spanish)
      b.  *En Joan ha sortit ahir.                            (Catalan)
        Lit.: John has left yesterday.

The sentences in (138) imply that the event took place at five o'clock of the current day. Note that even if it is true that in Spanish and Catalan, as well as in English, a sentence like *John has left yesterday* is ungrammatical, these languages are not alike, because (138) is ungrammatical *tout court* in English, even if it is clear that it is five o'clock of the current day. As Comrie (1985) points out, the correct way to formulate the relevant rule for Spanish and Catalan is not in terms of hours. Rather, the dimension involved seems to be *today* vs. *yesterday*, where the current *day* begins with the morning.

The semantics $S \subseteq R$ admits the stating of constraints on the temporal distance which can occur between the culmination of the event and $S$. The following picture exemplifies this constraint:

(140)

24 hours

This constraint also works, as expected, even if there is no time adverbial. Consider the following sentences:

(141)  a.  Juan ha salido.                                         (Spanish)
      b.  En Joan ha sortit.                                  (Catalan)
        Lit.: John has left.

Both (141a) and (141b) imply that the event took place today. This is another important difference with respect to the English system. In English a sentence such as *John has left*, provided that the leaving has "current relevance", does not exhibit any peculiar constraint concerning the temporal location of the event. That is, it does not necessarily have to be within the last 24 hours. Obviously, a constraint of this type would be impossible in English-like languages.

### 3.3.3. The analysis of the Portuguese periphrastic present perfect

As we have seen in chapter 2, in Portuguese we find two forms of the past tense — namely, a periphrastic one formed by the auxiliary verb *ter* plus a participle, *tenho comido* (I have eaten), and a simple one, *comi* (I ate). The compound form refers to a *habit* :[73]

(142)  Tem comido muito.
       Lit.: I have eaten a lot.
       I took the habit of eating a lot.

The meaning of (142) is not that of the literal English translation. As shown by the gloss, (142) has a sort of habitual meaning. Consider the following examples:

(143)  a.  O João come às cinco.
           John eats at five.
       b.  O João tem comido às cinco.
           Lit.: John has eaten at five.
           John took the habit to eat at five.

Sentence (143a) has the "normal" meaning of a present tense interpreted habitually, like the corresponding English sentence. Sentence (143b), on the other hand, has a different interpretation which can be glossed more or less as "John took the habit to eat at five", implying both a change in John's habits and the fact that the new habit is still present. We could define this interpretation as a *perfective habitual*. Consider also the following example:

(144)  (Desde outubro) o João tem comido muito.
       Lit.: Since October John has eaten much.
       Since October John has taken to eat much.

This sentence does not mean, contrary to the English one, that since October João ate a lot — that is, that the amount of food eaten since October is a lot — but that *starting* from October João took the habit of eating a lot.

Finally, note that this peculiarity is limited to the present perfect. Example (145), in fact, has the same meaning as the corresponding English (or Italian) sentence:

(145)  Tinha comido às cinco.
       I had eaten at five.

Thus, the special habitual reading is only found with the present perfect. The analytic past perfect has the same reading we find in other Romance and Germanic languages. Note also that, if a punctual temporal argument is used, as in (143) and (144), it can only be an indefinite. Definite temporal arguments yield unacceptable sentences:

(146)    *O João tem comido ahier.
        John has eaten yesterday.

Therefore, according to the approach developed in §3.2.5., these temporal arguments cannot move out of the VP.

Let us propose an account for these facts. Note that *ter* also has a lexical meaning (to keep), besides being used as an auxiliary. In this respect it is similar to English *do*, which has a lexical use, as well as a functional use — that is, it can be used as a semantically empty auxiliary. Furthermore, Portuguese did have an auxiliary corresponding to *have* which became obsolete (Vázquez Cuesta & Mendes da Luz 1989). In order to account for (142), we hypothesise, therefore, that *ter* is lexically ambiguous. It may behave either as a semantically empty auxiliary, or as a full verb. When it is a true auxiliary, we expect the construction it enters into to exhibit the same meaning as the corresponding auxiliaries of languages such as Italian and English. Our hypothesis is that in the pluperfect *ter* is interpreted as an auxiliary. In the case of the present perfect, however, *ter* must be interpreted as a full verb. Conversely, it cannot be interpreted as an auxiliary in the present perfect and as a full verb in the pluperfect. We relate the impossibility of a construction such as *tem(aux) comido* to the existence of the synthetic perfect *comei*. The two forms would have the same interpretation, and this possibility is ruled out. This situation is explained by resorting to the following principle of economy suggested by Chomsky (1995 §5.4):

(147)    $\alpha$ enters the enumeration only if it has an effect on the output.

Concerning PF, the relevant notion of *effect on the output* is defined in terms of strict identity — that is, identity of two phonetic forms, so that an item $\alpha$ that modifies the phonetic form can be entered into the initial numeration. With respect to LF, Chomsky observes that a weaker notion than strict identity is needed, embodying some form of logical equivalence. Returning to the Portuguese case, consider that the logical form of a sentence with *comei* and that of a sentence with *tem comido*, with auxiliary *ter,* express the same meaning.[74] Then a principle like (147) inhibits the insertion of the auxiliary *ter* in the initial numeration, because it is redundant with respect to the possibility of using the synthetic *comi*.[75] The only option available, then, is the full verb *ter*, which, by introducing its own eventive variable, causes LF to change. The habitual meaning of (143b) can be captured by hypothesising the presence in the participial clause of a hidden habitual operator *Gen* which binds the temporal variable of the event time (cf. Krifka et al. 1995 and chapter 4):

(148) $\lambda x.$ (Gen $t(\text{TP}(t, I) \wedge \text{TP}(x, I)] \exists e \exists e'(\text{eat}(e) \wedge$ five-o-clock$(t) \wedge$ at$(t, e) \wedge$ CS$(e', e))$.

Example (148) is the (tentative) logical form associated with the participial clause of (143b). It requires that for generically many times $t$ which are included in a contextually relevant interval $I$, and which are *five o'clock* times, there is an event $e$ of eating taking place at $t$, and the consequent state of $e$, $e'$. Notice, furthermore, that (148) yields a predicate of times. This is due to the fact that the contextually relevant interval $I$ must be connected with the speech time. Given the present tense on *ter*, the result will be $x = s$.

Concerning the inchoative meaning of Portuguese sentences with the analytic present perfect, let us hypothesise that verbal *ter* requires a stage level predicate. Therefore, when combined with an individual level predicate, it gives rise to an inchoative interpretation. In this sense, it behaves like the Spanish and Portuguese auxiliary *estar* (Schmitt 1991). *Estar*, when combined with an individual level predicate, such as *gordo* (fat) in (149a) or *um homen* (a man) in (149b), forces an inchoative interpretation:

(149)  a.  Juan está gordo.                                  (Spanish)
           Lit.: Juan *está* fat.
           Juan has fattened.
       b.  Ele está um homen.                                (Portuguese)
           Lit.: he *está* man.
           He has turned into a man.

In the literature (Bertinetto 1991; Carlson 1989; Vlach 1993), it has been observed that habituals and generics share many properties with stative sentences. In particular, Carlson (1989) proposes that they involve a semantic change from a stage-level to an individual-level predicate. Suppose this is correct. Then the inchoativity of (142) would correspond to the inchoativity of (149), and whatever explains this property of (149) could explain (142). That is, the inchoativity of Portuguese analytic perfects would be a consequence of the mismatch between the requirements of lexical *ter* and the nature of the complement it combines with, similarly to what happens with Spanish and Portuguese *estar*.

We still have to explain why the Portuguese pluperfect does not have the same meaning as the present perfect — that is, why (145) does not mean that "at a certain point I had taken to eat at five". According to our account, the peculiar interpretation of the Portuguese present perfect is due to the presence of the full verb *ter*. Furthermore, we argued that auxiliary *ter* cannot be used with the present perfect because the resulting form would compete with the synthetic present perfect. The situation with the pluperfect is exactly the opposite one: auxiliary *ter* is allowed, whereas verbal *ter* is forbidden. Consider that in the pluperfect there is both a T1 and a T2 category. The former T-marks *tinha*, and the latter T-marks the main verb. The consequent state variable is not directly connected with the speech event, but it can be connected to it through the auxiliary. If the nonauxiliary *ter* is selected, the variable of the consequent state cannot be identified with that of *ter*, given that they are two distinct entities.

### 3.4. Some observations on the temporal and aspectual properties of the Italian present perfect

Cinque (1994) proposes that the Italian adverb *appena* (just) occupies the specifier position of an aspectual projection, ASP1, which is higher than T2:

(150)  $[_{ASP1}$ appena $[ \ldots [_{T2P} \ldots T2 \ldots [_{VP}$   $]]]$

He bases this conclusion on observations concerning the distribution of *appena* (just) with respect to other items. In particular, he considers the floating quantifier *tutti* (all) which, he argues, occupies the *Spec* of an AGR position:

(151)  a.  *L'hanno appena tutti avuto.
            Lit.: they-cl have *appena* all had.
            They have all just had it.
       b.  L'hanno appena avuto tutti.
            Lit.: they-cl have *appena* had all.
            They have all just had it.
       c.  L'hanno avuto appena tutti.
            Lit.: they-cl have had *appena* all.
            They have all just had it.

Given the paradigm in (152), it can be hypothesised that such adverbs as *appena* (just) and *ora* (now) are incompatible with a *[+ past]* feature, since they cannot cooccur with the simple past tense, as in (152a):[76]

(152)  a.  *Mario appena arrivò.
            Mario *appena* arrived.
            Mario just arrived.
       b.  Mario è appena arrivato.
            Mario is *appena* arrived.
            Mario has just arrived.
       c.  Ieri Mario è arrivato.
            Yesterday Mario has arrived.
       d.  *Ieri Mario è appena arrivato.
            Yesterday Mario has *appena* arrived.

The Italian present perfect can cooccur either with a temporal locator, such as *ieri* (yesterday) in (152c), or with *appena* (cf. (151b), (151c) and (152b)), but not with both (cf. (152d)). One might propose, therefore, that the Italian past participle can assume either a temporal or an aspectual value, the cooccurrence of the two being somehow inhibited. Adverbs such as *appena* select (i.e., make visible) the aspectual value, explaining (152a), whereas temporal locators such as *ieri* in (152c) need *[+ past]* — that is, a temporal value.

This theory contrasts with the one we are proposing here in that it takes the Italian past participle to be ambiguous between an aspectual and a temporal value, the two being mutually exclusive. In the previous sections, however, we have suggested that the past participle has *both* an aspectual (perfective) and a temporal value, and that the two always cooccur. Let us reconsider the data in (152) and suggest an alternative explanation for them.

It is not the case that *ieri* (yesterday) suspends the aspectual value of the present perfect. The event seems to be perfective both when *ieri* is present and when it is not, as shown by (153):

(153)   a.   * Mario ha (appena) mangiato la mela e l'ha terminata oggi.
             Mario has (*appena*) eaten the apple without finishing it and has finished it today.
        b.   * Ieri Mario ha (appena) mangiato la mela e l'ha terminata oggi.
             Yesterday Mario has (*appena*) eaten the apple without finishing it and has finished it today.

Both (153a) and (153b) are unacceptable, independently of the presence of the temporal adverbial *ieri*. The present perfect *is* perfective, and an accomplishment predicate such as *mangiare la mela* (eat the apple), when perfective, entails that the telos (culmination) has been reached — in this case, that the apple has been consumed. If *ieri* suspended the aspectual value, we would expect (153b) to be acceptable, contrary to fact.

Consider now the distribution of *appena* (just). It is ruled out not only in sentences with the simple past tense (cf. (152a)) but also in every sentence with a non-compound tense:

(154)   a.   *Mario appena arriva.
             Mario just arrives.
        b.   *Mario appena arriverà.
             Mario just will arrive.
        c.   *Mario appena arrivava.
             Mario just arrived(IMPF).

On the other hand, *appena* is always grammatical with compound tenses:

(155)   a.   Mario è appena arrivato.
             Mario has just arrived.
        b.   Mario era appena arrivato.
             Mario had just arrived.
        c.   Mario sarà appena arrivato.[77]
             Mario will have just arrived.

The fact that *appena* is incompatible with simple tenses seems to suggest that it cannot simply be described as being incompatible with the feature *[+ past]*. Furthermore, even the impossibility for *appena* to cooccur with a temporal locator such as *ieri*, exemplified by (152d), is far from being absolute, as we will see in the following discussion. Our hypothesis is that *appena* is not an item selecting aspectuality, at least not in the sense we are using this term here — that is, to characterise the opposition between perfectivity and non-perfectivity. Rather, it behaves like an operator appearing in various contexts and with a range of different meanings which can be given a uniform analysis. Let us propose that *appena* selects the minimal element from a given domain. Consider the data in (156):

(156) a. Mario è appena arrivato.
         Mario has just arrived.
      b. Sono appena arrivato ieri (alle tre).
         I have just arrived yesterday (at three o'clock).
      c. Mario ha (appena) toccato (appena) Maria.
         Mario has (just) touched (just) Maria.
      d. Mario toccò appena Maria.
         Mario touched just Maria.

Example (156a) can mean "Mario has just arrived". Example (156b) has a similar meaning, despite the presence of a temporal specification concerning the time of the arrival (cf. (152c)). Note that (156b) needs a suitable context — namely, one according to which the time elapsed since yesterday (or since three o'clock) can be considered minimal.

To account for these data, we assign *appena* a structure similar to the one Krifka (1990) proposes for polarity items — namely, a structure $\langle A_\alpha \, a_\alpha \leq_\alpha \rangle$ such that:[78]

(157) (i)   $A_\alpha$ is (part of) the domain of *appena* (i.e., its restriction) and is a
            set of alternatives of a given semantic type $\sigma$.
      (ii)  $\leq_\alpha$ is a preorder (that is a transitive and reflexive relation) on $A_\alpha$.
      (iii) $a_\alpha$ is the unique element that is minimal in $A_\alpha$ according to $\leq_\alpha$.
      (iv)  there is at least one additional element $b \in A_\alpha$ such that $b \neq a_\alpha$.[79]

Given a restriction and its denotation $A_\alpha$, *appena* applies to a constituent with denotation $P(x)$ in such a way that $Appena_x[A_\alpha(x)]P(x)$ is true iff there is one $x$ in $A_\alpha$ that makes $P$ true and for every such $x$ it holds that $x = a_\alpha$.

Intuitively, in (156a) the domain of *appena*, $A_\alpha$, consists of temporal entities elapsing from the culmination of the event reported by the main verb. The relevant ordering on $A_\alpha$ is the inclusion relation so that $a_\alpha$, the minimal element, is the shortest one. Therefore, the meaning of (156a) could be paraphrased as "there is an event which is an arrival by Mario and the minimal temporal entity elapsing from its culmination is such that it contains the speech event, $s$". The same holds for (156b), with the caveat that in this case a contextual component is playing a role. Now consider (156c). When *appena* appears before the participle, two interpretations are possible. The first is again about the quantity of time that has elapsed since the main event (i.e. the touching of Maria by Mario) culminated. Such an interpretation can be treated on a par with (156a) and (156b). The other reading may be paraphrased by saying that Mario has *simply* (or *only*) touched Mary. He did not beat her, or attempt to kill her, or do anything involving any degree of violence to Mary. Here the set of alternatives is formed by the aforementioned types of events (all involving some sort of physical contact between Mario and Maria) ordered according to the amount of violence involved. As in (156b), a contextual component is at work, and *appena* picks up the event that is minimal, according to the relevant ordering, from the alternative set (such an interpretation is always available with the preverbal *appena*, given the right context). Finally, when *appena* appears after the participle — still (156c) — the only meaning available is the one we have just discussed.

To explain this pattern we hypothesise that there are two positions available for *appena* and that its domain is provided by (at least part of) the material it c-commands. When it is in the first position — call it position A — it can quantify over temporal entities elapsing from the culmination, whether the latter are localised by means of a temporal adverbial, as in (156b), or not. In the case in which a temporal locator is present (an *E*-temporal argument in the terminology of §3.2.5. in the preceding discussion), it must be within the scope of *appena* in the syntax. *Appena* can also quantify over predicates of events, ordered by means of a contextually salient ordering, as in (156c). When it is in the second position — call it position B — *appena* can only quantify over (predicates of) events.[80] Position A is higher than position B and c-commands everything that position B c-commands. Following Cinque (1994, 1995a), we hypothesise that participial clauses project two aspectual categories, ASP1 and ASP2, where ASP2 realises the perfective/imperfective opposition. Given that in every case the event is perfective, position B must c-command $ASP2^0$. On the other hand, given that from position A *appena* can quantify over something which is closely related to consequent states (see following discussion) we hypothesise that this position is higher than T2. Thus, in (152) *appena* occupies the *Spec* of $ASP1^0$. Finally, we propose that Cinque's ASP1 is actually the syncretic category ASP/T2 introduced in §3.2.4. Consequently, *appena* in (152) occupies the *Spec* of this category:

(158)     ASP1/T2-P

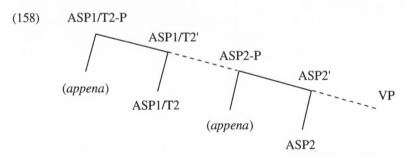

Let us consider in more detail what the term "temporal entity elapsing from the culmination", used in the preceding discussion means. In §3.2.3. we proposed that participial clauses introduce a relation *CS(e', e)* that holds between two events *e'* and *e,* iff *e'* is a consequent state of *e.* We hypothesise now that the domain of *appena* is the partially ordered set $A_\alpha = \langle 2^C, \propto \rangle$ obtained by ordering the power set of consequent states $2^C$ according to the relation of duration $\propto$.[81] In conformity with (157)iii, *appena* picks up the minimal such subset. Hence, in a participial phrase modified by *appena*, the relation *CS* is restricted in such a way that *CS(e', e)* holds iff *e'* is a minimal consequent state of *e*, according to $\propto$. Eventually, we obtain a logical form for (156a) where the speech event is localised within one of the minimal consequent states singled out by *appena* — that is, $\exists e' e(. . . CS(e', e) \wedge \rho(s, e') . . . )$. We call such a reading the *temporal reading* of *appena*.

Now consider (156c) and (156d), repeated here for simplicity:

(156) c. Mario ha (appena) toccato (appena) Maria.
      Mario has (just) touched (just) Maria.
   d. Mario toccò appena Maria.
      Mario touched just Maria.

The alternative set $A_\alpha$ is formed by all the *relevant kinds* of events, the agent of which is *Mario* and the theme of which is *Maria*. The notion *relevant kind* can be made more precise by recalling the observation made above concerning the fact that the *touching* in question is *minimal* among the events of physical contact possibly performed by Mario on Maria. This observation can be formalised by resorting to what Krifka (1990) calls the *generalised inclusion relations* $\subseteq$ (not to be confused with the temporal containment relation):

(159) If $\alpha$ and $\beta$ are of type $t$ then $\alpha \subseteq \beta$ iff $\alpha \rightarrow \beta$.

Therefore an expression $\alpha$ of type $t$ is in the generalised inclusion relation with respect to another expression $\beta$ of the same type iff the truth of $\alpha$ entails the truth of $\beta$. In our case, had Mario flogged Maria, then he would also have touched her; thus, touching is the most general eventive concept involved here. As in Krifka (1990), the ordering we are seeking is the reverse of the generalised inclusion relation. That is, the minimal element in the domain $A_\alpha$ is such that its truth is entailed by the truth of every other element. Therefore, in (156c) and (156d), we obtain $A_\alpha = \{P \mid touch \leq_\alpha P\}$ where $P$ is a predicate of events and $\leq_\alpha$ is the inverse of $\subseteq$, and furthermore, $a_\alpha = touch$. With this, the (relevant) meaning of (156c) is that "Mario has touched Maria and touching is minimal according to the given ordering (e.g., the involved degree of violence)". We will call such a reading a *contextual eventive* one.

Let us now go back to cases such as (152a), (154a), and (154b), repeated here:

(152) a. *Mario appena arrivò.
         Mario *appena* arrived.
         Mario just arrived.

(154) a. *Mario appena arriva.
         Mario just arrives.
   b. *Mario appena arriverà.
         Mario just will arrive.

Observe that neither the contextual eventive reading nor the temporal one (involving the consequent state) is possible. This might be due to the fact that simple tense clauses lack the projection ASP/T2 in whose *Spec* temporal *appena* is licensed. On the other hand, ASP2 is available with both compound and simple tenses, as shown by (156c) and (156d), which both exhibit the contextual eventive reading. These facts are consistent with our theory. The higher position, ASP/T2, being linked to the presence of consequent states, does not show up in simple tense constructions. The lower aspectual projection, on the other hand, is independently needed to fix the aspectual properties of the main verb (see, among others, Borer 1993) and is always available.

We have shown that, crucially, *appena* is compatible with an in situ overt *E*-temporal argument (cf. (156b)). However, when the same argument is in the leftmost position, the sentence is ungrammatical, as in (152d), repeated here:

(152) d. *Ieri Mario è appena arrivato.
      Yesterday Mario has *appena* arrived.

We account for this contrast by drawing a parallelism between (152d) and (126c). In both cases, there is an adverb (*appena* (just) in (152d) and *già* (already) in (126c)) which must take overt scope over the *E*-temporal argument. In §3.2.7., the behaviour of *già* (already) has been explained by claiming that the *E*-temporal argument must be in a checking relation with the adverb at LF. We also show that this assumption yields the correct predictions with respect to the grammaticality of specific temporal arguments in past perfect sentences. The extension of this analysis to (152d) is straightforward: as with *già* (already), *appena* (just) attracts the *E*-temporal argument which must be in a checking configuration with it at LF. Thus (152d) is ruled out because it violates this requirement.[82]

Before concluding this digression on the properties of *appena*, let us briefly discuss another use of this adverb, exemplified by the following sentences:

(160) a. Appena arrivò, Mario venne licenziato.
      Lit.: *Appena* he arrived, Mario was fired.
      Immediately after he arrived, Mario was fired.
  b. Appena è arrivato, Mario è stato licenziato.
      Lit.: *Appena* he arrived, Mario has been fired.
      Immediately after he arrived, Mario was fired.
  c. Appena arrivato, Mario è stato licenziato.
      Lit.: *Appena* he arrived (past-part), Mario has been fired.
  d. Appena arrivò alle tre, Mario venne licenziato.
      Lit.: *Appena* he arrived at three, Mario was fired.
      Immediately after he arrived at three, Mario was fired.
  e. Appena è arrivato alle tre, Mario è stato licenziato.
      Lit.: *Appena* he has arrived at three, Mario has been fired.
  f. * Appena arrivò ieri, Mario venne licenziato.
      Lit.: *Appena* he arrived yesterday, Mario was fired.

g. * Appena è arrivato ieri, Mario è stato licenziato.
   Lit.: *Appena* he has arrived yesterday, Mario has been fired.
   Immediately after he has arrived yesterday, Mario has been fired.
h. Appena arrivato alle tre, Mario è stato licenziato.
   Lit.: *Appena* he arrived at three, Mario has been fired.
   Immediately after he has arrived at three, Mario has been fired.

Here, we have bi-clausal constructions where the clause introduced by *appena* locates the event reported by the main clause. Example (160a) means that there is an arrival of *Mario* and a subsequent firing of *Mario*, and the latter immediately follows the former. This reading is very close to the one we analysed as involving "temporal entities elapsing from the culmination". The same holds for (160b) and for the absolute construction in (160c). Following the literature (e.g., Kratzer 1995; Bonomi 1995) on *when* clauses, we propose that in these sentences *appena* acts as a restricted quantifier whose restriction is supplied by the clause it introduces and whose nuclear scope contains the main clause. More precisely, *appena* quantifies over the variable of the *E*-temporal arguments of the main clause. Now consider (160a). The *alternative set* of (157), corresponding to the restriction, is formed by time spans beginning with the culmination of the event in the restrictive clause — that is, $A_\alpha = \{t \mid e < t\}$. The ordering $<_\alpha$ is the relation of temporal inclusion. We need not modify the truth conditions for *appena* given before. Therefore, we obtain for (160a) the logical form in (161):

(161)  $\exists e(\text{Appena } t[\text{arrive}(e) \wedge \text{Theme}(e, \text{Mario}) \wedge \underline{e \leq t}]\ \exists e'\exists t'(\text{fire}(e') \wedge \text{Theme}(e', \text{Mario}) \wedge \text{At}(t, e) \wedge t \leq t'))$

Example (160a) is true iff there is an arrival of Mario and a firing of Mario such that the firing obtains immediately after the arrival.[83]

   Sentences (160d) and (160)f have a slightly different meaning. Example (160d) does not assert that the firing immediately followed Mario's arrival (at three). Rather, it says that the very first time Mario arrived at three he was fired. That is, in (160d) *appena* quantifies over occasions of arrival. Notice that to obtain such a reading the *E*-temporal argument of the adverbial clause must be indefinite:

(162)  a.  ??Appena Mario arrivò giovedì scorso, venne licenziato.
           Immediately after Mario arrived on last Thursday, he was fired.
       b.  Appena Mario arrivò di giovedì, venne licenziato.
           As soon as Mario arrived on a Thursday, he was fired.

In (160f), (160g), and (162a) the temporal locator is definite, making the sentences quite marginal. To account for this fact, we propose, following Borer (1993), that (temporal) arguments that remain in the VP (as may be the case for temporal indefinites; cf. the preceding discussion in §3.2.7.) incorporates into the verb, yielding a complex predicate — that is, the predicate *arrivare-di-giovedì* (arrive-on-a-Thursday) in (162b). In this case, *appena* binds the eventive variable of the complex predicate, yielding (163):

(163)   Appena *e* [Complex-Pred(*e*) . . .] $\exists e'$ (main-clause-Pred(*e'*) . . . )

As above, the restrictive clause supplies the alternative set which, in (162b), is formed by all the events of *arriving on Thursday*, the theme of which is *Mario*. The ordering $\leq_\alpha$ is simply temporal precedence.[84] Therefore, *appena* singles out the first event which is an arrival on Thursday and (163) establishes that it corresponds to the firing of John.

Note that the reading we are discussing is also possible with (160a) to (160c). These sentences are ambiguous between the (already discussed) temporal reading (Mario was fired immediately after his arrival) and the "first time" one. This confirms our analysis: in (160a) to (160c) there is no overt *E*-argument. The latter is a variable which, we suggest, can behave as an indefinite and be analysed as part of the main predicate, yielding a logical form like the one in (163). If the variable corresponding to the null *E*-temporal argument is not analysed as part of the predicate, then *appena* ranges over temporal intervals spanning from the event culmination, yielding (161).

When the *E*-temporal argument is definite, as in (162a), it must be scoped out of the VP (cf. §3.2.7.):

(164)   [*E*-arg$_i$ . . . [$_{VP}$ . . . t$_i$]]

In this case, there is no variable that *appena* can bind in (162a), and the sentence is ruled out as an instance of vacuous quantification.

To summarise, we consider *appena* as having a semantics very similar to that which Krifka (1990) suggested for polarity items. It singles out the minimal element from an ordered set (the *set of alternatives*, cf. (157)). We also argued that there are two positions for *appena* within the participial clause — one in the *Spec* of ASP1, and the other in the *Spec* of ASP2. When *appena* is in the first position, its alternative set is the power set of the consequent states, the relevant ordering is temporal duration, and *appena* selects the subset of consequent states having minimal duration. When *appena* is in the second position, its alternative set is constituted by predicates of events, and the relevant ordering is the reverse of what Krifka (1990) calls the *generalised inclusion relation*. The unavailability of the first possibility in sentences with simple tenses is attributed to the fact that these sentences lack the ASP/T2 position. Finally, we also considered *appena* as introducing adverbial clauses, and we observed that the theory developed here can be extended to predict these cases as well.

## Appendix: The present perfect in Catanese and Vicentino

Let us briefly illustrate some data concerning the distribution of the present perfect in southern varieties, comparing it with the distribution of surcompounds in certain northern Italian dialects. These phenomena certainly deserve further study. However, here we only illustrate some data which might clarify the distribution of the present perfect in Italian.

We have already pointed out that in northern Italy the simple past is not very productive, and that, even if sometimes it is used, it has a literary flavour. In any case, northern Italian speakers do have judgements concerning the paradigm in (48). In southern Italy, on the contrary, the only productive past form is the simple past, even when it cooccurs with adverbials such as *adesso* or *ora* (now). However, a form corresponding to the present perfect does exist in southern dialects, but it has a special meaning, which we will consider in a moment.

Let us analyse the following paradigm of Catanese, a variety of west Sicilian:[85]

(165) a. Mangiai u pisci spada e mmi fici mali.
   I ate(SP) swordfish and it made(SP) me sick.
  b. Haju mangiatu u pisci spada e mma ffattu mali.
   I have eaten(PrPerf) swordfish and it made(PrPerf) me sick.
  c. Haju mangiatu u pisci spada e mmi fici mali.
   I have eaten(PrPerf) swordfish and it made(SP) me sick.
  d. *Mmi mangiai u pisci spada e mma ffattu mali.
   I ate(SP) swordfish and it made(PrPerf) me sick.

Observe first that even in Sicilian we find a verbal form composed of an auxiliary, *have*, plus a participle, *mangiatu* (eaten) and *ffattu* (lit: made) which seems therefore rather close to the Standard Italian present perfect. However, the distribution of this form is different from the one we have seen in (48) above:

(166) a. Gianni emigrò negli Stati Uniti, ma poi è tornato.
   Gianni emigrated(SP) in the States, but then he has come(PrPerf) back.
  b. *Gianni è emigrato negli Stati Uniti, ma poi tornò.
   Gianni has emigrated(PrPerf) in the States, but then he came(SP) back.

In (165c) and (165d), the sequence accepted by Sicilian native speakers is exactly opposite of the sequence accepted in Standard Italian. That is, the sequence PrPerf-SP is grammatical in Sicilian, but ungrammatical in Standard Italian. However, the sequence SP-PrPerf is acceptable in Italian, but unacceptable in Sicilian. That is, if the first clause contains the simple form and the second the periphrastic one (acceptable in Italian), the result is sharply ungrammatical in Sicilian. If, on the contrary, the present perfect precedes the simple past, which is the ungrammatical case in Italian, the result is acceptable in Sicilian.

Our proposal is that the Catanese data in (165) are due not to a temporal opposition but rather to an aspectual one. In other words, the emphasis is presumably not on the temporal distinction between the two events, even if such a distinction might exist, but on the aspectual properties which are collapsed together with the temporal ones. In fact, the meaning attributed by speakers to (165c) is that the first verbal form provides the *background* and, significantly, has no actual relevance, whereas the second one expresses the salient fact, which is relevant at the time of the utterance. Note that, coherently with such considerations, native speakers agree that in the case of sentences (165a) and (165c), the state of sickness might persist up to the present moment, a possibility which is ruled out in (165b).[86]

For speakers of central varieties of Italian (as the authors of this book are), it is difficult to understand which exactly is the aspectual meaning involved in the Sicilian sentences. We observed some similarities with the glosses provided for surcompounds in northern Italian dialects (see Poletto 1992), and, by asking native speakers, we found some surprising correspondences between the two cases. In northern Italian varieties, as already stated, the simple past is not productively used, and the present perfect is adopted to express past meanings (in addition to, obviously, the imperfect). In some northern dialects, however, such as Vicentino, it is possible to find another form, exhibiting an extra auxiliary. Consider the following sentence, from Poletto (1992, p. 293, ex. 8):

(167)   Stamatina go *bio* stirà.
        Lit.: This morning (I) have *had* ironed.

In addition to this sentence, we can also have *stamatina go stirà* (This morning I have ironed) — that is, *bio* is not to be obligatorily inserted, but contributes a certain semantic value. It is not clear what the exact meaning associated with *bio* is. Poletto (1992) points out that it is an aspectual auxiliary, meaning something like *completion*. As we said above, native speakers explain the semantics of these forms in ways very similar to that of the present perfect in Catanese. Interestingly, the surcompound of Vicentino has the same distribution of the present perfect in Catanese: [87]

(168)   a.  Go magnà e me ga fato mal.
            I have eaten it and it has made me sick.
        b.  Go *bio* magnà e me ga *bio* fato mal.
            I have *had* eaten it and it has *had* made me sick.
        c.  Go *bio* magnà e me ga fato mal.
            I have *had* eaten it and it has made me sick.
        d.  *Go magnà e me ga *bio* fato mal.
            I have eaten it and it has *had* made me sick.

We cannot give a full analysis of these facts here, because further work would be required concerning the distribution and the semantics of these items. Let us just make a few comments. In Standard Italian the value expressed by the Vicentino surcompound and by the Catanese present perfect seems not to be expressible by means of a *morphologically* codified form. A periphrasis must be used to translate the semantic content of the two dialects. For instance, the Standard Italian form *Una volta che ebbi mangiato . . .* (Once I had eaten . . . ) might be a good approximation to Vicentino (168c) and Catanese (165c) (this is not the case for other usages of the forms in question). Consequently, the structure projected in Italian, and to a certain extent, even the initial array, are different from those of Catanese and Vicentino.[88]

Putting aside these more general questions and returning to the topic of this appendix, our aim has been to provide more data in support of the thesis that the present perfect and the simple past of Standard Italian cannot simply be considered to be free variants, because they instantiate two different semantics which must somehow be connected to their morphological forms. The contrast between the two temporal forms of Standard Italian seems to be a *real* one, given that it can also be found in languages which have minimally different systems, such as Catanese and Vicentino.

## Notes

1. For a diachronic analysis, see Roberts (1993). On the analysis of the verbal projections of the Germanic languages, see among others Holmberg & Platzack (1988), Platzack & Holmberg (1989), Vikner (1994, 1995), Rohrbacher (1994).

2. On the lack of a present tense morpheme in English, see Enç (1991) and Thráinsson (1994). For a discussion of the value of the present in English, see Campbell (1991) and Guéron (1993).

3. The form in example (2b) is the *imperfect indicative*. We are using it for simplicity, and we will not consider the properties of the imperfect with respect to the simple past. See chapter 4 for a discussion of the imperfect in Italian and Romance.

4. But see Chomsky (1995) for a different view according to which there is no AGR projection at all. We will not discuss such a hypothesis in this work. Let us observe, however, that it would not provide a solution for the distributional problem we are addressing in the text.

5. Such an idea has also been suggested by Thráinsson (1994) and then further developed by Chomsky (1995), even if in a different perspective.

6. Vikner (1994; 1995) also discusses the previous literature. We refer the reader to his work and to references cited there.

7. For a discussion of the notion of paradigm, we refer the reader to Roberts (1993 ch. 3 §1), Rohrbacher (1994), Vikner (1995); see also Jaeggli & Safir (1989) for the notion of *morphological uniformity*.

8. According to certain authors, among others Poletto (1992), auxiliaries do not project their own verbal projections but are directly inserted in functional heads. We have not found strong reasons in favour of such an assumption. From the point of view of acquisition, it is presumably more adequate to hypothesise that items such as *have* and *be*, exhibiting the morphosyntactic properties of verbs (tense, agreement, the presence of VP adverbials, etc.), are classified by children as verbs, according to the positive evidence available.

9. See Chomsky (1995) for a proposal concerning the position of VP-adverbials such as *often*. The judgements on (11) seem to be more consistent with British

speakers than with American speakers. Thanks to C. Tortora for comments and suggestions on this point.

10. In French, as hypothesised by Pollock (1989; see also chapter 1 §1.1. of this book), the non-finite verb undergoes short movement. In French, the adverb appears to the right of the non-finite form, and the negation, to the left:

(i)     Ne pas manger souvent.

It seems, therefore, that the distribution of the English auxiliary cannot be traced back to a short-movement hypothesis, given that the word order is the opposite.

11. The data in (12) could be accounted for by resorting to Pollock's (1994) notion of *bilingualism*. He shows, for instance, that Elizabethan English speakers allowed the forms in (i) beside the one of contemporary English:

(i)     John kisses never Mary (Pollock, ex. 19c).

He accounts for these facts by assuming that the speakers could analyse a form like *kisses* in two different ways: (a) *kiss+suffix,* where the suffix enters a rich system of paradigmatic oppositions, or (b) *kiss+augment,* where the resulting word is not morphologically complex (in the relevant sense). Accordingly, the $\phi$-features of *kisses* are strong in the (a) case, yielding (i), and weak in the (b) case, yielding the situation of contemporary English.

The importance of this proposal, once applied to (12), consists in the fact that (12a) and (12b) do not express a true optionality — that is, free choice which is something unexpected within the minimalist framework. Rather, the choice is deterministically motivated by the morphological properties of a given item. Whenever *has* is analysed as *have+es(suffix)*, the $\phi$-features are necessarily strong. If it is analysed as *have+augment,* then they are weak. Thus, the ambiguity is not in the syntax but in the lexicon.

12. Notice that our reasoning does not extend to strong verbs, which do not differ in movement properties from the other ones. In the present tense, in fact, they undergo a regular derivation, and the apophonic derivations of the past and the participial forms are in some sense "regular" ones, even if not productive anymore. As a conclusion, we might say that there is no evidence for a speaker to hypothesise that a verb such as, for instance, *to write (wrote, written)* has strong features requiring movement before Spell-Out.

13. For an analysis of the verbal form *says*, which as far as pronunciation is concerned is an exception to the discussion above, see Roberts (1993, ch. 3 fn. 5). Though orthographically regular, this form is phonologically anomalous. Roberts points out that if the relevant factor were the morphological, or rather *morphophonological*, properties of the verb, its behaviour should be the same as *have* and *be*, because analogously to these verbs it is "irregular". Since, however, it behaves as a normal non-auxiliary verb, the relevant properties determining the distribution of these forms, according to Roberts, should be the ones related to $\theta$-theory, as originally proposed by Pollock (1989) and Chomsky (1993), because *have* and *be* have exceptional properties, whereas *say* does not. We think that such

evidence is not sufficient to justify these conclusions, even if *say* constitutes an exception which must be taken into account.

Notice that, interestingly, Roberts points out (ch. 3) that the -*s* morpheme could be analysed as the cliticisation of a third person pronominal form. In fact, in a 15th-century dialect spoken in northern England and Scotland, this ending was in complementary distribution with a pronominal subject. If this analysis is correct, we have an additional argument for claiming that there is no *paradigm* in English verbal morphology, in the sense of (9), because even the only surviving ending expressing φ-features is not a proper suffix. Under this view, the process of verbal inflection is actually a process of cliticisation.

14. Following Iatridou (1990a), one could object that the ordering of *often* and *never* is not a test for verb movement-either. She argues, in fact, that alternative explanations for their positions, not involving V-to-I movement, could be found. The paradigm in (10) to (12) calls for an explanation, whatever the theory assumed, and, if the verb movement hypothesis makes the correct predictions, we have no reason to reject it.

15. Notice that speakers prefer the following sentences with respect to (14b), even if it is judged acceptable:

(i)     John cannot sleep here often.
(ii)    Often John cannot sleep here.

16. The reason we tested sentences simultaneously containing an adverb such as *often* and negation is that in this way we can be sure that *often* does not appear in the Specifier of the VP projected by *sleep*, a possibility available if nothing intervenes between the two. Notice, in fact, that the sentence *John can often sleep here* is possible. In this case, however, the meaning is partially different from that of *John often can sleep here*, given that the scope relations between the modal and the adverb of quantification are not the same in the two cases.

17. In Scandinavian, on the contrary, modals do appear in non-finite forms (see Roberts 1993, p. 318 ff.), showing that in these languages they have the categorial status of verbs.

18. With respect to case assignment properties, we might hypothesise that MOD/T works exactly as AGR/T does (cf. chapter 2 §2.5.).

19. Modals can be modified by the same kind of adverbs that modify verbs, such as *often, never*, and the like. This fact can be explained by claiming that the properties, or, rather, the features, relevant for the presence of such adverbs are also present on modals. For instance, we might say that modals, like verbs, have an *e* position in their θ-grid which can be θ-identified with that of the adverb (see Higginbotham 1985).

20. On the properties which *do* seems to have in common with expletives, see also Roberts (1993, ch. 3, fn. 19).

21. On the ordering of *do* and negation see §3.3.

22. We thank for judgements and discussion T. Taraldsen, A. Holmberg, C. Platzack, S. Vikner, H. Sigurðsson, H. Thráinsson, and O. Olafsson.

23. In all Germanic languages there are strong (irregular) and weak (regular) verbs. We assume that the morphological component is responsible for the actual form a verb takes, along the lines suggested by Halle (1991) for Russian. See, however, Campbell (1991) for a different hypothesis.

24. Vikner (1995) proposes that negation appears in the highest possible *Spec* — namely, in *Spec*, TP. Recall that in English, on the contrary, negation always appears to the right of the auxiliary and of the supporting verb *do*.

25. Notice also that we are implicitly claiming that negation in English cannot appear above AGR, whereas this seems to be a possibility in other languages — for instance, in Basque, as hypothesised by Laka (1990). See following discussion.

26. The inheritance of the temporal specification is presumably due to a general constraint requiring that a predicate be temporally interpreted. If in a sentence such as (25) above the temporal interpretation remains on *do*, the predicate *leave* would not satisfy such a constraint. Notice that in these cases, the expletive is not a maximal projection but a head.

27. We follow Bach (1981) in using the term *eventuality* to refer to both events and states.

28. Notice that in principle the structure in (30) could be given even for MSc, the only difference being that in MSc the visible part of the negation is always the Specifier of the NEG projection. Such a structure in MSc would be the result of scattering. However, this possibility is ruled out because scattering can occur only if the *Spec* position made available by such a move belongs to one of the scattered categories. Economy considerations rule out the possibility that AGR and T are projected separately if (Spec,T) is not occupied by any phrase. Therefore, scattering in MSc can only occur if the (Spec,T) position must be made available for some phrase. As a consequence, for the derivation to converge, negation is necessarily located there.

The same reasoning holds for English: NEG-P cannot intervene between AGR and T, because scattering cannot take place simply to provide room for additional projections. The case of the infinitive, which will be analysed later in the text, is different. As we will see, no scattering occurs, but *to* projects a non-hybrid category T.

29. Covert movement of the modal to a position higher than $AGR_S$ is presumably a universal property. See Brennan (1993) for the possibility that modals take scope only on VPs.

30. The interpretation of forms such as *might, should, would*, and the like is similar to the one discussed in the text for *could*, given that these modals can be used as dependent on a past verb in indirect speech:

(i)     John said that I might borrow his umbrella.

*Might* corresponds to an unmarked form in direct speech: *John said, "You may (can) borrow my umbrella"*, and can be interpreted as *may+ED*. Similarly, *would* and *should*, corresponding to *will* and *shall*, can express future in the past:

(ii)    John said he would leave early.

Again, *would* corresponds to an unmarked form in direct speech: *John said, "I will leave early"*. In these cases the feature corresponding to *-ED* is *[+ past]*, whereas no feature value exists for *i-mod*.

31. On the importance of the present perfect puzzle for characterising the English present perfect, see Dowty (1979).

32. The data in (36) are not the only way in which the English present perfect differs from the simple past. For example, a sentence with the simple past seems to refer to a (contextually) well defined time, whereas the present perfect leaves the time of the event undetermined. That is, it is a sort of indefinite past. Consider (i) (from Partee 1973, 602):

(i)     I didn't turn off the stove.

When uttered by someone driving on his/her way to the office, the sentence refers to a specific time at which he/she did not perform the relevant action. The notion of *current relevance* is another property distinguishing between the two forms. The present perfect seems to describe events that have a more direct present relevance than those reported with the simple past. We will not directly address these issues here.

33. For instance, *John has left this morning* is acceptable if the sentence is uttered in the morning and not in the afternoon.

34. Cf. among others Hornstein (1990 ch. 3) and Bertinetto (1991) for a discussion.

35. See Rohlfs (1954, Ital. ed. 1969, §672 – 674).

36. For a list of phenomena which can be traced back to this kind of explanation, see Bertinetto (1991, p. 100).

37. Notice that the data we just discussed are cases in which the simple past cannot be used and the present perfect *must* be adopted. We have not found instances of the opposite phenomenon — that is, a context in which the simple past is obligatory and the present perfect is excluded. However, we might think of (48d) as a relevant example in this direction. In fact, if we substitute the present perfect *has emigrated* with the simple past, we obtain a grammatical sentence (cf. (48b)). Notice, though, that the same holds for the simple past *tornò* (came back). Once substituted with the present perfect, a grammatical sentence is obtained (cf. (48a)). This fact is expected under the analysis we will provide for the two tenses. Both the simple past and the present perfect express a past value, by means of T1 and T2, respectively, but the present perfect *also* expresses a consequent state; see §3.2. Therefore, the simple past appears in a subset of cases with respect to the present perfect.

38. Approaches to the semantics of perfect tenses based on a notion similar to Parsons's consequent state can also be found in Moens (1987) and Moens & Steadman (1987).

39. Parsons's *hold* is a relation between states (more generally, eventualities) and times such that *hold(s, t)* is true iff *s*'s subject is in state *s* at *t*. For our purposes, the logical form in (52b) could be simplified by dropping *hold* and requiring instead that a suitable temporal relation be established between the consequent state and the speech event, as in (i) (cf. Higginbotham 1994):

(i)      $\exists e\exists x(\text{eat}(e) \wedge \text{Agent}(e, \text{John}) \wedge \text{Theme}(e, x) \wedge \text{apple}(x) \wedge \text{CS}(e){\approx}S)$

In (i) we have indicated with $\approx$ a relation of temporal overlap, or inclusion.

40. In Reichenbachian terms, Parsons's account corresponds to the case in which the adverbial fixes the reference time, which is correctly excluded.

41. In other words, in Dowty's theory the adverbial takes wide scope over the *XN* predicate. Heny (1982) presents an extended now theory in which the adverbial can take both wide and narrow scope with respect to (the equivalent of ) *XN*. Discussing the narrow scope case, he concludes that the unacceptability of sentences such as (54a) in English is due to pragmatic factors.

42. Here, we assume a naive compositional semantics for negation in present perfect sentences, so that (ia) translates as (ib):

(i)     a.   John has not $\phi$-ed
        b.  $\neg(\exists e)(\phi(e) \wedge \text{Agent}(e, \text{John}) \wedge (\text{hold}(\text{CS}(e), S)))$

43. Thanks to J. Higginbotham for discussion on this point.

44. We propose here a demonstration. Suppose that there exist two events *a* and *b* that make (ia) and (ib) true and have the same consequent state:

(i)     a.   John has eaten an apple.
        b.  $\exists e(\text{eat}(e) \wedge \text{Agent}(e, \text{John}) \wedge \text{Theme}(e, \text{an-apple}) \wedge \text{hold}(\text{CS}(e), S))$

(ii)    a.   Mary has drunk a beer.
        b.  $\exists e(\text{drink}(e) \wedge \text{Agent}(e, \text{Mary}) \wedge \text{Theme}(e, \text{a-beer}) \wedge \text{hold}(\text{CS}(e), S))$

Then we have: *hold(CS(a), S)* and *hold(CS(b), S)*. Recall the meaning of Parsons's *hold*: if *x* is a state then *hold(x, t)* iff the subject of *x* is in state *x* at *t*, which we symbolise with *in-state(subject, x, t)*. Then we have for (i): *hold(CS(a), S) iff in-state(John, CS(a), S)*. Since *CS(a) = CS(b)*, then we obtain *in-state(John, CS(a), S) iff in-state(John, CS(b), S)*. Following Parsons, the latter statement can be spelled out as "John is in the state of having eaten an apple" iff "John is in the state of having drunk a beer", which is clearly false. Similarly, for (ii) we obtains "Mary is in the state of having drunk a beer" iff "Mary is in the state of having eaten an apple", which, again, is false. Therefore, it does not seem possible for two distinct events to have the same consequent state; see also fn. 45.

45. In the framework we will develop in chapter 4, the culmination (*telos*) of an event coincides with its right boundary.
Now, consider (i):

(i)

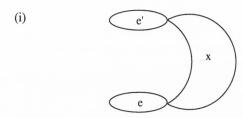

The requirement that the left boundary of the consequent state be the same object as the right boundary of the event, together with (70), correctly excludes situations such as the one depicted in (i), where $x$ is the consequent state of both $e$ and $e'$.

Our formulation makes consequent states strongly dependent on culminations, to the point that the consequent states of two events $e$ and $e'$ are distinct only insofar as the culminations of $e$ and $e'$ are distinct. We will not discuss here the more problematic cases where two events $e$ and $e'$ have the same right temporal boundary and neither one is part of the other. We will consider two simpler cases. Let $e$ be a culminated event and $e'$ a part of it which is final in $e$ — that is, it has the same right boundary as $e$. As an example, consider the culminated event of John's eating a certain apple and its subpart consisting of John's eating the second half of the same apple. Our approach predicts that the events in the following two sentences have the same consequent states:

(ii)     a.  John has eaten the apple.

         b.  John has eaten the second part of the apple.

This seems to be correct.

Consider now a situation in which *John and Mary* eat the same apple, and suppose that Mary's eating finishes before John's eating. Then, the right boundary of the sum of the two eating events does not coincide with John's eating right boundary. Correctly, we can exclude the possibility that (iiia) and (iiib) have the same consequent states:

(ii)     a.  John and Mary have eaten the apple.

         b.  John has eaten the second half of the apple.

46. We hypothesise that, if scattered, the feature *asp* gives rise to the category ASP1, proposed by Cinque (1994, 1995a). See §3.4.

47. Both Larson (1988, 1990) and Stroyk (1990) do not limit their proposal to temporal adverbials but extend it to other kinds of adverbials, such as manner adverbs, locatives, and so on.

48. According to Longobardi (1994), in cases such as (i) the article acts as a quantifier binding the variable supplied by the noun:

(i)      I saw the dog.

He also considers, however, the possibility of expletive articles, as in (ii), which give rise to a generic (kind referring) interpretation:

(ii)     I dinosauri mangiavano erba.
         Dinosaurs ate grass.

49. The presence of feminine agreement on *sola* (only+fem) shows that the relevant item is an adjective and not the adverb *solo* (only), which is homophonous with the masculine singular form of the adjective (cf. Longobardi 1994)).

50. It is not the case that whenever there is no article the $D^0$ position is occupied by the raised noun. Longobardi (1994) discusses examples with mass nouns, as in (i):

(i)     a. Ho bevuto vino.
           I drunk wine.
        b. Ho mangiato manzo.
           I ate beef.

He proposes that in these sentences the nominal head does not raise to $D^0$ and that the latter position is occupied by an empty determiner which is interpreted as an existential quantifier. Its range may be either the set of subparts of the masses *vino* and *manzo* or the set of members of the extension of a (plural) count noun, as in (ii), where an indefinite number of boys is met:

(ii)    Ho incontrato ragazzi.
        I met boys.

This possibility is naturally accounted for by the generalisation that every argument must be a DP. In (78) to (81), however, such interpretations are not available when the article is absent, showing that the nominal head has raised to $D^0$. The existential interpretation (due to the empty determiner) can be obtained by using a plural form, as in (iii), which parallels (ii):

(iii)   Ho passato natali interi ad annoiarmi.
        Lit.: I have spent Christmases whole getting bored.
        I spent whole Christmases getting bored.

    51. That the modifier plays a role in endowing the nominal with object referring properties is also showed by the fact that adjectives must be of the correct type. In our case, the correct type is a temporal adjective such as *scorso* (last) or *prossimo* (next). Nontemporal adjectives do not have the relevant property:

(i)     *Ho passato giovedì bello/lungo/interessante al mare.
        I spent the nice/long/interesting Thursday at the seaside.

The importance of an indexical anchorage to the speech time/event is also shown by the contrasts in (ii), where *tre settimane fa* (three weeks ago) indexical refers to the third but last week before the current one, whereas *la settimana prima* (the week before) only has an anaphoric interpretation:

(ii)    a. Giovedì di tre settimane fa / *Giovedì della settimana prima è stato un
           giorno orribile.
           Thursday of three weeks ago / * Thursday of the week before was a horrible
           day.
        b. Ho passato giovedì di tre settimane fa / *giovedì della settimana prima al
           mare.
           I spent the Thursday of three weeks ago / * Thursday of the week before at
           the seaside.
        c. Mario è arrivato giovedì di tre settimane fa / *giovedì della settimana
           prima.
           Mario has arrived the Thursday of three weeks ago / * Thursday of the week
           before.

52. The data discussed in the text cannot always be reproduced with other calendric units, e.g. month names:

(i)     a.  Mario è arrivato *(in) Marzo.
            Mario has arrived *(in) March.
        b.  Mario è arrivato *(lo) scorso Marzo.
            Mario has arrived *(the) last March.
        c.  ??Mario è arrivato Marzo scorso.
            Mario has arrived March last.
        d.  (Il) Marzo scorso è stato un mese terribile.
            Lit.: (The) March last has been a terrible month.
            Last March was a terrible month.
        e.  *(Lo) scorso Marzo è stato un mese terribile.
            Lit.: (The) last March has been a terrible month.
            Last March was a terrible month.
        f.  Ho passato (il) Febbraio scorso al mare.
            Lit.: I have spent (the) February last at the seaside.
            I spent last February at the seaside.
        g.  Ho passato *(lo) scorso Febbraio al mare.
            Lit.: I have spent (the) last February at the seaside.
            I spent last February at the seaside.

In particular, it must be observed that DPs with month names behave in the expected way when playing the role of subjects or objects — that is, (i)d-(i)g. However, they differ from day names because of the marginality of DPs headed by the raised noun which are not (canonical) arguments, (ic). Common nouns, however, give worse results if the nominal head is raised:

(ii)    *Ho visto tavolo vecchio.
        I have seen table old.

It seems that the ability of month names to refer to (temporal) objects is reduced with respect to that of day nouns. As a consequence, they can only marginally be endowed with the [+ ref] feature hypothesised by Longobardi (1994). The ability of month names to refer to (temporal) objects is nevertheless stronger than that of common nouns, explaining the contrast between (i) and (ii).

53. Cinque (1990, ch. 2) notices that preposed temporal adverbials have a different meaning than postverbal, VP-internal, ones:

(i)     Nel 1821 è morto Napoleone. (from Cinque 1990, p. 90–91))
        In 1821 Napoleon died.

(ii)    Napoleone è morto nel 1821. (ibid)
        Napoleon died in 1821.

In (ii), *nel 1821* (in 1821) provides the background. We suggest that in the case of (i) the adverbial is moved to a preverbal position to check an informational feature, for instance GIVEN, which is responsible for the different interpretation in question.

According to this view, the adverbial is always generated in the same position. See following discussion for an analysis of $R$-modifiers.

54. Note that it is not necessary to imply that $R$-modifiers are always complements of V, as opposed to specifiers in the VP shell.

55. The extraction of $R$-modifiers is more constrained than that of many other adverbials:

(i)     a.    *[A che ora]$_i$ credevi che Gianni fosse già partito t$_i$ ?
            At which hour did you believe that Gianni had already left?
         b.   Perché$_i$ credevi che Gianni fosse partito t$_i$ ?
            Why did you believe that Gianni had left?

The ungrammaticality of (ia) is presumably due to the fact that the reference time has a *[+ familiarity]* feature (cf. Delfitto & Bertinetto 1995b). That is, it always encodes information shared by the participants in the conversation. Phrases bearing such a feature can never be questioned, for obvious pragmatic reasons. Consider, in fact, the question in (ii) and the possible answers in (iii):

(ii)      Chi hai visto?
         Who did you see?

(iii)    a.   *L'ho visto.
          I cl-him saw.
       b.   Ho visto lui.
          I saw him.

It is widely assumed that clitic pronouns are *familiar* with respect to tonic pronouns (in the relevant sense). Therefore, the data on extraction of $R$-arguments seen in the text do not constitute evidence against the argumental status of $R$-adverbials. The hypothesis that $R$-arguments always bear the feature *[+ familiarity]* might also explain why they are always dislocated, as shown in (96). Thanks to Denis Delfitto for discussion on this point.

56. The examples in (101) are taken from Bianchi et al. (1995, fn. 7) who cite Paulino de Souza, *Grammaire portugaise raisonnée et simplifiée*, Paris, 1872.

57. Italian makes this distinction clear by using a different form for the indefinite temporal argument — namely, a PP introduced by the preposition *di* (of):

(i)     Ha lavorato di domenica.
       Lit.: He has worked prep-of Sunday.
       He has worked on a Sunday.

58. Note that, as a consequence of this definition, if $e$ is a culminated event then $e$ and $e'$ have the same right boundary. Furthermore, as a limiting case, the right boundary of $e$ is a final portion of $e$ — that is, $\rho(rb(e), e)$ holds.

59. Note that we do not accept Klein's view that whatever contains the speech time is definite.

60. The theory we are going to develop in the next section does not explicitly address the problem raised by (115).

61. Compare the TOP node hypothesised in Uriagereka (1994) and in Raposo & Uriagereka (1995), as well as the familiarity feature of Delfitto & Bertinetto (1995b).

62. In the terminology of Chomsky (1995), T-DEF is an obligatory feature of the English present tense AGR/T1. However, T-DEF is an optional feature for D/P.

63. We have implicitly extended to *R*-arguments the proposal made in §3.2.5. for *E*-temporal arguments: there is always an *R*-argument, possibly realised as an empty category.

64. It cannot happen that the temporal argument moves to D/P when the participial clause has been formed, given that *T-DEF* is weak. Consider also the possibility that one of the temporal arguments covertly raises to D/P. This could be an available option if our claim about the optionality of the raising of the auxiliary *have* in English is correct, so that after Spell-Out the auxiliary (with D/P incorporated) is still in V (or in some other position lower than AGR/T1). At this point, one of the two temporal arguments could raise and check the *T-DEF* of the auxiliary, before covert V-to-I movement of the auxiliary takes place. Example (i) illustrates the raising of the *E*-temporal argument:

(i)

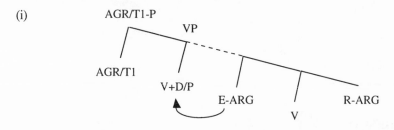

But then, the (T-DEF feature of the) raised temporal argument would be closer to AGR/T1 than the *R*-argument. Movement of the latter is then prevented, again yielding a violation of the MH.

65. Alternatively, one could simply assume that topics are adjoined to TP, as subjects are according to Chomsky (1995), and that checking obtains in this configuration.

66. Cf. Cinque (1994) for a discussion of the position of *già* and other adverbs in the participial clause.

67. Cases such as (i) still need to be discussed:

(i)    (This morning) John has read the book (this morning).

As pointed out in §3.1.5., the status of (i) is unclear. Some speakers find it fine, whereas others reject it. We do not have a satisfactory explanation for these facts. Let us point out, however, that the acceptability of (i) would follow if *this morning* were an *R*-argument and if the *E*-argument were realised as an indefinite empty category. Then, the *R*-argument would provide the range for an existential quantifier binding the event time variable.

68. Another observation in favour of this analysis comes from sentences such as (i):

(i)     ?Martedì Mario aveva telefonato a Maria qualche venerdì.
        Tuesday Mario had called Mary on some Friday.

Their relative acceptability, as compared to (125), follows from the fact that the *E*-temporal argument does not have to raise to comply with the MH, because it is non-definite.

69. According to the theory developed in the text, the solution to the present perfect puzzle crucially requires a head such as D/P, endowed with the T-DEF feature. This might raise a problem with Italian unaccusative. Kayne (1993) argues that the participial clauses of Italian ergative verbs are VPs, thus lacking the D/P projection:

(i)     [ BE [$_{VP}$ V . . . ]]

For our purposes, we assume that the only difference between unaccusative verbs, on the one hand, and unergative and transitive ones, on the other, in Italian is whether or not D/P incorporation into BE is overt. In transitives and unergatives D/P overtly incorporates into BE, whereas the incorporation is covert with unaccusative verbs.

70. Dahl (1985) shows that the Icelandic-like present perfect — that is, the one with an epistemic reading, can be found in other MSc languages as well.

71. One might wonder whether there are arguments suggesting that an epistemic modal requires both the checking of a feature in MOD and then covert raising to OP. Let us point out as evidence in favour of this view that epistemic (and deontic) modality can be expressed in several ways. Interestingly, in languages such as Italian, the epistemic value can be expressed by a modal, as in the following sentence:

(i)     Gianni deve essere partito.
        Gianni must have left.

Where modal verbs are certainly lower than AGR in $\Sigma$. Epistemicity can also be expressed by means of epistemic adverbs:

(ii)    Probabilmente Mario è partito.
        Probably Mario has left.

It has been argued (see Belletti 1990) that (in Italian) the basic position for these adverbs is above AGR. One might conclude, therefore, that the head position of the projection — where, in certain cases, we see the adverb — is the landing site of the covert movement of the modal. That is, it is the head of the projection OP.

72. We thank for judgements L. Grácia, A. Suñer, and L. Ripoll. J. Harris (personal communication) informs us that in American Spanish the present perfect can never cooccur with a definite temporal specification, contrasting with European Spanish. We have not been able to study these varieties in more detail, and further investigation is required. Let us only point out that our theory predicts that in English-like languages a definite temporal specification could *never* cooccur with a present perfect form. In Italian-like languages their cooccurrence, which is in general possible, could still be impossible, due to the intervention of other factors.

73. We thank R. A. Marques Pereira and A. M. Madeira for judgements.

74. The difference between the two is limited to the aspectual features of the syncretic ASP/T2 in the *ter comido* variant.

75. The fact that (147) does not yield the same results for English (or Italian) present perfect sentences vs. simple past ones shows that, at least with respect to the relevant notion of identity at LF, in these languages the two past forms are different. Given our framework, the difference can be attributed to the fact that in English and Italian the present perfect contains a T2 category, whereas the simple past contains only a T1. Furthermore, note that the reasoning in the text can be extended to the past perfect. As we saw in chapter 2, §2.3., contemporary Portuguese has an analytic past perfect *tinha comido* (he/she had eaten), with auxiliary *ter*, that has largely substituted the obsolete synthetic form *comeram*. We hypothesise that the disappearance of the synthetic form is attributed to the similarity of the two forms at LF so that (147) forced one of the two to be eliminated.

76. This proposal has been adopted by Brugger & D'Angelo (1994).

77. (155b) and (155c) need a suitable context to be fully acceptable:

(i)    Quando venne chiamato dal direttore, Mario era appena arrivato.
       When he was called by the director, Mario had *appena* arrived.

We believe, however, that our arguments go through independently of such a consideration.

78. The semantics we are giving for *appena* are very close to that often assumed for focus constructions, according to the analysis originally developed in Rooths (1985), and further elaborated in Rooths (1992) and Kratzer (1991b).

79. This condition, aiming at assuring that $a_\alpha$ is not the unique element in the set of alternatives, is meant to prevent trivial applications of (157).

80. We do not consider here the cases in which *appena* operates on other entities, although we think that the account developed in the text can be straightforwardly extended to them:

(i)    Mario mangiò appena una mela.
       Lit.: Mario ate *appena* an apple.
       Mario just ate an apple.

In (i), the domain $A_\alpha$ is formed by (contextually restricted) quantities of edibles, and the relevant ordering is one according to which an apple constitutes a minimal quantity.

81. That is, given $C, C_1$, and $C_2$, where $C$ is the set of consequent states of an event $e$, and $C_1, C_2 \subseteq C$, $C_1 \propto C_2$ iff $s_1 \propto s_2$, for every two consequent states $s_1$ and $s_2$ in $C_1$ and $C_2$, respectively. In the framework developed in Pianesi & Varzi (1996a), $s_1 \propto s_2$ iff $P(d(s_1), d(s_2))$ — that is, iff the *divisor* of $s_1$ is included in the divisor of $s_2$. See chapter 4, §1.4 for the notion of a *divisor* in an *eventive structure*. Furthermore, by letting the restriction of *appena* depend on the divisors of the consequent states, we can account for the context sensitivity of $\propto$ by relying on the choice of the dividing condition $\delta$ (cf. Pianesi & Varzi 1996b).

82. Even WH-like movement cannot override the constraint that $E$-temporal arguments must be within the scope of *già* (already) and *appena* (just) in the syntax:

(i)    a.  IERI, Mario è arrivato.
           YESTERDAY, Mario has arrived.
       b.  *IERI, Mario è già/appena arrivato.
           YESTERDAY, Mario has already/just arrived.
       c.  Quando è arrivato Mario?
           When has Mario arrived ?
       d.  *Quando è già/appena arrivato Mario?
           When has Mario already/just arrived?

See Cinque (1990) for evidence that left peripheral focus is a WH-like movement. These facts, together with those discussed in the text, can be explained by hypothesising that overt movement to a leftmost position (for the purpose of checking the Focus, *WH-*, or *Topic/Familiarity* features) does not allow the temporal argument to land in the position where it can check the weak feature of *già* (already) or *appena* (just), which, therefore, remains unchecked.

Note that the discussion in the text only applies to those instances of *appena* (just) which have a temporal meaning. Only in these cases we expect it to be able to attract the *E*-temporal argument. We therefore predict that, when *appena* has the eventive reading, the *E*-temporal argument can be moved to the left peripheral position. This prediction is borne out. A sentence such as (152d) can have a grammatical reading paraphrasable as: "concerning yesterday, Mario has only arrived".

83. A more precise analysis of (160a) would probably involve the notion of consequent state. Note, in fact, that the occurrences of *appena* when introducing a complex adverbial usually require a predicate that singles out a *telos*:

(i)    a.  ??Appena Mario mangiò una mela, Giuseppe bevve un bicchiere di birra.
           Immediately after Mario ate an apple, Giuseppe drank a glass of beer.
       b.  Appena Mario raggiunse la vetta, Giuseppe bevve un bicchiere di birra.
           Immediately after Mario reached the top of the mountain, Giuseppe drank a glass of beer.
       c.  *Appena Mario spinse il carretto, tutti lo rimproverarono.
           Immediately after Mario pushed the cart, everyone blamed him.

Example (ib), with the achievement predicate *raggiungere* (reach), is fine. However, (ia) and (ic), with an accomplishment and an activity predicate, respectively, are odd. They do not mean that immediately after the completion of the event in the restriction, the event in the main clause occurred. Rather, they have a reading more similar to the "first time reading" to be discussed shortly. We propose that this pattern is due to the fact that only achievement predicates refer to a *telos*. Accomplishments and activities can have a *telos*, but this is not linguistically available unless some functional category provides it. We argue that this is what the ASP/T2 category of past participial forms discussed previously does. It can form consequent states by accessing the structure of the event it combines with. As such, the data in (i) can be explained by hypothesising that the restriction of *appena* is formed by consequent states. They can only be construed from *teloses* which are linguistically available, as in (ib), where the predicate is an achievement, as opposed to (ia) and (ic). If this reasoning is correct, we expect (ia) and (ic) to improve if a verbal form, such as a perfect, is used that already makes available a consequent state. This prediction is borne out:

(ii)    a.  Appena Mario ebbe mangiato una mela, Giuseppe bevve un bicchiere di birra.
            Immediately after Mario ate an apple, Giuseppe drank a glass of beer.
        b.  Appena Mario ebbe spinto il carretto, tutti lo rimproverarono.
            Immediately after Mario pushed the cart, everyone blamed him.

Concluding, *appena* (just) in the temporal interpretation takes consequent states into its restriction.

84. Indeed, sentences such as (162b) do not exclude the existence of further arrivals of Mario on Thursday, which follow the relevant one. For instance, Mario may have been fired but then continued to work for a short period in order to finish his work.

85. Thanks to Salvatore Claudio Sgroi for these judgements on Catanese, which have also been confirmed by other speakers.

86. Interestingly, Bertinetto (1991, p. 99) lists this property, which he calls "inclusiveness", as a characteristic of the present perfect in Standard Italian. This means, therefore, that there is a real functional correspondence between the simple past of southern varieties and the present perfect of Standard Italian. Presumably an important difference is constituted by the fact that in these varieties there is no consequent state in the normal past form, given that consequent states are only expressed by means of past participles. See also chapter 2 for an analysis of modern Portuguese, which might provide further arguments in this direction.

87. We thank P. Benincà for having provided us with judgements from native speakers of Vicentino.

88. This consideration does not necessarily constitute an argument against the universality of the structure. We might reflect, however, on the fact that if languages were identical with respect to the functional categories they project, we would have to explain the lack of a literal translation in Italian as the impossibility of associating a lexical item with a functional projection already available to the speaker. On the contrary, according to the hypothesis we are developing in this book, we might explain the differences among Standard Italian, Vicentino, and Catanese as due to the impossibility of *acquiring* the category in question, because of the lack of positive evidence in favour of its existence. The difference between the two perspectives is subtle, but, we believe, important.

# 4

# The Present and the Imperfect
# in Germanic and Romance

In this chapter we consider in more detail the syntax/semantics interface of the continuous tenses — in particular, of the present tense and the imperfect indicative.

The observation from which we begin is the following. In the previous chapters we have shown that English and Mainland Scandinavian languages differ from Romance and from the other Germanic languages with respect to the morphosyntax of the present tense. We have argued that a wide range of phenomena follows from this difference, such as the facts concerning the interpretive properties of the present perfect. With respect to these properties, English and MSc pattern together, contrasting with Romance and the other Germanic languages. In chapter 2 and chapter 3 we considered the syntax/semantics interface with respect to the *temporal* properties of the present tense.

However, it must also be pointed out that English and MSc crucially differ from each other with respect to the interpretation of the present tense. As we will better illustrate in §4.1., in English the continuous reading of the present tense is impossible with all eventive predicates, whereas this is allowed in MSc. With respect to the continuous interpretation, MSc languages pattern with Italian and with all the other Romance and Germanic languages.

In this chapter we propose a theoretical account of this observation. We will argue that the English verb has special morphosyntactic properties, setting it apart from Romance and the other Germanic languages. As far as these properties are concerned, MSc patterns with Italian (and Italian-like languages). We will show that the morphosyntactic structure of the English verb largely determines its aspectual characteristics, and, consequently, the peculiar interpretive properties of the present tense. In this chapter, therefore, we investigate the syntax/semantics interface with respect to *aspectual* properties.

In particular, we will argue that a deeper understanding of perfectivity is necessary. We will propose that the way perfective events are related to *anchoring* events is universally constrained by means of what we will call the *punctuality constraint*.[1] We will show that it is impossible to relate a perfective event to the speech event, and that this impossibility accounts for the crosslinguistic differences observed in the interpretation of the present tense.

Furthermore, we will argue that the punctuality constraint, ruling the anchoring of the matrix event to the speech event, can be generalised to the anchoring of a subordinate event with a matrix event. Namely, we will propose that the punctuality constraint holds of all anchoring events.

We will show that the hypotheses which account for the crosslinguistic differences in the interpretation of the present tense can be extended to the interpretation of the (subordinate) imperfect indicative in Italian (and in the languages which have the imperfect in their tense inventory). More precisely, we will argue that the anchoring of the imperfect, in the so-called present-in-the-past interpretation, obeys the same constraints as the present tense in matrix clauses. We will also show that our theory correctly predicts the properties of the present-in-the-past reading in the Germanic languages, which do not have an imperfect tense in their systems that is morphologically distinct from the simple past. [2]

## 4.1. The present tense

The central observation concerning the present tense is that in English the (non-progressive) present tense cannot have the continuous — we will say *imperfective* — interpretation, contrasting with the other languages in the Romance-Germanic domain. Our goal is to find an explanation for the exceptional behaviour of English, on the one hand, and to clarify the relation between the present tense and the perfective/imperfective opposition, on the other. Our proposal will also shed light on some very general properties of the temporal interpretation of utterances. The interaction between morphosyntactic and aspectual properties emerges very clearly from our analysis of the differences among Italian, English, and German, with respect to the present tense.

### 4.1.1. Crosslinguistic evidence

We adopt the so-called Aristotle-Dowty-Vendler (Dowty 1979; Vendler 1967) classification according to which *predicates* are divided into statives (*to love, to be tall*), accomplishments (*to eat an apple*), achievements (*to reach the top, to find the book*), and activities (*to run, to sleep*). Consider first the behaviour of the present tense with stative predicates:

(1)     a.  John loves Mary.
        b.  Hans liebt Marie.
        c.  Giovanni ama Maria.

These sentences mean that a certain state holds of the subject at the speech time. As can be seen, there are no interpretive differences among Italian, German, and English.

Importantly, English predicates belonging to the class of accomplishments or activities do not allow a present tense imperfective reading, contrasting with German (and all the other Germanic languages) and Italian (and all the Romance languages):[3]

(2)    a.  John eats an apple.
        b.  John runs.

(3)    a.  Hans ißt einen Apfel.
        b.  Hans läuft.

(4)    a.  Gianni mangia una mela.
        b.  Gianni corre.

Example (2a) cannot mean that "John is presently the agent of an ongoing event of eating an apple", and, analogously, (2b) does not mean that "John is presently the agent of an event of running". However, these readings are available in Italian, German, and, notably, in Mainland Scandinavian languages:

(5)    a.  Sten äter ett äpple. (Swedish)
           Sten eats an apple.
        b.  Han skriver et brev. (Norwegian)
           He writes a letter.
        c.  Ole kommer. (Danish)
           Ole comes.

All of the sentences in (5) can have the continuous interpretation. MSc patterns with English with respect to other properties of the present tense — for instance, the presence of the syncretic AGR/T category (see chapter 3) — but it contrasts with English as far as the continuous reading of the present tense is concerned.

In English, in order to obtain the continuous reading, the progressive must be used. Consider the following examples:

(6)    a.  John is eating an apple.
        b.  John is running.

We will consider the progressive in more detail in §4.1.5.4. in the following discussion.

Interestingly, English is not different from the other languages as far as the other possible interpretations of the sentences in (1) to (4) are concerned. For instance, English, German, and Italian admit the so called *reportive* reading of the present tense, where an event is described as perfective but its time is not (directly) related to the speech event. For example, sentences (2a) and (2b) in English, like their counterparts in (3) to (4), are grammatical as commentary on a picture or a movie, or when uttered by a radio commentator. These similarities extend to sentences introduced by the so-called *contensive individuals*, discussed by Katz (1995):

(7)    a.  In "Via col vento" Rossella scrive una lettera.
        b.  In "Gone with the wind" Scarlet writes a letter.

When a sentence is introduced by a constituent of the form "in DP", where DP refers to a movie, a book, or the like, the present tense is grammatical with an accomplishment or activity predicate. In this work we will not further consider reportive readings and sentences introduced by contensive individuals. Note, however, that according to the theory to be developed in the following sections, the availability of these readings in English shows that the event is not (directly) anchored to $S$.

Furthermore, in both English and the other languages present tense sentences can express *habituality*. For instance, *John eats apples* can mean that John is an apple-eater, and *John runs* that John is a runner. See §4.1.5.3. in the following discussions for an analysis of habitual contexts.

Let us now consider the so-called achievement verbs:

(8)     a.  John finds a book.
        b.  Hans findet ein Buch.
        c.  Gianni trova un libro.

In all languages, the imperfective reading is not available with present tense achievement predicates. See §4.1.5.5. for an analysis of achievement predicates.

Another important characteristic of the present tense in *all* Germanic and Romance languages concerns the fact that it does not allow perfective readings *tout court*. For instance, it is not possible for sentences like (2a), (3a), and (4a) to mean that at the speech time a complete action of eating an apple has been performed.

To summarise, there are three (possibly related) problems showing up with present tense sentences. The first concerns a difference between English, on the one hand, and all the other languages of the Germanic and Romance domain, on the other. Present tense sentences with an accomplishment or an activity predicate can always have a continuous (imperfective) reading in Italian, German, and Mainland Scandinavian, but not in English.

The second problem is the unavailability of an imperfective reading with achievement predicates in all Germanic and Romance languages. Finally, the third problem concerns the impossibility of a perfective interpretation for present tense sentences *tout court*.

The three questions seem to be related. In fact, as we will show in the following sections, they are linked to the incompatibility of the present tense with perfectivity.

### 4.1.2. The structure of events

Before proposing an account of the phenomena illustrated in the previous section, we will discuss some relevant aspects of the structure of events.

We will show that in order to account for the interactions between aspectual properties and anchoring conditions, an ontological perspective must be adopted.[4] We will first illustrate the mereological properties of eventive domains — that is, the properties describable by means of the *part-of* relation. Then, we will argue that mereology does not suffice to characterise some crucial notions, such as the distinction between perfective and non-perfective events. To this purpose we will argue that the *topological* properties of events must also be considered.

The idea that mereology (that is, the theory of the *part-of* relation) plays an important role in the semantics and ontology of natural languages goes back at least to Davidson (1967). More recently, it has been revived by Link (1983, 1987), Bach (1986), Krifka (1989), and Landman (1989, 1990) among others. To illustrate the basic intuitions of this approach, consider (9):

(9)    John ate an apple. While eating the first bit of it, he remembered that he had to phone Mary.

The first sentence in (9) is true iff there is a (past) event which is an eating, the agent of which is John. Suppose $x$ is an event satisfying such requirements. Now consider the second sentence. The event of the *while*-clause is, intuitively, a part of $x$. More generally, we can imagine that every event of eating an apple has a subpart consisting of the event of eating the first bit of the apple, another subpart consisting of the event of eating the second bit of the same apple, and so on. We symbolise the *part-of* relation between two events $x$ and $y$ by means of the binary relation $P(x, y)$ which is true iff $x$ is a part of $y$.[5]

*Overlapping* is an important relation between events which can be derived from *part-of*. Consider three events — $x$, $y$, and $z$ — such that $x$ consists of Mary's eating a full course meal, $y$ consists of Mary's eating the first and the main course, and $z$ consists of Mary's eating the main course and the fruit. Then $y$ and $z$ overlap, since they share a common part — namely, the event consisting of Mary's eating the main course. Formally, overlapping can be defined in the following way:

(10)   $O(x, y) \equiv_{df} \exists z (P(z, x) \wedge P(z, y))$

By means of *part-of* and overlap we can say, for instance, that the event consisting of the battle of the Marne is a part of the event consisting of World War I, whereas the event consisting of the Russian Revolution overlaps World War I.[6] Mereology by itself does not suffice to account for the distinction between the *perfective* (bounded) and the *imperfective* (unbounded) aspect. Consider, for instance, the sentences in (11):

(11)   a.  Mario mangiò una mela.
           Mario ate an apple.
       b.  Mario mangiava una mela.
           Mario ate(IMPF) an apple.

Intuitively speaking, the Italian sentence in (11a) means that the event of eating is finished (bounded).[7] In Italian, a simple past verbal form always conveys this meaning. In (11b), on the other hand, the event in question is not necessarily finished — that is, it is unbounded. In Italian this is possible when the verbal form is an imperfect indicative. The two past tenses contrast with respect to perfectivity. On the imperfect see §4.2.

Pure mereological approaches, based on the *part-of* relation, cannot capture the contrast exemplified in (11). Both the event corresponding to the perfective predicate and the event corresponding to the imperfective one can have parts.

Intuitively, a perfective event can be a part of an imperfective one and vice versa, and both can be part of another perfective or imperfective event. We propose that in order to characterise the distinction between the two events in (11) we need a primitive notion, which deserves its own formal theory. More precisely, we propose that the formal counterpart of the notion of perfectivity is that of a *topologically closed* event.[8]

The classical notion of topological closure is based on the idea that, given a set $X$ of objects and a function $cl$ from $X$ into $X$, $cl$ is an operator of topological closure iff the following axioms hold:[9]

(12)   a.  $P(x, cl(x))$
       b.  $cl(cl(x)) = cl(x)$
       c.  $cl(x) + cl(y) = cl(x + y)$

Let us apply these ideas to the event domain. Suppose that $cl$ is a perfectivising function. Then (12a) holds of $cl$. In fact, let $x$ be the imperfective event contained in a sentences such as *John is eating an apple*, and let $cl(x)$ be the perfective event appearing in the sentence *John has eaten an apple*. Then, the event $x$ is part of the event $cl(x)$. Consider now (12b). If $x$ is a perfective event — that is if $cl(x) = x$ — then there is no smaller perfective event containing $x$ but itself. Therefore (12b) holds of perfective events. Finally, it is intuitively clear that if $x$ and $y$ are imperfective events and $z$ is their sum, then the perfective event corresponding to $z$ is the sum of the perfective events corresponding to $x$ and $y$. In other words, (12c) also holds of $cl$. In conclusion, the axioms (12a) to (12c) hold of the function $cl$ so that $cl$ can be regarded as an operator of topological closure. Therefore, the values of this operator — namely, perfective events — can be regarded as topologically closed entities.

We symbolise closure by means of the predicate $Cl$ . Example (13) is the logical form for (11a):[10]

(13)   $\exists e \exists x(\text{eat}(e) \wedge Cl(e) \wedge \text{apple}(x) \wedge \text{Theme}(e, x))$

Concluding, in this section we proposed that *topological closure* is the formal notion corresponding to the intuitive concept of perfectivity. Perfective predicates denote topologically closed events, and imperfective predicates denote topologically non-closed events.[11]

In the literature, it has been argued that the interpretive characteristics of perfectivity can be analysed by resorting to a quantificational apparatus. For instance, Delfitto & Bertinetto (1995b) and Lenci & Bertinetto (1995) propose that in perfective sentences the event time is existentially quantified, and they argue that imperfectivity involves a strong quantifier binding a temporal variable. We basically agree with these proposals. However, we also think that the quantificational behaviour of the event time variable cannot fully account for the perfectivity/imperfectivity distinction. Hence, we propose that such a theory be supplemented by the ontological distinction concerning events which we have been arguing for in this section. In the end, we hypothesise that (the morphological mark of) perfectivity is interpreted as requiring that the event denoted by the verb be closed, and that the temporal variable be existentially bound.[12]

### 4.1.3. Punctuality and the properties of the speech event

As we pointed out in the introduction, the temporal interpretation of an utterance involves the anchoring of the event denoted by the verb to the speech time — that is, to the time of the event which consists of the utterance itself. In this section, we discuss the properties of the speech event $s$ and argue that $s$, as an anchoring event for the utterance, is conceptualised as punctual.[13]

Discussing Taylor's (1977) theory of the English progressive, Dowty (1979, p. 167) observes that if the *utterance time*, that is, our speech time, is a moment, then the postulate in (14) (Taylor 1977) predicts that it is impossible to have a present tense with eventive predicates:

(14)    If $\alpha$ is an activity verb or an accomplishment/achievement verb then $\alpha(x)$ is only true at an interval larger than a moment.

According to this analysis, the impossibility of a sentence such as *John runs* is due to the intrinsic properties of eventive predicates and to the fact that the speech time is a *point*.

We think that the idea that the speech time is punctual is essentially correct. In the next sections we will show that it can explain why in no language, among those considered here, the present tense can have a perfective reading. However, in order to account for the crosslinguistic data, we will propose some revisions of this notion. Note that the theory discussed by Dowty cannot easily be extended to languages other than English, such as Italian. As we know, eventive predicates are acceptable in Italian with the continuous reading.

From a more theoretical perspective, it does not seem correct to hypothesise that the speech time is a moment — that is, a time point. In an interval structure such as the one Dowty (1979) adopts, time points are unextended intervals. Hence, time points in general, and the speech time in particular, are durationless. However, intuitively, utterances take time. We would like to propose, therefore, a notion of punctuality which does not entail absence of duration.

Furthermore, as we will argue in §4.2., an adequate theory of temporal anchoring should provide a uniform analysis of the anchoring events. That is, we need a theory capable of explaining the relevant facts both in matrix and in embedded clauses. Such a theory cannot consist in a straightforward extension to embedded contexts of the requirement that speech events are punctual. Consider the following example:

(15)    John said that Mary left.

In (15) the temporal anchor for the event of the embedded clause is the matrix event. Intuitively, however, the saying in (15) is not punctual. Hence, we will propose a theory which permits an analysis of an event as punctual when functioning as a temporal anchor, and as not punctual otherwise.

### 4.1.4. A revised notion of punctuality

When an event $e_1$ must be temporally anchored to another event $e_2$, it has to be determined whether $e_1$ precedes, follows, or is simultaneous with $e_2$. We will now sketch a theory of temporal relations in event domains.[14]

Consider a mereotopological domain of events $\mathcal{E}$ and an event $x$ which separates $\mathcal{E}$ into two disconnected parts $\mathcal{E}'$ and $\mathcal{E}''$; such an event is called a *divisor* for $\mathcal{E}$. Hence, as far as $x$ (and its parts) is concerned, it is possible to arbitrarily choose one of $\mathcal{E}'$ and $\mathcal{E}''$ and call it the *past* of $x$ (and of its parts) and call the other the *future* of $x$. That is, pairs such as $\langle y, x \rangle$, $\langle x, z \rangle$, and $\langle y, z \rangle$ (where $y$ and $z$ are, respectively, parts of $\mathcal{E}'$ and $\mathcal{E}''$) can be formed. Their intended meaning is that $y$ *precedes* $x$, $x$ *precedes* $z$, and $y$ *precedes* $z$, respectively. To provide $\mathcal{E}$ with a uniform and consistent temporal ordering — that is, to extend the relation of temporal precedence to arbitrary pairs of events— a collection $\delta$ of divisors covering $\mathcal{E}$ must be considered instead of a single divisor. This way, each event $x$ in $\mathcal{E}$ is associated with a divisor which determines the past and the future of $x$. Such a divisor is called *the divisor of $x$* and is symbolised by means of the function $d(x)$.

The pair $\langle \mathcal{E}, \delta \rangle$ consisting of a mereotopological eventive domain $\mathcal{E}$ and of a collection of divisors $\delta$ covering $\mathcal{E}$ is called *an oriented eventive structure*. The procedure just described amounts to defining in an oriented eventive structure a relation of temporal precedence $\leq_\delta$.[15] Other temporal relations such as *simultaneity*, can be derived. Two events $e_1$ and $e_2$ are simultaneous iff they have the same divisor — that is, iff $d(e_1) = d(e_2)$. In this case we will write $e_1 \approx_\delta e_2$. Another relation is that of *temporal part*, defined as follows:[16]

(16)   $e_1$ is a temporal part of $e_2$, written $\mathsf{TP}_\delta(e, e')$, iff $\mathsf{P}(d(e_1), d(e_2)))$

The subscripts emphasise the dependence of the temporal relations on the choice of the collection of divisors $\delta$. This is an important feature of oriented eventive structures: the temporal distinctions that can be expressed are all and only those allowed by the choice of $\delta$. Consider the two figures in (17). Examples (17a) and (17b) represent two oriented structures arising from the same event domain $\mathcal{E}$ by choosing two different $\delta$s. The event domain and the divisors are depicted as a portion of the plane and as vertical bars, respectively. In the oriented structure in (17a), according to the chosen divisor collection $\delta = \{d_1, d_2, d_3, d_4\}$, $e_3$ precedes $e_1$, $e_2$, and $e_4$; both $e_1$ and $e_2$ precede $e_4$. However, $e_1$ and $e_2$ are part of the same minimal divisor, that is $d(e_1) = d(e_2)$, so that as far as $\delta$ is concerned, $e_1$ and $e_2$ are simultaneous. In other words, $\delta$ does not distinguish the temporal properties of $e_1$ from those of $e_2$. The situation is different in (17b). A finer divisor collection $\delta' = \{d_1, d_2, d_3, d_4, d_5\}$ has been chosen by splitting the divisor $d_2$ of (17a). As far as $\delta'$ is concerned, $e_1$ precedes $e_2$. That is, $\delta'$ distinguishes the temporal properties of $e_1$ from those of $e_2$.[17]

(17)  a.

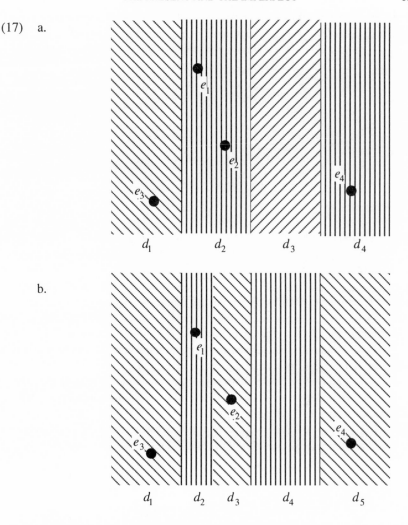

b.

Summarising, we have discussed a construction of temporal relations from events that relies on the auxiliary notions of *divisor* and *divisor collection*. Importantly, the resulting time structures are not absolute but depend on the choice of the divisor condition. This characteristic will allow us to unify the analysis of temporal anchoring in matrix and embedded contexts.

To formalise the notion of punctuality, we elaborate a proposal originally made by Russell (1936) and further considered by Kamp (1979), according to which an event is punctual iff it is not temporally partitioned by other events. That is, an event is punctual iff there are no events that *temporally overlap* it and that do not overlap each other. We define *temporal overlap* as follows:

(18)   $TO_\delta(e_1, e_2) \equiv_{df} O(d(e_1), d(e_2))$

Given an oriented event structure $\mathcal{H} = \langle \mathcal{E}, \delta \rangle$, two events temporally overlap in $\mathcal{H}$ iff their divisors $d(e_1)$ and $d(e_2)$ overlap in the ordinary mereological sense — that is, iff $d(e_1)$ and $d(e_2)$ have a common part:

(19)

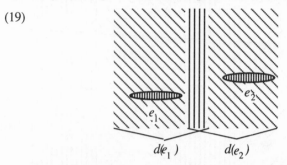

$$d(e_1) \qquad d(e_2)$$

Kamp's (1979) original notion of punctuality can now be rendered as follows:

(20)    $e$ is punctual in $\mathcal{H} = \langle \mathcal{E}, \delta \rangle \equiv_{df} \forall xy (TO_\delta(e, x) \wedge TO_\delta(e, y) \rightarrow TO_\delta(x, y))$

As required, $e$ is punctual iff every two events that temporally overlap it also temporally overlap each other. Example (20) meets the requirements we discussed above. Example (20) does not define punctuality on the basis of duration but characterises punctual events as being devoid of internal temporal structure. Furthermore, punctuality as defined in (20) is not absolute. In fact, the temporal properties and relations of an oriented event structure depend on the choice of the divisor collection $\delta$. As a consequence, whether two events overlap in an oriented event structure depends on $\delta$. Given that (20) defines punctuality by means of $TO_\delta$, punctuality itself depends on the choice of $\delta$. That is, an event can be punctual in a given oriented event structure and non-punctual in another one. A definition of punctuality equivalent to (20) is (21):

(21)    a.  An event is punctual in $\mathcal{H} = \langle \mathcal{E}, \delta \rangle$ iff its divisor is minimal.
        b.  A divisor is minimal in $\mathcal{H} = \langle \mathcal{E}, \delta \rangle$ iff it does not contain other divisors.

In the following discussion we will often refer to (21).

We can now state the following universal interpretative principle:

(22)    The anchoring event is punctual.

In (22) we refer to the anchoring event rather than to the speech event, since in §4.2. it will be shown that the anchoring of events in embedded clauses obeys the same constraints as in matrix clauses.

### 4.1.5. The present tense and perfectivity

In this section we provide an explanation for the impossibility of the perfective reading of the present tense. We will argue that the event denoted by eventive predicates has internal temporal properties which are incompatible with the punctuality of the speech event. Such properties are those characterising *processes*.

### 4.1.5.1. Processes and topological closure

The notion of *process* has often been used to characterise the actional (aktionsarten) properties of predicates. For instance, Mourelatos (1978) applies this term to Vendler's activities. On the other hand, Galton (1984) and Hoeksema (1984) use the feature *±process* and the feature *±definite* to provide a four-way classification of predicates. Consider (23) (from Verkuyl 1993, p. 35):

(23)

|          | - process    | +process        |
|----------|--------------|-----------------|
| - definite | states      | activities      |
| + definite | achievements | accomplishments |

Processes are events evolving in time and can be detected by means of the so-called *continuous tense criteria*. Example (24) illustrates the *progressive criterion* according to which a predicate is a process only if it can be progressivised.[18]

(24)   a.  *John is loving.
       b.  John is running.
       c.  John is eating an apple.
       d.  *John is winning the race.

Accordingly, both activities and accomplishments are processes. Concerning achievements, they are assigned the *-process* feature since they fail the progressive criterion. It has been noted, however, that some achievement predicates are compatible with progressive morphology (cf. Comrie 1976; Vlach 1981; Mourelatos 1978):

(25)   a.  John is winning this game.
       b.  Mary is reaching the top.

Kearns (1991) considers examples such as (25) and concludes that the successful application of the progressive criterion to achievement predicates depends on the availability of processes that typically lead to the *telos* denoted by the achievement predicate. Consider the example in (26):

(26)   a.  John is noting Mary.
       b.  John is dying.

Example (26a) is acceptable if uttered in a situation in which John is doing something that will lead him to note Mary. Similarly, the acceptability of (26b) is due to the existence, in the given situation, of an ongoing event that typically leads to death. It seems, therefore, that processes are relevant for the characterisation of achievements, as well as for the characterisation of activities and accomplishments. We propose that such relevance must be understood in the sense that every event denoted by an eventive predicate is either a process or contains a processual part. The first possibility obtains when the predicate is neutral with respect to the perfective/imperfective opposition, as is the case with the Italian present tense or the imperfect:

(27)    Mario corre/correva.
        Mario runs/ran(IMPF).

The meaning of these sentences involves reference to an ongoing, non-closed event. The second possibility arises with perfective predicates:

(28)    Mario ha corso.
        Mario has run.

The closed event of running in (28) contains a *processual part*. Conceptually, a topologically closed event is an entity containing its boundary, and a topologically non-closed event is an entity which does not contain its boundary.[19] In other words, a closed event corresponds to a non-closed event to which the boundary has been added. According to the preceding discussion, non-closed events are processes; therefore, a closed event can be decomposed into a processual part and a boundary.

Processes, such as running, are events evolving in time. They can be analysed as consisting of successive parts which are themselves runnings (Landman 1992). Similarly, the process involved in a sentence such as *John ate an apple* consists of a temporal sequence of elementary eating events. Therefore, for $e$ to be a process it must be the case that (a) $e$ has a mereological structure, consisting of event parts which are of the same type of $e$, and (b) $e$ has a temporal structure which, at least partially, mirrors the mereological one. Such intuitions can be formalised in the following way:

(29)    Let $\mathcal{H} = \langle \mathcal{E}, \delta \rangle$ be an oriented event structure and $e$ an event such that the
        predicate $\phi$ applies to it — that is, $\phi(e)$. $e$ is a $\phi$-*process* in
        $\mathcal{H} \equiv_{df} \exists e_1 e_2 (\phi(e_1) \wedge \phi(e_2) \wedge \text{TPP}(e_1, e) \wedge \text{TPP}(e_2, e) \wedge e_1 \neq e_2)$[20]

According to (29), an event $e$ is a process of running in a given oriented event structure iff there are distinct temporal proper parts of $e$ which are still events of running. The crucial point in (29) is the dependence of the notion of process on the notion of temporal structure. An event can be seen as a process only if a suitable temporal structure is available. If the temporal structure assigns $e$ a minimal divisor (cf. (21b)) — that is, if $e$ is punctual — $e$ cannot be considered a process, even if it has a mereological structure. As we saw in §4.1.4., in fact, punctuality amounts to neglecting temporal structure. For the same reasons, it follows that a process cannot be simultaneous with a punctual event. In this case, too, the temporal structure assigns $e$ a minimal divisor, and by the same token this means that $e$ cannot be regarded as a process.

Such properties carry over to closed events. As we saw, topological closure amounts to adding a boundary to processes, without affecting the temporal properties of the process. Therefore, a closed event maintains the temporal properties of its processual part. As a consequence, it cannot be simultaneous with a punctual event.

Recall, now, that we hypothesised that perfectivity amounts both to a requirement of topological closure on events, and to an existential quantification over event times. Thus the logical form of a perfective present tense sentence is (30):[21]

(30)    $\exists e \exists t (\phi(e) \land Cl(e) \land at(t, e) \land s \approx t)$

Note that $s$ is punctual and $e$ is closed. As a consequence, $s$ and $e$ cannot be simultaneous and the logical form in (30) is ruled out. As it turns out, the fact that the present tense has a perfective reading in no language depends on a conflict between the interpretative properties of the speech event, expressed by (29), and the presence of a process part in closed events. Let us formulate the following *punctuality constraint*:

(31)    A closed event cannot be simultaneous with a punctual event.

## 4.1.5.2. The English present tense

Let us now consider the problem introduced in §4.1. concerning the impossibility of English present tense eventive verbs having a continuous interpretation, which contrasts with Italian and German. In this section we argue that English associates the feature value *[+ perf]* to all eventive predicates. This is necessary in English but not in Italian (and the other Romance languages) and German (and the other Germanic languages), due to the morphological properties of the English verb. The presence of the feature *[+ perf]* on a verbal form entails closure. As we argued in the preceding section, a closed event cannot be mapped onto the punctual temporal anchor $s$. As a consequence, an eventive verb cannot have the same interpretation in English, as in German and Italian. In these languages, the event is not closed and hence can be mapped onto the punctual $s$. Let us first consider the morphosyntax of the English verb.

Roberts (1993) observes that in English verbs are well-formed words, even without the addition of any inflectional morphology, and that the change from a richer morphological structure, observable in Old English, to the present one had an important role in the development of Modern English. Here we will reformulate his observation, which we think is essentially correct, using the feature mechanisms adopted in this book.

A word such as *eat* is a "naked" form and can express one of several verbal values, such as the infinitive (without *to*), the first and second person singular, and the first, second, and third person plural. Many English words are even categorially ambiguous in that they can either identify an "object" or an "action", such as *dream, dress, want, fall*, and many others. This does not happen in Italian, where verbs are always complex words, consisting of a lexical morpheme plus inflection, as we have seen in the previous chapters, and where the verbal inflection is (usually) distinguishable from the nominal one. Furthermore, from a typological point of view, English is rather isolated in the Romance-Germanic domain.

Let us recall that Chomsky (1995) points out that the categorial features are *interpretable*. According to Chomsky, it is necessary to distinguish, for instance, between a verb and a noun, to attribute the correct referential properties to them. Here we will consider the role and the function of the verbal specification, presumably *[+ V;- N]*. Such interpretable features must be associated with the feature bundle corresponding to the lexical entry — that is, the form *eat* in English, or *mangiamo* (we eat) in Italian. Note that AGR also bears the categorial features, which however appear on this node only for attracting, overtly or covertly, the verb. The categorial features on AGR are consequently not interpretable. If this reasoning is correct, it follows that, for the derivation to converge, both in Italian and in English it is necessary to associate the categorial features with the verbal form. A word such as *mangiamo* (we eat) corresponds to the following bundle (irrelevant details omitted): *[ . . . + V; - N; 1st Pers; Plur . . . ]*. That is, it is a verb, and it is associated with typical verbal features, such as person and number. In other words, it is *recognisable* as a verb because of these features.[22]

On the other hand, the English form *eat* is not associated with any visible feature, corresponding to inflectional morphology. If the form *eat* enters the derivation without any further specification, the derivation itself does not converge because the categorial features on AGR cannot be checked.

Obviously, however, verbs *do* exist in English, and children are able to discern nouns and verbs quite early in this language, too. Our hypothesis is that the bundle is disambiguated — that is, it is identified as belonging to a certain lexical category, by being systematically associated with the aspectual features, which are typical only of verbs. The aspectual category bears the features *[+ perf; + V; - N]* — that is, it is associated with the categorial verbal features. ASP is a functional category, and therefore, once checked, the categorial features are erased. More precisely, let us propose that in English there are two feature bundles corresponding to a word such as *dress*. The first is associated with the nominal form, and the second, with the verbal form. Crucially, the latter is distinguished from the former because it is associated with the *perfective* value. If this analysis is correct, we can predict that a verb in English is always perfective, given that in this language this is the only way for it to get the correct categorial features and for allowing the derivation to converge.

The natural question which can be raised at this point is the following: Why is the English verb always associated with the feature value *[+ perf]* and never associated with the value *[- perf]*? In principle, this should be possible.

The analysis we are going to develop in §4.2. provides evidence in favour of the idea that in English and in Italian the only marked value is constituted by the feature *[+ perf]*. In other words, we propose that *[- perf]* is never instantiated in Italian and English, in that it does not correspond to any morpheme (cf. §4.2.).

To summarise, our hypothesis is that in English the only way for the verb to acquire the categorial features is by means of its association with the aspectual marker. The category ASP contributes the feature *[+ perf]*. As a consequence, English eventive predicates denote closed events which cannot be simultaneous with *S* (cf. the preceding section). In Italian, on the contrary, there is no need to associate the verb with the aspectual feature, because it is always defined as *[+ V; - N]*, thanks to the presence of the inflectional verbal morphology. In other words, at the relevant level of abstraction, in Italian a word is (unambiguously) associated with the categorial features. Hence the derivation can converge. In English, on the other hand, the derivation converges only when the verb is marked as perfective.[23]

Given this proposal, the logical form associated with a sentence such as (32a) is (32b):

(32)  a.  John eats an apple.
      b.  $\exists e \exists t \exists x (\text{eat}(e) \wedge \text{Theme}(e, x) \wedge \text{apple}(x) \wedge \text{Agent}(e, \text{John}) \wedge \text{Cl}(e) \wedge t \approx S \wedge \text{at}(t, e))$

According to (32b), the truth conditions for (32a) require that there is a closed event of eating, due to the presence of *[+ perf]*, which is simultaneous with the speech time. However, the speech event is punctual, and, as argued above, a closed event cannot be simultaneous with a punctual one. As a consequence, (32a) is assigned no interpretation.

Additional evidence in favour of the idea that English verbs denote bounded events comes from perceptual reports. Consider the following examples:[24]

(33)  a.  John saw Mary eat an apple.
      b.  John saw Mary eating an apple.

In English, perception verbs can take as their complements either "naked" verbs (i.e., infinitives without *to*), or Acc-ing constructions. It is well known that naked forms allow only a perfective reading. Therefore (33a), where the complement is an accomplishment predicate, means that "John saw an event *e*, where *e* is an event of *eating*, the *agent* is *Mary*, the *theme* is *an apple* and *e* has reached the *telos*". According to what we said in the preceding discussion, the complement event in this case is interpreted as a *bounded* one. On the other hand, the complement verb in (33b) is progressive — that is, it refers to a *non-bounded* event. As a consequence, it is not possible to infer that the apple was eventually eaten. Notice that both in Italian and in German the corresponding forms with an embedded infinitive are ambiguous:[25]

(34)  a.  Ho visto Gianni *mangiare* una mela.
          I saw Gianni eat-INF an apple.
      b.  Ich sah Hans einen Apfel *essen*.
          I saw Hans eat-INF an apple.

That is, these sentences do not specify whether or not the *telos* has been reached.

Let us add a few words on performatives in English. Dowty (1979, pp. 189-190) points out that in performative constructions, the predicate does not need to appear in the progressive form, even if these predicates clearly are not statives:

(35)  a. I pronounce you man and wife.

      b. I am pronouncing you man and wife.

Interestingly, (35a) contrasts with (35b), in that (35b) loses its performative value. We propose the following explanation. In (35a) the *pronouncing* is the same event as the speech event. Therefore, the punctuality constraint is not violated. As soon as there are two events — the pronouncing event and the speech event, as in (35b), which is not a performative — the progressive form must be used to avoid a violation of such a constraint.

### 4.1.5.3. Statives and habituals

In §4.1.1. we saw that the present tense of English eventive verbs can have the habitual interpretation and that the entity denoted by stative verbs can be interpreted as simultaneous with the speech event. We must explain, therefore, how it is possible that in these cases the verb gets its categorial features even if it cannot be said to be associated with a perfectivity mark.

To solve this problem, we adopt the proposal by Chierchia (1995a), who convincingly argues that habituals and statives can be analysed as having similar properties — namely, the presence of a quantificational feature associated with a generic operator.[26] We propose that in these cases — that is, the eventive habitual and the stative — the head receives the categorial features in a way analogous to the one seen above. The only difference is that, instead of being associated with the perfectivity feature, the categorial features $[+ V; - N]$ are associated with the quantificational feature and the generic operator hypothesised by Chierchia (1995a).[27]

The explanation we proposed in the preceding discussion for the impossibility of the continuous reading of English present tense sentences relies on the hypothesis that the (eventive) verbs of this language always denote closed events. As we showed in the last section, this is due to the morphosyntactic properties of English verbs. The impossibility of a continuous reading for a sentence such as *John eats an apple* then follows as a consequence of (a) the interpretative principle (22), which requires the speech event to always be punctual, and (b) the general impossibility of punctual events to be simultaneous with closed events (cf. (31)). In this section we show that our theory makes the correct predictions with respect to the possibility for an English present tense sentence to have the habitual reading. We show that the acceptability of habituals is due to the fact that in these sentences the conflict between the punctuality of the speech time and the closure of the event denoted by the verb does not arise.

In this work we adopt an analysis based on the so-called *relational theory* of generic and habitual sentences (cf. Carlson 1988; Krifka 1988; Krifka et al. 1995). According to this theory, the logical form of a habitual sentence contains a dyadic operator similar to the one which has been hypothesised for *when*-clauses and for conditionals.[28] A dyadic operator is an operator relating two sets of conditions: the *restrictor* and the *nuclear scope* (or *matrix*). Typical dyadic operators are quantifying adverbs such as *always*, *often*, and the like. Consider (36):

(36)  a.  When Mary comes John always leaves.

　　　b.  $\forall e[\text{come}(e) \wedge \text{Subj}(e, \text{Mary})]\ \exists e'(\text{leave}(e') \wedge \text{Subj}(e, \text{John}))$

In the logical form for (36a), *always* is translated by means of a universal quantifier ranging on the events provided by the formula in its restriction. This formula corresponds to the meaning of the *when*-clause of (36a). The *nuclear scope*, on the other hand, corresponds to the main clause of (36a). The logical form in (36b) is true iff, every time the restrictor is satisfied, the nuclear scope is true. That is, (36b) is true iff every time there is an event of Mary's coming, there is an event of John's leaving. The general form for a semantic representation containing a dyadic operator is the following (see Krifka et al. 1995):

(37)  $Q[x_1, \ldots, x_n; y_1, \ldots, y_m]$　$(\text{Restrictor}[x_1, \ldots, x_n]; \exists y_1, \ldots, y_m$
　　　$\text{Matrix}[\{x_1\}, \ldots, \{x_n\}, y_1, \ldots, y_m])$

That is, the dyadic operator is a quantifier binding the variables $x_1, \ldots, x_n$. The variables $y_1, \ldots, y_m$ are bound by an existential quantifier with scope only over the matrix. The notation $\{x_i\}$ means that $x_i$ can be free in the formula containing it.

In the case of habitual sentences, the relevant operator is usually symbolised by *Gen*:

(38)  a.  John smokes.

　　　b.  $\text{Gen}\ t(\exists e\ (\text{smoke}(e) \wedge \text{Agent}(e, \text{John}) \wedge \text{at}(t, e)))$

Here, the generic quantifier *Gen* ranges over temporal locations. The truth conditions in (38b) require that for every generic time $t$ there is an event of smoking $e$ such that the agent of $e$ is John.

Notice, now, that Italian past tense habituals are odd if uttered out of the blue:

(39)　Gianni andava al mare con Maria.

　　　Gianni went(IMPF) to the seaside with Maria.

Example (39) requires a time interval where the reported habit can be located. Such a time interval can be supplied either by the context or by what Bonomi (1995) calls a *background phrase*:

(40)　*L'anno scorso*, Gianni andava al mare con Maria.

　　　*Last year*, Gianni went(IMPF) to the seaside with Maria.

Ordinary, punctual temporal arguments, which set the event time, do not by themselves provide the relevant time interval:

(41)    a.  L'anno scorso, alle cinque Mario prendeva il tè.
            Last year, at five Mario had(IMPF) tea.
        b.  L'anno scorso, Mario prendeva il tè alle cinque.
            Last year, Mario had(IMPF) tea at five.

Examples (41a) and (41b) are odd if uttered without the temporal location for the habit. It seems, therefore, that at least past habitual sentences need a contextually provided external time. Adopting a term proposed by Chierchia (1995a), we call such a contextually specified time interval the *external time* of the habitual. We hypothesise that in habitual sentences the tense contributes to the restrictor. More precisely, it establishes a relationship between the external time interval and the speech time. Therefore, the logical form for (41a), with the background phrase, is the following:

(42)    Gen $t$[TP($t$, $I$) $\land$ last-year($I$) $\land$ five-o-clock($t$) $\land$ $I{<}S$] $\exists e$ (drink-tea($e$) $\land$ at($e$, $t$))

(Where TP stands for Temporal Part). The meaning of (42) is that for every time $t$, which (a) is part of the temporal interval referred to by *last year* (the external time), and (b) is a *five o'clock* time, there is an event of drinking tea occurring at $t$. Generalising, the logical form scheme for a habitual is the following:[29]

(43)    Gen $t$[TP($t$, $I$) $\land$ contextually-relevant($I$) $\land$ R($I$, $s$)] $\exists e$ ($\phi(e)$ $\land$ at($e$, $t$))

Here *R(I, s)* stands for whatever relation between the event time and the speech time is contributed by the tense.[30] In a present tense habitual sentence, we obtain (44b) for the sentence in (44a):

(44)    a   John smokes.
        b.  Gen $t$[TP($t$, $I$) $\land$ contextually-relevant($I$) $\land$ TP($s$, $I$)] $\exists e$ (smoke($e$) $\land$ Cl($e$) $\land$ at($e$, $t$))

The present tense still relates the contextually relevant external time to the speech time. It requires the speech time to be a part of the external time. As a consequence, (44b) is true iff for generically many times $t$ which are part of the contextually relevant interval $I$, where $I$ contains the speech event, there is an event of smoking occurring at $t$. Note that the event is closed, since we argued in the previous section that English verbs only denote closed events. However, (44b) does not establish any direct relation between the speech event $s$ and the eventive variable. Example (44b) only requires that $s$ be a temporal part of the interval where the habit holds. As a consequence, (44b) does not violate the constraint according to which closed events cannot be simultaneous with (or, more generally, overlap) the speech time, and (44a) is an acceptable sentence.

Therefore, the acceptability of present tense habitual readings in English is due to the fact that the present tense is not interpreted as requiring the event time to be directly related to *S*. As a consequence, even if the eventive variable in the matrix of (44b) denotes closed events, the punctuality constraint does not apply, and no ungrammaticality arises. This property is an instance of a more general characteristic of habitual sentences. They always require the tense to connect the speech time to the *external time*.[31]

## 4.1.5.4. Progressives

Another question concerns progressive forms in English. Observationally, a V-*ing* structure has the continuous interpretation. Recall, however, that we have argued that the English verb always has the *[+ perf]* feature, and therefore the anchoring with the punctual events should be ruled out. A violation similar to that found with the non-progressive present tense should arise, but this is not the case.

The solution to this problem lies in a better understanding of the properties of the progressive. We will argue that the presence of the feature *[+ perf]* is compatible with the continuous reading of the progressive.[32] Following the literature, we hypothesise (a) that the progressive morphology contributes an intensional operator and (b) that the English progressive refers to an *intensionally* perfective (i.e., closed) event. Recall that all eventive predicates have a processual part (cf. §4.1.4.). Given that the perfectivity is only intensional, the continuous interpretation is possible on the (extensional) processual part. We also show that the Italian progressive has properties similar to the English progressive, contrasting with the other Italian non-progressive, continuous forms.

Bennett & Partee (1972) argued that an event can be said to be ongoing at a given interval *I* iff it will continue beyond such interval. Consider the following example:

(45)    John is eating an apple.

According to Bennett and Partee's proposal, in (45), the event of eating an apple is ongoing at an interval *I* containing the speech event, iff there is a larger interval *I',* where the corresponding perfective sentence is true:

(46)    John has eaten an apple.

This proposal has some shortcomings. In (46) nothing seems to require the existence of a larger interval. Furthermore, there are cases in which the larger interval does not exist, at least in the actual world:

(47)    John was crossing the street when a car hit him.

Suppose that (47) is true at an interval *I*. Given that John was hit by a car, he did not complete the crossing, and as such there is no interval containing *I* where the perfective sentence *John has crossed the street* is true. These considerations led Dowty (1979) to propose an *intensional* theory of progressives. The larger interval where the event is completed is not in the actual world *w,* but in an *inertia world* for *w*. According to Dowty, an *inertia world* for *w* is a possible world that (a) is identical to *w* up to the interval *I*, and (b) can differ from *w* from that point on. Therefore Dowty's analysis of the progressive is the following:

(48)    *John is eating an apple* is true in *w* at an interval *I* iff in every inertia
        world *v* for *w* there is an interval *I'* containing *I* where *John has eaten an
        apple* is true.

Following Dowty (1979), other scholars developed the idea that the progressive
is an intensional operator. For instance, Landman (1992) argues that the
progressive is a relation between an event *e* and an event type *P*:

(49)    ⟦PROG(*e*, *P*)⟧ $^{w,g}$=1 iff ∃*f* ∃*v*:⟨*f*, *v*⟩ ∈ CON(g(*e*), *w*) and ⟦*P*⟧ $^{v,g}$(*f*)=1

*CON(g(e), w)* is the *continuation branch* of g(*e*) in *w* and *g* is an assignment of
values to variables. As an exemplification, let us consider (50) and the
representation in (51) (from Landman 1992, p. 27):

(51)

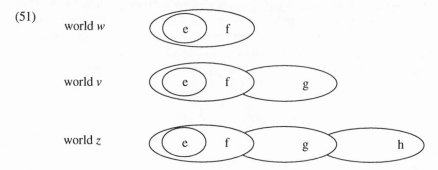

world *w*

world *v*

world *z*

Suppose that *e* is the ongoing event of eating mentioned in (50), and that, in the
actual world, *e* is a *stage* of another event *f*. Landman's notion of *stage* is the
following: *e* is a *stage* of *e'* iff *e'* can be seen as a more developed version of *e*.
That is, *e'* is *e* at a later stage of development. That *e* in the actual world is a
stage of *f* means that *f* is an event which is a more developed version of *e*. If *f* is
a completed event of eating an apple, then the process stops. If *f* is not a
completed event of eating, then we consider a suitable world *v* accessible from
*w*.[33] Suppose that *g* is an event in *v* such that *f* is a stage of *g*. The *stage*
relation is transitive, so *g* is a more developed version of both *f* and *e*. If *g* is a
closed event of eating an apple, then the procedure stops; otherwise it continues
and considers the next accessible world *z*, and so on. In other words, we travel
through possible worlds following the *stage-of* relation until we find an event *f*
which is a completed event of eating an apple. The *continuation branch* of an
event *e* in a world *w* is the (smallest) set of pairs of events and worlds that are
obtained by means of this construction. Example (49) establishes that
*PROG(e, P)* is true in a world *w*, relative to a variable assignment *g*, iff in some
world of the continuation branch of g(*e*) and *w* some event realises *P*.

    Kearns (1991) conceptualises the meaning of the progressive by appealing to
the notion of *typical immediate preludes* — that is, processes that *typically* (but
not necessarily) lead to a (bounded) event of the kind referred to by the verb. In
our terminology, the denotation of V+ing is a non-bounded process. More

explicitly, Higginbotham (1994) proposes a view of the progressive according to which the affix -*ing* is a modifier of the event:

(52)　-*ing* is $(e, [\pi(e') \mid \phi(e')])$

The suffix -*ing* has an event position that is identified with the eventive variable of the verbal stem, and another position containing an attribute, in the form of an intensional abstract. Then, V+*ing* is true of an event $e$ iff $e$ is *sufficiently similar* to the processual part $(\pi)$ of an event in the extension of the verb predicate. To exemplify, *eating an apple* is true of an event $e$ iff $e$ is sufficiently similar to the processual part of a typical event of eating an apple. As can be seen, these approaches share the idea that the progressive morpheme is an intensional operator.

Our proposal is that the progressive operator relates an event $e$ belonging to the actual world and a closed event $e'$ belonging to a suitable possible world — that is, an inertia world, adopting Dowty's terminology, or in a continuation branch of $e$ and $w$, according to Landman's theory. Following Higginbotham (1994), $e$ is a process — that is, a non-closed event. We hypothesise that $e$ is anchored to the speech event giving rise to the continuous reading.

Rephrasing our proposal in Landman's (1992) terms, the predicate $P$ incorporates the topological closure, due to the *[+ perf]* feature of the verb: $P = \lambda e.(\phi(e) \wedge Cl(e))$, where $\phi$ is the predicate contributed by the verb. In Higginbotham's (1994) terms, we obtain (53):

(53)　-*ing* is $(e, [\pi(e') \mid \phi(e') \wedge Cl(e')])$

To show that the progressive involves an intensionally closed event, we consider the following example, discussed by Landman (1992, ex. 9):

(54)　God was creating a unicorn, when He changed His mind.

Verbs such as *create* are extensional in that they normally presuppose the existence of their objects. Importantly, Landman considers a reading of *create* which excludes the existence of partial unicorns.[34] Therefore, the unicorn comes into existence only when the event reaches the *telos*. Landman conclusively shows that since (54) does not commit us to the existence of actual unicorns, such a sentence is intensional and the intensionality is due to the progressive operator. Hence, the unicorn referred to in (54) exists in some possible world.

However, as we said, the created object comes into existence only when the creation reaches the *telos*. Therefore, Landman's example shows that in the same world where there is the unicorn, there is also a closed event of creating that unicorn. That is, the truth of (54) entails the existence in a possible world of both a unicorn and a closed event of creating.

These conclusions also apply to the Italian progressive forms. They create intensional contexts:

(55)　Quando venne interrotto da Lucifero, Dio stava creando un unicorno.
　　　When He was interrupted by Lucifer, God was creating a unicorn.

Even (55) does not presuppose the existence of actual unicorns. Moreover, if we consider Landman's reading, no partial object exists, and we must conclude that even the Italian progressive creates an intensional context.

Interestingly, in Italian the progressive contrasts with the imperfect. Consider the following example:

(56)  a.  Quando Artù entrò, Merlino creava un unicorno.
          When Arthur entered, Merlin created(IMPF) a unicorn.
      b.  Quando Artù entrò, Merlino stava creando un unicorno.
          When Arthur entered, Merlin was creating(PROG IMPF) a unicorn.

Our understanding of (56a) is that the unicorn must exist in the actual world, contrasting with (56b), which does not entail the existence of actual unicorns. These data provide additional evidence in favour of the idea that the progressive is an intensional operator. Moreover, they show that the Italian imperfect must be kept distinct from the progressive.

Concluding, the fact that progressive sentences have a continuous reading is fully compatible with our hypothesis that English verbs always have the feature *[+ perf]* and denote closed events. The progressive is an intensional operator; thence closure (perfectivity) is intensional as well. Furthermore, because of its semantics, the progressive make a process available, the temporal variable of which is bound by a default universal quantifier, giving rise to the continuous reading.[35]

### 4.1.5.5. Achievements

Recall that in §4.1.5.1. we argued that closed events contain their boundaries. Achievements have the lexical property that the event they denote always contains a *telos* (cf. Verkuyl 1993). Therefore, achievements always denote closed events. This property, being a lexical one, holds crosslinguistically. As a consequence, we expect achievements in Italian to behave like English eventive predicates. This expectation is borne out.

Consider the following sentence:

(57)  #Gianni raggiunge la vetta.
      Gianni reaches the top.

As we pointed out in §4.1.1., a sentence such as (57) cannot have the continuous reading. This fact directly follows from our theory. In order to have a continuous reading, the progressive must be used:

(58)  Gianni sta raggiungendo la vetta.
      Gianni is reaching the top.

Again, this is predicted by our theory.

## 4.2. On the present-in-the-past interpretation of embedded events in Germanic and Romance

The aim of this section is to show that the analysis we gave in §4.1. to account for the crosslinguistic differences in the interpretation of the present tense can successfully be extended to embedded contexts, to capture the pattern of the so-called present-in-the-past reading in Italian, English, and German.[36] Such a generalisation provides further evidence in favour of our hypothesis — namely, that the mechanisms determining the anchoring of the events are the same both when the event in question is the matrix event and when it is a subordinate event. In other words, we propose that the speech time $S$ — that is, the indexical anchor — and a contextually given temporal anchor have the same properties, *as far as they are considered anchoring times*. To provide evidence in favour of this conclusion, we will consider the distribution of the imperfect in Italian and its equivalent forms in German and English. The imperfect is the verbal form used in Italian to express the present-in-the-past reading, which we will henceforth call the *simultaneous* interpretation. In Germanic languages, however, there is only *one* past form, the simple past, which in certain contexts can have the simultaneous interpretation exhibited by the Italian imperfect.

In this section we will first illustrate the properties of the Italian imperfect, with a special emphasis on its interpretation in embedded contexts. We will then provide an analysis of its distribution. Finally, we will consider the equivalent forms in Germanic languages.

### 4.2.1. The Italian imperfect: a characterisation

In this section, we illustrate the properties of the imperfect in Italian. Our hypothesis is that this form is a *past, anaphoric, continuous* verbal form, *unmarked* with respect to the opposition perfectivity/ imperfectivity.

#### 4.2.1.1. The anaphoricity of the imperfect

By *anaphoric* we mean that the imperfect must, on the one hand, be interpreted as a past with respect to $S$, and, on the other, that it requires that the temporal argument of the predicate be overtly specified. This property has been studied by many authors, among others Kamp & Rohrer (1983), Eberle & Kasper (1991), Bertinetto (1991), and Delfitto & Bertinetto (1995a).

The present, simple past, and future tenses are fully acceptable even when the temporal argument of the predicate is not overtly specified (see chapter 3, §3.2.5.), and are interpreted relative to $S$. The imperfect, on the contrary, cannot be interpreted in such a straightforward way, but rather needs a temporal reference somewhere in the context:

(59)    Mangio/ho mangiato/mangerò una mela.
         I am eating / ate / will eat an apple.

(60)   Mangiavo una mela.
       I eat(IMPF) an apple.

The sentences in (59) are perfectly interpretable, even in the absence of any context, and convey the information that the event time either coincides (*mangio*), is in the past (*ho mangiato*), or is in the future (*mangerò*) with respect to the speech time $S$. The sentence in (60), however, is odd if uttered "out-of-the-blue". It is appropriate as an answer to questions such as, What were you doing yesterday? or What were you doing when John arrived? which explicitly provide a temporal location from which the imperfect can take its temporal reference — in these cases, *yesterday* and *when John arrived*. The temporal expression can also appear in the same sentence, as in the following cases (the temporal location appears in italics):

(61)   *Ieri* Gianni non sapeva se andare al cinema o no.
       Yesterday Gianni did not know(IMPF) whether or not to go to the movie.

(62)   Mentre Gianni disegnava, Maria leggeva.
       While Gianni was drawing(IMPF), Maria was reading(IMPF).

(63)   *Quando Gianni uscì*, Maria guardava la TV.
       When Gianni went out, Maria was watching(IMPF) TV.

These sentences can be uttered "out-of-the-blue", unlike example (60).[37] These examples show that the time of the event, or state, referred to by the imperfect is anaphoric.

As stated, the imperfect is a *past* tense. Consider, for instance, the following sentence:

(64)   *Quando Gianni uscirà, Maria guardava la TV.
       When Gianni will go out, Maria watched(IMPF) TV.

Example (64) cannot be coherently interpreted. The matrix predicate, *uscirà* (will go out), provides a temporal anchor which is in the future with respect to $S$ and which cannot be exploited by the imperfect. We will discuss this property further in §4.2.1.2.

### 4.2.1.2. The present-in-the-past reading

Now consider the well-known fact that, when embedded under a past tense, the imperfect can express simultaneity. Interestingly, as we will illustrate in a while, only the imperfect and the subjunctive can have this reading. The other (past) tenses of the indicative do not have this property. Consider the following examples:[38]

(65)   Mario mi ha detto che Gianni mangiava una mela.
       Mario told me that Gianni ate(IMPF) an apple.

In (65), Gianni's eating can be understood as simultaneous with Mario's saying. In this case, there is an accomplishment predicate, but the same reading also arises with stative and activity predicates:

(66)  a.  Mario mi ha detto che Gianni era felice.
          Mario told me that Gianni was(IMPF) happy.
      b.  Mario mi ha detto che Gianni correva.
          Mario told me that Gianni ran(IMPF).

Note that in these cases the temporal anchor is provided by the superordinate predicate. Finally, the following examples show that with achievement predicates, in order to obtain a simultaneous interpretation, there is a strong preference for a progressive (imperfect) form, and that a simple imperfect gives rise to an odd sentence (the symbol # signals lack of a simultaneous interpretation):

(67)  a.  #Mario mi ha detto che Gianni raggiungeva la vetta.
          Mario told me that Gianni reached(IMPF) the top.
      b.  Mario mi ha detto che Gianni stava raggiungendo la vetta.
          Mario told me that Gianni was reaching (PROGR-IMPF) the top.

As mentioned, when the subordinate sentence contains other indicative past tenses, such as a present perfect or a simple past, the simultaneous interpretation is not available, contrasting with the imperfect:

(68)    #Mario mi ha detto che Gianni ha mangiato/mangiò una mela.
        Mario told me that Gianni has eaten/ate an apple.

We will discuss these cases in the next section.

Notice also that a non-simultaneous reading is impossible in sentences such as (65) and (66) above. The non-simultaneous interpretation is available only if the context provides a temporal reference which is *not* the superordinate predicate. This is another instance of the more general phenomenon observed above — namely, the fact that the time referred to by an imperfect verb is anaphoric. Consider the following example:

(69)    Mario mi ha detto *questa mattina* che *ieri* Gianni mangiava una mela.
        Mario told me this morning that yesterday Gianni ate(IMPF) an apple.

The embedded imperfect in (69) can have a non-simultaneous interpretation and can be interpreted as past with respect to the saying, as a derivative effect of the presence of the temporal argument provided by *ieri* (yesterday). Example (69) contrasts with (68) where a present perfect tense appears in the subordinate clause and the shifted reading is the only one available even though the temporal argument (yesterday) is missing. The imperfect predicate is interpreted as simultaneous with respect to *ieri* (yesterday) and not with respect to the saying. The final result is a *pseudo*-shifted reading (*pseudo*-shifted because the shifting is obtained only indirectly).

Consider finally the following example:

(70)    Gianni dice che Teresa mangiava una mela.
        Gianni says that Teresa ate(IMPF) an apple.

The embedded imperfect in (70) must be interpreted as past. However, as in (60), it requires the temporal argument to be overtly given:

(71)    Gianni dice che *ieri alle cinque* Teresa mangiava una mela.
        Gianni says that yesterday at five Teresa was eating an apple.

Now consider the interpretation of the imperfect when it is dependent on a future tense:

(72)    Gianni dirà che Teresa mangiava una mela.
        Gianni will say that Teresa ate(IMPF) an apple.

In (72) the eating is interpreted as past with respect to the saying. Again the sentence where a temporal location is overtly provided gives better results. For instance:

(73)    a.  Gianni dirà che *il giorno precedente* Teresa mangiava una mela.
            Gianni will say that the day before Teresa ate(IMPF) an apple.
        b.  Gianni dirà che *ieri* Teresa mangiava una mela.
            Gianni will say that yesterday Teresa ate(IMPF) an apple.

Given the presence of the time specification *the day before* in (73a), the imperfect is interpreted as past with respect to the saying. Analogously, in (73b), because of the presence of *yesterday* the imperfect verb is interpreted as past with respect to the utterance time.

Concluding, the imperfect is a past tense requiring an anaphoric (familiar) event time. Such a time can be provided by the context, by an explicit temporal argument, or, finally, by the embedding matrix event, yielding a simultaneous interpretation.

### 4.2.1.3. Continuity

Before addressing our main question, the present-in-the-past reading, let us illustrate an important property of the imperfect — namely, the continuous interpretation. According to the evidence which we will discuss in this section, imperfectivity is *not* a prerequisite for continuous readings. We will see, in fact, that continuous readings are compatible with achievement predicates, predicates entailing that the *telos* has been realised. Therefore, the continuous reading is possible even with perfective predicates. In the framework we are developing here, this shows that it does not require non-closed events.[39]

To show that the imperfect is a continuous tense, we adopt the traditional test — namely, the compatibility with *mentre* (while). Only the continuous tenses can appear in a clause introduced by *while* (cf. Bertinetto 1991):[40]

(74)    Mentre Gianni guardava la TV, Maria cucinava.
        While Gianni was watching(IMPF) TV, Maria was cooking (IMPF).

(75)    a.  *Mentre Gianni ha suonato, Maria cantava.
            While Gianni has played(PrPerf), Maria was singing.
        b.  *Mentre Gianni suonò, Maria cantava.
            While Gianni played(SP), Maria sang.

In Italian neither the present perfect nor the simple past can appear in this context, contrasting with the imperfect.

As mentioned, we suggest that the compatibility of the imperfect with *mentre* does not entail that it is always imperfective. We propose that the imperfect is continuous and that continuity can be a property both of imperfective and perfective predicates. The relevant evidence comes from the distribution of the imperfect with achievement predicates. We have illustrated that achievement predicates always instantiate bounded sequences. In this sense, it can be said that they are always perfective. Achievement predicates are compatible with the imperfect morphology, and, moreover, they can appear in *mentre* contexts. Consider the following examples:

(76)    a.  Ieri alle cinque, Gianni raggiungeva la vetta.
            Yesterday at five, Gianni was reaching(IMPF) the top.
        b.  Ieri, mentre Gianni raggiungeva la vetta, sua madre pregava.
            Yesterday, while Gianni was reaching(IMPF) the top, his mother was praying.

The hypothesis that the imperfect tense always gives rise to imperfective predicates would be incompatible with these examples. As we have already seen, achievement predicates are intrinsically perfective. Consider the following examples:

(77)    a.  #Ieri Gianni raggiungeva la vetta, quando un violento temporale glielo impedì.
            Yesterday Gianni was reaching(IMPF) the top, but then a violent storm prevented him.
        b.  #Mentre Gianni raggiungeva la vetta, un violento temporale gli impedì di arrivarci.
            While Gianni was reaching(IMPF) the top, a violent storm prevented him from getting there.
        c.  Ieri Gianni stava raggiungendo la vetta, quando un violento temporale glielo impedì.
            Yesterday, Gianni was reaching(PROG IMPF) the top, when a violent storm prevented him.

Sentences such as (77a) and (77b) do not make sense (besides perhaps a reportive reading, at least for some speakers). In fact, the achievement predicate *reach the top* is telic and, therefore, its semantics contrast with the meaning of the other predicate (*prevent*). Examples (77a) and (77b) contrast with (77c), because the progressive form does not entail that the culmination has been reached, at least in the real world (see §4.1.5.4.). From these data it might be concluded that continuous readings are possible with closed (telic) predicates. We propose that the imperfect (and the present) are aspectually unmarked, and that the only marked aspectual value, in Italian (and we would like to say in Romance in general), is perfectivity.

### 4.2.1.4. Modal meanings

For the sake of completeness it is important to point out that the imperfect can have several uses often called *modal* in the literature. The data are quite consistent crosslinguistically. That is, the languages which have the imperfect in their tense inventory can often associate it with some modal usage. Among the several modal meanings of the imperfect, we mention two. The imperfect can be used as a quasi-epistemic modal. In this circumstance it is compatible with future temporal arguments:[41]

(78)   a.   Domani cantava Pavarotti.
            Tomorrow Pavarotti sang(IMPF) (meaning that *he is supposed to sing*).
       b.   Partivo domani.
            Tomorrow I left(IMPF) (meaning that *as far as I am concerned, I will leave tomorrow, but something might happen to make me change my plans*).

Another modal usage is the so-called *imperfait preludique* (a French term which approximately means *the imperfect used in children plays*):[42]

(79)   a.   Facciamo che io ero il re e tu la regina.
            Let's pretend that I was(IMPF) the king and you the queen.
       b.   Adesso io uscivo e tu mi seguivi.
            Now I went(IMPF) out and you followed(IMPF) me.

We will not discuss here the reasons the imperfect can have these meanings; we will only derive from these considerations some conclusions on the temporal systems of English and German. Let us only point out that, interestingly, in these cases the imperfect loses its past temporal value, as shown, for instance, by its compatibility with *adesso* (now) in (79b).

   These phenomena are reminiscent of the interpretation of English modals (see chapter 3 §3.1.4.), where the past interpretation is in complementary distribution with a modalised interpretation.

### 4.2.1.5. An account of the Italian imperfect

Let us sketch an analysis of the temporal properties of the imperfect in embedded contexts. According to the revised Reichenbachian approach discussed in chapter 1, a past tense is represented as the composition of $E,R$ and $R\_S$ — that is, $E\_S$. We will give a characterisation of the imperfect which is compatible both with the above observations and with the formal apparatus proposed thus far.

We consider the imperfect to be a past tense, in that it establishes a relation between two temporal entities such that the final interpretation turns out to be a past one. We represent the temporal entities in question by means of two *variables*, $t_E$ and $X$. Informally speaking, $X$ is the equivalent of the anchoring time $S$, appearing in indexical tenses, and $t_E$ is the event time. The relation characterising the imperfect can therefore be represented as follows:

(80) $t_E\_X$

Observationally, three constraints hold on the interpretation of these variables: (a) they *must* both receive a reference; (b) $t_E$ cannot take reference from $S$, because it must be bound by a temporal argument; and (c) $X$ must be the time of an anchoring event — either $S$ or the time of the event of the matrix clause (for instance, given by the superordinate verb of saying in the examples given above). As we pointed out in the previous sections, when the variables cannot take their values within the sentence, they must be interpreted by means of the context. Here we are going to generalise the mechanism sketched in §4.1. for matrix clauses to subordinate contexts as well, and will propose that the relation holding between an event and its anchoring event obeys the same constraints discussed therein.

Let us represent the tense of the superordinate clause by means of the Reichenbachian relations between $E$ and $S$ — that is, $E\_S$, for the past tenses, and $S\_E$ for the future. The simultaneous interpretation of the imperfect under a past tense (ex. 65) is obtained by interpreting $X$ as $S$, and $t_E$ as the moment of the saying — of the speech event mentioned in the sentence (cf. (81)):

(81) (ex. 65)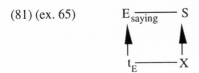

If $X$ is interpreted as the time of the saying, then $t_E$ must be located by the context. This way we obtain the shifted reading of (25) (cf. (82)):

(82) (ex. 69)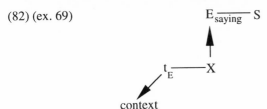

The only interpretation available for an imperfect under a present tense is given in picture (83). $X$ can only be $S$, since the speech time and the time of the matrix event coincide. Therefore, $t_E$ cannot be $S$, given that the imperfect is a past tense. Consider the following representation:

(83) (ex. 71)

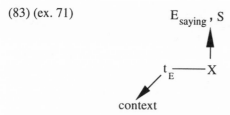

If the imperfect is embedded under a future, there is no way to coherently interpret $t_E$ as the time of the superordinate event. It must always be interpreted by means of the context. The possible representations are the following:

(84)

(85)

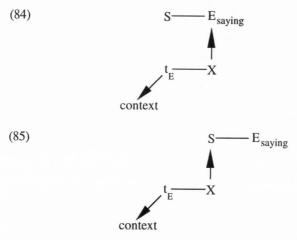

Recall that $t_E$ cannot be linked to $S$. Therefore, in (84) and (85) it must be temporally located by the context. In (85) a link to the superordinate saying event would be incoherent, given that $X$ refers to $S$ and given that, because of the semantics of the imperfect, $t_E$ precedes $X$.

Concluding, the anaphoricity of the imperfect is captured by means of the hypothesis that the time of the event is not autonomous but rather must be interpreted by resorting to the context. Normally, past (and future) tenses do not have this requirement and can be interpreted even in the absence of any contextually given temporal reference. The obligatoriness of a temporal reference provided by the context, when the imperfect appears in main clauses, follows from this hypothesis.

Let us consider now the distribution of achievement predicates in embedded contexts, as illustrated by example (67a), repeated here for simplicity:

(67)   a.   #Mario mi ha detto che Gianni raggiungeva la vetta.
           Mario told me that Gianni reached(IMPF) the top.

As pointed out, this sentence is odd, and there is a strong preference for the corresponding progressive (*stava raggiungendo*, was reaching). As we will better develop in §4.2.3., the theory sketched in §4.1. can account for this observation. The explanation is the same one we gave for the impossibility of the non-reportive reading of the present tense with achievement predicates. In particular, we claimed that the closed event identified by these predicates cannot be simultaneous with the speech event. Such a configuration would violate the punctuality constraint — that is, that a closed event cannot be mapped onto a punctual one. Our proposal is that punctuality is not a property of $S$ but a more general property of anchoring events, which as such are conceptualised as punctual. According to this proposal, given the fact that the mapping in (67a) would entail the same kind of operation (the embedded closed event should be mapped onto the superordinate punctual anchoring event), it is ruled out by the interface conditions. We will provide further evidence in favour of this hypothesis by means of an analysis of the present-in-the-past reading in Germanic languages.

### 4.2.2 Comparative evidence

Let us now compare the Italian picture with that of English and German, which do not have the imperfect in their tense inventory. Special attention will be devoted to the present-in-the-past reading. As we have seen, in Italian only the imperfect can have this function, with statives, accomplishments, and activities.

In English, only stative predicates (in the simple past) exhibit the simultaneous reading. For the other kinds of predicates, when they appear in the non-progressive simple past only the shifted reading is possible.

German is more similar to Italian. In this language past predicates embedded under another past can have the simultaneous interpretation, even when the embedded predicate is an activity or an accomplishment. Let us consider the data:

(86)  a.  Gianni ha detto che Mario era felice.
          Gianni said that Mario was(IMPF) happy.
      b.  Gianni ha detto che Mario mangiava una mela.
          Gianni said that Mario ate(IMPF) an apple.
      c.  Gianni ha detto che Mario correva.
          Gianni said that Mario ran(IMPF).

As we already discussed, in Italian the simultaneous interpretation is available with statives (86a), with accomplishments (86b), and with activities (86c).

In English, an embedded stative predicate appearing in the simple past form can display the simultaneous reading, whereas the same does not hold for the embedded simple past of eventive verbs (Stowell 1992; Enç 1987; Abusch 1990), both accomplishments and activities:

(87)  a.  John said Mary was happy.
      b.  #John said Mary ate an apple.
      c.  #John said Mary ran.

With eventive predicates, the simple past can only be interpreted as past with respect to the saying — that is, shifted. In order to obtain the simultaneous reading, the progressive form must be used:

(88)    a.  John said that Mary *was eating* an apple.
        b.  John said that Mary *was running*.

In German, both stative and eventive predicates can appear in the past tense under another past tense with the simultaneous interpretation, as in Italian:

(89)    a.  Hans sagte, daß Marie glücklich war.
            Hans said that Marie was happy.
        b.  Hans sagte, daß Marie einen Apfel aß.
            Hans said that Marie ate an apple.
        c.  Hans sagte, daß Marie rannte.
            Hans said that Marie ran.

Let us provide an explanation of these facts. As we have seen above, English eventive verbs always denote perfective events, and for this reason they can never be simultaneous with a punctual event. The explanation for (87b) and (87c) is exactly the same as the one we gave for the non-progressive present tense, provided that the anchoring event for the embedded clause is punctual. With respect to the progressive forms in (88), again, what we said in §4.1.5.4. holds.

The relevant generalisation seems therefore to be the following:

(90)    Anchoring events are punctual.

The principle in (90) predicts that the effects due to punctuality observed in the interpretation of non-dependent verbal forms must also be found in dependent contexts. More precisely, we observed that present tense predicates, in order to be interpreted as simultaneous with $S$, must identify a non-bounded event — that is, they must be non-perfective. This effect is also found in dependent contexts and explains the distribution of the simultaneous present-in-the-past reading in Italian, English, and German. In Italian the imperfect is neutral with respect to the perfective/imperfective distinction, as we have already seen. Thus, non-bounded readings can arise and the predicate can always be related to an anchoring event (i.e., to the utterance, thought, wish, etc. mentioned in the embedding clause) to obtain a simultaneous interpretation.[43] As we have seen, the only exceptions are achievement predicates, for the reasons already discussed.[44]

In English and German there is no imperfect tense, and the simple past is used to express the present-in-the-past relation. In English the verb is always perfective, and the past tense morpheme does not modify the perfective value of the verb. Therefore, a past tense eventive verb, embedded under a verb of saying, can be interpreted as simultaneous neither with respect to $S$, nor with respect to another anchoring event, by principle (90).[45] As happens with present verbs, however, stative verbs are not subject to the same restriction and may give rise to simultaneous readings.

In German, as in Italian, the event denoted by the predicate is non-bounded. The past tense morpheme in German is neutral with respect to the perfective value, like the Italian imperfect. Consequently, it might have both a perfective interpretation and an imperfective one. Native speakers of German assign it an imperfective interpretation in a present-in-the-past construction. Compare (91a), with the simultaneous interpretation, with (91b):

(91)   a.  Hans sagte, daß Marie einen Apfel aß.
          Hans said that Marie was eating an apple.
      b.  Hans sagt, daß Marie einen Apfel aß.
          Hans says that Marie ate an apple.

As expected, with the simultaneous reading, the perfective interpretation is ruled out. However, if for independent reasons the simultaneous reading is impossible, as in (91b), such an interpretation is available.

In Italian the simple past is always perfective. For this reason it can never appear in a present-in-the-past construction. This is the case in all languages which have the imperfect in their tense inventory. The past tense yields a perfective predicate. Finally, the event of a perfect tense is always perfective, since the notion of consequent state makes sense only if the culmination has been reached (see chapter 3). For all these reasons, the simple past and the present perfect cannot have the simultaneous interpretation in embedded contexts, as can be seen in (68), reproduced here for simplicity:[46]

(68)    #Mario mi ha detto che Gianni ha mangiato/mangiò una mela
       Mario told me that Gianni has eaten/ate an apple

However, the imperfect in Italian and Romance is a verbal form which has specific properties which are not shared by the simple past of Germanic languages. On the one hand, the simple past of German and English can appear in contexts where the Italian requires the imperfect, such as in the present-in-the-past readings. On the other, however, the simple past in Germanic languages does not have the same distribution.

Consider first that the interpretive requirement of the imperfect, which establishes that it must always have a temporal reference provided by the context, is not shared by the simple past in English and German. In fact, it can be interpreted with the shifted reading, without providing a temporal location. With respect to this property, as we have seen, the German verbal form contrasts with the Italian imperfect.

Moreover, in English and German the simple past cannot have the modal meanings usually attributed to the imperfect:

(92)   a.  *Tomorrow I left.
      b.  *Now let's pretend that I was the king and you queen.

The same is true in German:

(93)   a.   *Morgen sang Pavarotti.
             Tomorrow Pavarotti sang.
       b.   *Laßt uns ein Spiel machen: ich war der König und du warst die
             Königin.
             Let's do a play: I was the king and you were the queen.

Analogously, in Italian real past forms, such as the simple past and the present
perfect, never can:

(94)   a.   *Domani cantò/ha cantato Pavarotti.
             Tomorrow Pavarotti sang/has sung.
       b.   *Facciamo che io fui/sono stato il re e tu la regina.
             Let's do that I was/have been the king and you the queen.

Furthermore, our suggestion seems to be confirmed by the behaviour of
achievement predicates in Italian which parallel the general case in English. Even
in Italian achievements cannot have continuous interpretations in the present
tense. This is consistent with our observation that achievements only denote
closed events. Coherently, to obtain a continuous present form, the progressive
morphology must appear:

(95)   Mario sta raggiungendo la vetta.
       Mario is reaching the top.

In (95), the closed event is intensionalised by the progressive morphology. As
stated, the progressive introduces in the semantics a process that gives rise to the
continuous reading.


## Notes

1.   The term *anchoring* must be understood in the sense of Enç (1987).

2.   These phenomena are usually considered by Sequence of Tense theories. Let us
stress, however, that our aim here is *not* to develop a full theory of Sequence of Tense
phenomena but only to investigate some syntax/semantics interface effects. See also
chapter 5 and chapter 6 for an analysis of some data concerning the *consecutio
temporum et modorum* in Romance and Germanic.

3.   We will see in §4.2. that the contrast perfectivity/imperfectivity is
independent of the notion of continuity, even if, in several cases (but interestingly
not in all of them) they overlap.

4.   Alternatively, one could disregard the properties of eventive domains and
adopt a mere quantificational view. We think, however, that such an approach would
not suffice to capture the relevant interactions. For interesting proposals in this
direction, see Delfitto & Bertinetto (1995b) and Lenci & Bertinetto (1995).

5.   For an introduction to mereology, see Simons (1987). Landman (1991)
discusses many applications to natural language semantics. Finally, Moltmann
(1997) critically reexamines the pros and cons of classical mereology and proposes a

modalised view of the *part-of* relation. Our treatment here is inspired by Pianesi & Varzi (1996a, 1996b).

6.   The mereological setup includes the following definitions (see Pianesi & Varzi 1996a):

| (i) | $x=y$ | $=_{df}$ | $P(x, y) \wedge P(y, x)$ | $x$ is identical with $y$ |
|---|---|---|---|---|
| (ii) | $O(x, y)$ | $=_{df}$ | $\exists z \, (P(z, x) \wedge P(z, y))$ | $x$ overlaps $y$ |
| (iii) | $X(x, y)$ | $=_{df}$ | $O(x, y) \wedge \neg P(x, y)$ | $x$ crosses $y$ |
| (iv) | $PO(x, y)$ | $=_{df}$ | $X(x, y) \wedge X(y, x)$ | $x$ properly overlaps |
| (v) | $PP(x, y)$ | $=_{df}$ | $P(x, y) \wedge \neg P(y, x)$ | $x$ is a proper part of $y$ |
| (vi) | $\sigma x \phi x$ | $=_{df}$ | $\iota x \forall y \, (O(y, x) \leftrightarrow \exists z \, (\phi z \wedge O(z, y)))$ | sum of all $\phi$ers |
| (vii) | $\pi x \phi x$ | $=_{df}$ | $\sigma x \, \forall z \, (\phi z \rightarrow P(x, z))$ | product of all $\phi$ers |
| (viii) | $x+y$ | $=_{df}$ | $\sigma z \, (P(z, x) \vee P(z, y))$ | sum of $x$ and $y$ |
| (ix) | $x \, y$ | $=_{df}$ | $\sigma z \, (P(z, x) \wedge P(z, y))$ | product of $x$ and $y$ |
| (x) | $x - y$ | $=_{df}$ | $\sigma z \, (P(z, x) \wedge \neg O(z, y))$ | difference of $x$ and $y$ |
| (xi) | $\sim x$ | $=_{df}$ | $\sigma z \, (\neg O(z, x))$ | complement of $x$ |
| (xii) | $U$ | $=_{df}$ | $\sigma z \, (z=z)$ | universe |

Here, $\phi x$ stands for any formula, and $\phi z$ is the result of substituting each free occurrence of $x$ in $\phi$ with $z$; $\iota$ is the definite description operator. Among the operators and relations introduced by means of (i) to (xii) the sum operator $\sigma$ plays a crucial role in the mereological theory. Given a (possibly infinite) number of events, $\sigma$ builds the unique event which is the sum of all of them. For instance, if $\phi x$ identifies the (possibly infinite) collection of past, present, and future eating events, then $\sigma x \phi x$ is the sum of all the events of eating which have occurred, are occurring, and will occur. In the finite case, if $x$ is the event of Mary's eating the first course, $y$ is the event of Mary's eating the main course, and $z$, that of Mary's eating the fruit and the cake, then applying $\sigma$ to them yields the entire event consisting of Mary's lunch.

7.   In the literature the opposition bounded/non-bounded is often used to characterise the aspectual properties of sentences such as (11). See, for instance, Smith (1991) and Guéron (1995). In the following sections we will define a more precise notion — namely *topological closure* — corresponding to boundedness.

8.   See Desclés (1989) and Jackendoff (1991) for topological approaches to aspect.

9.   The axioms in (12) are the mereological rendition of the Kuratowskian axioms for standard set-theoretic topology. See Kelley (1955).

10.   For the sake of simplicity, the formal theory takes the relation $B(x, y)$ as primitive, to be read as "$x$ is a boundary in $y$" (cf. Chisolm 1984). We could have started from the closure predicate directly, obtaining the same results. Examples (i) to (ix) reproduce a sample of derived topological relations and operators discussed in Pianesi & Varzi (1996a):

| (i) | $b(x)$ | $=_{df}$ | $\sigma z \, (B(z, x))$ | maximal boundary of $x$ |
|---|---|---|---|---|
| (ii) | $c(x)$ | $=_{df}$ | $x+b(x)$ | closure of $x$ |
| (iii) | $i(x)$ | $=_{df}$ | $x \sim b(x)$ | interior of $x$ |
| (iv) | $e(x)$ | $=_{df}$ | $\sim x \sim b(x)$ | exterior of $x$ |

| (v)    | $Cl(x)$     | $=_{df}$ | $x=c(x)$                                     | $x$ is closed                       |
|--------|-------------|----------|----------------------------------------------|-------------------------------------|
| (vi)   | $Op(x)$     | $=_{df}$ | $x=i(x)$                                     | $x$ is open                         |
| (vii)  | $C(x, y)$   | $=_{df}$ | $O(c(x), y) \vee O(c(y), x)$                 | $x$ is connected with $y$           |
| (viii) | $EC(x, y)$  | $=_{df}$ | $C(x, y) \wedge \neg O(x, y)$                | $x$ is externally connected with $y$ |
| (ix)   | $Cn(x)$     | $=_{df}$ | $\forall y \forall z\, (x=y+z \rightarrow C(y, z))$ | $x$ is self-connected        |

Here, $Cl$ is the closure predicate discussed in the text.

Such a topology maintains, within a mereological setting, the basic insights of classical set-theoretic topology (see, among others, Kelley 1955). Importantly, the basic axioms can be proven to be equivalent to the mereological counterpart of the Kuratowskian ones:

(x)     $B(x, y) \rightarrow B(x, \sim y)$

(xi)    $B(x, y) \wedge B(y, z) \rightarrow B(x, z)$

(xii)   $P(z, x) \wedge P(z, y) \rightarrow (P(z, b(x \times y)) \leftrightarrow P(z, b(x)+b(y)))$

11. The notion of *closure* and that of *telicity* must be kept separate (cf. Comrie 1976, Ch. 1 §1.1.1; de Praetere 1995, for a discussion). A sentence contains a telic event if the presence of a *telos* is entailed, that is, if the existence of a natural end point for the event is asserted. For instance, a perfective sentence such as *John ate an apple* is telic. The *telos* is the event at which the apple has been completely consumed. However, it is not the case that every sentence that is perfective is also telic, as in *John ran*. Therefore, the notion of telicity and that of perfectivity must be kept distinct. Comrie (1976, Ch. 1 and Ch. 6) points out that in many languages (for instance, the Slavonic languages) the perfective is the aspectually marked form, even if it is not possible to identify the marked member on the basis of language independent criteria. Simplifying the proposal we will argue for in this chapter, and rephrasing it in typological terms, we suggest that the perfective/imperfective opposition is not an equipollent opposition, but a privative one, in the sense of the Prague School, where the perfective is the marked option.

12. In Italian, the present tense is not perfective, whereas the past tense can be. Perfectivity in Italian can be associated with a morphological mark. The present perfect is marked by -*t*-, see chapter 3. The mark appearing on the imperfect — -*v*- —marks tense. The Italian simple past is a perfective past tense, where perfectivity is directly marked on the verbal stem (see fn. 27). The English verb is always marked as perfective (see §4.1.5.2.).

13. As will become clear later, the speech time and the speech event have the same status with respect to punctuality. More generally, it will be shown that whenever an event is punctual, so is its time, and vice versa.

14. The idea that time can be derived from events goes back at least to Russell (1936), where time instants were conceived of as maximal sets of pairwise simultaneous (or temporally overlapping) events, and to Whitehead (1929). More recently, Kamp (1979) and van Benthem (1983) have developed formal systems which take events as primary entities and time instants and intervals as derivative. However, they maintain that the temporal relation of *precedence* is primitive, though it applies directly to events. The procedure sketched in the text is inspired by Pianesi

& Varzi (1996a 1996b), who show that even temporal relations can be derived from the mereotopological properties of eventive domains.

15. For a formal proof, see Pianesi & Varzi (1996a).

16. We will drop the subscript, when indicating a temporal relation, whenever the divisor collection is recoverable from the context or not relevant for the discussion.

17. In general, it holds that the finer the divisor collection in an oriented event structure, the more temporal distinctions can be captured. Such a property can be exploited, for instance, to account for the shifts of perspective that are often found in temporal discourses:

(i)     John arrived when Mary did.

For (i) to be true it is not required that John's arrival be exactly simultaneous with Mary's arrival. What is needed is that the two events are parts of the same minimal divisor — for instance, the same hour or day. Therefore, the simultaneity requirement of a *when*-clause in a sentence such as (i) corresponds to a constraint on the oriented eventive structures available for interpreting (i). Only the oriented structures in which $d(arrival\text{-}of\text{-}John) = d(arrival\text{-}of\text{-}Mary)$ are admissible. Such a property will turn out to be useful to account for the notion of punctuality, to which we will return in a while.

Time entities — that is, time points and/or intervals, can be construed from oriented eventive structures by adopting the strategies discussed by Kamp (1979) and by van Benthem (1983). We will not consider the details here. Note, however, that even the temporal entities so derived will depend on the choice of the particular oriented eventive structure and, ultimately, on the choice of $\delta$. More generally, different choices of the divisor collection give rise to different temporal structures which differ both according to the time entities they contain and to the relations holding among them. This way, to a given eventive domain $\mathscr{E}$, an entire family of temporal structure can be associated (see Pianesi & Varzi 1996b).

18. See Verkuyl (1993) for an extensive discussion of the continuous tense criteria.

19. See Kelley (1955). For a discussion of these questions in a mereotopological setting, see Pianesi & Varzi (1996a).

20. The notion of *temporal proper part* is defined in the obvious way:

(i)     $TPP_\delta(e_1, e_2) \equiv_{df} PP(d(e_1), d(e_2))$

Here *PP* is the *proper part-of* relation introduced in fn. 6.

21. The relation $at(t, e)$ can now be understood in the following way: $at(t, e)$ holds iff $d(e) = t$.

22. Consequently, it can easily be *classified* as a verb by a child who is learning the language.

23. These considerations hold independently of the precise structure which is associated to the initial numeration. For the sake of completeness, however, let us point out that, in accordance with the proposals discussed in chapter 3, the aspectual category mentioned in the text is lower than T2 and higher than V. That is, it is Cinque's (1994, 1995a) ASP2. We will not delve into structural details any further. We are discussing the inherent properties of the verb — namely, its features, which must

be checked by means of overt or covert movement, without directly addressing structural questions here.

24. We will not investigate here whether (33a) entails that John witnessed the entire act of eating — that is, up to the *telos*. Van der Does (1991) expresses this opinion. However, judgements are not clear on this point. Consider the following sentence:

(i)     Queen Elizabeth saw Shakespeare write Hamlet.

According to some informants, for the report to be true it is not necessary that Queen Elizabeth witnessed every phase of the event of writing Hamlet. However, it is true that the completion of the perceived event must be entailed. Concluding, it seems possible that what is perceived and what is reported are not the same thing, even if the latter entails the former.

25. Consider also that neither in English nor in Italian can a stative predicate be the complement of a perception verb:

i.      *I saw John know/knowing mathematics.
ii.     *Ho visto Gianni sapere la matematica.

Predicates belonging to the other classes — that is achievements and activities — on the contrary are perfectly acceptable in both languages. On Italian, see Cinque (1995b, Ch. 8), Guasti (1993), and Rizzi (1992).

26. Chierchia (1995a) suggests that in the case of the habitual interpretation, the quantificational feature and the generic operator are the head and the specifier, respectively, of an aspectual projection. In the case of stative predicates, however, they are internal to the VP projection. In this respect we differ from Chierchia because we propose that in both cases there is an aspectual projection specifying the verb as an habitual or as a stative.

27. Let us briefly consider what happens in Italian. As we said in §4.1.5.2., in Italian (and in all the other languages of the Romance and Germanic domain) the verb is marked $[+ V; - N]$ without the need to associate it to an aspectual feature. Therefore, the verb can have the continuous reading in the present tense. If the present tense verbal form is instead either an eventive predicate with an habitual reading or a stative, it must be associated with Chierchia's aspectual projection. Finally, in Italian there is a verbal form — the simple past — which does not bear any explicit aspectual morpheme but turns out to be perfective. Consider the following examples:

(i)     Gianni legge un libro.
        Gianni reads a book (continuous).
(ii)    Gianni lesse un libro.
        Gianni read(SP) a book (perfective).
(iii)   Gianni leggeva un libro.
        Gianni read(IMPF) a book (imperfective).

Example (i) has the usual continuous (imperfective) reading which eventive verbs have in Italian. The simple past in (ii) only has the perfective reading, contrasting with the imperfect form in (iii). Notice however, that even if the form appearing in (ii), *lesse* (read-SP), has no explicit aspectual morpheme, it is derived from a stem which differs with respect to the one of the present and the imperfect, *legge* (reads) and *leggeva* (read-IMPF). In the first case we have *less-* and in the second *legg-*. We propose that the stem *less-* corresponds to a lexical entry which has some properties in common with the English verbal form, in that it is inherently marked for perfectivity, contrasting with the present stem (from which the imperfect is also derived). The habitual reading of the present tense and the properties of statives are obtained as in English. In other words, the two languages do not differ to this extent.

28. See Kratzer (1981, 1991a), Farkas & Sugioka (1983), and Schubert & Pelletier (1987, 1989) for an analysis of conditional sentences and *when*-clauses exploiting dyadic operators. See also chapter 5.

29. In a habitual sentence the restriction and the matrix are largely determined by topic and focus considerations. In general, a topic contributes to the restriction (Partee 1995) and a focus contributes to the matrix (Diesing 1992). A logical form scheme such as (43) in the text applies to sentences where time arguments are topics, such as (ia):

(i)     a.   L'anno scorso, *alle cinque* Mario prendeva il tè.
            Last year, *at five* Mario had(IMPF) tea.
        b.   L'anno scorso, Mario prendeva il tè *alle cinque*.
            Last year Mario had(IMPF) tea *at five*.

When the time argument is focused, it contributes to the matrix, as in (ib), and the following scheme applies:

(ii)     Gen $e$[TP$(e, j) \land$ contextually-relevant$(I) \land \phi(e) \land$ R$(e, s)$] $\exists t$ (at$(e, t)$)

Such differences, however, do not affect the argument in the text.

30. In Chierchia (1995b), as well as in Lenci & Bertinetto (1995), the external interval is bound by an existential quantifier taking scope over the whole logical form. That is, these authors propose (i) as a logical form for (41a), instead of (42) in the text:

(i)     $\exists I$(C$(I) \land$ R$(I, s) \land$ Gen[.........].........)

Where, again, $R(I, s)$ is whatever relation the tense contributes.

We prefer to maintain that the external time $I$ and the tense contribution both enter into the restriction, to emphasise the fact that $I$ is contextually determined — that is, it is familiar. Apart from this fact, there are no relevant differences between the two representations.

31. On this point, cf. Chierchia (1995a) and Lenci & Bertinetto (1995).

32. We will not provide a theoretical account for all the phenomena concerning the progressive in English. We will only focus on the aspectual properties which are relevant for our analysis.

33. For the relevant notion of accessibility, see Landman (1992).

34. Following Parsons (1989, 1990), one might argue that an extensional semantics for the progressive can be maintained if we admit the existence of partial

objects in our worlds. Such a move seems independently necessary to account for sentences such as (i), uttered by pointing to a not yet finished house:

(i)      This is my new house.

The phrase *my new house* does not refer to an object that completely satisfies the predicate *house*, since it is still being built. In this sense, such an object is a partial one.

Normally, processes of creation go through a series of stages. At each stage some new part of the object comes into existence. That is, the direct object of such verbs is an *incremental theme* (Dowty 1991). If this is the case for (54), then the extensional, partial object semantics of Parsons can account for the truth conditions of (54). When God was interrupted, He had already created some parts of a unicorn. That is, He had already created a partial unicorn. Therefore, although (54) does not commit us to the existence of actual complete unicorns, it requires us to believe in the existence of partial unicorns. Landman excludes the reading of *create* in which Parsons's partial object semantics could apply (from Landman 1992, p. 9): "There is nothing incoherent about the assumption that the process (or this particular process) of creating a unicorn is indeed a process of the above form [*during which no object whatsoever exists*]: a lot of preparatory work and at the end — flash — a unicorn. ... The point is that in this situation we cannot claim that in (9) [*ex. (54) in our text*] we quantify over an incomplete, an unfinished unicorn, because there is no such thing" .

35. Once the semantics of the progressive are properly defined, the continuous reading of the progressive can be accounted for without any further stipulation. For instance, partially adopting a proposal by Delfitto & Bertinetto (1995a), we can hypothesise that continuous readings involve a hidden universal quantifier over times. Hence, (i)b is the logical form for the Italian sentence (i)a:

(i)      a.   Maria corre.
              Maria runs(continuous).
         b.   $\exists e(\text{run}(e) \land (\forall t[\text{TP}(t, S)]\text{TP}(t, e)))$

That is, (ia) is true iff there is a non-closed event $e$ of running, such that every temporal part of the speech event is a temporal part of $e$. The general scheme for continuous readings is the following:

(ii)     $\exists e(\phi(e) \land (\forall t[\text{TP}(t, I) \land \text{contextually-relevant}(I)]\text{TP}(t, e)))$

In (ii) $\phi$ is the predicate contributed by the VP, and $I$ is a contextually relevant temporal interval (cf. Delfitto & Bertinetto 1995a for the reasons requiring such an entity). When the verb is in the present tense, $I$ is the speech time and logical forms such as the one in (ib) are obtained.

Returning to progressive sentences, the predicate $\phi(e)$, that is, the denotation of the VP — must be substituted by $PROG(e, \lambda e'.(\phi(e') \land Cl(e')))$ — that is, the denotation of the complex V+-*ing*. Therefore the logical form of (iiia) is (iiib):

(iii)    a.   John is running.
         b.   $\exists e(PROG(e, \lambda e'.(\phi(e') \land Cl(e'))) \land (\forall t[\text{TP}(t, S)]\text{TP}(t, e)))$

36. This analysis can also be extended to the other languages of the Romance-Germanic domain, which, however, will not be directly investigated here.

37. In our discussion we will disregard the cases in which the temporal reference is provided by the extralinguistic context. In fact, as far as our hypothesis is concerned, these cases do not seem to make any difference.

38. In this chapter we consider only the present-in-the-past reading provided by the imperfect. In chapter 5 and chapter 6 we will extend our analysis to subjunctive contexts.

39. See Guéron (1995) for similar considerations concerning French.

40. Consider the following example:

(i)　　　*Mentre Mario ha cantato, Carlo disegnava.
　　　　　While Mario has sung, Carlo drew(IMPF).

The incompatibility of *mentre* with perfective tenses can be accounted for by assigning the logical form scheme in (iib) to the structure (iia):

(ii)　　a. Mentre $\phi$, $\psi$
　　　　b. $\exists e(\psi(e) \wedge (\forall t[TP(t, e)] \exists e'(\phi(e') \wedge at(t, e'))))$

The temporal variable bound by the universal quantifier is that of the $\phi$ clause. In §4.1.2. we argued that the eventive variable of perfective tenses is existentially bound. Therefore, if the tense of the $\phi$-clause in (iia) is perfective, the temporal variable of the event is already bound, and a vacuous quantification arises. This discussion also entails that in (iib) such devices as Existential Disclosure (Chierchia 1995b) are not available.

41. Cf. Inclán (1991) for the same data in Spanish.

42. Cf. Vet (1983) for a discussion of similar French examples.

43. See Higginbotham (1995a) for a discussion of the role of utterances, thoughts, wishes, and the like in the interpretation of clauses.

44. Let us stress again that, as remarked in §4.1.3., (90) does not require the anchoring time/event to be intrinsically punctual. Example (90) states that the event in question has the relevant properties as far as it functions as an anchor. The framework outlined in §4.1.4. permits to express such a fact by hypothesising that the interpretation of clauses is performed not only with respect to a world parameter but also with respect to a *temporal structure* parameter. That is, we have $[\![ 'clause' ]\!]^{w, \tau}$, where $\tau$ ranges on temporal (oriented eventive) structures. Thus (90) amounts to requiring that $\tau$ be such that the temporal anchor is punctual in it. In this sense, a temporal anchor $t$ provides a set of minimal constraints on the temporal structure to be considered for interpretive purposes. Only those in which $t$ is punctual are available.

45. Notice that a past tense in English can be continuous, despite its being perfective:

(i)　　　While Mary ate an apple, John sang a song.

The event of eating must be interpreted continuously — otherwise, the sentence would have no interpretation at all (*while* semantically selects a continuous event).

Furthermore, (i) clearly implies that the apple has been eaten; compare it with the following sentence:

(ii)    While Mary was eating an apple, John sang a song.

In (ii) there is no entailment that the apple has actually been eaten.

46. Similarly, achievement predicates cannot appear in embedded contexts with the simultaneous interpretation, even in the imperfect. Consider the following contrast:

(i)    a. #Mario mi ha detto che Gianni raggiungeva la vetta.
           Mario told me that Gianni reached (IMPF) the top.
       b. Mario mi ha detto che ieri alle cinque Gianni raggiungeva la vetta.
           Mario told me that yesterday at five Gianni reached the top.

Sentence (ib) seems to have, at least for certain speakers, a reportive flavour. This reading is similar to that obtained with the present tense in sentences such as:

(ii)    Messner raggiunge la cima del K2.
        Messner reaches the top of K2.

The same pattern can be observed when the imperfect appears in non-embedded contexts:

(iii)    Ieri alle cinque Messner raggiungeva la cima del K2.
         Yesterday at five Messner reached(IMPF) the top of K2.

Hence the generalisation seems to be that continuous tenses (i.e., the present tense and the imperfect) force reportive readings of perfective predicates. An exception to this generalisation is constituted by *while* contexts, where in spite of the perfectivity of the predicate, no reportive interpretation is obligatory.

# 5

# On the Semantics and Morphosyntax of the Italian Subjunctive

## 5.1. Toward a semantics of the subjunctive

In this section we consider the distribution of the subjunctive and the indicative in Romance and Germanic languages. We will argue that the observed patterns can be explained on semantic grounds. Within the so-called *possible world* approaches to semantics, it is commonplace to assume that the contribution of a subordinate clause to the meaning of the sentence is computed by relativising its truth conditions to a set of worlds (mainly) determined by the matrix verb. We will see that the properties of such a set of worlds, constituting the *context of evaluation* of the clause, play a crucial role in the explanation of mood choice. The core of this idea is not new: it constitutes the basis of the traditional view according to which the indicative/subjunctive dichotomy is a manifestation of the *realis/irrealis* opposition. We will argue that an analysis in terms of realis/irrealis is not empirically adequate, and we will develop a semantic component providing a fine grained classification for the contexts of evaluation. On the other hand, we will argue that since the indicative/subjunctive distinction is a binary one, the typology identified by the semantic component must be collapsed into two main classes: the indicative one and the subjunctive class. Our proposal with respect to crosslinguistic variation is the following: languages might differ in the way they reduce the classes identified by the semantic component into the binary *grammatical* distinction. We will show that the various contexts can be ordered along a *continuum*, and that languages tend to behave alike at the extremities, selecting consistently the indicative or the subjunctive, whereas they differ with respect to the intermediate contexts, which in some languages emerge with the indicative and in other ones with the subjunctive.

In §5.1.1. we present the basic facts illustrating the distribution of the indicative and the subjunctive moods in the Romance and Germanic languages. We will then discuss some previous accounts and conclude that among the various theories which have been proposed, the realis/irrealis theory is probably the most promising. According to such an account, the indicative is the mood of *realis* contexts, whereas the subjunctive is employed in *irrealis* contexts. As we stated above, such a simple binary distinction will be shown to be too coarse grained in that it cannot account for crosslinguistic variation. We will propose that a correct account of mood choice must incorporate the distinction between the *notional* mood, which is a semantic classification of the evaluation contexts, and the *grammatical* mood. To implement these ideas we will adopt a framework according to which notional mood is closely related to modality (Farkas 1992a, b), where modality is to be understood in the sense of Kratzer (1991a), as discussed in §5.1.3.

In §5.1.4. we will develop our account by discussing mood in subordinate clauses.

Section 5.1.5. considers factive contexts. These sentences constitute a counterexample for many approaches to mood choice, including those based on the realis/irrealis distinction. It is well known, in fact, that the truth of the complement of a factive verb is presupposed; therefore, the indicative is expected. We will see that in some languages, however, such clauses require the subjunctive.

In §5.1.6. we will discuss sentences with fiction verbs such as *dream*. These too are problematic for many current theories. Clearly, they create irrealis contexts, yet the mood of the complement clause is always the indicative. The final sections, §5.1.7. and §5.1.8., are devoted to a discussion of the factors determining the intralinguistic variation in mood choice and to the effects of negation and topicalisation.

In the appendix to this chapter we will consider Italian conditionals, focusing on *if*-clauses. We will see that a proper account of the data requires the extension of the notion of counterfactuality and a modification of the proposals by Kratzer (1981, 1991a) on the interpretation of counterfactuals.

### 5.1.1. The data

As is well known, the indicative is the mood of matrix clauses with affirmative illocutionary force. The data are consistent across languages:

(1)    a.  Gianni è/*sia arrivato.               (Italian)
            Gianni has(IND)/(SUBJ) arrived.
      b.  Jean a/*ait arrive.                (French)
            Jean has(IND)/(SUBJ) arrived.
      c.  Hans ist/*sei angekommen.        (German)
            Hans has(IND)/(SUBJ) arrived.
      d.  John has/*have(SUBJ) arrived.      (English)

The subjunctive appears in matrix clauses only if they have a special illocutionary force, such as optatives, again consistently across languages:

(2)     a.  (Che) Dio ci aiuti!                                    (Italian)
            (That) God us-help(SUBJ)!
        b.  (Que) Dieu nous aide!                                  (French)
            (That) God us-help(SUBJ)!
        c.  Gott hilfe uns!                                        (German)[1]
            God help(SUBJ) us!
        d.  God help(SUBJ) us!                                     (English)

The subjunctive is also used in matrix contexts when commands are expressed:[2]

(3)     a.  (Che) Mario parta!                                     (Italian)
            Lit. : (that) Mario leave(SUBJ)!
            Let Mario leave!
        b.  Gehe Paul weg!                                         (German)
            Lit. : go(SUBJ) Paul away!
            Let Paul go!

Although possible in matrix clauses, the subjunctive is mainly used in subordinate clauses. Interestingly, mood choice varies crosslinguistically, depending on the matrix predicate.

Before proceeding to analyse the determinants of mood choice, however, a classification of the different subordinate contexts is needed. In this work we adopt Hooper's (1975) proposal, which has the advantage of providing a rather extensive classification of verbal predicates. Given our purposes — namely, the analysis of the factors determining mood choice — we will at times depart from Hooper's classification, as for instance, in the case of her *strong assertive* predicates. This class is rather heterogeneous with respect to the subjunctive/indicative distinction, and we prefer to restrict our attention to a subset — namely, the so-called *verba dicendi*.

Finally, we will also consider predicates that have not been discussed by Hooper, because their behaviour is particularly interesting for our purposes. For instance, we will discuss the volitional verbs *to want, to wish*, as well as fictional verbs such as *to dream*.

Hooper (1975) considers two orthogonal dimensions for classifying English predicates. The first concerns the *factive/non-factive* divide, and the second, the *assertive/non-assertive* divide. This produces a fourfold classification: assertive factive, non-assertive factive, assertive non-factive, and non-assertive non-factive predicates. Furthermore, the assertive non-factive predicates are further split into *weak* and *strong* assertives. The resulting classification is reported in the following tables (from Hooper 1975):

(4) a.

| | Assertive | | | | Non-assertive |
|---|---|---|---|---|---|
| | Weak Assertive | Strong Assertive | | | |
| Non-factive | think | acknowledge | insist | agree | be likely |
| | believe | admit | intimate | be afraid | be possible |
| | suppose | affirm | maintain | be certain | be probable |
| | expect | allege | mention | be sure | be conceivable |
| | imagine | answer | point out | be clear | be unlikely |
| | guess | argue | predict | be obvious | be impossible |
| | seem | assert | prophesy | be evident | be improbable |
| | appear | assure | postulate | calculate | be inconceivable |
| | figure | certify | remark | decide | doubt |
| | | charge | report | deduce | deny |
| | | claim | say | estimate | |
| | | contend | state | hope | |
| | | declare | suggest | presume | |
| | | divulge | swear | surmise | |
| | | emphasise | testify | suspect | |
| | | explain | theorise | | |
| | | grant | verify | | |
| | | guarantee | vow | | |
| | | hint | write | | |
| | | hypothesise | | | |
| | | imply | | | |
| | | indicate | | | |

(4) b.

| | Assertive (semifactive) | Non-assertive (true factive) |
|---|---|---|
| Factive | find out | regret |
| | discover | resent |
| | know | forget |
| | learn | amuse |
| | note | suffice |
| | notice | bother |
| | observe | make sense |
| | perceive | care |
| | realise | be odd |
| | recall | be strange |
| | remember | be interesting |
| | reveal | be relevant |
| | see | be sorry |
| | | be exciting |

The factive/non-factive distinction is a traditional one (Kiparsky & Kiparsky 1971). Factive predicates presuppose the truth of their complements:

(5)    John knows/regrets that Mary left.

In order for (5) to be true it must be the case that Mary actually left. Furthermore, this is not so by virtue of (5). That is, (5) does not assert the truth of the complement. Rather, knowledge about such a fact must already be present in the discourse. This is not the case with non-factive predicates:

(6)    John said that Mary left.

The truth of (6) does not require the truth of the complement. Concerning the distinction between assertive and non-assertive predicates, both Bolinger (1968) and Hooper (1975) provide a number of syntactic tests justifying this distinction. Assertive predicates allow their complements to be preposed:

(7)    a.  The wizard will deny your request, I think. (Hooper 1975, ex. 3)
       b.  *Many of the applicants are women, it's probable.

According to Hooper, there are two assertions in (7a): one concerning the fact that the wizard will deny the request and the other expressing a particular attitude of the speaker toward such a proposition. Note that complement preposing cannot be accomplished under negation:

(8)    *The wizard will deny your request, I don't think.

Under negation and interrogation, strong assertive predicates allow the operator scope to be restricted to subparts of the complement (neg raising):

(9)    a.  The boss didn't say that he wanted to hire a woman, the personnel
           director said that. (Hooper 1975, ex. 27)
       b.  John was not surprised that Hilda was so competent.
       c.  Did he say it was raining? (ibid., ex. 32)
       d.  Was he surprised that Hilda was so competent? (ibid., ex. 37)

In (9a), negation focus may either be on the main clause predicate or on the complement clause. In the former case, the meaning is that *the boss didn't say such and such*; in the latter, the sentence means that what the boss actually said was that he didn't want to hire a woman. In (9c), the question is ambiguous between a situation paraphrasable as *Did he say x?*, where *x* happens to be *it was raining*, and a situation in which the questioner is asking about the weather. On the other hand, with factive (non-assertive) verbs, such as *surprise* in (9b) and (9d), negation and interrogation only involve the main predicate.

Furthermore, assertive predicates allow so-called root transformations:

(10)   a.  Sally plans for Gary to marry her, and it seems that marry her he will.
       b.  *Sally plans for Gary to marry her, and it's likely that marry her he
           will.

Complement preposing permits a distinction of the factive predicates into assertive (also called *semifactives*) and non-assertive (also called *true factives*):

(11)    a. She was a compulsive liar, he soon realised.  (Hooper 1975, ex. 137)
        b. *She was a compulsive liar, she forgot.  (ibid., ex. 141)

Consider also (12):

(12)    a. It will be probable that Mary will regret that John left early.
        b. It will be probable that Mary will discover that John left early.

In (12a) the complement of the true factive predicate *regret* is presupposed.
Example (12b) has two readings: in the first the complement of the semifactive
*discover* is presupposed, whereas in the second it is not.
    Let us now go back to the distribution of the subjunctive and the indicative in
the various contexts across languages. With semifactives (e.g., *to know*, *to
discover*), the indicative appears consistently, both in Romance and in Germanic:

(13)    a. Gianni sa che Paolo ha/*abbia scritto una lettera.          (Italian)
           Gianni knows that Paolo has(IND)/(SUBJ) written a letter.
        b. Hans wißt, daß Paul einen Brief geschrieben hat/*habe.   (German)
           Hans knows that Paul has(IND)/(SUBJ) written the letter.

With volitional verbs (e.g., *to want*, *to wish*) the subjunctive is the common
choice in Romance:[3]

(14)    a. Paolo vuole che tu venga.                                (Italian)
           Lit. : Paolo wants that you come(SUBJ).
        b. Paul veut que tu viennes.                               (French)
           Lit. : Paul wants that you come(SUBJ).
           Paul wants you to come.

This is also the case in Romanian (see Farkas 1992a), Spanish, Catalan, and
Portuguese.
    The Germanic languages that have a productive subjunctive, such as German
and Icelandic, exhibit a similar pattern:[4]

(15)    Ich wollte, du wärest hier.                                 (German)
        Lit. : I wanted you were(SUBJ) here.
        I wish you were here.

(16)    Jón vill að Mária fari.                                     (Icelandic)
        Lit. : Jón wants that Mária leave(SUBJ).
        Jón wants Mária to leave.

In many cases, however, languages diverge as to the choice of the mood of the
subordinate clause. This is the case with verbs of reported communications
(*verba dicendi*):

(17)  a.  Gianni ha detto che Mario ha/*abbia scritto la lettera.     (Italian)
          Gianni said that Mario has(IND)/(SUBJ) written the letter.
      b.  Jean a dit que Marie a/*ait ecrit une lettre.          (French)
          Jean said that Marie has(IND)/(SUBJ) written a letter.
      c.  Hans sagte, daß Paul einen Brief geschrieben hat/habe.    (German)
          Hans said that Paul has(IND)/(SUBJ) written the letter.
      d.  Jón segir að tveir *eur/séu fjórir.     (Thráinsson 1990, ex. 8)
                                                              (Icelandic)

          Jón says that two plus two is(IND)/(SUBJ) four

Thus, Italian *dire* (to say) selects the indicative, as does the corresponding French
verb. The same happens in Romanian, Spanish, Catalan, and Portuguese.[5] In
German, however, *sagen* admits both the indicative and the subjunctive, whereas
Icelandic only selects the subjunctive. Languages also differ with respect to the
*true factives* :

(18)  a.  A Maria dispiace che Paolo sia/?*è partito.        (Italian)
          To Maria displeases that Paolo has(SUBJ)/(IND) left.
      b.  Marie regrette que Paul soit/est parti.           (French)
          Maria regrets that Paul has(SUBJ)/(IND) left.
      c.  Maria regreta ca Paul a plecat.      (Farkas 1992a, ex. 2)
                                                              (Romanian)

          Mary regrets that Paul has(IND) left.

In Italian these verbs select the subjunctive, while in Romanian they require the
indicative, and in French they admit both. See §5.1.5. in the following
discussion for a more detailed analysis of these facts.

   Crosslinguistic differences can also be found with *belief* predicates. Italian,
Portuguese, Icelandic and German can select the subjunctive, whereas French,
Spanish, and Catalan require the indicative:[6]

(19)  a.  Mario crede che Andrea abbia mangiato.           (Italian)
          Mario thinks that Andrea has(SUBJ) eaten.
      b.  Je croi que il est/*soit parti.                  (French)
          I think he has(IND)/(SUBJ) left.

Finally, there are subordinate contexts where we find intralinguistic variation in
mood choice, at least in certain languages. This is the case, for instance, with
*believe* in Italian, German, and Portuguese:

(20)  a.  Gianni crede che Mario abbia/ha mangiato troppo.     (Italian)
          Gianni believes that Mario ate(SUBJ)/(IND) too much.
      b.  Hans glaubt, daß er krank sei/ist.                  (German)
          Hans believes that he is(SUBJ)/(IND) sick.

The subjunctive is also used in adverbial clauses — for example, in the protasis
of counterfactual conditionals, both in Italian and in German (see the appendix
for further discussion):

(21)   a.  Se Mario fosse arrivato in orario, lo avrei incontrato.    (Italian)
           If Mario had(SUBJ) been on time I would have met him.
       b.  Wenn Mario pünktlich wäre, hätte ich ihn getroffen.      (German)
           If Mario had(SUBJ) been on time I would have met him.

Furthermore, observe that mood choice is also affected by the presence of certain items such as negation and the interrogative operator:

(22)   Mario non ha (mai) detto che Giuseppe è/sia impazzito.
       Mario never said that Giuseppe has(IND)/(SUBJ) gone crazy.

(23)   Sai se Giuseppe è/sia partito?
       Do you know whether Giuseppe has(IND)/(SUBJ) left?

Negation in (22) and the interrogative operator in (23) make the subjunctive possible in the complement clause of a *verbum dicendi* and of a semifactive, respectively. This also happens in French with *croire* and in Icelandic with past semifactives, such as *know*:

(24)   a.  Jean ne croit pas que Marie soit parti.                  (French)
           Jean does not believe that Marie has(SUBJ) left.
       b.  Jón vissi ekki að María hefði farið.                     (Icelandic)
           Jón did not know that M. had(SUBJ) left.

Finally, syntactic operations, such as clitic left dislocation, can affect mood choice:

(25)   a.  Che Mario fosse/era sciocco, Carlo lo sapeva.
           Lit. : That Mario was(SUBJ)/(IND) silly, Carlo it-cl knew.
           Carlo knew that Mario was silly.
       b.  Carlo sapeva che Mario *fosse/era sciocco.
           Carlo knew that Mario was(SUBJ)/(IND) silly.

In the topicalised complement clause of (25a) the subjunctive is acceptable, in contrast with (25b).

From the analysis of the data presented here, it can be concluded that the indicative is selected in assertive matrix clauses and in the complements of Hooper's semifactive predicates consistently across languages. The same holds of the subjunctive in matrix clauses which have a special illocutionary force (such as optatives, commands, etc.) in the complement clauses of volitional verbs, and in the protasis of counterfactuals. The cross-linguistic differences show up with the other predicates analysed above: *verba dicendi*, Hooper's true factives, and *belief* verbs. Here languages exhibit a seemingly fuzzy pattern of mood choice that will be more deeply investigated below. The existence of intralinguistic variation was noted too, as in the case of the Italian verb *credere* (believe), exemplified in (20). Furthermore, other factors (aside from the illocutionary force of matrix clauses and the matrix predicate of embedded clauses) can affect mood choice: negation (cf. ex. 21), the interrogative operator (cf. ex. 22), and such syntactic operations as clitic left dislocation (cf. ex. 23).

### 5.1.2. Previous accounts

In this section we discuss some existing accounts of mood choice. It will be noted that, although many of them correctly capture part of the relevant data, they often fail to account for crosslinguistic variation. This observation is particularly important in connection with the realis/irrealis view, to be discussed in a while. We will conclude that such a theory is on the right track but that the kind of distinction it considers is too coarse grained to achieve a correct account of all the relevant phenomena. It will be argued that a better theory should allow for finer distinctions to be captured. These ideas will be further developed in the following sections.

Suppose that the choice between the subjunctive and the indicative were due only to the idiosyncratic selectional properties of the matrix predicate. Then, for a given verb, the mood of the complement clause should be fixed once and for all. This way, however, the pattern in (22) to (25) and in (20) cannot be easily captured. Furthermore, such an analysis could not be extended to non-subordinate contexts — that is, it could not explain the occurrences of the subjunctive in main clauses (cf. exx. 2 and 3).[7] Therefore, the presence of the subjunctive in a subordinate and in a matrix clause should be regarded as two completely distinct phenomena. This, however, hardly seems a line of investigation worth pursuing.

On the other hand, it is also clear that the predicate of the main clause does play a role in the choice of the mood of the complement. Let us propose the following intuitive idea, which will be discussed in more detail in a while. Suppose that there is a set of semantic factors X which directly and possibly uniquely determine the mood of a clause, and that X is largely, though not exclusively, determined by the matrix predicate.[8] In the next sections we propose that X consists of certain properties of the semantic context the subordinate clause is evaluated in. The notion of *evaluation context* for a clause will be made clearer below. For the moment, let us observe that each clause needs a semantic environment with respect to which its truth is assessed. Such a semantic environment constitutes the evaluation context of the clause. According to this view, the subjunctive/indicative distinction corresponds to the different kinds of properties of such contexts. Finally, matrix predicates affect mood selection by contributing to the determination of the characteristics of the evaluation contexts.

The traditional explanation of mood choice as connected to the realis/irrealis opposition can be understood in light of these considerations. According to such a view, the indicative mood appears whenever the (proposition corresponding to) a given clause is true of the actual world (realis), and the subjunctive appears when it is not true of the actual world.

This theory can explain the fact that in counterfactual *if*-clauses and in the complements of volitional verbs the subjunctive is (almost) always found, whereas the mood of affirmative main clauses is the indicative. On the one hand, in fact, counterfactuals presuppose the falsity of their *if*-clauses. On the other, the complement of volitional verbs need not be true (and usually are not true) of the actual world.

However, the realis/irrealis distinction is too coarse grained to account for the whole pattern of data presented above. Consider, for example, true factive and semifactive predicates. Both take complements the truth of which is presupposed. Therefore we would expect the indicative in their subordinate clauses. This is not the case, however, as examples (13) and (18), reproduced here, show:

(13)    a.   Gianni sa che Paolo ha/*abbia scritto una lettera.       (Italian)
            Gianni knows that Paolo has(IND)/(SUBJ) written a letter.
        b.   Hans wiβt, daβ Paul einen Brief geschrieben hat/*habe.   (German)
            Hans knows that Paul has(IND)/(SUBJ) written the letter.

(18)    a.   A Maria dispiace che Paolo sia/?*è partito.           (Italian)
            To Maria displeases that Paolo has(SUBJ)/(IND) left.
        b.   Marie regrette que Paul soit/est parti.             (French)
            Marie regrets that Paul has(SUBJ)/(IND) left.
        c.   Maria regreta ca Paul a plecat  (Farkas 1992a, ex. 2)      (Romanian)
            Maria regrets that Paul has(IND) left

*Know* is a semifactive predicate, and, consistently with the realis/irrealis view, its complements always have the indicative. *Regret* is a true factive verb, according to Hooper's (1975) classification. However, its subordinate clause can have either the subjunctive or the indicative in Italian and French (Italian speakers prefer the subjunctive), and only the indicative in Romanian (and in Icelandic). This crosslinguistic variation is unexpected, since according to the realis/irrealis thesis only the indicative should appear. Similarly, Farkas (1992a) notes that verbs such as *to dream*, *to fantasise*, and the like (the so-called fiction verbs) obviously never force the hearer to assume the truth of their complements. Therefore they should select the subjunctive. However, the subordinated clauses of *to dream* always take the indicative in Italian, French, and Romanian, whereas the complements of *to imagine* take the indicative in French and Romanian, and both the subjunctive and the indicative in Italian:

(26)    a.   Gianni ha sognato che Pietro ha/*abbia ricevuto il premio Nobel.
                                                (Italian)
            Gianni dreamed that Pietro has(IND)/(SUBJ) received the Nobel Prize.
        b.   Jean a reve que Pierre a/*ait reçu le Nobel          (French)
            Jean dreamed that Pierre has(IND)/(SUBJ) received the Nobel Prize.
        c.   Ion a visat ca Petru a primit/*sa fit primit premium Nobel.
                                           (Romanian)
            Ion dreamed that Petru has(IND)/(SUBJ) received the Nobel Prize.

Finally, the realis/irrealis view also fails to account for the intralinguistic variability that many contexts exhibit. That is, it cannot easily accommodate the fact that a language allows both the indicative and the subjunctive in a given context (cf. ex. 20).

Another theory that deserves mentioning is the one tracing back the mood distinction to the assertive/non-assertive opposition. Originally proposed by

Bolinger (1968), it has been further elaborated by Hooper & Terrel (1974) and by Hooper (1975). According to this view, *assertive* predicates, such as *to say, to communicate*, and the like, select the indicative, whereas *non-assertive* ones select the subjunctive.

Similarly to the theory based on the realis/irrealis distinction, this one, too, successfully predicts certain patterns while failing to account for others. In particular, true factive and semifactive predicates do not fit with this picture. As seen above, Hooper classifies the former as non-assertive, and the latter as assertive, predicates. Consequently, it is not clear why Italian has the indicative under *to know* and the subjunctive under *to regret*, as predicted, whereas Icelandic has the indicative in both cases, contrary to expectations. Similar considerations also hold for fiction verbs. Finally, Hooper does not provide a precise theoretical account of what her assertive/non-assertive distinction amounts to. She only suggests that assertive predicates commit the speaker to the truth of the embedded proposition whereas non-assertive predicates do not. As we saw, however, fiction verbs provide a counterexample.

Despite their different perspectives, the theories we briefly reviewed take mood choice to be largely determined by semantic factors. The role of the main predicate, as anticipated, is to *set the stage*. That is, it affects certain properties that are relevant for mood choice, whether those properties are the veridicality (realis/irrealis) of the complement proposition or the fact that the complement is asserted or not. These theories fail to predict the crosslinguistic variation in the subordinated clauses of factive (e.g., *to regret, to be surprised, to worry*, etc.) and fiction verbs, and the intralinguistic variation seen in (20).

Another line of reasoning led other researchers to propose that the source of mood choice is a *[± definite]* feature on the complement clause.[9] Working on French, Tsoulas (1994) observes that there is a parallel between extraction out of so-called picture nominals and extraction out of complement clauses:[10]

(27)  a.  *Que te demandes-tu qui a dit qu' Alex a vu? (Tsoulas 1994, ex. 13)
          What$_i$ you/refl wonder [who$_j$ [t$_j$ said that Alex saw t$_i$]]
      b.  Que te demandes-tu qui a decide de voir? (ibid., ex. 14)
          What$_i$ you/refl wonder [who$_j$ [t$_j$ decided to see t$_i$]]
      c.  Que te demandes-tu qui a voulu que Sophie voie? (ibid., ex. 15)
          What$_i$ you/refl wonder [who$_j$ [t$_j$ wanted that Sophie see(SUBJ) t$_i$]]

(28)  a.  *What do you want to see these pictures of?
      b.  What do you want to see pictures of?
      c.  What do you want to see a picture of?

Extraction is possible out of indefinite picture nouns (cf. (28)). Similarly, extraction out of infinitive and subjunctive clauses, as in (27b) and in (27c), improves with respect to extraction out of indicative clauses (cf. 27a). To explain the parallelism, Tsoulas (1994) resorts to a notion of *clausal definiteness,* arguing that this property can be realised either at the level of C or at the level of I. He then proposes the following generalisation:

(29)  (i)   *[- definite]* in C gives rise to (inflected) infinitive type structures with particular COMPs.

      (ii)  *[- definite]* in I results in specific morphology, sometimes bound, e.g. French subjunctive, and sometimes not, e.g. English infinitival *to*. (Tsoulas 1994, ex. 51)

According to Tsoulas the indefiniteness/definiteness distinction affects the time of the event (or the event itself) of the complement clause. More precisely, he suggests that the complement of a sentence such as (30a) should be treated on a par with an indefinite such as (30b):

(30)  a.   Maria vuole che Sofia venga.
           Maria wants that Sofia come.
      b.   A man in the garden.

In (30b) the indefinite does not refer to any particular individual. In frameworks such as those developed by Heim (1982) and Kamp (1984), it would simply introduce an individual variable. The same holds, according to Tsoulas, of the time of the complement event in (30a).

Sentences such as (31) may constitute a problem for theories hypothesising that the crucial factor in determining mood choice is the definiteness of the time (or event) variable:

(31)  Mario vuole che Giovanna parta/*parte domani alle tre.
      Mario wants that Giovanna leave(SUBJ)/leaves(IND) tomorrow at three.

The mood of the verb in the subordinate clause of (31) is the subjunctive, yet the event time is definite, because of the definite $E$-adverbial *alle tre* (at three) (cf. chapter 3), contrary to what a theory like Tsoulas's would predict. The problem cannot be solved straightforwardly by claiming that the definite/indefinite distinction affects the eventive variable rather than the temporal one. Following the standard view that the eventive variable of the verb is existentially bound, it is not even clear what its indefiniteness amounts to. Furthermore, assuming that eventive variables can be bound by other operators as well, the following example should count as counterevidence to the idea that definiteness is the crucial factor:

(32)  Mario credeva che Carlo telefonasse sempre alle tre.
      Mario believed that Carlo always phoned(SUBJ) at three.

Here the eventive variable of the subordinate verb is bound by the strong adverbial quantifier *sempre* (always). Strong quantifiers are definite, so (32) is unexpected. To conclude, this theory seems too vague on a crucial issue — namely, what is to count as a definite/indefinite time or event. Moreover, how could such an approach explain the intra- and interlinguistic variation described above? If a given language uses the subjunctive because, for instance, the time of the dependent clause is *[- definite]*, why can other languages use the indicative under the same conditions?

We conclude this review by observing that the importance of semantic factors in mood choice is widely acknowledged. In this respect, we think that the traditional realis/irrealis distinction, albeit too coarse grained to provide an adequate account, is on the right track. More precisely, the important insight is that mood selection depends on the kind of context in which the subordinated clause is evaluated and, furthermore, that the matrix predicate is just one of the factors which contributes to establish it. This view opens the way toward a unified account of mood in complement and main clauses, and permits an account of the influence of negation, interrogative operators, and of such syntactic operations as clause preposing. However, as seen above, the realis/irrealis distinction fails to yield the correct predictions in many cases. Most notably, it does not capture the crosslinguistic differences.

In the next sections we propose a view according to which mood is still a manifestation of a binary classification of the contexts in which a clause is evaluated.[11] Such a classification, however, differs from language to language. More precisely, it will be argued that (a) the contexts of evaluation for clauses are ordered according to their similarity with respect to a *basic* designated one which will be identified with that of simple assertions and (b) languages crosscut such an ordering, assigning the indicative to the contexts which are (judged to be) the closest to the basic one, and the subjunctive to those which are the farthest away. Eventually, the distinction between the indicative and the subjunctive is to be connected to the way languages classify evaluation contexts as similar or different, respectively, to that of assertions.

### 5.1.3. Mood and modality

In this section we introduce the background necessary to develop the account of mood choice just sketched. Following many authors (see, among others Farkas 1985, 1992a, 1992b; Portner 1994) we consider mood to be a manifestation of modality. In fact, we hypothesised that in the subordinate clause of a sentence such as *Mario crede che Carlo sia partito* (Mario thinks that Carlo has(SUBJ) left), mood choice is determined by the condition which rules the interpretation of the subordinate clause itself. Such conditions have traditionally been analysed by hypothesising the presence of a modal operator requiring the clause to be true in a particular set of worlds, distinguished from the actual ones, the so-called *doxastic alternatives* (Hintikka 1962; Cresswell & von Stechow 1982). Similarly, all the cases in the previous discussion involve clauses the truth conditions of which require the consideration of possible states of affairs that are different from the actual one, albeit possibly connected with it.

Our understanding of modality crucially involves the conversational backgrounds active when a sentence is uttered or introduced by modal words and predicates (Kratzer 1979, 1981, 1991a). As the term suggests, the notion of *conversational background* originates from the theory of assertions and, in particular, from the work of Stalnaker (1979).[12] Given a communicative setting (e.g., a conversation or a text), the relevant notion of context includes what is common to all the participants in the communicative exchange. When a speaker utters a sentence, he/she *presupposes* something concerning the other participants, and his/her assertion is evaluated with respect to this set of presuppositions. In turn, presupposed propositions are those that the speaker takes to be granted by the background of the conversation. As such, they constitute what Stalnaker calls the *common ground* of the conversation.[13] Such a set of propositions determines the *context set* of the conversation — that is, the set of all possible worlds which compatible with every proposition in the common ground.

Formally: Let $\mathcal{P}$ be the *common ground* of a conversation at a certain point — that is, the set of propositions that the speaker takes for granted. Then the *context set* determined by $\mathcal{P}$ is as follows:

(33)    $C(\mathcal{P}) = \{w \mid w \in p,$ for every proposition $p$ in $\mathcal{P}\}$

Equivalently, given that a proposition is a set of possible worlds, $C(\mathcal{P}) = \cap \mathcal{P}$. That is, the context set is the intersection of all the propositions in the common ground.

Both context sets and common grounds play a major role in the understanding of the nature of assertions. Propositions describe the world as being a certain way. The idea behind their formal correspondence with sets of possible worlds is that, in all generality, a given set of propositions may not provide enough information to pick up a single world but usually determines a set thereof, which the actual, real world (the true object of the propositions) belongs to. The notion of context set models such "live", active options — that is, the set of possible worlds each compatible with every proposition of the common ground and containing the actual world, the one the conversion aims at characterising. When a new proposition $p$ is added to a common ground, the effect is to filter out from the live options all the possible worlds that do not comply with $p$. This way, an assertion maps the current context set into one of its proper subsets. A conversation, viewed as a sequence of assertions, progressively narrows down the context set, at each step adding information (or, equivalently, reducing the uncertainty) about the way the world should be conceived of. Therefore the characterisation of the actual world is an asymptotic process, the state of complete knowledge possibly never being attained.

To exemplify, let $p$ be the propositional content of a sentence $s$ uttered in a conversation, and let $\mathcal{P}$ be the set of presuppositions (the common ground) at that point. Then $\mathcal{P}$ is transformed into $\mathcal{P} \cup \{p\}$ — that is, the set of propositions compatible with the new assertion, which becomes the new common ground. From the point of view of the corresponding context sets, in order to understand $p$ the participants in the conversation have to discard all the worlds in the current context sets $C$ that are not compatible with $p$ (i.e., any world $w$ such that $w \notin p$). Therefore, the new context set is $C' = C \cap \{p\}$. That is, the new context set consists of all the worlds that are compatible with the assertions previously made, as well as with the current assertion. Consider the following simple utterance:

(34)    Mary has climbed Mount Toby.

The assertion of (34) is felicitous only if the intersection of the current context set $C$ with the corresponding proposition $p$ is not empty. That is, it is felicitous only in case there are worlds, among those compatible with the current presuppositions, in which Mary has actually climbed Mount Toby.

We saw that asserted propositions are evaluated with respect to the current conversational background, the so-called common ground. The effect of the evaluation procedure is to add the new proposition to the set of presupposed ones and, at the same time, to narrow down the set of worlds (the context set) that corresponds to those presuppositions. Context sets can be seen as approximations to the actual world, and the conversation is a process, possibly converging at the limit, continuously refining such approximations.

This picture, though adequate for "normal" assertions, must be modified when dealing with modalised sentences. In particular, in these cases it might be necessary to consider not the whole common ground but one of its subsets. Consider (35):

(35)    Mary must have climbed Mount Toby.

This sentence has an epistemic meaning due to the modal *must*.[14] It could be paraphrased as: given the current state of knowledge, it must be the case that Mary has climbed Mount Toby. According to Kratzer's (1981, 1991a) analysis, two basic components (besides the modal operator) are crucial to the analysis of modality: the *modal base* and the *ordering source*. Both are sets of contextually determined propositions, thus bearing many similarities to common grounds.

Modal bases play the role of the more conventional *accessibility relations* of modal logic. They determine the set of worlds with respect to which the truth of modalised propositions is evaluated. Sometimes modal bases are explicitly introduced — for example, by means of phrases such as *according to what we know, according to the available evidence*, and so on. More often, however, they are made available by the context. This is the case with (35), where the context provides an epistemic modal base — that is, a modal base consisting of the known facts, and the available evidence (as the paraphrase given in the preceding discussion shows).

Formally, modal bases are sets of propositions associated with worlds by a function $f: W \rightarrow 2^{2^W}$. In the following paragraphs we will use the term *modal base* to refer both to the set of propositions this way determined and to the function $f$, and we will let the context disambiguate the intended meaning. Thus in (35), the modal base (function) is a function such that for each world $w$, $f(w)$ (the real modal base) describes what is known in $w$. Since a modal base is a set of propositions, we can associate it with the set of worlds where each such proposition is true, that is, $\cap f(w)$. We will call this set the *derived context set* (Roberts 1989).

An ordering source, again a set of propositions, orders the worlds in a derived context set according to the degree in which they realise a certain ideal, represented by the ordering source itself. Ordering sources can be formalised in a way similar to modal bases — that is, by representing them as functions mapping worlds into sets of propositions. As before, we will use the term *ordering source* ambiguously, to refer to both the function and its value. The ordering induced on possible worlds by a set of propositions can be defined as follows (Kratzer 1991a):

(36)  Let $A \subseteq W$, where $W$ is the set of possible worlds, and let $B$ be a set of propositions, i.e., $B \subseteq 2^W$, then $w_1 \leq_B w_2$ iff $\{p \mid p \in B \text{ and } w_2 \in p\} \subseteq \{p \mid p \in B \text{ and } w_1 \in p\}$ for every two worlds $w_1$ and $w_2$ in $A$.

Suppose $w$ is a world, $f$ is the function corresponding to a modal base such that $f(w) = A$, and $g$ is the function corresponding to an ordering source such that $g(w) = B$. Definition (36) establishes that, for every two worlds $w_1$ and $w_2$ in $A$, $w_2$ is not less than $w_1$ according to (the set of propositions) $B$ if and only if every proposition of $B$ that is true in $w_2$ is also true in $w_1$. Thus, worlds are ordered according to how many propositions in the ordering source they realise. If $B$ represents some sort of ideal or norm, then the greater the number of propositions of $B$ that are true in a world $w$, the closer $w$ is to realising the ideal.

As with modal bases, ordering sources can be introduced by phrases such as *in view of what is normal, in view of what is legal, rational, according to the law*, and so on. The context also plays an important role in providing the relevant information. This is what happens in (35), where the propositions of the ordering source describe what is the normal course of events. In (35) the modal *must* has a universal force. Let the relevant epistemic modal base be $f(w) = A$ (in view of what is known) and the ordering source be $g(w) = B$ (what the normal course of events is). Then the proposition corresponding to (35) is true in a world $w$ iff the proposition in the scope of the modal, *she has climbed Mount Toby*, is true in all the worlds of the derived context set $A$ come closest to the ideal established by $g$. That is, the proposition is true in all the worlds in which the relevant facts that belong to the epistemic modal base are true and that come closest to "what the normal course of events is".[15]

What is the relationship of modal bases and ordering source to common grounds? We already saw that they can be contextually determined. With respect to a conversation, this means that a modal base can be a subset of the conversational background itself. This is the case of epistemic modality (cf. ex. 35): "the known facts" of the epistemic modal base are presuppositions the participants share.[16] Given the relationship that modal bases of this sort entertain with common grounds, they can be called *realistic*:

(37)  Given a common ground $\mathcal{P}$ and its context set $C$, a modal base $f$ is *realistic* iff $f(w) \subseteq \mathcal{P}$, for every world $w$ in $C$.[17]

Realistic sets of propositions capture portions of the reality as it is described by the common ground. As a matter of fact, their derived context sets contain the conversational set.

On the other hand, when a modal base, or, more generally, a set of propositions, coincides with the common ground (that is, whenever it completely and only characterises the current context set), we speak of a *totally realistic* modal base:

(38)    Given a common ground $\mathcal{P}$ and its context set $C$, a modal base is totally realistic iff $f(w) = \mathcal{P}$, for every world $w$ in $C$.

Thus, in the case of assertions, the proposition is evaluated against a totally realistic modal base. Normal epistemic modal bases are simply realistic; therefore they more liberally admit worlds that are not in the current context set. This way they signal that the truth of the relevant proposition is attributed a greater degree of uncertainty than that ascribed to assertions. Finally, let us observe that while modal bases can be realistic this is hardly so with ordering sources. In fact, ordering sources are often normative, dictating ideals which the actual world cannot be completely assimilated to.[18]

Before we conclude this review of the semantics of modality, notice that it is possible to unify the analysis of simple assertions, such as (35), with that of modalised sentences. We proposed that assertions are evaluated with respect to the common ground, the effect of such an evaluation being one of narrowing the corresponding context set. In the literature (cf. among others Stalnaker 1978; Chomsky 1995), it has often been proposed that assertive force is due to a (null) operator. Let us assume that such an operator is one of necessity.[19] Then, we can unify the analysis of (35) and (34). In fact, the only difference between them concerns their respective modal bases (we neglect the modal ordering for the moment). In both cases, in fact, the new context set $C'$ is given by (39):

(39)    $C' = \{w \mid w \in C \text{ and for every } w' \in \cap f(w), Z(w', p)\}$

Here, $p$ is the proposition corresponding to *Mary has climbed Mount Toby*; $C$ is the current context set, $f$ is the modal base function, and $Z$ is a relation holding between worlds of the derived context set and $p$. In the case of (35), $f$ is totally realistic, that is, $f$ is such that for every world $w \in C$ it holds that $f(w) = \mathcal{P}$, where $\mathcal{P}$ is the current common ground (cf. ex. 38); $Z(w', p)$ reduces to $w' \in p$. Therefore the new context set, according to (39), is $C' = \{w \mid w \in C \text{ and } w' \in p\} = C \cap \{p\}$. That is, we obtain the formulation of $C'$ discussed at the end of the previous section.

In the case of (35), $f$ is required to be realistic — that is, $f(w) = \mathcal{P}' \subseteq \mathcal{P}$ (cf. (37)), and $Z(w', p)$ is complex, given that it incorporates the effect of the ordering source, along the lines of the preceding discussion.[20] In the next section we will consider the effect of ordering sources more closely.

To conclude, in this section we have presented Kratzer's (1981, 1991a) account of the semantics of modalised sentences. Such a theory is based on two different sorts of conversational backgrounds: modal bases and ordering sources, both specified by means of functions from possible worlds into sets of propositions. Modal bases play the role of the *accessibility relation* found in standard (possible world theoretic) approaches to modal semantics. In other words, a modal base specifies the worlds in which the proposition in the scope of the modal is to be evaluated. Ordering sources, on the other hand, capture the observation that the understanding of a modalised sentence often implies the use of idealised states of affairs describing the way the world should be — that is, *according to the law*, or *according to what is the normal course of events*, and so on. The joint effect of modal bases and ordering sources is to force the evaluation of the modalised proposition in those worlds of the modal base that better realise the given ideal or norm.

In the next section this theory will be applied to the semantics of mood. In particular, we will argue that the contexts of evaluation for a proposition can be ordered along a number of dimensions, according to their resemblance to the *standard* constituted by totally realistic modal bases (i.e., common grounds). The rationale of this idea is that notional mood is a way for classifying clauses, or, better, utterances and parts of utterances, with respect to the standard constituted by assertions. Grammatical mood — in our case, the distinction between the subjunctive and the indicative — corresponds to a simplification of such classifications into a binary one. For a given language, contexts of evaluations classified as *similar* to the standard require the indicative, whereas those classified as *different* require the subjunctive. This account renders explicit an intuition already present in the theory based on the realis/irrealis distinction: the indicative is the mood of assertion-like clauses, and the subjunctive, that of non-assertion-like ones.

Let us finally add a few comments. Here we understand *notional mood* to be the complex of semantic factors concerning the classification and ordering of the contexts in which the truth conditions of clauses are assessed. This view is related to the original proposal by Jespersen (1924) according to which notional mood describes a characteristic of sentence use. More precisely, it concerns the speaker's commitment about the truth of the sentence in the actual world. The notion of speaker commitment, in turn, can be formalised by means of the properties of the semantic environment in which the truth of the sentence is to be evaluated; that is, given the framework developed above, by means of the properties of the relevant modal base and ordering source. Extending these ideas to clauses, we arrive at the conclusion sketched above: notional mood amounts to a classification of the contexts of evaluation for a clause according to the properties of the modal base and of the ordering source.

Such a classification can be complex and affected by many parameters. As suggested above, *grammatical mood* corresponds to simpler classifications obtained from more complex ones. In this work, given that we are only considering the indicative and the subjunctive distinction, we will assume that such a simpler classification is a binary one. Grammatical mood, however, cannot be reduced to a (simplified) semantic classification. The two notions are partially independent: each of them obeys the rules and principles of the module it belongs to — that is, semantics and syntax, respectively. In particular, grammatical mood is a morphosyntactic property encoded by means of a feature, *mood*. Therefore, the properties of grammatical mood can be understood in the usual ways — in terms of such concepts as the strength or the interpretability of the feature *mood*, of its capability of triggering the movement of other items (Attract/Move-F), and so on. We return to a closer analysis of some syntactic phenomena which crucially involve the feature *mood* in §5.2. Notional mood, on the other hand, involves the properties of the semantic context in which a clause is evaluated. As such, it plays a role in every language, even in those having a very impoverished system of grammatical moods, such as English. The relationship between the two notions is an interpretive one: a given grammatical mood, such as the subjunctive, is interpreted as signalling that the clause it appears in must be evaluated in a semantic environment having certain properties. In other words, such a relationship is established at the point where LF representations are processed by the semantical-conceptual system. In the following discussion we will not specify the relationships between grammatical and notional mood any further. Given what we have stated, the problem is part of the more general question of how LF representations are mapped onto semantical-conceptual representations, a question we will not address here. What we are interested in is clarifying the formal correspondences between the two abstract notions. The proposal sketched above, which will be discussed at length in the next sections, goes in this direction: the relevant correspondence is that between a complex classification and a simplified one encoded by means of the values of the feature *mood*.

### 5.1.4. Mood in subordinate clauses

Let us reexamine a divide that is intuitively close to the realis/irrealis one — namely, the realistic/non-realistic distinction. In discussing (34) and (35), the property of being realistic was attributed to conversational backgrounds — that is, modal bases and ordering sources. In particular, a realistic conversational background is a subset of the common ground. Within the theory of modality developed above, the main role of modal bases and ordering sources consists in determining the actual context against which the truth of propositions is to be evaluated. In the case of (35), the interaction of the epistemic modal base with the ordering source (the normal course of events) gives rise to a non-realistic *context of evaluation*. To see this, consider the worlds where the modalised proposition is evaluated. Among the worlds belonging to the context set, they are the closest to the ideal established by the ordering source. That is, according to (36), they contain maximal sets of normative propositions.

We already pointed out that often ordering sources consist of non-realistic sets of propositions, this being a manifestation of a general property of norms and ideals: they are never true of the actual world. This is the case with (35), where the ordering source corresponds to the norm given by *what is the normal course of events*. As a consequence, *Mary has climbed Mount Toby* is evaluated in a context which is non-realistic. In the case of (34), a simple assertion, the modal base is totally realistic, the ordering source is null, and the evaluation context is totally realistic.[21]

Let us consider now other types of ordering sources, such as deontic ones:

(40)    John must go.

Example (40) involves a deontic code such that the evaluation of the truth of the corresponding proposition $p$ requires *John goes* to be true in all the worlds complying with such a code.

More precisely, let $\mathcal{P}$ and $\mathcal{C}$ be the common ground and the context set, respectively, of the current conversation at the point where (40) is uttered. Assume that the modal base is empty — that is, that $f(w) = \varnothing$ for every $w \in \cap \mathcal{P}$. Then the derived context set is $W$, the set of all possible worlds. The deontic code imposes a normative ideal on possible worlds. Thus, there is an ordering source $g$ corresponding to it. The modal force is *necessity*, and (40) is true in a world $w \in \mathcal{C}$ iff *John goes* is true in every possible world that is closest to the ideal established by $g$ (cf. n. 15). This set of worlds forms the domain of evaluation for the complement proposition. It is clearly non-realistic, for the same reason given above: we do not assume that the actual world complies with deontic standards.

Among the contexts considered in §5.1.1., the following ones induce non-realistic domains of evaluation for the embedded clause: volitionals, desideratives, and directives. Consider sentences with volitional and desiderative predicates:

(41)    a.  Gianni vuole che Maria parta.
            Lit. : Gianni wants that M. leaves(SUBJ).
            Gianni wants Maria to leave.
        b.  Gianni desidera che Maria parta.
            Lit.: Gianni wishes that Maria leaves(SUBJ).
            Gianni wishes that Maria would leave.

In both cases, the proposition *Mary leaves* is evaluated with respect to the set of John's wishes and desires. Such a set being normative, John's desires contribute the ordering source by establishing a *bouletic* conversational background. Bouletic backgrounds are non-realistic, since we cannot assume that anyone's desires are realised in the current world.[22]

The two main verbs in (41) differ with respect to the kind of modal bases they require. A verb such as *want* requires the subject to believe it possible for the embedded proposition to become true. A verb such as *wish*, on the other hand, does not impose such a condition. This difference explains the relative oddity of (42a) and the relative acceptability of (42b):

(42)    a.  #Gianni vuole che Maria attraversi l'Atlantico a nuoto.
            Lit. : Gianni wants that Maria swims across the Atlantic.
            Gianni wants Maria to swim across the Atlantic.
        b.  Gianni desidera che Maria attraversi l'Atlantico a nuoto.
            Lit. : Gianni wishes that Maria swims across the Atlantic.
            Gianni wishes that Maria would swim across the Atlantic.

For (42a) to be true in the actual context set, it must be the case that we attribute to John the belief that it is possible for Mary to swim across the Atlantic. Example (42b), on the other hand, does not require any such belief of John's. John may wish something without believing it to be realisable. Such a contrast between wants and wishes explains the possibility of wishes being counterfactuals (see Portner 1994):

(43)  a.  John wants the earth to be flat.
      b.  John wishes the earth were flat.

Suppose the roundness of the earth is shared common knowledge. Then an utterance of (43b) merely reports a desire by John. On the contrary, by uttering (43a) a speaker is attributing to John the belief that the relevant state of affairs can somehow be brought about (e.g. by magic).[23] Similar considerations hold for hopes with respect to wishes (cf. Portner 1994):

(44)  a.  ??Jill hopes that Jane won, though she knows that she didn't.
      b.  Jill wishes that Jane won, though she knows that she didn't.

We can account for this pattern of data by hypothesising that a verb such as *wish* has an empty modal base. In the case of *want*, the modal base is non-empty and consistent with the subject's beliefs. Eventually, the evaluation context of the subordinated clause is consistent with the subject's beliefs.[24]

This analysis of volitional and desiderative predicates can be extended to desiderative main clauses by considering them as implicitly modalised:

(45)  Che Dio ci aiuti!
      God help us!

In (45) an implicit desiderative operator is present which has an effect similar to that of the explicit desiderative predicates just discussed. As in the case of *want* and *wish*, the ordering source is bouletic. In the case of commands and directives, the ordering source is deontic:

(46)  Gianni richiede che Maria parta alle tre.
      Gianni demands that M. leave at three o'clock.

In (46) the modal base is empty and the ordering source is deontic. Again, the analysis can be extended to directive main clauses, by assuming an implicit modal operator:

(47)  Che Mario vada!
      Lit. : that Mario go(SUBJ)!
      Let Mario go!

Interestingly, desiderative, volitional, and directive contexts consistently induce the subjunctive across languages. Moreover, a non-empty ordering source is always involved and the relevant evaluation bases are non-realistic. Thus, observationally, non-realistic evaluation contexts and non empty ordering sources pattern together with respect to the choice of the subjunctive as the (grammatical) mood of the modalised clause. The cases considered so far do not allow us to say whether the two factors are independent with respect to mood choice. It could be, in fact, that both non-null ordering sources and non-realistic evaluation contexts influence the mood of the clause, or that only one of them has an effect. To see which is the case, let us consider non-realistic contexts with null ordering sources, such as those provided by belief predicates and *verba dicendi*.

To understand a sentence such as (48)

(48)　　John believes that Mary is sick.

one must consider the way reality is according to John. This can be conceived of in terms of John's doxastic alternatives to the actual world. Roughly speaking, we can imagine that John is presented with different states of affairs — for instance, by means of a video screen. The believer is requested to indicate those which he could think to be in. The singled-out states of affairs (possible worlds) form John's doxastic context set. Thus, instead of sets of propositions characterising the real world, it is now necessary to consider sets of propositions depicting a private view of reality. As a consequence, a modal base for (48) need not share anything with the current common ground, at least in principle; therefore, it is non-realistic. The ordering source for (48) is null, and the evaluation context for the embedded clause of (48) is non-realistic.

Recall that non-null ordering sources crosslinguistically require the subjunctive. Such a consistency is lost if the evaluation base is simply non-realistic. In the case of belief verbs, French and Romanian select the indicative, whereas Italian, Icelandic, and German select the subjunctive (cf. (19), repeated here for simplicity):

(19)　　a.　Mario crede che Andrea abbia mangiato.　　　　　　(Italian)
　　　　　　Mario thinks that Andrea has(SUBJ) eaten.
　　　　b.　Je croi que il a/*ait parti.　　　　　　　　　　　(French)
　　　　　　I think he has(IND)/(SUBJ) left.

We argue that the variation in mood choice with belief predicates reflects a corresponding variation concerning the classification of the contexts of evaluation they induce. On the one hand, in fact, the modal bases of belief predicates are similar to common grounds: as pointed out in note 20, ordering sources have the effect of making truth conditions local to certain subsets of the derived context set. On the other hand, when the ordering source is null, each world in the derived context set is relevant for the truth of the modalised proposition, at least in principle.[25] In this respect, the contexts of evaluation created by belief predicates are similar to common grounds. In both cases all the worlds in the (derived) context set are relevant for the truth conditions of the proposition in question.[26]

On the other hand, common grounds and the modal bases of belief predicates differ in that the former consist of the shared facts about the current world, whereas the latter depict private, internal realities. Importantly, this means that the two context sets may have nothing in common (i.e., their intersection can be empty).

We propose that languages such as Italian (and Icelandic and German) which require the subjunctive under belief predicates, are sensitive to these differences with respect to common grounds. French and Romanian, on the contrary, assimilate the derived context sets of belief predicates to common grounds, for the reasons seen here. Accordingly, the indicative is required with these verbs. Therefore, the presence of a non-null ordering source is one of the parameters along which the similarity between evaluation contexts and common grounds is assessed. Contexts determined on the basis of non-null ordering sources are the farthest away from ordinary common grounds. This explains the crosslinguistically consistent choice of the subjunctive.

When the ordering source is null, other considerations may be relevant for mood choice. For instance, while discussing belief predicates we concluded that their modal bases do not (necessarily) share anything with the common ground. We also saw that, in the case of belief predicates, the choice of the subjunctive in Italian can be explained by hypothesising that this language is sensitive to such a parameter.

It can be concluded, therefore, that Italian is sensitive to a parameter constituted by the properties of the intersection between a modal base and the common ground. When such an intersection can be empty, Italian requires the subjunctive. Other languages, such as French and Romanian, are not sensitive to such a property. On the contrary, they classify the modal bases of belief predicates as similar to common grounds, along the lines of the preceding discussion. Consequently, they use the indicative.

Let us now consider the so-called *verba dicendi* — that is, predicates such as *say, tell, report, write,* and so on. The crucial property of these verbs is that they refer to a communicative setting which is not the current one. The communicative setting can consist of another conversation, as with *say* and *declare,* or a different discourse situation, as with *write.* We hypothesise that the ordering source is null and that the modal base consists of the shared facts, the presuppositions, valid in the reported communication setting. Consider the following examples:

(49)   John said that Mary wrote a letter.

(50)   a.  Gianni ha detto che Mario ha/*abbia scritto la lettera.     (Italian)
           Gianni said that Mario has(IND)/(SUBJ) written the letter.
       b.  Jean a dit que Marie a/*ait ecrit une lettre.              (French)
           Jean said that M. has(IND)/(SUBJ) written a letter.
       c.  Hans sagte daß Paul einen Brief geschrieben hat/habe.      (German)
           Hans said that Paul has(IND)/(SUBJ) written the letter.
       d.  Jón segir að tveir *eur/séu fjórir. (Thráinsson 1990, ex. 8)
                                                                      (Icelandic)
           Jón said that two plus two is(IND)/(SUBJ) four.

Example (49) is true with respect to the current conversational background iff the complement clause is true in the conversational background of the reported conversation. Examples (50a) and (50b) show that the Romance languages select the indicative mood with *verba dicendi*. German usually requires the subjunctive, although the indicative is admitted (cf. (50c)). Finally, in Icelandic we only find the subjunctive (cf. (50d)).

It should be noted that, while all the languages considered here select with a *verbum dicendi* the same mood as they select with *belief* verbs, Italian requires the indicative. This fact must be due to some property of *verba dicendi* which, at least for Italian, differentiates them from *belief* verbs. Such a property cannot be the realistic/non-realistic distinction, for the modal bases of *verba dicendi* are clearly non-realistic. A sentence such as (49) is true even if nothing of what is said, written, reported, and so on is taken as true in the current common ground.

We will show that the relevant property is essentially the same we saw above when discussing belief verbs. Italian is sensitive to the nature of the intersection between the modal base and the common ground. Consider the two discourse fragments in (51):

(51)   a.   John said that donkeys fly.
       b.   John thinks that donkeys fly.

Example (51a) is odd, at least when compared with (51b). The latter reports a (wrong) belief of Johns'. Its acceptability shows that belief reports are not affected by the correctness of what is believed. Therefore, the oddness of (51a) cannot be due to the fact that John must have believed that *donkeys fly* in order to say what he is reported to have said. We argue that the contrast between (51a) and (51b) is due to the different context of evaluation that verbs such as *say* and *believe* create. Beliefs are private to the believer. One may believe, counterfactually, that donkeys fly. As seen above, in fact, the derived context set of *belief* is not required to share anything with the current common ground. Things are different, however, with *verba dicendi*. When a proposition $p$ is asserted (be it *said, written, reported,* etc.), it must match the current common ground. The latter consists not only of the propositions asserted up to the point when (the sentence corresponding to) $p$ is uttered but also of some facts, shared among the participants of the conversation, without which no communication would be possible — for instance, facts concerning the way the physical and human world is conceived of; culturally established facts; and so on. Such propositions are part of the common ground of *every* communicative setting.[27] Hence the common grounds of every two conversations share a number of presuppositions. Formally, let $\mathcal{P}_1$ and $\mathcal{P}_2$ be two common grounds pertaining to two different conversations. Then it is always the case that $\mathcal{P}_1 \cap \mathcal{P}_2 \neq \varnothing$. As we saw, this is not necessarily so with beliefs: when talking about someone else's opinions we need not attribute to him/her any other belief beyond the one reported. We argue that it is the existence of such a common set of presuppositions among communicative settings that makes the difference with respect to belief predicates and also explains the contrast between (51a) and (51b).

For John to have said what he said, it is required that he acted as if the content of his assertion was appropriate with respect to the original conversation. For the content of his assertion to be reported as in (51a), without any further qualification (e.g., that no one believed him), it must be the case that such a content is actually compatible with the common ground of the *reported* conversation. The latter, however, shares a number of basic facts with the common ground of the *current* conversation; among them there is information excluding the fact that donkeys can ever fly. Eventually, (51a) is odd because it reports an assertion that contradicts presuppositions that are shared by different communicative settings.

To make these considerations more precise, let us introduce the notion of a *weakly realistic modal base*:

(52)  Given a common ground $\mathcal{P}$ and its context set $C$, a modal base $f$ is weakly *realistic* iff $f(w) \cap \mathcal{P} \neq \varnothing$, for every world $w$ in $C$.

*Realistic* modal bases associate each world in the context set to subsets of the current common ground. *Weakly realistic* ones, such as those created by *verba dicendi*, are only required to have a non-null intersection with the common ground. In (51a), the complement proposition is evaluated in a derived context set that is weakly realistic. That is, it shares some presuppositions with the actual common ground. This is not necessarily so with the belief predicate of (51b).[28]

Returning to mood choice, the fact that Italian *verba dicendi* require the indicative in their subordinate clauses shows that in this language the indicative/subjunctive distinction corresponds to the distinction between weakly realistic modal bases and non-realistic ones. In French and Romanian, grammatical mood reflects the non-null/null ordering source divide. Thus, we see how two parameters, one concerning the presence/absence of a non-null ordering source, and the other the status of the evaluation context as to the realistic/non-realistic distinction, may affect mood choice crosslinguistically.[29] The two parameters are only partially independent. As already shown, in fact, whenever the ordering source is non-null the context of evaluation is non-realistic, and the subjunctive is consistently selected across languages. When the ordering source is null, languages can differ on the other parameter. Taken together, the two parameters determine an ordering of the contexts of evaluation that can be represented in the following way:

(53)  non-null  > non-realistic > weakly  > realistic > totally
                                   realistic              realistic

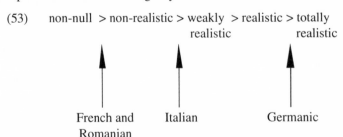

French and       Italian          Germanic
Romanian

At the end of the previous section we argued that notional mood is a property of the contexts of evaluation of clauses. In light of the considerations presented there, it can be concluded that such properties include both the two parameters discussed and the ordering they induce. Since these parameters reflect formal properties of the context of evaluations, and given that they are employed to classify them with respect to common grounds, we will use the term *structural similarity* to refer to both of them. The subjunctive/indicative distinction — that is, grammatical mood — corresponds to a reduction of an ordering such as the one depicted in (53) into a binary classification. As shown, the indicative mood is associated with the contexts to the right of the chosen point — that is, contexts that the given language classifies as structurally similar to common grounds. The subjunctive is found in the contexts to the left of the division — that is, the contexts classified as structurally different from common grounds.

### 5.1.5 Factive predicates

In §5.1.1. we saw that the predicates which Hooper (1975) calls *true factives* provide counterexamples to many an account of mood choice. In particular, the realis/irrealis theory has problems explaining why propositions whose truth is clearly presupposed require the subjunctive in languages such as Italian (cf. (18)), repeated here:

(18)  a.  A Maria dispiace che Paolo sia/?*è partito.             (Italian)
          To Maria displeases that Paolo has(SUBJ)/(IND) left.
      b.  Marie regrette que Paul soit/est parti.                 (French)
          Marie regrets that Paul has(SUBJ)/(IND) left.
      c.  Maria regreta ca Paul a plecat.  (Farkas 1992a, ex. 2)  (Romanian)
          Maria regrets that Paul has(IND) left.

As seen in §5.1.1., Romanian requires the indicative with true factives. Italian and French, on the other hand, have the subjunctive, even if the indicative is sometimes marginally accepted.

We follow Farkas (1992a), who claims that the property explaining the behaviour of these predicates is their emotional/evaluative character. For our purposes, we distinguish here between emotional and evaluative factives. Emotional factives, such as *be surprised*, *regret*, and *be worried*, depict a situation in which the event described in the complement clause causes the subject to be in a certain emotional state. On the other hand, evaluative true factive predicates such as *be strange*, *be odd*, *be relevant*, *be important*, and the like report an evaluation of a fact by the speaker.

Consider a sentence such as (54):

(54)   It is odd that John wrote a long letter to Mary.

Suppose that (54) is uttered during a conversation at a point where the common ground and the context set are $P$ and $C$, respectively. The effect of (54) is to restrict $C$ to the subset of strange worlds, that is, to those worlds where strange things happen, given that it is true that *John writes a long letter to Mary*. The worlds in $C$ which are "normal" are discarded. We can formalise these intuitions by hypothesising that the modal base $f$ describes *what is strange* and that the ordering source is the totally realistic background — that is, the common ground. Then (54) is true in $w$ iff in the *strange* worlds of the derived context sets, $f(w)$, which are maximally similar to the common ground, the embedded proposition of (54) is true.

Concerning emotional true factives, they can be analysed as involving causation. The event described by the complement clause (or the related fact) causes the subject to be in a state of *astonishment*, *regret*, *worry*, and so on. Causation has often been analysed as requiring counterfactual reasoning (see Lewis 1973; Bennett 1988). Consider (55):

(55)    It surprises me that John wrote that letter to Mary.

Understanding (55) amounts to setting up chains of counterfactual reasonings, concerning what my emotional state would have been like had John not written that letter to Mary. For instance, I did not expect him to write that letter, and the fact that my expectations have not been fulfilled causes my surprise. Thus, asserting (55) requires presupposing the truth of the complement and asserting the emotional state as well, as in (56):

(56)    Had John not written the letter, I would not have been surprised.

In the appendix, counterfactual conditionals will be analysed as crucially involving a non-empty ordering source.

Thus, there are two aspects that must be considered when accounting for such sentences as (54) and (55): (a) the truth of the complement clause is presupposed, and (b) there is a component of their meaning requiring the complement clause to be true with respect to a modal environment — that is, a modal base and an ordering source.

Following Farkas (1992a), we argue that (b) explains the obligatoriness of the subjunctive in Italian. In other words, the presence of a modal component with an ordering source forces the subjunctive in such a language, consistently with what we saw above (cf. (53)). Note, in fact, that if the modal component is absent, then the indicative is the only possible choice, as in the following sentence:

(57)    Mario sa che Giuseppe è/*sia arrivato.
        Mario knows that Giuseppe has(IND)/(SUBJ) arrived.

*Sapere* (know) presupposes the truth of its complement. However, differently from a predicate such as *rimpiangere* (regret), no modal component is involved, so that the mood of the subordinate clause is the indicative.

On the other hand, there are languages such as Romanian, Icelandic, and German which are sensitive only to the relationship of the complement proposition with the current common ground. Since in (54) and (55) the truth of those propositions is presupposed, these languages require the indicative in both of them. Finally, French, which admits both the indicative and the subjunctive with semifactive predicates, has an intermediate position between languages which select the subjunctive, such as Italian, and languages which require the indicative, such as Romanian.[30]


### 5.1.6. Dream *and its companions*

In §1.1 we saw that fiction predicates such as *to dream* are problematic for most of the current approaches to mood choice. In fact, their complement propositions are prototypically non-veridical; yet the indicative is the mood that all the Romance languages require in the complement of verbs such as *rever, sognare, a visa* (to dream), etc.:

(58)   a.  Gianni ha sognato che Pietro ha/*abbia ricevuto il premio Nobel.
                                                         (Italian)
           Gianni dreamed that Pietro has(IND)/(SUBJ) received the Nobel Prize.
       b.  Jean a reve que Pierre a/*ait recu le Nobel.              (French)
           Jean dreamed that Pierre has(IND)/(SUBJ) received the Nobel Prize.
       c.  Ion a visat ca Petru a primit/*sa fit primit premium Nobel.
                                                         (Romanian)
           Ion dreamed that Petru has(IND)/(SUBJ) received the Nobel Prize.

In §5.1.4. we hypothesised that mood choice is determined by the way a given language reduces a complex ordering of the evaluation contexts of clauses into a binary scheme. Contexts that, according to this scheme, are classified as structurally similar to common grounds require the indicative, whereas those that are classified as dissimilar require the subjunctive. We also saw that languages differ as to the way such a split is performed. French and Romanian distinguish strongly non-realistic contexts from the other contexts, the relevant factor being the absence versus the presence of a non-empty ordering source. Italian takes a lower threshold, corresponding to what we called weakly realistic contexts. Finally, languages such as Icelandic and German require the indicative (almost) only for contexts which are identical to common grounds — namely, totally realistic ones.

     Fiction verbs do not easily fit into this account. On the one hand, they create contexts that do not exhibit any clear ordering source and are obviously strictly non-realistic. Thus, we would expect the indicative mood to be used in French and Romanian, and the subjunctive to be used in Italian, contrary to fact (cf. (58)). Some parameter other than the structural similarity discussed above is presumably ruling mood choice in these cases.

     We propose that the relevant factor is connected with what has been called in the literature the *persistency* or *discourse scope* of modal operators (see Farkas 1992a). Such a notion has been discussed in connection with discourse anaphora (cf. Roberts 1989). Consider (59):

(59)  a.  Mario ha sognato che Carlo comprava una casa.
          Mario has dreamed that Carlo bought(IMPF) a house.
      b.  Era bella e spaziosa.
          (It) was beautiful and spacious.

The antecedent of *it* (*pro* in Italian) in (59b) is the indefinite *una casa* (a house) of the previous sentence. That is, it is an object existing only in Mario's dreams. Anaphoric connection of this type, however, is not always possible. Consider the following sentences:

(60)  a.  Mario pensa che Giuseppe abbia comperato una casa.
          Mario thinks that Giuseppe has(SUBJ) bought a house.
      b.  (Secondo lui), sarebbe bella e spaziosa.
          (According to him), it is(COND) nice and spacious.
      c.  Crede che sia bella e spaziosa.
          He thinks that it is(SUBJ) nice and spacious.
      d.  #E' bella e spaziosa.
          (It) is(IND) nice and spacious.

(61)  a.  Maria ha chiesto a Mario di prepararle un dolce.
          Maria asked Mario to prepare her a cake.
      b.  Deve essere alla cioccolata.
          (It) must be a chocolate one.

Example (60a), with the narrow scope reading of the indefinite, can only be followed by (60b) or (60c), but not by (60d). As argued by Roberts (1989), discourse anaphora require the antecedent to be accessible by the pronoun. Therefore, the proposition of the antecedent and that of the pronoun must be evaluated in the same context set. Such a condition is satisfied if the (derived) context set of the first proposition carries over to the second one. This is the case of normal assertions; each of them is evaluated in the same (though updated) context set of the previous ones. However, when the first proposition is evaluated in a (non-trivial) derived context set $C$, then an explicit modalisation is required in the second sentence, signalling that $C$ is to be used for it, too.

Alternatively, discourse anaphora is possible if the first proposition is accommodated in the derived context set of the second one.[31] When none of these strategies is applied, the anaphoric connection cannot be recovered.

The indefinite *una casa* in (60) introduces a referent into Mario's doxastic derived context set, and this referent can only be accessed from within it. Example (60d), in the normal case, is interpreted with respect to the current context set, which describes the actual world. However, there is no available antecedent for *pro*, and (60d) is ruled out. On the other hand, (60b) and (60c) explicitly signal, by means of the conditional mood and by iterating the belief predicate, respectively, that the corresponding propositions should be interpreted with respect to the same derived context set introduced by (60a). This way, the referent introduced by *una casa* (a house) can function as an antecedent for *pro*. Similarly, in (61), the possibility for the pronominal to take the indefinite *un dolce* (a cake) as an antecedent is due to the presence in (61b) of an explicit modal. Consider now (62):

(62)   a.   Mario ha detto che Gianni ha comperato una casa.
            Mario said that Gianni has bought a house.
       b.   E' bella e spaziosa.
            (It) is nice and spacious.

Here, the anaphoric relation is possible because the embedded proposition of (62a) can be directly *accommodated* in the current context set in such a way that it becomes a presupposition of the current conversation.

Examples (60) to (62) contrast with (59). In (60)-(62) the referent introduced by the indefinite is not available from within a different clause, unless some explicit connection is established — for example, by means of other modal operators, as in (60) and (61), or by means of accommodations, as in (62). Neither move is required in the case of (59). The referent introduced by the indefinite DP in (59a) is available to the pronominal in (59b), but the second clause is not explicitly modalised, nor is the first proposition accommodated. Rather, the second sentence is directly evaluated in the same derived context set as the clause containing the indefinite. In this respect *dream* creates a context of evaluation which is similar to that created by the assertive operator — that is, a common ground:

(63)   a.   John bought a house.
       b.   It is in a pleasant place.

In both (63) and (59) the referent introduced by the indefinite in the first sentence is readily available to the pronoun in the second sentence. Common grounds and the contexts created by *dream* are *persistent*. That is, once introduced, they remain available to the following sentences. On the contrary, doxastic context sets, those of desiderative predicates, and, in general, the derived context sets introduced by the predicates discussed in the previous sections are not persistent, so that some means is required in order for the anaphoric connection to be possible.

If we accept the degree of persistency of a conversational context as another possible measure of its similarity to common grounds, then the Italian fact in (58) can be explained by hypothesising that this language is sensitive to this parameter, too, in addition to the one discussed in the previous sections. Persistency need not play the same role in other languages. For instance, there is no reason to resort to this parameter to explain the indicative in French and Romanian with *rever* and *a visa* (dream). The structural similarity (of contexts of evaluation) is sufficient to make the correct predictions.

## 5.1.7. Intralinguistic variations in mood choice

In §5.1.1. we saw that in many languages there are contexts which accept either the subjunctive or the indicative. This is the case with the subordinate clauses of *belief* verbs in Italian and of *verba dicendi* in Romanian (and German):

(64)   a.   Gianni pensa che Mario abbia/ha mangiato una mela.
            Gianni thinks that Mario has(SUBJ)/(IND) eaten an apple.
       b.   Ion a spus ca Maria a plecat.
            Ion has said that Maria has(IND) left.
       c.   Ion a spus ca Maria sa plece imediat.
            Ion has said that Maria leave(SUBJ) immediately.

In the literature (see, among others, Farkas 1992a; Manzini 1994a) these alternations have often been associated with different meanings. As (64b) and (64c) indicate, this seems to be the case with Romanian *verba dicendi*. When the indicative is used, as in (64b), the sentence is a report about someone else's assertion. With the subjunctive, on the other hand, the sentence reports a directive, as in (64c). This pattern is predicted by our theory: directives entail the presence of an ordering source, so that the subjunctive is required.

However, in other cases, differences between the subjunctive and the indicative are not easily detected. This is what happens with the Italian example (64a). To our ears its meaning is not affected by mood changes in the complement clause.[32] Furthermore, it should be noted that the acceptability of the indicative in such contexts is largely affected by the idiolect of the speaker. In the colloquial register, many speakers tend to use the indicative under belief verbs to a greater extent than in other circumstances.

Such intralinguistic variation in mood choice, without corresponding meaning differences, are not unexpected in our theory. In §5.1.4. it was pointed out that belief verbs create evaluation context sets which can be classified as patterning with (assertion) context sets or not, according to the parameter considered. Thus, French classifies them as similar to assertion context sets because the relevant parameter is the presence/absence of a non-null ordering source. Standard Italian, on the other hand, also exploits the realistic/non-realistic properties of the modal base. In the case of belief predicates, it classifies their evaluation contexts as different from context sets. Example (64a) shows that it is possible for (a certain register of) Italian to consider only the first parameter, classifying the relevant contexts of evaluation as similar to conversational context sets.

If this is correct, then we expect such contexts of evaluation to behave like conversational context sets even in other respects — for example, we expect them to exhibit the same discourse scope as conversational context sets. Recall that in general it is not the case that discourse anaphora can pick up an antecedent from within a belief context, unless the clause containing the pronoun is explicitly modalised:

(65)    a.  *Mario pensa che Gianni abbia comperato una casa. E' bella e
            spaziosa.
            M. thinks that Gianni has(SUBJ) bought a house. (It) is(IND) nice and
            spacious.
        b.  Mario pensa che Gianni abbia comperato una casa. Sarebbe bella e
            spaziosa.
            M. thinks that Gianni has(SUBJ) bought a house. (It) is(COND) nice
            and spacious.

Consider, however, the following discourses:

(66)    a.  Mario crede che Ercole ha/??abbia fissato i confini del mondo tramite
            una colonna. E' di marmo rosa ed alta più di 50 metri.
            Mario believes that Hercules has(IND)/(SUBJ) fixed the boundaries of
            the world by means of a column. (It) is(IND) made of pink marble and
            more than 50 meters high.
        b.  Andrea riteneva che Gianni aveva/??avesse visto tre marziani. Erano
            verdi e venivano da Venere.
            Andrea believed that Gianni saw(IND)/(SUBJ) three martians. (They)
            were green and came from Venus.

As (66) shows, the pronominal in the second sentence can take the indefinite in
the subordinate clause of the first sentence as its antecedent, provided that the
mood of the clause introducing it is the indicative. The same possibility does not
obtain with the subjunctive. This fact cannot be accounted for by assuming that
the complement clause of the belief verb is accommodated in the common
ground, so that the referent introduced by the indefinite is available for the
pronominal in the second sentence. Indeed, as in the case of the verb *dream*
discussed in the previous section, nothing requires the participants in the
conversation to assume the existence of marble columns delimiting the world or
of martians. Instead, it seems that the doxastic context for the subordinated clause
of (66) can have a discourse scope wider than usual, so that the second sentences
are interpreted with respect to it. The data in (66) follow from our hypothesis:
the indicative in the subordinated clauses of the belief verb in (66) is possible
because the relevant contexts of evaluation are judged as similar to the
conversational context set. Therefore, the former share with the latter the
property of having discourse scope.

### 5.1.8. Other factors affecting mood choice

In §5.1.1. we briefly mentioned some situations in which mood choice can
diverge from the normal case. This is what happens with negation, interrogative
operators, and topicalisation. In this section we will briefly discuss these.

### 5.1.8.1. Negation

It is widely held that negation licenses the subjunctive:

(67)    a.  Mario non ha detto che Gianni è/?sia malato.
            Mario has not said that Gianni is sick(IND)/(SUBJ).
        b.  Mario non sapeva che Gianni era/fosse arrivato.
            Mario did not know that Gianni had(IND)/(SUBJ) arrived.

According to a number of scholars (Brugger & D'Angelo 1994; Giannakidou 1994), the data in (67) are evidence in favour of the view that the subjunctive is a negative polarity item, the indicative being a negative anti-polarity item. We are not going to present here a comprehensive account for the effects of negation on mood choice. We only point out some problems that any theory must address, and propose a possible direction of investigation along which a solution could be pursued.

Structurally, in order to affect mood choice, negation must appear in the superordinate clause. Negation has no such effects on the verb of its own clause:

(68)    a.  Mario non ha/*abbia mangiato una mela.
            Mario has(IND)/(SUBJ) not eaten an apple.
        b.  Mario ha detto che Giuseppe non è/*sia malato.
            Mario said that Giuseppe is(IND)/(SUBJ) not sick.

Note that this also holds for relative clauses:

(69)    Mario non ha mangiato una mela che Maria gli ha/*abbia regalato.
        Mario didn't eat an apple that Maria has(IND)/(SUBJ) given him.

However, these sentences improve if a polarity item, such as *mai* (never), or a particular intonation is used:

(70)    a.  Mario non ha mai mangiato una mela che Maria gli ha/?abbia regalato.
            Mario never ate an apple that Maria has(IND)/(SUBJ) given him.
        b.  Mario non ha mangiato UNA mela che Maria gli ha/?abbia(SUBJ) regalato.
            Mario never ate AN apple that Maria has(IND)/(SUBJ) given him.

Another problem concerns the fact that there are contexts where negation does not uniformly license the subjunctive. This is the case of the semifactive predicate *sapere* (to know):

(71)    a.  Mario non sa che Gianni è/*sia arrivato.
            Mario does not know that Gianni has(IND)/(SUBJ) arrived.
        b.  Mario non sapeva che Gianni partiva/partisse l'indomani.
            Mario did not know that Gianni had(IND)/(SUBJ) left the day after.

It seems that, in addition to negation, the tenses on both the main and the embedded predicates may also play a role in mood choice.[33]

Within the framework for mood choice developed here, an explanation for the effects of negation on mood selection could be pursued on the basis of modifications negation induces on the interpretation context of the complement clause.[34] More generally, negation makes the interpretation contexts more different than they normally are with respect to common grounds. This would explain why in no case negation induces a change from the subjunctive to the indicative. The contexts where the former mood is licensed are by themselves distant enough from common grounds for the change induced to happen without consequences on mood choice. On the other hand, the fact that the mood of normal matrix assertions is not affected by negation may be explained by noticing that in these cases negation is in the scope of the assertive operator so that it does not change the context of evaluation.[35]

### 5.1.8.2. Dislocated complement clauses

Before concluding the discussion of the factors affecting mood choice, let us consider dislocated clauses:

(72)    a.   Mario mi ha detto che Giuseppe è/*sia partito.
             Mario told me that Giuseppe has(IND)/(SUBJ) left.
        b.   Che Giuseppe è/sia partito, Mario me l'ha detto.
             That Giuseppe has(IND)/(SUBJ) left, Mario to me it-cl has told.
             Mario told me that Giuseppe has left.

As we know, *dire* (tell) requires the indicative in Italian (cf. (72a)). However, if the complement clause is (clitic) left dislocated, the subjunctive becomes acceptable (cf. (72b)). This property is not limited to *verba dicendi* but extends to other verbs that normally select the indicative:

(73)    a.   Mario sa che Giuseppe è/*sia sciocco.
             Mario knows that Giuseppe is(IND)/(SUBJ) silly.
        b.   Che Giuseppe è/sia sciocco Mario lo sa.
             That Giuseppe is(IND)/(SUBJ) silly Mario it-cl knows.
             Mario knows that Giuseppe is silly.

Note that to obtain this effect it is crucial that the complement clause be topicalised. Focused clauses, even if preposed, do not exhibit the same behaviour:

(74)    CHE GIUSEPPE *SIA/E' PARTITO, Mario mi ha detto.
        That Giuseppe has(SUBJ)/(IND) left, Mario told me.

Furthermore, it is not necessary that the relevant proposition be presupposed. Consider the discourse in (75), where the two sentences are uttered by two different speakers:

(75)    a.   Mario mi ha detto che Andrea è innamorato.
             Mario told me that Andrea has fallen in love.
        b.   Che Andrea è/sia innamorato a me lo ha (già) detto Carlo.
             That Andrea has(IND)/(SUBJ) fallen in love Carlo has (already) told me.

The proposition *Andrea has felt in love* is clearly not presupposed in (75), since it is introduced in the domain of discourse by a *verbum dicendi*. However, because of (75a), it is old, familiar information. Furthermore, as observed by Manzini (1994a), even focusing the matrix verb suffices to license the subjunctive:

(76)   Mario DICE che Maria sia partita.
       Mario SAYS that Maria has(SUBJ) left.

In this case, too, the complement proposition is background information.

Now consider what it means for a proposition to be background information at a given point in a conversation. It must either have been previously asserted, hence belonging to the current common ground, or it corresponds to the complement clause of a predicate such as *believe, say, want*, or the like — in this case belonging to the modal base introduced by the predicate. Uttering a sentence containing a topicalised clause is appropriate only if it is possible to retrieve the corresponding proposition in such an enlarged conversational background — namely, that consisting of (a) the common ground, and (b) all the modal bases used so far. Notice, now, that topicalised clauses with the subjunctive can refer to propositions contained either in (a) or in (b). Consider the following discourses:

(77)   a.   Mario è sciocco.
            Mario is silly.
       b.   Che Mario sia/è sciocco ce la ha già detto ieri Carlo.
            That Mario is(SUBJ)/(IND) silly Carlo has already said it to us yesterday.

(78)   a.   Carlo pensa che Mario sia sciocco.
            Carlo thinks that Mario is(SUBJ) silly.
       b.   Che Mario sia/#è sciocco ce lo ha detto ieri Andrea.
            That Mario is(SUBJ)/(IND) silly Andrea has said it to us yesterday.

The topicalised clause with the subjunctive in (77b) is to be connected with the content of the previous assertion — that is, a proposition belonging to the common ground. On the other hand, in (78b) the topicalised clause with the subjunctive refers to the complement proposition of the verb *believe* in (78a) (that is, to a proposition belonging to a modal base). The indicative has a more restricted distribution in topicalised clauses (this is signalled by "#"). It is acceptable in (77b), where the relevant proposition is not only familiar but also presupposed when (77b) is uttered. It is not appropriate in (78b), however, where the proposition *Mario is silly* belongs to the modal base of *believe*. Notice, in fact, that the indicative improves if the relevant proposition — namely, the one corresponding to the complement of (78a) — can be accommodated. In this case the *silliness* of Mario becomes part of the common ground, and (78b) is therefore a report about a shared fact. This effect can be seen more clearly with a *verbum dicendi* which, as seen in §5.1.7., normally permits its complement proposition to be accommodated:

(79)   a.   Giuseppe ha detto che Mario è sciocco.
            Giuseppe said that M. is(IND) silly.
       b.   Che Mario sia/#è sciocco lo ha detto anche Carlo.
            That Mario is(SUBJ)/(IND) silly also Carlo has said it.

Finally, when uttered *out of the blue*, (80) is acceptable only if the proposition corresponding to the topicalised clause is accommodated:

(80)   Che Mario è stupido Carlo me lo aveva detto.
       That Mario is(IND) silly Carlo had told it to me.

Therefore, topicalised clauses always allow the subjunctive, even with complements of verbs that would normally only admit the indicative, as in (78b). On the other hand, the indicative seems acceptable only (a) with clauses that would admit it even in the normal, base position, and (b) if the relevant proposition is either presupposed or accommodated. Therefore, the generalisation seems to be that the subjunctive in a topicalised clause permits the retrieval of the background proposition from whichever component of the enlarged conversational background — both in the common ground and in the different modal bases — is used that far. The indicative in a topicalised clause, on the other hand, only permits the retrieval of presupposed propositions.

Let us speculate on the source of this difference. We propose that in the case of the subjunctive it is due to the presence of a discourse operator in the topicalised clause that permits the enlargement of the conversational background mentioned in the preceding discussion.[36] If the mood is the indicative, such an operator is absent, and the topicalised clause is interpreted with respect to the closest operator available, which is the assertive operator of the whole sentence. Independent evidence in favour of this hypothesis will be provided in §5.2., where it will be shown that it explains some facts concerning Complementiser Deletion in Italian. In particular, it accounts for the fact that topicalised clauses with the subjunctive never delete the complementiser.

### 5.1.9. Concluding remarks

We have proposed a theory according to which notional mood is to be understood as a manifestation of modality. That is, it is to be understood in terms of such entities as the modal force and the ordering source set up by the embedding predicate or by (possibly invisible) operators. Such entities, in turn, determine the context which the clause is interpreted in. An interesting feature which the approach proposed here shares with others (e.g., Portner 1994) is the existence of a sort of *continuum* comprising assertions and the different kinds of modalised clauses, in which the relevant differences are reduced to those involving contextual backgrounds — that is, modal bases and ordering sources and their combinations. Such a continuum is specified by means of a number of parameters. Among these parameters we discussed the null/non-null ordering source parameter, the realistic/non-realistic distinction for modal bases, and the persistency of the (derived) context set. Importantly, we proposed that the correspondence between notional and grammatical mood is not direct. That is, the subjunctive/indicative distinction does not have an immediate counterpart in the ordering of evaluation contexts. Rather, it corresponds to a simplified, in our case, binary, classification obtained from the more complex one by choosing a threshold. Crucially, languages can differ as to the choice of the threshold, which explains (at least part of) the crosslinguistic variation discussed in §5.1.1. This approach allowed us to give a uniform account of mood choice in such contexts as those created by *verba dicendi*, fiction predicates, and Hooper's (1975) true factives. Finally, we discussed some phenomena concerning intralinguistic variation, showing that our ideas can be extended to them, too.

It is important to stress that the simplified classification must be consistent with the full-fledged ordering it derives from. More precisely, let $A$ and $B$ be the partition of the original ordering in a given language, where $A$ is the set of assertion-like contexts. Then it must be that for every context $c_i$ in $A$ and for every $c_j$ in $B$ $c_j > c_i$.[37] This leads to a falsifiable statement: since we claimed that the subjunctive is associated with the contexts in $B$ (that is, with the contexts that are judged as different from the context set), our theory would be falsified by a language in which the distribution of the subjunctive or the indicative is not consistent with the original ordering. That is, our theory would be falsified by a language in which there is a context requiring the subjunctive $c_S$ and one requiring the indicative $c_I$ such that $c_I > c_S$.

Concerning the parameters, it is possible that others are required besides the ones we hypothesised, or, on the contrary, that some, possibly all, of them have to be reduced to a single more fundamental one. Nothing in our theory rests on the assumption that the relevant parameters are the ones we discussed. They simply serve the purpose of providing a classification. The important point is that grammatical mood corresponds to a simple, limited classification of the contexts of evaluation obtained from a more complex one. The simplification is necessary because of the way the computational system $C_{HL}$ works: it processes features, and features can only encode a limited number of distinctions. That is, *mood* cannot accommodate all the facets of notional mood. Finally, the simplification idea serves another important purpose: it makes it possible to account for crosslinguistic differences by letting languages vary in the way the simplification is performed. We think that, in addition to correctly predicting a number of interesting phenomena, such an idea is also quite natural. On the one hand the determinant(s) of crosslinguistic differences in mood choice cannot be located at the level of semantic representation, because this level is immune to crosslinguistic differences. On the other hand, syntax cannot help: there we only find the morphological feature *mood,* the properties and behaviour of which are fully and exclusively determined by the rules and principles of syntax. The remaining possibility, therefore, is that crosslinguistic differences in mood choice correspond to properties of the mapping from LF representations to semantical-conceptual structures — that is, the mapping from grammatical to notional mood.[38]

## 5.2. The morphosyntax of the Italian subjunctive

In this section we consider the morphosyntactic properties of the Italian subjunctive. We have shown in §5.1. that in Italian the subjunctive occurs in embedded clauses when the evaluation context of the clause is at least weakly realistic. From a morphosyntactic point of view, we propose that a feature *mood* appears in subjunctive clauses, whereas no such feature appears in indicative ones. In the (revised) minimalist framework adopted here (Chomsky 1995), the presence of such a feature has a wide range of consequences, because the grammar requires it to be checked and interpreted.

Here we examine Complementiser Deletion (henceforth CD) facts and extraction from subjunctive clauses, with special reference to non-D-linked adjuncts such as *come* (how) and *perché* (why). We argue that the hypothesis concerning syncretic categories presented in chapter 1 plays a major role in explaining the data discussed here.

The phenomena observed in CD contexts with respect to the position of the subject are also found in interrogative sentences. As we will illustrate in a while, in both cases the subject can appear neither preverbally nor in a position occurring between the auxiliary and the participle. These two empirical domains — CD and subject inversion in interrogatives — have usually been considered to be independent and, at least as far as we know, have never been related to each other. Here we argue that they are both instances of the same morphosyntactic property of the agreement features in Italian. That is, we argue that they are the effect of the possibility for agreement to be realised syncretically, in the sense defined in chapter 1, with other features — in particular, with the *mood* feature of the subjunctive and the *Wh-* feature of the interrogative clauses. In other words, interrogative clauses, even if not immediately related to subjunctive contexts, will be shown to share with them an important property of the Italian verbal morphology — namely, the presence of syncretism in the inflectional verbal system. Interrogative contexts, therefore, provide independent evidence in favour of our morphosyntactic analysis of the subjunctive and of the general view we are proposing in this book for verbal morphology across languages.

### 5.2.1. Syncretic categories and the Feature Scattering Principle

Let us briefly summarise the relevant notions concerning the clausal architecture which will be useful in this section. In chapter 1 it is proposed that the syntactic universal component of the language faculty is constituted by (a) the inventory of features among which a child selects those relevant to his/her language and (b) the order of checking. The latter is expressed by means of the following principle:

(81) **Universal Ordering Constraint**
Features are ordered so that given $F_1 > F_2$, the checking of $F_1$ precedes the checking of $F_2$.

The child learns a language by associating morphemes to features. If the association is one to one, the result is the grammar of an agglutinative or isolating language. If the same morpheme is associated to more features, the grammar of an inflected language such as Italian is obtained. When a category expresses more than one feature, we call it a *syncretic category*. In chapter 3 we also illustrated the properties and the effects of hybrid categories such as AGR/T in English. In this chapter we will not further consider hybrid categories, since they do not seem to be present in the subjunctive morphological system. The features collapsed in a syncretic head can, under certain circumstances, be projected separately. In chapter 1, we introduced the principle in (82) ruling the projection procedure:

(82) **Feature Scattering Principle**
Each feature can head a projection.

A (syncretic or hybrid) category, which is nothing more than a set (of sets) of features, must project at least one node, otherwise the initial numeration cannot be consumed. A consequence of the Feature Scattering Principle is that, since each feature can head a projection, the upper limit on the number of nodes is given by the number of features selected in the array. The criterion which permits the choice between the scattered and the non-scattered option is constituted by the principles of economy discussed in chapter 1. Recall, however, that Chomsky (1995) points out that economy considerations hold only for different realisations of the *same* array. *Different* arrays cannot be compared with each other and consequently cannot be ordered with respect to economy conditions. We will see in a while that such a consideration is important in defining the formal properties of Feature Scattering.

We hypothesise the existence of two slightly different kinds of scattering. The first kind can be described as follows: given a numeration $N$ containing a bundle of features corresponding to a syncretic category, scattering can determine more than one projection in $\Sigma$, in correspondence with the features of that bundle. We will call this scattering process *Scattering A*. The second type can be characterised as follows: instead of applying to the array, scattering can take place at a *pre-numeration* level — that is, at the point in which the numeration is created by selecting the lexical entries. Scattering in this case can be conceived of as a process that, starting from a syncretic category, creates an array partitioning the syncretic feature bundle into various different ones. Let us call this kind of scattering *Scattering B*.

Under which circumstances do Scattering A and Scattering B take place? Scattering A can occur only when there is no other way to project the bundles contained in $N$ — that is, it is ruled by economy conditions. We know that all the bundles of the initial $N$ must be projected. Scattering A is allowed only when an extra head is needed to provide a *Spec* position for some feature (or feature bundle) which must be merged there. If no such additional position is needed, Scattering A cannot take place, due to the intervention of economy considerations which bar longer derivation — that is, derivations requiring a higher number of applications of Merge.

Scattering B by itself is not subject to economy conditions, because, as we stated above, according to Chomsky (1995) such conditions cannot be used to compare various arrays with each other. In other words, it cannot be stated whether a scattered array gives rise to a better derivation from an economical point of view with respect to a non scattered one. In this case, the only condition which the scattered structure has to satisfy is that the heads must correspond to a lexical entry, so that morphological (and phonological) conditions can be met. Recall in fact that morphology can only handle $X^0$ objects — that is, well-formed words — otherwise, the derivation will not converge.

Let us give some abstract examples. Assume a syncretic category $C = [F_1; F_2; F_3]$. Scattering A can apply in the course of the computation from an array $[... [F_1; F_2; F_3] ... ]$ yielding a structure $\Sigma$ containing the terms $\alpha_1$ and $\alpha_2$, such that $\alpha_1$ is $[F_1]$ and $\alpha_2$ is $[F_2; F_3]$, or whatever combination of categories that realises the content of $C$ and that does not violate the Universal Ordering Constraint. This is obtained in accordance with (82), by letting Merge apply not only to bundles but also to the features, or subset of features, which constitute a bundle.

Consider now Scattering B. Starting from a syncretic category $C$ it can give rise to various arrays. For instance $[ ... [F_1] ... [F_2; F_3] ... ]$, or $[ ... [F_1; F_2] ... [F_3] ... ]$, etc. From each array the computation proceeds as usual to form $\Sigma$.

Let us briefly discuss now the interaction of Scattering A and B with Move. From what we stated above, the *Spec* positions made available by Scattering A cannot be landing sites for movement, because they are already filled by some feature of $N$. Scattering A, in fact, is simply a sub-case of Merge, and the features it applies to are given in $N$. Move, on the other hand, targets an *already existing* portion of $\Sigma$, which therefore must already be construed. Scattering, as we defined it, cannot take place in order to provide a landing site.

The *Spec* position created by Scattering B, on the contrary, is a possible landing site for movement, provided that the other conditions of grammar are met. The cases we are dealing with in this section are all instances of Scattering B.[39]

### 5.2.2. Subject-Verb inversion phenomena in Italian

#### 5.2.2.1. On Complementiser Deletion phenomena in Italian

In this section we consider the well-known facts concerning the (optional) absence of a complementiser in embedded contexts in Italian.[40] CD is typically allowed when a subjunctive is present, even though this is not a sufficient condition. For instance, a context introduced by the verb *credere* (believe) admits CD, but a context introduced by the verb *rammaricarsi* (regret) does not, in spite of the fact that they both require a subordinate subjunctive clause. Consider the following examples:

(83)    Crede (che) sia partito.
        He believes (that) he left(SUBJ).

(84)    Si rammarica *(che) sia partito.
        He regrets (that) he left(SUBJ).

Verbs such as *pensare* (think), *supporre* (suppose) and the like, or belief verbs; and *volere* (want), *sperare* (hope) and the like, or volitionals and desideratives admit CD, whereas true factives do not (see §5.1.). Verbs requiring a subordinate indicative both in non-factive, as in (85), and in semifactive contexts, as in (86), never admit CD:[41]

(85)    Ha detto *(che) è partito.
        He said (that) he left(IND).

(86)    Ha confessato *(che) è partito.
        He confessed (that) he left(IND).

Poletto (1995) proposes that this phenomenon is due to the movement of the verb to C; Scorretti (1991) argues instead that the clauses appearing without *che* are IPs and not CPs. Both proposals face some empirical problems related to the position of the subject in the embedded clause, which we are going to analyse in the following discussion.

    To complete the survey, observe that topicalised and focused clauses, as well as subject clauses in preverbal position, do not admit CD:[42]

(87)    a.  Che fosse partito, lo credeva.
            That he had left, he believed.
        b.  *Fosse partito, lo credeva.
            He had left, he believed.

(88)    a.  CHE FOSSE PARTITO, credeva.
            THAT HE HAD LEFT, he believed.
        b.  *FOSSE PARTITO, credeva.
            HE HAD LEFT, he believed.

(89) a.     Che sia già partito, è probabile.
            That he has already left, is probable.
        b.  *Sia già partito, è probabile.
            He has already left, is probable.

With respect to the subject position in CD clauses, Poletto observes that there is an important difference between these constructions and other phenomena, such as Aux-to-Comp sentences, which might at first glance be considered to be of the same type. In CD cases the subject can never appear between the auxiliary and the participle, whereas this is possible in Aux-to-Comp constructions. Consider the contrast between (90) and (91):[43]

(90)    *Credeva fosse Gianni arrivato.
        He believed had Gianni arrived(SUBJ).

(91)    Essendo Gianni arrivato, fummo più contenti.
        Had Gianni arrived, we were happier.

Example (90) is a CD context, whereas (91) is an Aux-to-Comp case, as discussed in Rizzi (1982). Note that, as can be inferred from her paper, in clauses with CD Poletto also accepts a full lexical subject appearing to the left of the subjunctive:

(92)    Credeva Gianni fosse arrivato.
        He believed Gianni had arrived(SUBJ).

However, we observed that Italian speakers do not homogeneously share this judgement. For some speakers, (92) is grammatical, while for others it is not. Moreover, this fact does not seem to be related to regional variation. Significantly, the two authors of this work do not have the same judgement, in spite of the fact that both originate from Central Italy. For one of them the sentence in (92) is grammatical, while for the other it is almost a "*".[44] For speakers who do not accept (92), the only grammatical forms are those with either a postverbal subject or a referential *pro*:[45]

(93)    Credeva fosse arrivato Gianni.
        He believed had arrived Gianni.

(94)    Credeva fosse arrivato.
        He believed (he) had arrived.

Notice that if the preverbal subject is the second person singular pronoun, the sentences are grammatical for all speakers:[46]

(95)    Credeva tu fossi arrivato in tempo.
        He believed you had arrived in time.

The contrast with the third person is quite sharp, even if perhaps the pronoun *lui* is slightly better than a full NP such as *Gianni* in (92):

(96)    ?*Credeva lui fosse arrivato in tempo.
        He believed he had arrived on time

In §5.2.4.1. a solution will be proposed to account in a principled way for the variation among speakers with respect to the acceptability of sentences such as (92).

*5.2.2.2. Subject-Verb inversion in Italian interrogatives*

In this section we consider word order phenomena in interrogative constructions. These sentences instantiate the same kind of phenomena found in CD contexts: the subject cannot occur preverbally.[47] It is a very well known fact that in Italian and in several other Romance languages (Spanish, Portuguese, Catalan, Romanian), the subject follows the verb in interrogative contexts and cannot appear preverbally (see Rizzi 1991):[48]

(97)  Che cosa ha visto Gianni?
      Lit.: What has seen Gianni?

(98)  *Che cosa Gianni ha visto?
      Lit.: What Gianni has seen?
      What has Gianni seen?

The position following the auxiliary and preceding the participle is not available for the subject, neither when it is a full lexical subject nor when it is a pronominal one:

(99)  *Che cosa ha Gianni visto?
      What has Gianni seen?

(100) *Che cosa hai tu visto?
      What have you seen?

With respect to this pattern, interrogative constructions strongly resemble CD constructions.

Consider, moreover, that the phenomenon in question is not a *root* one; it can also take place in subordinate clauses, even if in this case the ungrammaticality of non-inverted sentences is perhaps less strong:

(101) Gianni si domanda che cosa ha visto Mario.
      Gianni wonders what has seen Mario.

(102) ?*Gianni si domanda che cosa Mario ha visto.
      Gianni wonders what Mario has seen.

Interestingly, if a subjunctive appears in the subordinate interrogative, a preverbal subject is admitted:

(103) Gianni si domanda che cosa Mario abbia fatto.
      Gianni wonders what Mario has(SUBJ) done.

In the following section we will review some of the solutions proposed in the literature to the problems raised by CD and interrogative inversion in terms of movement of the verb to a complementiser position. We will then illustrate our solution. We will show that our proposal concerning CD structures can be successfully extended to the pattern found in interrogative constructions.

### 5.2.3. The V-to-C solution

Rizzi (1991) and Poletto (1995) propose very similar solutions, even though Rizzi only considers the problem of interrogative inversion, while Poletto only considers the CD phenomena. They both claim that the verb moves to a complementiser position and that such a movement destroys the environment for nominative case assignment to a phrase in the *Spec* of $AGR_S$ — that is, to a post-auxiliary subject.[49]

Rizzi (1991, §7) compares Italian with French and points out that the inversion pattern of French distinguishes between full NPs and pronouns, contrasting with Italian, as illustrated by the examples in (99) and (100):[50]

(104)   Où est-elle allée? (From Rizzi 1991, ex. 48)
        Where is she gone?

(105)   *Où est Marie allée?
        Where is Marie gone?

According to Rizzi's theory, I to C movement destroys the possibility of nominative case assignment in a Spec-head configuration with AGR, and as such (105) is ruled out.

Example (104) is grammatical because the clitic is incorporated in the verb, satisfying the case requirements in a different way. Italian rules out the equivalent of (104) because of the absence of subject clitics. We will not argue against Rizzi's proposal with respect to French, because his solution seems to yield the correct predictions in this language; we will only point out that its extension to Italian is not completely satisfactory.

The main problem with this account, also discussed by Poletto (1995), concerns the fact that there are instances of V to C in Italian which do not destroy the environment for nominative case assignment — namely, Aux-to-Comp constructions.

Let us only point out that if the landing site of the auxiliary in both classes of phenomena — Aux-to-Comp and interrogative inversion — is taken to be the same, it is not clear how the difference between the two could be acquired by a child. It seems to us that a more precise explanation for (99) and (100) must be provided to obtain a satisfactory theory.

Let us consider now the explanation proposed by Poletto for CD phenomena. Given the differences between the Aux-to-Comp construction and CD cases, she concludes that the head the verb moves to is not the same in the two cases and that the subjunctive moves to a lower position, which she calls AGR/C. Poletto in fact hypothesises that two complementiser positions are available in Italian. The higher complementiser head has only complementiser-like properties, whereas the lower one also exhibits nominal characteristics. To support her proposal she observes that in many northern Italian dialects, as well as in Occitan varieties, two complementisers can be simultaneously realised :

(106)  A venta **che** Majo **ch**'a mangia pi' tant.  (from Poletto 1995, ex. 50c)
       (Piedmontese of Turin)
   Lit.: Need that Majo that eat more.
   It is needed that Majo eats more

The two complementisers have the same lexical form *che*. The first precedes the
subject, and the second follows it. Poletto proposes that the subject in (106)
occupies the *Spec* position of the lower complementiser. She also points out
that similar phenomena take place in Germanic languages, such as Dutch and
Mainland Scandinavian, as noted by Vikner (1994) and Hoekstra (1992), among
others. Her conclusion is that the complementiser positions appearing in (106)
are also available in Standard Italian and that the indicative selects the higher one,
whereas the subjunctive selects the lower one. The only difference between the
dialects admitting sentences such as (106) and Standard Italian is that in the latter
there is a constraint inhibiting the simultaneous realisation of both. To
summarise, in Italian, the higher C position is the one filled by the
complementiser in indicative contexts, and the lower position — Poletto's
AGR/C — is the one exploited by the subjunctive verbal form and can be filled
either by a complementiser or by the verb itself through movement. CD effects
arise as a consequence of the latter possibility.

Finally, Poletto excludes sentences such as (90), in which the subject
intervenes between the auxiliary and the participle, by means of a proposal very
similar to Rizzi's: nominative case cannot be assigned to the subject because
AGR/C, unlike C, cannot assign case under government.[51]

Poletto proposes that the movement of the subjunctive to AGR/C is a
phenomenon which must be treated similarly to V2 phenomena — that is, as a
type of V-to-C movement. To support this idea she claims that the class of verbs
triggering V2 in subordinate contexts in Germanic is the same one displaying
CD effects in Italian. That is, the fact that in some languages a certain context
gives rise to overt verb movement to C is taken by Poletto as an argument in
favour of claiming that Italian CD cases are an instance of the same type of
movement.

Our proposal, though acknowledging the role of movement, does not unify
CD with V2 and maintains that the only trigger for overt verb movement in
Italian is constituted by strong agreement features.[52]

Let us point out first that the class of verbs triggering V2 in Germanic —
that is, the so-called bridge verbs — in embedded contexts cannot be identified
*tout court* with the class exhibiting CD phenomena in Italian. Consider the list
of German bridge and non-bridge verbs given by Vikner (1994, p. 133–134):[53]

(107) **Bridge verbs**
   *andeuten* (hint), *angeben* (indicate), *antworten* (answer), *behaupten*
   (**claim**), *berichten* (report), *betonen* (emphasize), *entscheiden* (decide),
   *erfahren* (learn), *sich erinnern* (remember), *feststellen* (ascertain), *finden*
   (**think**), *glauben* (**believe**), *hoffen* (**hope**), *meinen* (**mean**), *sagen*
   (say), *sehen* (see), *spüren* (feel), *vermuten* (assume), *wissen* (know)

(108)  **Non-bridge verbs**
        *bedauern* (be sorry), *bestätigen* (confirm), *bereuen* (regret), *beweisen*
        (prove), *bezweifeln* (**doubt**), *darum bitten* (ask for), *daran denken* (think
        of), *erklären* (explain), *erlauben* (permit), *geheim halten* (keep secret), *gern*
        *haben* (be happy), *hassen* (hate), *übersehen* (overlook), *überzeugen*
        (convince), *vergeben* (forgive), *verlagen* (demand), *verschweigen* (conceal),
        *zeigen* (show), *zugeben* (admit)

Vikner (1994) provides these lists for German (and Danish). In both languages
bridge verbs trigger embedded V2, unlike non-bridge verbs. The verbs allowing
CD in Italian (those in boldface) fall into both classes. As can be seen from the
lists, it is possible to find bridge verbs which do not admit CD and non-bridge
verbs which do admit it (even if there is only one case in the lists given here).
The fact that CD verbs in Italian (mostly) belong to the bridge class could be
taken as an argument in favour of the movement analysis of CD effects. As an
objection to this view, however consider the fact that in English, bridge verbs, as
opposed to non-bridge verbs (see Stowell 1981; Kayne 1981), permit CD, yet
they do not trigger V2:

(109)  a.  John said Mary had left.
       b.  *John said had Mary left.

Moreover, it does not seem to be obvious that (109) should be accounted for as
an instance of (covert) movement of V to C. Notice, furthermore, that it is not
clear at all why (109b) should be ungrammatical, given that auxiliaries can
normally overtly raise in English, even to the leftmost head, as happens with
interrogatives:

(110)  *Have* you eaten an apple?

Therefore it might be concluded that the fact that *most* verbs which admit CD in
Italian belong to the class of bridge verbs is not necessarily an argument in
favour of an analysis of CD in terms of overt movement of the verb to a
complementiser position.[54]

  In our opinion, the problems which remain open under a V2 view of CD
phenomena are the following: Why is the (Spec, AGR$_S$P) position not available
for a subject — that is, why are sentences such as (90) ungrammatical? Why
does a consistent group of speakers reject (92)? That is, why could a preverbal
subject give rise to an ungrammatical sentence?

  Note also that Poletto points out that a negative quantifier can precede the
verb in CD constructions. Such a consideration obviously holds only for the
speakers who accept a preverbal subject with CD:

(111)  Mario crede Gianni arrivi stasera.
       Mario believes Gianni arrives tonight.

(112)  Mario crede nessuno arrivi stasera.
       Mario believes nobody arrives tonight.

Given that negative quantifiers cannot undergo topicalisation, the (relative) acceptability of (112) shows that the subject does not occupy a derived position.[55] This is an important observation that any theory dealing with these facts should account for.[56] Let us propose an alternative approach in a different framework.

## 5.2.4. The syncretic category solution

### 5.2.4.1. An alternative proposal for CD contexts

In this section we propose an account of CD constructions which can also be extended to interrogative sentences (see §5.2.6.). Our idea is that CD effects are due on the one hand to the movement of the verbal head to the AGR position as usually happens in Italian, and on the other hand to the fact that, due to the presence of the subjunctive mood, this head has some special properties distinguishing it from the head appearing in indicative clauses. We propose that the subjunctive morphology realises a syncretic category — namely, a category projecting the agreement and the modal (*mood*) features. Such a category will be called MOOD/AGR.[57]

Let us consider in more detail the nature of the features lexicalised by means of the syncretic category MOOD/AGR. AGR is the label for the φ-features and NOM, and MOOD is the label for the feature corresponding to the complementiser of the subjunctive.[58] Therefore, following Poletto, we implicitly claim that such a complementiser is not the same one that introduces indicative clauses.[59] If this idea is correct, the *Spec* position associated with the syncretic category can have the properties of either an AGR Specifier (an A-position) or a complementiser Specifier (an A'-position). The speakers who accept a preverbal subject in CD contexts take the first option (however see §2.5 below for an analysis of what happens under extraction). For the other speakers, this *Spec* can only function as an A'-position. As a consequence, it can only be filled by an operator and is not available for a subject. These speakers reject (92) and require the subject to appear to the right of the participle.[60] Furthermore, according to the hypothesis developed here, no subject position is provided between the raised verb and the participle — that is, CD cases are not instances of Aux-to-Comp.

Finally, as will be seen in the next section, the subjunctive always moves to check the feature *mood*. Movement is overt when mood is projected syncretically with AGR, given that the AGR features are strong. In these cases, therefore, the checking of *mood* is parasitic on the checking of the φ-features. Movement is covert when mood is expressed by means of a complementiser — that is, when the scattering option has been taken, given that mood is weak. The scattering we are talking about in this case is Scattering B. A subset of the features of the syncretic category, in fact, is lexicalised by means of the complementiser — that is, a lexical item. Moreover, the *Spec* of MOOD can be filled by a moved phrase (see §5.2.5. below), whereas this is not allowed with Scattering A, as stated earlier.

With factive verbs CD is impossible, as illustrated by (84). Our hypothesis is that in this case the complementiser cannot be syncretically realised because it bears an extra feature, let us call it *[+ fact]* (cf. §5.1.). The presence of this feature is presumably to be connected with the presence of a factive operator in the *Spec* position, as has often been proposed in the literature (see Rizzi 1990; Cinque 1990; Melvold 1991). For similar reasons, the complementiser *se* (if) cannot be deleted in the case of indirect questions because it bears the feature *[+ Wh]*, which again is not syncretic with the other subjunctive features:

(113)   Mi domando *(se) abbia mangiato.
        I wonder (whether) he has eaten.

Both *[+ fact]* and *[+ Wh]* are neither intrinsic nor optional, in the sense of Chomsky (1995), for the subjunctive verb; they are lexicalised by the complementisers *che* and *se,* respectively. Thus, CD is impossible. The same conclusion can be reached for left contexts (subjects or topicalised sentences), where presumably a (topic) operator is realised, licensed by a feature in the complementiser (see §5.1.). We will illustrate the various cases in a while.

Summarising, the contexts where CD is impossible — that is, factives, indirect questions, topicalised clauses, and left subjects — are characterisable by the presence of a feature in the initial numeration not belonging to those of the subjunctive bundle. Crucially, such a feature is lexicalised by the complementiser. In the case of factive clauses and indirect questions, the relevant feature is due to the selectional requirements of the matrix verb. In the case of topicalised clauses and subjects, it is added to the numeration and determines the leftward movement of the phrase in question. As a consequence, in all these cases an overt complementiser is needed to realise such extra-features, on the basis of the observation that in Italian we do not find null complementisers.[61]

Let us add a few words on the acquisition of syncretic categories. We proposed in chapter 1 that syncretic categories are acquired only on the basis of positive evidence. In Italian, as in many other languages, the subjunctive is morphologically marked with respect to the indicative and the presence of the feature *mood* in the array is the marked option.[62] However, the fact that a certain verb is embedded under a factive has nothing to do with the inherent morphological properties of the embedded verb, but is only a function of the superordinate predicate. As a consequence, the feature *[+ fact]* cannot be acquired as syncretic with any other feature of the verb.

Let us consider the projection of $\Sigma$ starting from the various possible arrays. When the complementiser is realised, the scattered array contains the following bundles of features (non-relevant details omitted):

(114)   . . . ;[+ mood]; [φ; nom]; [+ V; - N; φ; nom; + mood]; . . .

The corresponding $\Sigma$ is the following, for sentences such as: *Credo che Maria sia partita* (I believe that Mario left):

(115)

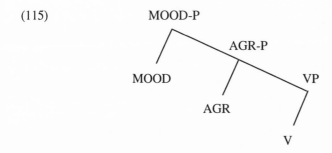

Example (115) corresponds to the *scattered* option — that is, the one in which *mood* and *agr* ($\phi$ and *nom*), are projected separately. The subjunctive verb moves before Spell-Out to check agreement, and then moves covertly to check *[+ mood]*.

Consider the non-scattered option. In this case the array contains the following bundles of features, for sentences such as: *Credo Maria sia partita* (I believe Maria left):

(116)  . . . ;[+ mood; $\phi$; nom]; [+V; -N; $\phi$; nom; +mood] ; . . .

*Only one* head position is projected above the VP (besides, if needed, a temporal one). As in the case considered above, the $\phi$-features, being strong, trigger movement of the verb.[63]

Before proceeding further, let us consider the important question concerning the availability of a preverbal null subject position in pro-drop languages. It has been proposed (see Cardinaletti & Roberts 1991; Cardinaletti 1994) that *pro* is located in an AGR projection lower than the one hosting the lexical subject. We argue that such a position is still available in subjunctive clauses. If this is correct, the scattering mechanism hypothesised so far can be extended to the agreement features. Note, in fact, that, as discussed in chapter 2 §2.4., AGR is comprised of two different (sets of) features: $\phi$ and Case (NOM). In principle, $\phi$-features and NOM could also be scattered, giving rise to two separate projections. The tests on the availability of a preverbal *pro*, in fact, seem to predict its presence both in the scattered and in the non-scattered option. We consider here only one of various tests which have been proposed in the literature. Consider the following contrast (see Burzio 1986):

(117)  a.  Tutti i ragazzi sono partiti.
            All the boys have left.
       b.  I ragazzi sono tutti partiti.
            The boys have all left.

(118)  a.  Sono partiti tutti i ragazzi.
            Have left all the boys.
       b.  *Sono tutti partiti i ragazzi.
            Have all left the boys.

These data show that a floating quantifier is impossible with a postverbal subject (cf. ex. 118b), contrasting with a preverbal one (cf. ex. 117b). Therefore in (119) *pro* must be preverbal:

(119) *pro* sono tutti partiti.
(They) are all left.

Consider now subjunctive contexts:

(120) Mario crede che siano tutti partiti.
Mario believes that (they) are(SUBJ) all left.

(121) Mario crede siano tutti partiti.
Mario believes (they) are(SUBJ) all left.

According to the reasoning developed above, one is led to conclude that a preverbal *pro* is available in both cases.[64] The impossibility of a preverbal subject would therefore be limited to lexical subjects and would not be extended to null subjects, either referential or expletive. Consider now the array in factive contexts:

(122) . . . ;[+ fact]; [+ mood; $\phi$; nom]; [+ V;- N; $\phi$; nom; + mood]; . . .

The situation is similar to that described above. The difference is due to the presence of the feature *[+ fact]* in the array. This feature is lexicalised by the complementiser *che*, which heads a projection higher than the subjunctive MOOD. The SPEC position in this case is filled by an operator licensed by the feature *[+ fact]*.

There is another possibility available in principle — namely, that the feature *[+ fact]* appears in an array where *[+ mood]* is not syncretic with the other AGR features (Scattering B):

(123) . . . ;[+ fact]; [+ mood]; [$\phi$; nom]; [+ V;- N; $\phi$; nom; + mood]; . . .

We hypothesise that this structure is ruled out because it yields a structure with two adjacent identical complementisers, one lexicalising *fact* and the other lexicalising *mood*. Such a possibility is not available in Italian. Evidence in this direction is independently provided by the following contrast:

(124) *Ritengo *che* [*che* Gianni sia partito] sia improbabile.
I think that that Gianni left is improbable.

(125) Ritengo *che* sia improbabile [*che* Gianni sia partito].
I think that it is improbable that Gianni left.

If the two complementisers are contiguous, the sentence is ungrammatical. Notice that this happens only if the complementisers are identical. Consider the following case:

(126) Pensi *che* [*se* Gianni fosse partito] Mario lo saprebbe?
Do you think that if Gianni had left Mario would know it?

The *che se* sequence does not give rise to the same effect. Consider also the following contrast:

(127)  a.  *Penso *che* [*che* Mario sia partito] lo preoccupi
       I think that that Mario left worries him
     b.  Penso *che* [il fatto *che* Mario sia partito] lo preoccupi
       I think that the fact that Mario left worries him

The reasons for the existence of such a constraint are not clear to us. Let us stress that whatever explains the ungrammaticality of (127a) and (124) might also explain the impossibility for (123) to converge.

### 5.2.4.2. A proposal for inversion phenomena in interrogative clauses

Our hypothesis on interrogative inversion is that, similarly to what we proposed for CD constructions, the subject cannot appear preverbally because agreement and C form a syncretic category, and as such there is only one *Spec* position available. Since the Wh- operator in Italian overtly moves there, the lexical subject has to appear elsewhere — namely, inside the VP, whereas in CD structures *pro* can stay preverbally. This movement is triggered by the strong *Wh-* feature of the complementiser (Rizzi 1990). Therefore we propose the existence of a syncretic WH/AGR head.

Before proceeding further, let us briefly discuss Guasti's (1995) proposal concerning interrogative inversion, which points to conclusions very similar to ours. According to her, in interrogative sentences, the verb does not raise to C overtly but rather raises covertly, to check the *Wh-* feature. This explains the lack of the Aux-to-Comp word order — that is, of a lexical subject appearing between the auxiliary and the participle. On the other hand, Guasti points out that a null subject *pro* is obligatorily present in the *Spec* of the lowest AGR projection, following Cardinaletti's (1994) analysis of the subject positions in Italian:

(128)  [$_{AGR1}$ DP [$_{AGR2}$ pro . . . ]]

The lexical subject occupies the *Spec* of AGR1, and *pro* occupies the *Spec* of AGR2. Guasti proposes that the DP in AGR1 is not licensed if embedded in a +*Wh* phrase because the verb, in its (covert) raising to the WH complementiser head, cannot enter into an agreement configuration with two different elements — that is, the one appearing in AGR1 and the other occupying the *Spec* of AGR2 (where AGR1 and AGR2 are not the AGR projections we introduced in chapter 2). The subject in these constructions must therefore appear postverbally, whereas in preverbal position the *pro* is independently licensed.[65]

The account we are going to present also hypothesises the existence of two subject positions. Moreover, we argue that a lexical preverbal subject position is not available. Differently from Guasti, however, we propose that the incompatibility of a +*Wh* specifier with a preverbal lexical subject is due to the fact that these two elements realise the same abstract feature. We propose that *Wh* and *D* — that is, the feature requiring an interrogative phrase in (Spec,C) and the one requiring a preverbal subject in (Spec,AGR) (Chomsky 1995) — are two different realisations of the *same* formal feature. Consequently, only *one* specifier position can be licensed. If it is filled by a Wh-phrase it cannot be filled by a subject, and vice versa.[66] This fact can be captured by hypothesising that the agreement properties of the verb are realised syncretically with the *Wh*-feature. Moreover, we maintain that in Italian the only trigger for verb-movement is constituted by the strong $\phi$-features. We will also show that this framework predicts the possibility of a lexical preverbal subject in (subjunctive) embedded questions.

As stated earlier, in Italian the only instances of verb movement to C are Aux-to-Comp constructions. We propose that in all the other cases, agreement is collapsed together with the higher node, either *mood* or C. Given that the $\phi$-features in Italian are strong, movement to MOOD/AGR or, analogously, to WH/AGR takes place overtly.

A major difference between the *inversion* in interrogative constructions and CD is constituted by the optionality of the latter. Let us consider the various cases.

In matrix interrogative contexts only an indicative verb can appear, and the inversion is obligatory. The hypothesis of a syncretic category straightforwardly predicts this pattern: there is only one *Spec* position which must be filled by the operator. Consequently there is no room for the subject. According to this analysis, the subject cannot appear between the auxiliary and the participle. The contrast with languages which have real instances of V to C movement, and consequently which exhibit the order Aux-Subject participle, is therefore accounted for.

To put it differently, since there is a position where the subject can appear without resorting to the scattered option, a convergent derivation exists which is more economical than the one obtained by scattering the *Wh*-features and the AGR features.

A possible explanation is the following: according to Chomsky (1995), the subject must raise in (Spec,AGR$_S$) to check the feature *D*. In this case the Wh-phrase must occupy the relevant *Spec*, because of the presence of the (equivalent) feature +*Wh*. No other feature is present to trigger movement of the subject, and, therefore, by economy, it cannot move.

Note furthermore that *Wh*- and AGR cannot be scattered. In Standard Italian interrogative contexts the following sentence is ungrammatical:

(129)   *Quando che ha mangiato una mela?
        When that has eaten an apple?

The two possible structures are given in (139a), the syncretic structure, and (139b), the scattered structure. We must explain why (130b) is ruled out in Italian:

(130)   a.

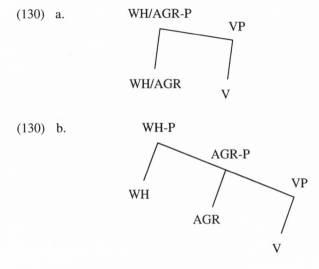

(130)   b.

Let us propose the following generalisation:

(131)   A strong *Wh* feature needs to be in a checking configuration with a verbal one.

Thus, verb movement in sentences such as (132) could be due to a (strong) *v* feature in the complementiser:

(132)   What did John eat?

Suppose that no such complementiser is available in Italian. Then, when the scattering option has been taken and an independent WH projection is present in $\Sigma$, nothing requires the verb to move to such a position. However, the resulting configuration violates (131) both in root and embedded questions. When the syncretic category WH/AGR is not scattered, no violation arises. The Italian verb, in fact, overtly raises there to check the strong $\phi$-features, and (131) is satisfied by the categorial feature of the verb.[67]

A possible explanation for (131) could be that in Italian, root contexts features triggering overt movement need a lexical support.[68] This permits capturing the empirical content of Rizzi's *Wh*-criterion. It follows as a consequence of the combined effect of the following two factors: (a) the interrogative XP is attracted by a strong +*Wh* feature, and (b) an empty head cannot satisfy such a requirement. Therefore, the functional category bearing the *Wh*-feature requires a lexical support (but see below for interrogatives embedded under a subjunctive). Therefore, the scattering option — (130b) — cannot produce a converging structure. The only possibility in Italian is the realisation of the syncretic category WH/AGR. This option, however, rules out the possibility of having an intervening subject.

An important question to be considered at this point concerns the acquisition process of the syntactic category WH/AGR. Let us speculate as follows: as we stated above, Chomsky (1995) proposes that (Spec, AGR) is filled by a subject in order to satisfy the (strong) feature $D$, which also appears on the head AGR. As proposed above, the feature $+Wh$ can be considered to be a variant of $D$. If this is the case, no additional problem arises with respect to the acquisition of the syncretic category WH/AGR, because the requirement that the *Spec* of $AGR_S$ must be filled is simply due to UG. Under this perspective, the child faces the same problem when acquiring *normal* sentences in addition to interrogative ones: in both cases a category syncretising some variant of $D$ and agreement must be hypothesised.

Let us now consider embedded contexts — that is, indirect questions. If an indicative appears, the situation is exactly the one we described for main clauses. When the embedded sentence contains a subjunctive verb, on the other hand, the subject can be preverbal, as shown in example (103), repeated here with minor variation for simplicity:

(133)  Gianni si domanda che cosa Mario abbia/*ha fatto.
       Gianni wonders what Mario has(SUBJ/ *IND) done.

Let us propose that the necessity of having a subjunctive in an embedded question, if the subject is preverbal, is due to the fact that the only convergent derivation must include a *mood* feature:

(134)  WH/MOOD-P

Our reasoning goes as follows: as we argued in the preceding discussion, an empty WH head cannot license the operator. That is, it cannot license movement of the operator to its *Spec*.[69] Let us propose that on the contrary WH/MOOD has this possibility and that this is so because the verb raises covertly to check the *mood* feature, whereas the verb normally does not raise to check a *Wh* feature. The presence of the verb in the head position is enough to license a Wh operator in the *Spec*.[70] Therefore, sentences such as (133) are analogous to (135):

(135)  Mario crede che Maria sia partita.

In both cases there is a Scattering B configuration: $[ \dots [_{. \; WH/MOOD} \; che \; [_{AGR} \dots ]] \dots ]$ in (133), and $[ \dots [_{MOOD} \; che \; [_{AGR} \dots ]] \dots ]$ in (135). A position for the subject is therefore available in both cases. Independent evidence in favour of this view is provided by the observation that although in standard Italian there is no complementiser lexicalising WH/MOOD, such a possibility seems to exist in northern Italian dialects in examples where we find a subjunctive in the embedded clause:

(136)  Mi domando cossa *che* Nane fasesse casa. (From Poletto 1993, ex. 41)
       I wonder what that John do(SUBJ) at home.

In summary, we proposed that in Italian the AGR features can be syncretic with the feature *mood* (CD contexts) and with the feature *Wh* (interrogative inversion). When this happens, an overt lexical subject cannot be licensed to the left of the verb, in the same way it is in the scattered cases, where the *Spec* of MOOD or WH and the *Spec* of the AGR features are both simultaneously realised in $\Sigma$.[71] The subject, therefore, must occur VP internally, or more generally, in a position to the right of the verb. A preverbal *pro* is present in the structure, because another AGR projection, AGR2, is available, as independently argued in the literature (Cardinaletti & Roberts 1991; Cardinaletti 1994; Guasti 1995).

Interestingly, we observed that some speakers accept a subject in the *Spec* of MOOD/AGR. In other words, for some speakers a lexical subject can coexist with CD. According to our hypothesis, even for these speakers there must be only *one Spec* available to the left of the verb. In the following section we will provide an independent argument in favour of this hypothesis, showing that in spite of the different surface realisations (presence versus absence of a lexical preverbal subject), the structure instantiated in CD cases is always the same.

### 5.2.5. Extraction from subjunctive clauses

In this section we provide further arguments in favour of our proposals: (a) the subjunctive verb moves to the MOOD position, either overtly (to check the agreement features) or covertly (because of scattering) and (b) due to the presence of the syncretic category MOOD/AGR, in CD constructions there is only one head position and consequently only one specifier available for XP movement. To illustrate these points we will consider extraction of non-D-linked adjuncts. This type of construction involves movement of the phrase in question through a *Spec* to the left of the subject, as argued by many scholars.[72]

It can be observed that sentences which contain a subjunctive more easily allow extraction of adjuncts in comparison to the corresponding sentences with the indicative. Consider the following data:

(137)  Perché$_i$ credi che Gianni sia fuggito di prigione t$_i$?
       Why do you believe that Gianni escaped(SUBJ) from prison?

(138)  *Perché$_i$ hai detto che Gianni è fuggito di prigione t$_i$?
       Why did you say that Gianni escaped (IND) from prison?

(139)  Come$_i$ credi che Gianni sia fuggito di prigione t$_i$?
       How do you think that Gianni escaped(SUBJ) from prison?

(140)   ?*Come$_i$ hai detto che Gianni è fuggito di prigione t$_i$?
        How did you say that Gianni escaped(IND) from prison?

Extraction of arguments does not give rise to the same contrasts:

(141)   Chi credi che Gianni abbia invitato alla festa?
        Who do you believe that Gianni invited (SUBJ) to the party?

(142)   Chi hai detto che Gianni ha invitato alla festa?
        Who did you say that Gianni invited (IND) to the party?

The presence of a D-linked adjunct in the sense of Pesetsky (1987) improves the
grammatical status of sentences (138) and (140), even if it contains an indicative:

(143)   ?Per quale ragione$_i$ hai detto che Gianni è fuggito di prigione t$_i$?
        For which reason did you say that Gianni escaped(IND) from prison?

(144)   ?In quale modo$_i$ hai detto che Gianni è fuggito di prigione t$_i$?
        In which way did you say that Gianni escaped(IND) from prison?

According to Cinque's (1990) theory, the conditions a phrase must satisfy in
order to undergo long movement are more restrictive than just being D-linked, in
that it must also be θ-marked and in an A-position. An adjunct, even when
D-linked, violates the other two conditions, and as such, it cannot resort to long
movement. Weak islands have the property of blocking successive cyclic
movement. An indicative clause is not a weak island for D-linked adjuncts, even
if it is a sort of *very* weak island for the non-D-linked adjuncts, such as *perché*
(why) and *come* (how). Subjunctive clauses are not weak islands either, because
they admit extraction of both D-linked and non-D-linked adjuncts. Note, in fact,
that extraction of a non-D-linked adjunct out of the (*traditional*) weak islands
gives still worse results than with the indicative:

(145)   *Wh-island:*        *Come ti domandi chi si fosse comportato t?
                            How do you wonder who behaved?

(146)   *Inner island:*     *Come non ti eri comportato t?
                            How didn't you behave?

(147)   *Factive island:*   *Come rimpiangi che Gianni si fosse comportato t?
                            How do you regret that Gianni behaved?

(148)   *Extraposition island:* *Come è ora di comportarsi t?
                            How is it time to behave?

Even the worst cases of extraction out of an indicative clause are still much
better than (145) to (148), independently of the fact that in certain cases, such as,
for instance, (145) and (147), a subjunctive appears.

In other words, the effect of the indicative on non-D-linked adjunct extraction
cannot be assimilated to a weak island violation for two reasons: (a) it is much
weaker, and (b) weak islands do no seem to be sensitive to the presence of an
indicative versus a subjunctive.

Notice that questions construed by extracting a phrase embedded in the complement of *dire* (say) might also have a special *echo* interpretation. Such an interpretation, however, has a typical intonational pattern and only occurs in contexts where the missing information can be immediately retrieved, as, for instance, in the following dialogues:

(149)  A: Gianni è partito indossando il suo vestito migliore.
           Gianni left wearing his best suit.
       B: Come hai detto che è partito?
           How did you say he left(IND)?
       A: Indossando il suo vestito migliore!
           Wearing his best suit!

(150)  A: Gianni è partito perché era arrabbiato.
           Gianni left because he was angry.
       B: Perché hai detto che è partito?
           Why did you say that he left(IND)?
       A: Perché era arrabbiato!
           Because he was angry!

Example (149) to (150) contrast with (138) and (140), where no background for an echo interpretation is provided. Typically, this effect is not obtained with verbs other than *dire* (say), such as *raccontare* (tell). We will propose an explanation for this property later.

There is another rather interesting fact: non-D-linked adjunct extraction seems to be limited to just one cycle. Consider the following examples:

(151)  *Perché$_j$ pensi che tutti credano che Gianni sia fuggito di prigione t$_j$?
        Why do you think that everybody believes that Gianni escaped from prison?

(152)  *Perché$_j$ hai detto che tutti pensano che Gianni sia fuggito di prigione t$_j$?
        Why did you say that everybody thinks that Gianni escaped from prison?

(153)  *Perché$_j$ pensi che tutti abbiano detto che Gianni è fuggito di prigione t$_j$?
        Why do you think that everybody said that Gianni escaped from prison?

(154)  *Come$_j$ pensi che tutti credano che Gianni sia fuggito di prigione t$_j$?
        How do you think that everybody believes that Gianni escaped from prison?

(155)  *Come$_j$ hai detto che tutti pensano che Gianni sia fuggito di prigione t$_j$?
        How did you say that everybody thinks that Gianni escaped from prison?

(156)  *Come$_j$ pensi che tutti abbiano detto che Gianni è fuggito di prigione t$_j$?
        How do you think that everybody said that Gianni escaped from prison?

In these cases there is no significant contrast among any combination of indicative and subjunctive verbal forms. Moreover, even if all the intervening verbs are in the subjunctive the sentence is still unacceptable. In other words, it does not seem that the pattern in (151)- (156) can be explained as a simple degradation due to the increased length of the sentence, as is, on the contrary, the case with argument extraction:

(157)   Che cosa pensi che Gianni abbia acquistato?
        What do you think that Gianni bought?

(158)   (?)Che cosa pensi che tutti credano che Gianni abbia acquistato?
        What do you think that everybody believes that Gianni bought?

(159)   Che cosa hai detto che Gianni ha acquistato?
        What did you say that Gianni bought?

(160)   (?)Che cosa hai detto che tutti pensano che Gianni abbia acquistato?
        What did you say that everybody believes that Gianni bought?

Notice also that the effect in question is not detectable with D-linked adjuncts:

(161)   Per quale ragione$_j$ pensi che tutti credano che Gianni sia fuggito di prigione t$_j$?
        For which reason do you think that everybody believes that Gianni escaped from prison?

(162)   In che modo$_j$ pensi che tutti credano che Gianni sia fuggito di prigione t$_j$?
        In which way do you think that everybody believes that Gianni escaped from prison?

The solution we are going to propose is a refinement of Cinque's (1990) theory. According to him, long Wh-movement is limited to phrases which are (a) in an A-position, (b) receive a referential θ-role (see Rizzi 1990), and (c) are intrinsically referential — that is, are D-linked (see Pesetsky 1987). Phrases not satisfying these conditions can only move by successive cyclic Wh-movement. Long movement is ruled by principles of binding. Successive cyclic movement is ruled by principles of government.[73] As a consequence, D-linked arguments can be extracted over a weak island, whereas non-D-linked ones cannot. On the other hand, D-linked and non-D-linked adjuncts are predicted to behave alike. However, this is not entirely correct, as the indicative effects illustrate. The indicative in fact (weakly) disallows extraction of non-D-linked adjuncts.

    A correct theory should therefore explain (a) the indicative effect on non-D-linked adjuncts and (b) the impossibility of repeating their extraction for more than one cycle.

    Our hypothesis is that the movement properties of the subjunctive allow extraction of non-D-linked adjuncts (observed in the preceding discussion), whereas the indicative does not.

    If an item does not satisfy *all* the conditions proposed by Cinque, then according to his theory, it can only be successive cyclically moved. However, in the cases usually considered in the literature, at least *one* of the requirements mentioned above is satisfied. In the cases considered here, none of the requirements is satisfied. That is, the adjunct is neither D-linked, nor generated in

A-position, nor referentially θ-marked. On the other hand, *come* (how) and *perché* (why) must be interpreted as belonging to a predicate of a certain clause. This seems to be the minimal requirement they must satisfy at LF. Intuitively, it is easy to interpret an adjunct as modifying the clause it appears in. In order for it to be interpreted as belonging to a different clause — that is, in order for a trace to be retrieved — some identification requirement must be met at LF. In other words, if the trace does not satisfy any of the constraints discussed by Cinque, we propose that it must be identified at LF. Non-D-linked adjuncts must enter a θ-identification configuration (see Higginbotham 1985, 1989) with the eventive variable of the verb. This is a Spec-head configuration.

Recall now that it was argued that a subjunctive verb moves to MOOD/AGR, whereas an indicative verb does not move to C, as shown by the lack of CD phenomena in the latter case. If movement is not overt — that is, when the syncretic category MOOD/AGR has been scattered — the subjunctive verb covertly moves to MOOD. There is no reason to hypothesise a similar movement for an indicative. Let us further propose, as claimed by Longobardi (1983) and Cinque (1990, ch. 2), that (at least in certain cases) adjuncts can directly originate in the *Spec* of a complementiser projection. A subjunctive verb moves to the head MOOD, either before or after Spell-Out, and can therefore identify an adjunct trace in its *Spec*. An indicative form could not satisfy such a requirement, given that, according to our hypothesis, it does not move to a complementiser head. Consequently, movement out of an indicative clause is admitted only for D-linked adjuncts, i.e. for those which already satisfy at least one of Cinque's requirements.

The combination of this property plus the requirement of being successive cyclically moved — in Cinque's terms, the impossibility for adjunct traces to establish a binding relation with their antecedents — determines the *single cycle* requirement. In fact, nothing prevents the adjunct from being moved through more than one clause, provided that at each cycle the trace satisfies the identification requirement. In other words, at each step the trace of the adjunct can be successfully identified by the raised subjunctive. Only the *last* identification of the trace, however, is available at LF, because a lexical item can be interpreted only once.[74] The consequence of this hypothesis is that sentences (153) and (156) are at most two ways ambiguous. In fact, the construal of the adjunct with the most embedded clause is ruled out, whereas the other two possibilities are available. Indeed either the phrase in question is interpreted as an adjunct of the highest verb, with no movement at all, or a movement derivation has taken place, constrained by the identification requirement. On the other hand, sentences (152) and (155) are not ambiguous. In this case, the verb of the first embedded clause is indicative; therefore, it does not raise to C, and consequently successive cyclic movement fails, given that the intervening trace of the adjunct is not identified at LF. Recall, in fact, that an indicative verb in Italian can only raise to AGR. However, this is not sufficient to establish a Spec-head relation with an adjunct trace in the Specifier of the complementiser.

More formally, we propose the following principles:

(163)  A trace must be identified at LF.

(164)  A trace is identified iff *at least one* of the following conditions is satisfied: it is θ-marked; it is in an A-position; it is D-linked; it enters a Spec-head agreement relation with the relevant predicate.

The principles in (163) and (164) permit an identification of the predicate a trace belongs to. If the trace in question is D-linked, it is obviously identified by the discourse; if it is not, it can be an argument, or can appear in an A-position, and as such is identified thanks to its argumenthood. If none of these conditions is met, the predicate must identify the trace in a Spec-head configuration, as proposed above. It has been argued (Cinque 1990; Longobardi 1983) that *why* and *how* can either originate from within the VP or outside it. The two possibilities correspond to different interpretations: VP-internal *why* and *how* yield a purpose and an instrumental interpretation, respectively. A VP-external *why* however, is interpreted as expressing a cause, and a VP-external *how*, as expressing a manner specification. Accordingly, it can be argued (see Larson 1988) that in VP-internal position, adverbs have a quasi-argumental interpretation, being generated in an A-position, and they therefore satisfy the principle in (164) without resorting to the Spec-head agreement strategy. Our theory predicts that the extraction from indicative contexts of VP-internal *why* and *how* should improve with respect to the extraction of VP-external *why* and *how*. This can be tested by forcing the VP-internal reading of the adjunct by means of the context. Consider the following examples:

(165)    Come ti ha detto che ha cotto la carne?
         How did he tell you that he cooked the meat?
    a.   (?)Con la pentola a pressione.
         With the pressure cooker.
    b.   *Indossando un berretto da cuoco.
         Wearing a chef hat.

(166)    Perché ti ha detto che è partito?
         Why did he tell you that he left?
    a.   Per andare a trovare la sorella.
         To visit his sister.
    b.   *Perché era arrabbiato.
         Because he was angry.

If the trace can be located inside the VP, as in the case of instrumentals and final clauses, it can be identified without resorting to movement of the verb. As a consequence, even the indicative is grammatical (cf. (165a) and (166a)). This does not happen, however, if a manner or causal interpretation of the adjunct is forced by the context. In this case, the adjunct is generated directly in C, and an indicative verb cannot identify the trace, given that it does not raise to such a position (cf. (165b) and (166b)). Let us finally emphasise again that the ungrammaticality we find in (165b) and (166b) is less strong than a typical weak island violation. Our theory, which attributes the effects to the violation of two different requirements, can correctly capture this observation.

If this proposal is on the right track, we have an additional argument in favour of the analysis of CD contexts as being due to the movement properties of the subjunctive. As discussed in §5.2.4.1., in CD clauses the verb overtly moves to MOOD/AGR, because of the strong $\phi$-features. If the category is not syncretic — that is, there are no CD effects — movement of the subjunctive verb is covert but can still be detected by means of extraction phenomena, as shown by the preceding examples.

Consider finally that we predict the grammaticality of sentences (157) to (160). Arguments, even non-D-linked ones, satisfy *at least one* of Cinque's requirements and as such can be extracted out of indicative clauses, without exhibiting any constraint on the number of clauses they cross.

Let us now illustrate another piece of evidence showing that in CD structures there is only *one Spec* position available, as predicted by our hypothesis concerning syncretic categories. As pointed out in the previous section, for some speakers a lexical preverbal subject is acceptable in CD constructions, as in the following case:

(167)   Credevo Gianni fosse partito.
        I believed Gianni had(SUBJ) left.

Note, however, that when *perché* (why) or *come* (how) are extracted out of the embedded clause, the same speakers strongly prefer the sentences in which the subject is inverted or not realised at all (for the relevant reading — that is, with the adjunct constructed with the lower clause):

(168)   ?* Perché$_i$ credevi Gianni avesse telefonato t$_i$?
        Why did you believe Gianni had(SUBJ) phoned?

(169)   Perché$_i$ credevi avesse telefonato t$_i$?
        Why did you believe (he) had(SUBJ) phoned?

(170)   Perché$_i$ credevi avesse telefonato Gianni t$_i$?
        Why did you believe had(SUBJ) phoned Gianni?

(171)   ?* Come$_i$ credevi Gianni fosse scappato di prigione t$_i$?
        How did you believe Gianni had(SUBJ) escaped from prison?

(172)   Come$_i$ credevi fosse scappato di prigione t$_i$?
        How did you believe (he) had(SUBJ) escaped from prison?

(173)   Come$_i$ credevi fosse scappato Gianni t$_i$?
        How did you believe had(SUBJ) escaped Gianni?

This pattern of data follows from our account. For these speakers, the *Spec* of MOOD/AGR can be occupied by the subject — that is, it can be an A-position. If (Spec,MOOD/AGR) has to be filled by a trace, the subject appears postverbally. The adjunct must land in this position, because movement is necessarily cyclic. This fact provides further evidence in favour of the idea that there is *only one* Spec position available in CD constructions.[75]

Let us briefly return to echo-questions. For simplicity, we reproduce the relevant dialogues here:

(149)  A: Gianni è partito indossando il suo vestito migliore.
           Gianni left wearing his best suit.
       B: Come hai detto che è partito?
           How did you say he left(IND)?
       A: Indossando il suo vestito migliore!
           Wearing his best suit!

(150)  A: Gianni è partito perché era arrabbiato.
           Gianni left because he was angry.
       B: Perché hai detto che è partito?
           Why did you say that he left(IND)?
       A: Perché era arrabbiato!
           Because he was angry!

*Why* and *how* are normally non-D-linked forms, contrasting with *per quale ragione* (for which reason) and *in che modo* (in which way). Therefore, we expect them to be ungrammatical in indicative contexts. In (149) and (150), however, they are grammatical. The explanation is trivial: the adjunct trace can easily be identified by means of the context without resorting to the verb movement strategy. In some sense, in fact, the adjunct trace turns out to be discourse linked, given that the domain the interrogative operator ranges over is clearly provided by the context. In other words, it is *discourse old*. According to this view, we do not expect echo-questions to be sensitive to the distinction between the indicative and the subjunctive mood.

Another interesting property of the embedded contexts is the fact that for some speakers, especially those from central and southern Italy, the imperfect indicative can replace the subjunctive, at least in some cases.[76] For instance, the imperfect indicative is quite common with verbs which belong to the *credere* (believe) class, whereas for many speakers of the same area it is still quite marginal with volitional verbs, such as *volere* (want). In §5.1. of this chapter it was argued, in fact, that volitional contexts constitute the core class of verbs requiring a subjunctive and that in this respect there is almost no variation across the languages which have a productive indicative/subjunctive distinction.

Consider the following examples (where "#" identifies the central and southern Italian varieties):[77]

(174)  a.  Credeva che fosse partito.
           He believed that he had(IMPF SUBJ) left.
       b.  #Credeva che era partito.
           He believed that he had(IMPF IND) left.

(175) a. Voleva che partisse.
He wanted that he leaved (IMPF SUBJ).
b. # *Voleva che partiva.
He wanted that he left (IMPF IND).

Sentence (174b) is grammatical for (some) central and southern Italian speakers, whereas (usually) it is not for northern Italian speakers. Notice that for the speakers who accept (174b), the imperfect indicative patterns with the other indicative tenses, as far as CD phenomena are concerned; that is, CD is impossible:

(176) # *Credeva era partito.
He believed he had (IMPF IND) left.

One might wonder what happens in these contexts with respect to extraction phenomena. Given the lack of CD effects, we also predict extraction to pattern together with the indicative, contrasting with the subjunctive. This prediction is borne out:[78]

(177) a. Perché$_i$ credevi che Gianni fosse partito t$_i$?
Why did you believe that Gianni had(IMPF SUBJ) left?
b. *Perché$_i$ mi hai raccontato che Gianni è partito t$_i$?
Why did you told me that Gianni has(PRES IND) left?
c. # *Perché$_i$ credevi che Gianni era partito t$_i$?
Why did you believe that Gianni had(IMPF IND) left?

(178) a. Come$_i$ credevi che Gianni fosse partito t$_i$?
How did you believe that Gianni had(IMPF SUBJ) left?
b. *Come$_i$ mi hai raccontato che Gianni è partito t$_i$?
How did you told me that Gianni has(PRES IND) left?
c. # *Come$_i$ credevi che Gianni era partito t$_i$?
How did you believe that Gianni had(IMPF IND) left?

These contrasts show that for the speakers in question, the imperfect indicative, even though it can appear in (almost) the same contexts where the subjunctive does, does not share with the latter its movement properties. It therefore excludes the possibility of licensing a non-D-linked adjunct. The ungrammaticality of (177b) and (c) and (178b) and (c), in fact, points to the conclusion that the imperfect indicative does not raise to the relevant position, even if it appears in the contexts where in other Italian varieties the subjunctive is used. In the next chapter, an observation of this kind will be shown to hold in English exactly in the same contexts — that is, *believe* contexts. We will show that the indicative form appearing in English in *believe* contexts has many properties in common with the Italian imperfect indicative and, crucially, not with the simple past form.

## 5.2.6. Conclusions

In this section we have shown that in Italian the weak feature *mood* can be analysed as constituting the syncretic category MOOD/AGR together with the φ-features. Furthermore, it has been proposed that mood must be checked by a corresponding feature on the verb. These two hypotheses provide a simple and elegant account for CD phenomena in Italian, and they also play a crucial role in the explanation of a number of interesting and hitherto largely ignored facts about extraction from subordinate clauses. It has been shown, in fact, that extraction of non-D-linked adjuncts from complement clauses is more marginal when the verb is an indicative form than when it is a subjunctive form. Moreover, non-D-linked adjunct extraction is limited to one cycle. These phenomena have been accounted for by hypothesising that such adjuncts are generated in the *Spec* of the scattered MOOD position and that their traces need to be in a Spec-head configuration with the verb at LF in order for identification requirements to be met. A subjunctive verb can serve for these purposes because, contrary to an indicative verb, it moves to MOOD to check its feature *mood*. The same requirement on trace identification rules out non-D-linked extraction longer than one cycle. Finally, the analogies between CD contexts and interrogative subject inversion in Italian have been argued to stem from a deeper formal principle. In Italian the feature *Wh* and the φ-features are syncretic, forming the category WH/AGR. This shows that the syncretism of AGR in Italian is a general property of this language and that our theory of features and of their realisations has been shown to be descriptively and explanatorily adequate.

## Appendix. Conditionals and counterfactuals

In this appendix we analyse some of the factors affecting mood choice in conditional sentences, mainly considering Italian, even if we cannot provide here a consistent theory of mood choice in conditional contexts.

A conditional is formed by a matrix clause, the so-called *apodosis,* and by an adverbial clause, introduced by a special conjunction, *se* (if). The adverbial clause is called the *protasis*, or the *if*-clause, of the conditional.[79] There are two basic types of conditional sentences: the so-called indicative conditional sentences, exemplified in (179a), and the counterfactual conditionals, exemplified in (179b):[80]

(179)  a.  If John has been to Paris, he has gone to visit the Louvre.
       b.  If John had arrived on time, we would have gone to the cinema.

We will also provide some suggestions for future research to explain the presence of the indicative in counterfactual conditionals in languages such as French, which, as we will see, in these contexts only uses the *imperfect* indicative.

An important feature of counterfactual conditionals is that the falsity of the protasis is presupposed. Thus, (179b) is appropriate in a situation in which *John* has not arrived on time. In Italian, the protases of counterfactual conditionals have the subjunctive mood (cf. (21a), repeated here):[81]

(21)   a.   Se Mario fosse arrivato in orario, lo avrei incontrato.
            If Mario had(SUBJ) been on time, I would have met him.

Indicative conditionals, on the other hand, do not presuppose anything about the truth of the protasis. In this case, the mood of the *if*-clause is always the indicative.

Notice that in Italian, as well as in other Romance languages, the imperfect indicative can appear in counterfactual protases (and in the apodosis), even if only marginally:[82]

(180)   Se Mario arrivava primo, la squadra vinceva.
        If Mario arrived(IMPF) first, the team would(IMPF) have won (counterfactual).

(181)   Se Mario è arrivato primo, la squadra ha vinto.
        If Mario arrived (PRES PERF) first, the team has won (non-counterfactual).

Other tenses of the indicative, however, cannot. Therefore when we mention *indicative* conditionals, we mean the conditionals where tenses of the indicative *other than the imperfect* appear. We will consider these cases in a while.

Kratzer (1991a) analyses indicative conditional sentences as implicitly modalised. For instance, she argues that there is a morphologically null necessity operator in sentences such as (179a), so that it must be treated on a par with (182):

(182)   If John has gone to Paris, he must have visited the Louvre.

Let *if $\alpha$ then $\beta$* be the general template of conditionals. A major difference between conditionals and the sentences discussed in the previous sections concerns the role of the proposition expressed by the *if*-clause. According to Kratzer (1991a) such a proposition is added to the modal base. Therefore, the following truth conditions for conditionals can be given (Kratzer 1991a, Definition 13):

(183)   $[\![$ if $\alpha$ (then) $\beta ]\!]^{f,g} = [\![$ must $\beta ]\!]^{f',g}$ where, for every world $w$, $f'(w) = f(w) \cup \{[\![ \alpha ]\!]^{f,g}\}$

The denotation of the *if*-clause is added to the modal base, and $\beta$ is then evaluated with respect to such a modified conversational background. The different kinds of conditional sentences can be distinguished according to the characteristics of the modal base or ordering source they select. For example, bare indicative conditionals, as in (179a), have a totally realistic modal base and an empty ordering source (i.e. each world in the modal base is as close to the ideal as any other world). Thus, if $\mathcal{P}$ is the common ground at the point where (179a) is uttered, and $C$ is the corresponding context set, then it follows that $f(w) = \mathcal{P}$ for every world in $C$, $f'(w) = \mathcal{P} \cup \{[\![ John \ has \ gone \ to \ Paris ]\!]^f\}$, and the apodosis *John has visited the Louvre* is evaluated with respect to $f'$. Therefore, (179a) is true in a world $w \in C$ iff *John has visited the Louvre* is true in each world of the derived context set $C' = \cap(\mathcal{P} \cup [\![\textit{John has gone to Paris}]\!]^f)$. Ultimately, it is true in $w$ iff in each world which is like $w$ and in which *John has gone to Paris* is true, *John has visited the Louvre* is also true.

According to Kratzer, counterfactuals have an empty modal base and a totally realistic ordering source. Thus $f'(w) = [\![\alpha]\!]$ for every world in the context set.[83] The ordering source is totally realistic — that is, the ideal is the actual world as described by the current common ground. Eventually, (179b) is true in a world $w$ iff for every world $w' \in [\![\alpha]\!]$, $\beta$ is true in all the worlds that are closer to the ideal than $w'$.

Kratzer's account of conditionals, together with the account developed here for mood choice, provides a straightforward explanation for the indicative in the *if*-clause of (179a). The protasis is evaluated with respect to a context which *is* the common ground. Therefore, the indicative is consistently selected across languages.[84]

Her account of counterfactuals, however, does not immediately fit the proposal we made in the previous section about the factors determining mood choice. It has been noted in the literature (see among others Palmer 1986), in fact, that not every subjunctive conditional needs to be strictly counterfactual, in the sense of presupposing the falsehood of the protasis:

(184)  Se Maria danzasse, tutti l'applaudirebbero.
        If Mary danced(SUBJ), everyone would applaud(COND) her.

Here, a hypothetical situation is depicted in which if Mary dances, everyone applauds her. No presupposition concerning the falsity of the protasis is involved in (184). In general, even past tense subjunctive conditionals need not be strictly counterfactual:

(185)  Se Mario fosse arrivato, Andrea sarebbe uscito.
        If Mario had(SUBJ) arrived, Andrea would have(COND) left.

Example (185) does not entail that *Mario è arrivato* (Mario has arrived) is currently false. Finally, (184) and (185) have almost synonymous indicative counterparts:

(186)  a.  Se Maria danza, tutti l'applaudiranno.
            If Maria dances(IND), everyone will(IND) applaud her.
        b.  Se Mario è arrivato, Andrea è uscito.
            If Maria has(IND) arrived, Andrea has(IND) left.

Given their similar meanings, what determines the subjunctive in (184) and (185) and the indicative in (186)? If (184) has the same meaning as (186a) — that is, if a null ordering source is involved — then the generalisation made in the previous section would predict the presence of an indicative in (184). Furthermore, there are problems even with respect to indicative conditionals:

(187)  Se Mario parcheggia in sosta vietata, deve pagare una multa.
        If Mario parks(IND) in a non-parking zone, he must(IND) pay a fine.

The modal base for (187) is null, but the ordering source is deontic. Thus, we would expect the mood of the *if*-clause to be the subjunctive.

To solve these problems, notice that a closer comparison between (184) and (185), on the one hand, and (186), on the other, reveals some differences. For instance, (186a) can be used in a situation in which the speaker has neither any information about, nor any attitude toward, the truth of *Maria danza* (Mary dances). Example (186a) simply expresses the speaker's conviction that were Mary to dance, the audience would applaud her. Example (184) on the other hand, is not appropriate in such a situation. To use it, the speaker *must* have some attitude toward *Maria danza* (Mary dances). For instance, he/she must assume that, for some reason, it is unlikely that she will do so. That is, the speaker's expectations exclude that *Maria danza* is true. Let us now consider (186b) and (185). Example (186b) simply reports a necessary connection between Mario's arrival and Andrea's leaving: if the former is true, the latter is true as well. Thus, (186b) could be uttered by someone before entering a room, without any knowledge about the presence of Mario and Andrea in the room. Example (185), however, is not felicitous in the same situation. In order to be uttered, it requires an epistemic commitment by the speaker. For instance, he/she enters a room and finds Andrea there; then he/she can utter (185), meaning that, according to what he/she knows, the presence of Andrea is evidence for the fact that Mario has not arrived. Therefore, the conditionals in (184) and (185) differ from their indicative counterparts in that the falsity of the *if*-clause is presupposed (or asserted, as in (185)) within a special modal context: an expectation-based one in (184), and an epistemic one in (185).

Consider now the following sentences, adapted from Kartunnen & Peters (1979) (see also McCawley 1993):

(188)   Se Maria fosse allergica alla penicillina, avrebbe gli stessi sintomi che mostra ora.
        If Mary were(SUBJ) allergic to penicillin, she would have(COND) the same symptoms she is having now.

Example (188) could be uttered by a physician trying to convince his sceptical colleagues that Mary's symptoms are actually due to her allergy to penicillin. Thus, as far as the physician is concerned, the protasis is true. However, his colleagues are assuming that Mary is not allergic to penicillin and that her symptoms cannot be attributed to this fact. On the basis of examples such as this one, Portner (1994) argues that the falsehood of the *if*-clause need not be relative to the common ground. In (188), in fact, the common ground of the conversation between the physician and his colleagues does not contain any proposition concerning whether Mary is allergic to penicillin. Some participants, in fact, are assuming that the proposition is false, and at least one of them assumes it to be true. Rather, a doxastic conversational background seems to be involved here, concerning the colleagues' opinions. It is with respect to this that the *if*-clause of (188) is false.

Generalising these observations, there is an ordering source in subjunctive conditionals such that the *if*-clause is false in every possible world which is closest to the corresponding ideal. Concerning (188), let us assume, as suggested by Kratzer, that the modal base is empty — that is, that the derived context set is the set of all possible worlds $W$. The ordering source, $g$, is formed by the doxastic propositions shared by the physician's colleagues, such that in every world of $W$ which is close to the (doxastic) ideal it is false that Mary is allergic to penicillin. Consider what the evaluation context is for the apodosis. According to (183), let us add the meaning of the *if*-clause $p$ to the modal base. The derived context set is now $\cap\{p\}$, that is, the set of worlds where it is true that Mary is allergic to penicillin. The doxastic ordering source $g$, however, contained $\neg p$.

Therefore, the ordering source for the apodosis $g'$ cannot be the same as that for the protasis. We propose that $g'$ is such that, for every world $w$, $g'(w) = g(w)-\{\neg p\}$. That is, the apodosis ordering source is like that of the protasis, except for the proposition concerning Mary's allergy to penicillin. As a consequence, (188) is true in $w$ only if the apodosis is true in every world $w'$ in which Mary is allergic to penicillin (this being contributed by the protasis) and which is closest to the ideal represented by $g'(w)$; the latter, in turn, consists of the doxastic propositions of the colleagues minus that concerning Mary's allergy.[85]

Thus, the evaluation of a counterfactual conditional *if $\alpha$ then $\beta$* requires an ordering source $g$ such that the protasis is false in $g(w)$, for every $w$. The evaluation procedure amounts to: (a) forcing in the (empty) modal base the propositional content of the protasis, as in Kratzer (1991a), this way obtaining the derived context set $⟦\alpha⟧$, and (b) computing the new ordering source $g'$ which is exactly like $g$ apart from the fact that $\neg p \notin g'(w)$, for every $w$. The evaluation of the apodosis then proceeds as usual.[86]

According to this proposal, examples such as (184), (185), and (188) are all counterfactual, albeit not necessarily so with respect to a totally realistic ordering source. We saw that in (188) a doxastic ordering source is present; in (184) the speaker's expectations are relevant, so that the sentence could be paraphrased as "I do not expect Mary to dance, but if she did she would be clapped". Ordinary counterfactuals, as in (62), have a totally realistic ordering source:

(189)   Se Maria avesse organizzato la festa ieri, ci saremmo divertiti di più.
        If Mary had(SUBJ) organised the party yesterday, we would have(COND) enjoyed it much more.

Thus, counterfactuality always requires some attitude of the participants in the conversation toward the truth of the protasis, be it believed, expected, or presupposed to be false. The difference between (184) and (186a), on the one hand, and (185) and (186b), on the other, is due to the fact that no such attitude toward the truth of the protasis is involved in (186). In (186), a direct relationship between the truth of the two clauses is established, the truth of the apodosis being dependent on the truth of the protasis. The same holds with respect to (187). What unifies (186) and (187) is the fact that the modal base is realistic, and the ordering source, be it empty or deontic, does not affect the *if*-clause. In these cases, the role played by the protasis consists only in restricting the modal base, according to (183).

This is different from what happens with counterfactuals, where it is crucial that the protasis is false in each world that is closest to the ideal, as established by *g*. Thus, it is not surprising that the indicative is chosen in (186a), (186b), and (187), whereas the subjunctive appears in the counterfactuals. The contexts where the *if*-clauses of these sentences are evaluated are (totally) realistic — that is, identical to the relevant common grounds. Thus, the indicative is expected, given the kind of parametrisation we proposed in the previous section. On the other hand, with counterfactuals, a non-empty ordering source crucially affects the evaluation of the *if*-clause, creating a context which is quite different from common grounds. As a consequence, the subjunctive is required.

Therefore, we conclude that in languages such as Italian the mood of the protasis of conditionals follows from the theory proposed. Interestingly, it has been shown that the conclusion carries over to cases such as (184) and (189), where there is no factual presupposition concerning the falsity of the *if*-clause. This result has been achieved by observing that the falsity concerns not the current context set but rather some other context sets — for example, referring to the speaker's expectations or beliefs — which contributes to forming the ordering source for the counterfactual. We also proposed that the apodosis needs a revised ordering source differing from that of the protasis in that $\neg p$ does not belong to it, where $p$ is the proposition associated with the *if*-clause. In the end, we claim that subjunctive conditionals are always counterfactual, albeit not necessarily so with respect to the common ground. Such a property distinguishes them from indicative conditionals that always have an empty ordering source, as suggested by Kratzer (1991a).

We have seen in the preceding examples (cf. (180) and (181)), that in Italian and in other Romance languages the imperfect indicative is a possible, even if slightly substandard, option in counterfactual contexts. The imperfect indicative is also the standard way of expressing the counterfactuals in French:

(190)   Si Mario avait été anglais il n'aurait pas repondu de cette façon.
        If Mario were (IMPF) English, he would not have answered that way.

Let us suggest a possible line of reasoning to solve this problem. These facts might seem counterexamples to our generalisations; however, also in the light of what we argued for in chapter 4, they are not. In chapter 4 §4.2.1.4. in fact, we pointed out that in Italian and French, as well as in other Romance languages such as Spanish, the imperfect indicative can be used in modal contexts, as, for instance, the so-called *imperfait preludique*:

(191)   Facciamo che tu eri il re ed io la regina.
        Let's pretend that I was(IMPF) the king and you the queen.

There we suggested that in these contexts the past interpretation of the imperfect is lost, in favour of a modal reading. This mechanism, of expressing modality with a temporally marked form, is also observed in certain modal contexts of English, see chapter 3 §3.1.4. Notice that the contexts in (191) share with counterfactuals the presupposition that the relevant proposition is false in the common ground. It is not surprising, therefore, that the same verbal form appears in counterfactual conditionals in standard French, and as a substandard variant in Italian (and other Romance languages). Further research is indeed required to explain why counterfactual contexts, but not other ones, might have this additional option in Italian and why in French the subjunctive is excluded.[87]

## Notes

1. In this work we will not consider the distinction between the two types of German subjunctives: Konjunktiv I and Konjunktiv II.

2. The subjunctive is the standard way to express commands where the verb is in the third person (both singular and plural). The second person always requires the imperative:

(i)     Vai!

        (you) go!

On imperatives in Italian, see Zanuttini (1995) and Graffi (1995).

3. As anticipated in the text, these predicates are not included in Hooper's classification. However, they are important for the understanding of the factors determining mood choice, as we will see.

Some speakers of Italian accept the imperfective indicative in the subordinate clause of a volitional verb, as in (i)a. However, they consistently reject the present indicative, as in (i)b:

(i)     a.   ?Mario voleva che Carlo partiva.

             Mario wanted that Carlo left(IMPF-IND).

        b.   *Mario vuole che Carlo parte domani.

             Mario wants that Carlo leaves(PRES-IND) tomorrow.

4. In German an indicative is also possible:

(i)     Ich will, daß du kommst.

        I want that you come(IND).

We will not investigate here the different meanings which German speakers attribute to (i) with respect to the corresponding sentence with a subjunctive.

5. Notice that if the verb *say* appears in the impersonal form, the subjunctive is also allowed:

(i)     Si dice/dicono che Maria sia partita.

        One says/ people say that Maria has(SUBJ) left.

6.  Italian, Portuguese, and German also admit the indicative. See following discussion of this possibility. Furthermore, French requires the indicative if the matrix *believe* verb is negated.

7.  Another problem for selectional accounts of mood choice is presented by relative clauses:

(i)      a.  Mario saluta chiunque incontri/?incontra.
             Mario says good-bye to everyone he meets(SUBJ)/meets(IND).
         b.  Mario saluta tutti quelli che *incontri/incontra.
             Mario says good-bye to every person he meets(SUBJ)/meets(IND).

In (i) the acceptability of the subjunctive vs. the indicative mood does not depend on the predicate in any obvious way.

8.  Notice that this account leaves open the possibility for other items, such as negation and the interrogative operator, to determine mood choice insofar as they affect the properties of evaluation contexts.

9.  Roussou (1994), developing ideas by Manzini (1994a), hypothesises that the subjunctive corresponds to an indefinite T which is bound by a sentential operator supplied by the verb of the matrix clause.

10.  Tsoulas (1994) also discusses Modern Greek data corresponding to (27) and (28), showing that the pattern is the same as in French.

11.  The relevant mood distinction might be taken to be a binary one since we are not considering here such moods as the imperative and the conditional.

12.  According to Stalnaker (1979, p. 315) "An act of assertion is, among other things the expression of a proposition, something that represents the world as being a certain way" Furthermore "... assertions are made in a context" and "... sometimes the content of an assertion is dependent on the context in which it is made". Finally, (ib.) "[...] acts of assertion affect, or are intended to affect such contexts".

13.  It must be noted that Stalnaker's (1979) theory does not require a common ground to be actually formed by common or mutual knowledge. The speaker may not even believe the relevant propositions; what is necessary is that he/she *treats* them as a common ground and acts *as if* the audience does the same. That is, what is important is the commitment overtly expressed by the speaker toward the truth of such propositions, not whether he/she actually believes them to be true.

14.  It should be noted that the tense of both the modal and the subordinate verb can influence the meaning of sentences with modals such as *must*:

(i)      a.  Maria deve andare a trovare sua madre.
             Maria must go to visit her mother.
         b.  Maria deve essere andata a trovare sua madre.
             Maria must have gone to visit her mother.
         c.  Maria è dovuta andare a trovare sua madre.
             Lit.: Maria is must(past-part) go to visit her mother.
             Maria had to go to visit her mother.

Example (i)a is ambiguous between a deontic and a (slightly more marginal) epistemic reading: it can either mean that Mary has the obligation to go to visit her mother or that, according to the available evidence (e.g., according to the fact that she is not at home), she is going to visit her mother. This is not the case with (i)b: the perfect tense on the subordinate verb makes available only the epistemic reading. On the other hand, with the present perfect modal of (i)c only the deontic reading is possible. We will not consider here these phenomena. For more on this point, see Brennan (1993) and references cited there.

15. More precisely, a proposition $p$ is a *necessity* in a world $w$ with respect to a modal base $f$ and an ordering source $g$ iff:

(i)    For every $u \in \cap f(w)$ there is a $v \in \cap f(w)$ such that $v \leq_g u$ and for every $z \in \cup f(w)$, if $z \leq_g v$ then $z \in p$.

16. One may go further by noticing that the common ground is by itself epistemic, being formed by shared common knowledge.

17. Equivalently, $f$ is realistic iff $f : \cap \mathcal{P} \to 2^{\mathcal{P}}$. Both the definitions of a realistic and of a totally realistic modal base are generalisations of the similar notions of Kratzer (1981; 1991a). See also Roberts (1989).

18. This is not to deny that ordering sources are shared among participants. However, ordering sources have a different status in that they aim to characterise the world not as it is but as it *could* or *should* be, provided that certain conditions are met.

19. Actually, Chomsky (1995) proposes that assertive illocutionary force is encoded by means of a weak feature in the complementiser C. The difference is immaterial for our purposes.

20. Cf. also n. 15.

21. To exemplify how the interaction between modal bases and ordering sources determines the evaluation context, consider the conditions given in n. 12 for a proposition $p$ to be a necessity in a world $w$. It is required that for every world $w'$ in the modal base there exists another world (in the same modal base) that is closer to the ideal established by the ordering source than $w'$, and such that, for every other world $w''$ closer than $w'$ to the same ideal, $p$ is true in $w''$. Let us now suppose that a non-empty ordering source $g$ and a realistic modal base $f$ are given. According to (23), the order induced by $g$ on the derived context set is a preorder (i.e., it is transitive and reflexive). Therefore, the structure $\langle \cap f(w), \leq_g \rangle$ is a preordered set of possible worlds. Let us now introduce some terminology:

(i)    Given a preorder $O = \langle A, \leq \rangle$, $Q \subseteq A$ is a *down set* of $O$ iff for every $x \in Q$, if $y \leq x$ then $y \in Q$.

(ii)   Let $O = \langle A, \leq \rangle$ be a partial order. Then $\downarrow x = \{ y \mid y \leq x \}$ is the *principal down set* generated by $x$.

For the purposes of our discussion we will then strengthen the ordering condition induced by the ordering source to a partial ordering — that is, to one which is transitive, reflexive and antisymmetric. The condition in n. 15 for the proposition $p$ to be a necessity amounts to requiring that $p$ be evaluated in the principal down sets of

$\langle \cap f(w), \leq_g \rangle$. More precisely, we can restate the relevant portion of the condition in n. 15 as follows:

...... for every $u \in \cap f(w)$ there is a $v \in \cap f(w)$ such that $z \in p$ for every $z \in \downarrow v$.

Thus, the context for evaluating the truth of $p$ with respect to $\langle \cap f(w), \leq_g \rangle$ is a subset of the set of principal down sets $I = \{ \downarrow x \}$. Given one such principal down set $Q$, each world it contains is such that there are propositions of the ordering source that are true in it. If the ordering source provides norms, and norms are non-realistic, then $I$ as a whole can be regarded as a non-realistic context for $p$; that is, the context of evaluation for $p$ is non-realistic. Such a characterisation extends to the case where the modal force is *possibility*, the only difference being the kind of quantification (existential) that is required (at the level of the metalanguage) for a proposition $p$ to be a possibility in a world (see Kratzer 1991a).

Other cases can be treated in a similar way. Suppose that the modal base is empty, whereas the ordering source is non-null. Thus, for each world $w$ in the common ground $f(w) = \varnothing$; an empty modal base is a degenerate case of a realistic one, since $\varnothing \subseteq P$, for every set of proposition $P$. Applying the same reasoning as before, we conclude that the set of principal down sets $I$ in the structure $\langle W, \leq_g \rangle$ is again the evaluation set for the proposition. $I$, as a context set, is non-realistic. Finally, consider the case in which the ordering source is empty — $g(w) = \varnothing$ for every world $w$. Then, each world in the modal base is as close to the ideal as every other world in the same modal base. That is, there is just one down set, $f(w)$, whose status, concerning the realistic/non-realistic distinction, only depends on whether or not the modal base is realistic.

22. See Heim (1992) for a different implementation of similar ideas. The fact that wishes and desires require ordering sources accounts for the observation that one may entertain inconsistent wishes — for instance, one might want that $p$ and also that $q$, where $p$ and $q$ are mutually inconsistent. For instance, a person may want to spend his holidays in Spain and at the same time want to spend them in Iceland, without being charged for any inconsistency. The wished propositions, in fact, are required to be true in some world of the modal base that is closest to the ideal represented by the subject's wishes. In the terminology introduced in n. 21, we require that, for each world in the modal base, there is a principal down set where $p$ is true and a principal down set where $q$ is true. The two sets need not be the same. That is, closest worlds need not realise the same set of wishes. Thus it may be that in a principal down set where $p$ is true, $q$ is false and vice versa. Therefore, an effect of having a non-null ordering source contributing to the evaluation base is that the truth of a proposition remains local, within down sets.

These considerations have more general import: the existence of a non-null ordering source always has the effect of localising the truth conditions for a clause to particular subsets of the domain itself — namely, the down sets of n. 21. When the ordering source is null, all the worlds in the derived context set are maximally close to the ideal. In this case, the truth conditions for necessity require the relevant clause to be true in every such world.

In this respect, modalised sentences with null ordering sources are structurally similar to normal assertions: let $C$ be a context set, as usual, and $C_a = C$ and $C_b = \cap f(w)$

be the two derived context sets for an assertion and for a modalised proposition having a null ordering source and a modal base $f$ (cf. ex. 26). In both cases the whole of $C_a$ and $C_b$ are relevant to the purpose of evaluating the clause.

23. In a language such as Italian, the same distinction is expressed by mood choice — namely, indicative vs. conditional:

(i)     a. Voglio che tu sia felice.
           I want(IND) you to be(SUBJ) happy.
        b. Vorrei che tu fossi felice.
           Lit.: I want(COND) that you were(SUBJ) happy.
           I wish you were happy.

When *volere* (want) is in the indicative mood it behaves as the English verb *want* — that is, the embedded proposition does not express a counterfactual. When *volere* is in the conditional, the embedded proposition is, normally, a counterfactual. In this case the verb of the subordinated clause must be an imperfect subjunctive — that is, *fossi* (you were(Imp-SUBJ)); the present subjunctive, *sia* (you are/Pres-SUBJ), is ungrammatical.

24. Therefore, *want* is similar to *believe* verbs in having a doxastic modal base (see following discussion). It differs from them in that it has a non-null *bouletic* ordering source.

25. Here we are abstracting away from considerations about the modal force.

26. Formally, in one case the domain of evaluation is a set of sets of worlds, $B \subseteq 2^{\cap f(w)}$. In the other case it is simply $B = \cap f(w)$. Portner (1994) speaks of the cumulativity of belief and conversational contexts, meaning that every believed/asserted proposition is entailed by the doxastic/conversational information. Wants and wishes, instead, create non-cumulative contexts, for the same reasons discussed here.

27. Therefore, a common ground is always non-empty, even at the very beginning of a conversation.

28. Actually, the requirement in question seems to be stronger than that stated in the text by (52). If the considerations made above are correct, it is not the case that every subset of a common ground suffices to identify weakly realistic modal bases. Rather, it must be that every such set contains some sort of minimal common knowledge required from every participant in a conversation — for instance, information about the way speakers and hearers must behave. Besides this common core, it is conceivable that the commonalties between the current and the reported conversations are subject to changes. Thus, if *John* in (50a) is a baby child, and the relevant sentence has been uttered during a conversation between children, then (50a) is completely acceptable. This is so because the participants of the adult, current conversation do not extend the relevant presupposition to the children involved in the reported conversation.

29. Portner (1994) characterises Italian mood choice in the following way (Portner 1994, (54) and (55)):

(i)     The subjunctive is the default mood, employed whenever the indicative is not appropriate.

(ii)    The indicative may only be used with a factive modal context and with the modal force of necessity.

Although Portner does not discuss independent evidence in favour of the idea that the subjunctive is a default mood, such evidence is needed, given that, from a purely morphological point of view, the subjunctive is clearly the marked choice and the indicative is the unmarked one.

Secondly, (i) and (ii) predict that the indicative is impossible under a belief verb, since it creates a non-factive context. However, this is not the case:

(iii)   Mario pensa che Giuseppe è intelligente.
        Mario thinks that Giuseppe is(IND) intelligent.

Furthermore, the fact that *verba dicendi* select the indicative in Romance does not easily fit with Portner's characterisation of this mood. Given that the contexts these predicates create are non-factive, he constraints the factivity requirement to the worlds (situations) in the given conversational setting and observes that "... in many contexts it is entailed that reported claims are true and ... this has resulted in the indicative having been grammaticalised as the default mood for complements of verbs of assertion" (p. 15). The assumption that the indicative is the default mood for a particular class of contexts contradicts the characterisation Portner provides for mood choice in Italian, according to which it is the subjunctive that acts as the default.

This, of course, does not deny the validity of Portner's observation. Actually, it is true that reported claims may turn out to be true in the current conversational context. Our approach correctly admits such a possibility, making it dependent upon the choice of the propositions that are shared between the actual conversational context and the reported one. More generally, an assertive predicate, as in (iv), might introduce chains of assertive acts linking the original utterance by John to the actual one performed by the speaker:

(iv)    John said Mary arrived.

Thus, it must be the case that either the speaker participated in the reported communication, or heard a report about it from someone else who participated in it, or heard it from someone else who heard of it from someone else, etc. In the simplest case where the speaker directly heard John's utterance, he/she must have accepted the relevant proposition, $p$, in the (then active) common ground. Unless he/she has changed his/her mind, the speaker still believes $p$ — that is, at least in principle, the present common ground is compatible with $p$. Thus $p$ is true of it. The more complicated cases involving longer chains of communicative acts can be analysed in a similar way, provided that at each intermediate point the active common ground is consistent with the original proposition.

Indirect evidence in favour of the view that the truth of reported claims might carry over to the current conversation is provided by the following sentence:

(v)    Mario ha detto che Giuseppe starebbe ancora a casa.
       Mario said that Giuseppe is(COND) still at home.

In Italian, a particular mood — that is, the conditional — is available to the speaker
to express an explicit doubtful attitude toward the content of the embedded clause.

   30. Farkas (1992a) reports that in earlier stages of French true-factive predicates
such as *regret* admitted only the indicative. If so, the present pattern could be
explained as due to an ongoing change from a situation in which this was not
sensitive to the modal component to another situation in which such a sensitivity is
present. The proposal in the text explains why the indicative is possible in these
contexts in French. We do not explain, however, why the subjunctive is also
possible, given that in French counterfactual conditionals only have the indicative.
On possible lines of future research on this topic see the appendix below.

   31. Our use of the notion of *accommodation* follows that of Roberts (1989). The
notion of proposition accommodation has been proposed by Lewis (1979), who
defines it as a means to enrich a conversational background with a proposition by
turning it into a presupposition. Such a move is needed to correctly interpret another
proposition that presupposes the previous one.

   32. According to Brugger & D'Angelo (1994), when the speaker uses the
indicative mood in sentences such as (64a), he/she asserts the truth of the embedded
clause, whereas with the subjunctive, he/she merely expresses an attitude toward its
complement. Hence (64a), with the indicative, could be paraphrased as in (i):

(i)    Mario ha mangiato una mela e Gianni lo pensa.
       Mario has eaten an apple and Gianni believes it.

However, this seems not to be the case. A speaker may assert (64a) without
necessarily asserting the embedded clause. Consider the following discourse:

(ii)   Gianni pensa che la terra è piatta. Ovviamente ciò è falso.
       Gianni thinks that the earth is(IND) flat. Obviously, this is false.

If by uttering the first sentence the speaker had asserted the embedded proposition,
then the second sentence would be false as a continuation. This is not the case,
however. Note, furthermore, that it cannot even be proposed that the indicative
signals that the embedded proposition is presupposed. Consider, in fact, (iii):

(iii)  La terra è rotonda. Tuttavia Mario pensa che è(IND) piatta.
       The earth is round. However, Mario thinks that it is flat.

Since the first assertion explicitly introduces the proposition concerning the
roundness of the earth in the common ground, we would expect (iii) to be infelicitous,
in case the complement proposition of the second sentence were presupposed.
Actually, this is what happens when presupposition is a real issue:

(iv)   #Mario non ama Maria. Preoccupa/stupisce Gianni che Mario ami Maria.
       Mario does not love Maria. It worries/amazes Gianni that Mario loves Maria.

In (iv) the presupposition of the factive verbs *preoccupare, stupire* (worry, amaze) contrasts with the content of the first sentence, and the whole discourse is anomalous.

33. The data in (71) seem problematic for any account, such as the one given by Portner (1994), which attributes the effect of negation to a tendency of modals and negation to form a semantic unit. For Portner, in a sentence such as (71b) the operator arising from the combination of the negation with the main predicate has a modal force which is not that required by the indicative mood. This view predicts that in these contexts the subjunctive should uniformly be chosen, and the indicative should always be disallowed. However, both predictions are not borne out by the data in the text.

34. For instance, Farkas (1992a) notes that negation affects mood only in those cases where there is a change in the type of epistemic commitment. At least in French and Romanian, mood is constant under negation in the case of *verba dicendi*, emotive and evaluative factives, and deontics. For instance, as shown in (24a), French requires the subjunctive in negated belief contexts.

We may conjecture that negation interacts with predicates such as *believe* to change the kind of interpretation context for the embedded clause. Given that the relevant parameter for mood choice in French is the one relative to the ordering source, it seems that the combination of negation with *believe* yields a non-null ordering source.

35. We follow Chomsky (1995), who proposes that assertive force is encoded by means of a feature in C. We also hypothesise that at the interface, the semantical-conceptual system reads off such a feature as an operator. Therefore, the assertive operator (or any other operator encoding illocutionary force) need not be present in the syntax.

36. Discussing the properties of the protasis of inverted conditionals, Iatridou & Embick (1994) propose that such an operator is located in a position higher than AGR-P.

37. According to (53), the ordering on the contexts of evaluation is a total one. This need not be so; it may well be a weaker ordering — for instance, a partial one. In this case the statement in the text should be amended as follows: . . . for every context $C_i$ in $A$ there is not $C_j$ in $B$ such that $C_i > C_j$.

38. These considerations raise the question of whether notional mood is a property of the mapping from LF to semantical-conceptual structures, or a property of the latter alone. If the first hypothesis is correct, then it could be possible that languages also vary according to the parameters they use to classify contexts of evaluations and, ultimately, that there are language specific notional moods. If the second hypothesis is correct, notional mood is a property of semantical-conceptual structures and therefore is crosslinguistically invariant. In the text we tentatively adopt such a view. However, further work is required for a complete assessment of this issue.

39. In the previous chapter, we saw a case of Scattering A, when considering the position of negation in Mainland Scandinavian languages.

Let us give a more formal definition for *Scattering*:

(i)      Let $C = [F_1 \ldots F_n]$ be a syncretic category and let $\alpha_1$ and $\alpha_2$ be two terms of $\Sigma$.
         Then Scattering is a binary relation between $C$ and the pair $<\alpha_1, \alpha_2>$ only if
         $\alpha_1 + \alpha_2 = C$.

The two options illustrated in the text correspond to the following two possibilities:
in Scattering A, $C$ is in the numeration. In Scattering B, $C$ is in the lexicon and $\alpha_1$ and
$\alpha_2$ are in the numeration. By defining Scattering as a *relation* we avoid introducing
new operations into the theory. In fact, the configurations created by means of
Scattering A are a product of Merge, as discussed in the text. Scattering B structures
are due to the operations mapping the lexicon into the numeration, which are also
independently given.

　　Notice finally that Scattering A configurations are different from Chomsky's
(1995) multi-Spec ones in that the former also create head positions which can be
used as landing sites for head movement. This permits an account of the data discussed
by Cinque (1994; see also chapter 1 §1.2.). Chomsky's multi-Spec hypothesis, on
the contrary, would not account for the same range of facts.

　　40. As far as we know, there is no context in Standard Italian where CD is
obligatory.

　　41. CD can take place in the environments considered in the text even if the
embedded verb is not a subjunctive. For instance, it can be a future or a conditional
(see Poletto 1995):

(i)      Crede (che) verrà.
         He believes (that) he will arrive.

(ii)     Sperava (che) sarebbe venuto.
         He hoped (that) he would arrive.

These cases are not further considered here. Note, however, that to our ears (i) and (ii)
are slightly more marginal than (92).

　　Scorretti (1991) points out that CD phenomena in Spanish and Portuguese are
similar to CD in Modern Italian. In Old Italian, and in Old Romance in general, CD
was much more widespread and could be found even in indicative contexts. No CD
exists in Modern French.

　　42. Poletto points out that postverbal subject clauses admit CD, even if to our
ears it is a bit more marginal:

(i)      E' probabile sia partito.
         It is probable he has(SUBJ) left.

In this work, these cases will be assimilated to the other contexts optionally
admitting CD and will not be considered separately.

　　43. Exclamative contexts and Inverted Conditionals are instances of
Aux-to-Comp (in the sense of Rizzi 1982), and not CD, as illustrated by the fact that
the subject can intervene between the auxiliary and the participle, whereas this is
never possible in CD:

(i)    Oh, fosse Gianni arrivato in tempo!
       Oh, had Gianni arrived on time!

(ii)   Fosse Gianni arrivato puntuale, non avrebbe perso il treno.
       Had Gianni arrived on time, he would not have missed the train.

We will not consider here the properties triggering Aux-to-Comp and the reasons why it is different from CD. Let us only point out that such a phenomenon is very similar to the phenomenon of V2 in the Germanic languages. Our proposal here is that V2 phenomena are due to the presence of a feature in C (see Tomaselli 1989; Rizzi 1992), which triggers verb movement, and not to the presence of a syncretic category. In §5.2.3. we discuss the V-to-C analyses which have been provided in the literature for CD and interrogative inversion and propose an alternative view. We think that V-to-C, on the one hand, and CD and interrogative inversion, on the other, must be explained by means of different theories. The results derived in this section seem to show that such a distinction is empirically adequate.

44. Note that in all the relevant examples the matrix verb appears in the third person. This is a crucial methodological point for investigating this domain. A matrix verb in the first person usually gives much better results. This can be due to independent properties of these forms. First person forms in fact can be used as parentheticals, whereas third person forms cannot (see also Hooper 1975):

(ii)   Gianni, credo/?*crede, è partito.
       Gianni, I believe / he believes has left.

It could be the case, therefore, that the first person in CD contexts is more easily analysed in a fashion similar to a parenthetical than the third person one, and, therefore, the construction would turn out to be grammatical for reasons other than the properties of CD.

45. A postverbal subject is associated with a marked informational pattern. In order to obtain the "unmarked" informational value, the speakers who reject (101) must obligatorily introduce a complementiser — that is, the CD variant is not available at all.

46. With respect to the properties of *tu* (you), see Benincà (1994). See also Cardinaletti (1994) for a distinction between weak and non-weak pronominal forms in Italian, where it is shown that *tu* can be analysed as a weak pronoun.

47. But see following discussion for embedded questions with the subjunctive.

48. For data and theories concerning the same kind of phenomenon in other Romance languages, see, in the recent literature, Bonet (1989), Solà (1992), Suñer (1994), and Friedeman (1995). We will not discuss at length their proposals here. For a discussion of the IP analysis of interrogatives provided by Solà and Bonet, see Guasti (1995); in general we agree with her observations.

49. There are several interesting proposals for V to C in Romance which have been suggested to explain various patterns of cliticisation. For an analysis of Portuguese phenomena along these lines, see Madeira (1993), Manzini (1994b), and

Kayne (1991). For a comparison between Modern and Old Portuguese and Medieval Romance languages, see Benincà (1995).

50. For a detailed discussion of French complex inversion see Rizzi and Roberts (1989).

51. A problem left open by this approach is constituted by the need to exclude the possibility that the verb can assign case in a Spec-head configuration on its way to AGR/C. In languages admitting V2, in fact, such an option has to be possible, because the phrase moved to (Spec,CP) is not necessarily the subject. In other words, the verb in C must assign case to a subject in a lower position, presumably in a Spec-head configuration with the verb trace.

52. With the exception of Aux-to-Comp constructions, on which we have nothing to say here.

53. Finding out a principled reason for classifying verbs as bridge and non-bridge constitutes an interesting topic for further research. The solution to such a problem might also shed light on the reason most (although not all) Italian verbs admitting CD belong to the bridge class.

54. Poletto discusses another argument in favour of her analysis — namely, the distribution of the epistemic adverbial *sicuramente* (surely). She observes the following contrast:

(i)     a.   *Credo sicuramente arrivi. (Poletto ex. 14a and 15)
             I think surely he comes(SUBJ).
        b.   Credo arrivi sicuramente.
             I think he comes(SUBJ) surely.

She concludes that the grammaticality of (i)b is due to movement of the verb past the adverbial. However she also notes that the postverbal position for *sicuramente* (surely) is available even in non-CD contexts:

(ii)    Credo che (sicuramente) arrivi (sicuramente).
        I think that he (surely) comes(SUBJ) (surely).

Moreover, verbs such as *dire* (say), which do not trigger CD, also admit both positions for the adverb:

(iii)   Ha detto che (sicuramente) arriverà (sicuramente).
        He said that he (surely) will come (surely).

These observations weaken the argument, because a postverbal position of *sicuramente* is not necessarily due to movement of the verb to a complementiser position.

55. See Belletti (1990) and references cited there.

56. It seems to us that, strictly speaking, Poletto's solution for CD contexts actually assigns the preverbal subject a derived status, because the subject should be moved in (Spec,AGR/C) from a lower *Spec* position — that is, from its canonical position in the *Spec* of AGR$_S$.

The question, however, is highly controversial, and therefore we will not further discuss it here.

57. We also proposed that the Universal Ordering Constraint orders the *mood* feature as following the φ-features. This seems reasonable on the basis of the crosslinguistic evidence, given that the subjunctive complementiser always precedes the verb.

58. For completeness, a form such as *mangiasse* (3rd pers sing, imperfect subjunctive of *to eat*) projects a T node bearing the feature *[+ Past]*, an AGR with the features *3rd pers sing* and a (possibly syncretic) feature *mood*. A present subjunctive such as *mangi* (eat(SUBJ)) does not bear any tense specification, similarly to the present tense of the indicative.

59. This idea is supported by evidence from several languages having the subjunctive as a mood distinct from the indicative, such as Modern Greek and Romanian, and by many Italian dialects, such as, for instance, Salentino. We will not consider these cases here; let us only point out that a similar claim is independently needed for these languages.

60. What the position of the postverbal subject might be is not discussed here. For discussion, see among others Delfitto (1993), Samek-Lodovici (1994), and Guasti (1994). Note also that in principle it is possible that for some speakers the *Spec* in question is *only* an A-position: if so, extraction of a non-D-linked adjunct from an embedded subjunctive clause, as discussed in §5.2.5. below, should be altogether impossible. We actually found some speakers exhibiting the relevant pattern, — they do not accept non-D-linked adjunct extraction from the embedded clause at all.

61. The whole question concerning null complementisers will be better investigated in §5.2.4.2. Let us just point out here that presumably the presence of a null complementiser is the correct hypothesis with respect to English CD facts. In this language, as we previously stated in the text, there is no evidence of V2 movement when the complementiser is omitted, nor is there any evidence in favour of the existence of a syncretic category in this case. The subject, contrary to what happens in Italian, normally precedes the verb, and, more importantly, it remains in the preverbal position even when an embedded phrase undergoes cyclic movement:

(i)     a.  John said Mary visited Bill.
        b.  Who did John say Mary visited?

The relevance of the grammaticality of example (i)b will be clearer after the discussion in §5.2.5. on extraction phenomena. Let us only point out that it shows that a landing site must be available between the subject and the superordinate verb. This observation shows that in (i)b there must be two embedded specifiers: one filled by the subject and another one available for Wh-trace. For the time being, on the basis of this empirical evidence, it can be concluded that English obeys different constraints than Italian.

62. The agreement series of the subjunctive exhibits some characteristics typical of marked items, such as, for instance, *syncretism* in the traditional sense: a *syncretic* form is a form that corresponds to more than one value. For instance, *mangi* (eat(SUBJ)) can correspond either to the first person singular, to the second, or to the third. This fact might be connected with the reduced possibility for certain forms of the subjunctive — in particular, the singular ones — to license a null referential

subject. If a singular form is used, in absence of a lexical subject, it can only be interpreted as third person, and not as first or as second:

(i)     Credo che abbia comprato un'auto.
        I believe that he/?*I/*you have(SUBJ) bought a car.

63. We think that the data of Albanian and of Arbëresh, the Albanian dialects spoken in southern Italy, might elegantly fit in this picture. In Albanian (see Turano 1995) there is a special complementiser for subjunctive clauses, që. If this complementiser is present, the subject can precede the verb, whereas in CD cases the order is obligatorily VOS. The subjunctive in these languages is realised as a periphrastic form consisting of a particle, të, (immediately) followed by the indicative verbal form. Consider, for instance, the following Albanian examples (from Turano 1995, p. 120, ex. 27):

(i)     a.  Dua që Maria të lexojë.
            I want that Maria reads(SUBJ).
        b.  *Dua Maria të lexojë.
            I want Maria reads(SUBJ).
        c.  Dua të lexojë Maria.
            I want reads(SUBJ) Maria.

We propose that të is the morphological realisation of the feature *mood* on the verb. In CD constructions të raises to check mood in MOOD/AGR. If the special subjunctive complementiser që is present, the checking takes place after Spell-Out, exactly as in Italian. The same seems to hold also for Romanian (see Motapanyane 1991; Farkas 1992a) and Modern Greek (see Tsoulas 1994; Roussou 1994).

64. If the presence of a preverbal *pro* is obligatorily required, then it is predicted that only languages licensing a null subject could manifest CD effects. At first glance such a prediction seems to be borne out. In French, in fact, no CD effects are observed. Further work is indeed required.

65. Guasti (1995) points out that if the preverbal *pro* is obligatory, only pro-drop languages can have the Italian-like interrogative inversion. This prediction seems to be correct because French seems to obey different constraints. See also n. 64.

66. Notice that further evidence in favour of the idea that the *Wh* feature and *D* are actually the *same* feature, can be provided by the so-called English *vacuous-movement* (Chomsky 1986) cases. If the subject is questioned, it remains *in situ* and *do* insertion is not required:

(i)     a.  Who left?
        b.  *Who did leave?

That is, *Who* fills the position in which the subject usually appears. Consider also that, as we said in n. 65, if *pro* is obligatory, English is predicted to exhibit no interrogative inversion. In fact, in this language, the auxiliary raises to C and the subject remains in preverbal position. This evidence is in some sense contradictory. On the one hand, it must be concluded that in English +*Wh* and *D* are separately realised, and, on the other, that when a *Wh*- coincides with the subject, no movement is necessary, because D and *Wh-* actually are the *same* feature. We do not investigate this question here. This might be a consequence of the impossibility of licensing a *pro* in this language.

67. If we follow Chomsky (1995) in assuming that the functional category AGR has an affixal feature $v$ triggering movement of the verb, then the relevant requirement is satisfied by WH/AGR itself. If this is correct, then we expect that the category WH/MOOD also satisfies (i). We will see shortly that this is indeed the case.

68. Some varieties spoken in Central Italy — for example, in Lazio and Umbria — allow a sentence such as (138). Consequently, we might argue that the complementiser is compatible with the feature *Wh-*. Notice that, in Romance, inversion in interrogative contexts is a widespread phenomenon; in addition, in Germanic, interrogative V2 or V1 order is obligatory. This happens even in English, which in affirmative sentences does not usually exhibit such a word order. The following generalisation could be proposed in order to capture the facts: in Germanic and Romance, it is impossible to license an empty $+Wh$ head in root contexts.

69. Notice that in this case both the $D$ feature and the *Wh* feature are present in the structure. This property resembles the one of English, as illustrated in n. 66.

70. This analysis has some points in common with Rizzi's (1990) *Wh*-criterion, at least in the sense that a verb can license an operator. In our opinion, however, there is no convincing evidence showing that the verb itself is endowed with a $+Wh$ feature. If this were the case, in fact, we would predict the V2 order in all interrogative contexts, with the shortcomings we already discussed. Moreover, dialectal varieties, such as the central Italian dialects, which admit (138), and the northern Italian dialects, which admit (145), would remain unaccounted for.

71. Let us point out that such an analysis, as it stands, is incompatible with Kayne's (1994) proposals concerning the position of clitics. Kayne, in fact, argues that clitics occupy a head position higher than $AGR_S$ but lower than C. In interrogative sentences with clitics, however, we still find obligatory subject-verb inversion:

(i) Cosa gli ha dato Gianni?
    Lit.: What to him-cl has given Gianni?

(ii) *Cosa Gianni gli ha dato?
    Lit.: What Gianni to him-cl has given?
    What did Gianni give him?

The two approaches, however, could be made compatible along the following lines. Kayne proposes that the functional head where the clitic appears — call it $f$ — also triggers movement of the subject in its *Spec* position (for reasons which are not clear). Therefore, we might say that such a head bears the feature $D$, responsible for the position of the subject at Spell-Out. Moreover, $f$ should also contain some (strong) feature overtly triggering clitic movement. Let us maintain that the AGR head can be syncretically realised with the superordinate categories — that is, $f$ and *Wh*. If this is the case, we can conclude that besides the features *Wh*, $D$, and $\phi$, the feature $f$ must also appear in the bundle projecting a syncretic agreement head. If cliticisation takes place, the feature $f$ must be scattered, because it must be projected separately from the *Wh*-feature on the one hand and the φ-features on the other in order to host the clitic. According to our proposal, in this case the presence of a *pre-clitic* subject is correctly ruled out, as shown by the ungrammaticality of (ii).

We argued in the text that the features $D$ and *Wh* are actually variants of the same strong feature, requiring a preverbal phrase. If *Wh* is present, no overt lexical subject can be realised in the pre-clitic, preverbal position in interrogative contexts, because it would require the presence of another strong feature, $D$, which in this case could not appear there.

72. See among others Cinque 1990; Rizzi 1990; Longobardi 1985; Chomsky 1986.

73. For definitions, see Cinque 1990, ch. 1, p. 55.

74. In principle there is also another possibility available; a trace cannot be identified more than once. In this case extraction through more than one cycle would simply be blocked.

75. We have shown that in English even when the complementiser is missing, no inversion is required under extraction from the embedded clauses (see n. 61). This is an argument in favour of a non-syncretic analysis of CD phenomena in English.

76. Thanks to Anna Cardinaletti for judgements and fruitful discussion on this point.

77. In central Italian varieties such as those spoken in Lazio, it seems that the indicative present and the present perfect are quite widespread options under a present form of *credere* (believe):

(i)     Mario crede che Luisa ha vinto.
        Mario believes that Luisa has(IND) won.

(ii)    Mario crede che Luisa è intelligente.
        Mario believes that Luisa is(IND) intelligent.

Such a possibility, however, also seems to be available, at least to a certain extent, in Northern Italian varieties. See also §5.1.7. An indicative form embedded under a past such as *credeva* (believed) seems, on the contrary, to be a more marked option and is ungrammatical even in central varieties:

(iii)   *Mario credeva che Luisa ha mangiato / mangiò una mela.
        Mario believed that Luisa has(IND) eaten / ate(IND) an apple.

78. Recall that, as stated in the previous chapter, the (simple) imperfect is interpreted as simultaneous with the event of the main clause. This property is also shared by the subjunctive. It is rather natural, therefore, that the form which can substitute the subjunctive is the imperfect indicative, and not, for instance, the simple past. The temporal dependencies can in fact be the same in both cases.

79. See Iatridou (1990b) for a deeper analysis of conditionals.

80. Many languages admit the so-called *conditional inversion*: besides normal *uninverted* conditional sentences, as in (i)a, there are also cases in which the protasis is a V1 clause, as in (i)b:

(i)    a. If John had arrived on time, we could have met him.

        b. Had John arrived on time, we could have met him.

It must be notice that while in English conditional inversion is limited to counterfactual conditionals, many languages, such as German, also admit it with indicative conditionals (from Iatridou & Embick 1994, ex. 2):

(ii)    a. Wenn Hans kommt, dann geht Susanne.

        b. Kommt Hans, dann geht Susanne.

         If Hans comes then Susanne goes.

The following table reproduces the conclusions Iatridou & Embick (1994) arrive at concerning the distribution of conditional inversion in a number of languages.

| | Counterfactual Inversion | Indicative Inversion |
|---|---|---|
| English | + | - |
| German | + | + |
| Dutch | + | + |
| Yiddish | + | + |
| Icelandic | + | + |
| Swedish | + | + |
| Old English | + | + |
| Middle English | + | + |
| Greek | - | - |
| French | (-) | - |
| Italian | + | - |
| Spanish | - | - |
| Eur. Portuguese | + | - |
| Romanian | + | - |
| Galician | (-) | - |
| Russian | + | (+) |
| Bulgarian | + | - |
| Polish | (-) | - |

We will not consider conditional inversion in this work, limiting our discussion to uninverted conditionals. See Iatridou & Embick (1994) for more discussion of this topic.

    81. The mood of the apodosis of counterfactual conditionals varies across languages. For instance, Italian and French have the conditional:

(i)    Se Mario fosse arrivato in tempo, saremmo andati al cinema.

        If Mario had(SUBJ) arrived on time, we would have(COND) gone to the movie.

German has the subjunctive:

(ii)    Wenn Hans gekommt wäre, dann wäre Susanne abgefahren.

        If Hans had(SUBJ) arrived, then Susanne would have(SUBJ) left.

We will not address the problem of mood choice in the apodosis of conditionals.

82. Consider the following data:

(i)     Se o João tivesse chegado a tempo, não teríamos perdido o comboio.

                                                                (Portuguese)

        If J. had(SUBJ) arrived on time, we would not have lost the train.

(ii)    Se o João chegava a tempo, não perdíamos o comboio.    (Portuguese)

        If J. arrived(IMPF) on time, we would not have lost the train.

(iii)   Si en Joan venia, en Pere se n'anava.                  (Catalan)

        If Joan arrived (IMPF), Pere would have gone.

(iv)    Si Maria venia, Juan se iba.                           (Spanish)

        If Maria arrived(IMPF), Juan would have gone.

All these sentences are counterfactuals, and the verb of the protasis is in the imperfect indicative. As in Italian, (i) to (iv) have a more or less marked status.

83. Actually, we should have written $f'(w) = [\![\alpha]\!]^{f,g}$, cf. (183). However, $\alpha$ is not modalised; therefore both $f$, which is the empty modal base, and the ordering source $g$ do not have any effect on it. Therefore $[\![\alpha]\!]^{f,g} = [\![\alpha]\!]$.

84. It also accounts for the indicative of the apodosis of indicative conditionals. According to (183) the ordering sources is null and the modal base is at least weakly realistic.

85. Formally, let $p$ be the propositional content of the protasis and $q$ that of the apodosis. Let $f$ be a modal base and $g$ an ordering source such that (i) holds:

(i)     For every $u \in \cap f(w)$, there is a $v \in \cap f(w)$ such that $v \leq_g u$ and such that for every $z \in \cap f(w)$ if $z \leq_g v$ then $z \notin p$.

or, in the terminology of n. 21, for every world $u \in \cap f(w)$, there is $v \in \cap f(w)$, $v \leq_g u$ such that $p$ is false in the principal down set $\downarrow u$. According to (183), $q$ must be evaluated with respect to the modal base $f'(w) = f(w) \cup \{p\}$. But then the new ordering source is the $g'$ defined in the text. In fact, assuming bivalency and according to (36), for any two worlds $w'$, $w''$ in $\cap f'(w)$, $w' \leq_g w''$ iff $\{r \mid r \in g(w) \text{ and } w'' \in r\} \subseteq \{r \mid r \in g(w) \text{ and } w' \in r\}$. However, by construction, $p$ is true in both $w'$ and $w''$ so that it is not the case that $\neg p$ is ever relevant for the purposes of ordering.

86. Starting from different considerations, Heim (1992) arrives at similar conclusions. She observes that if the protasis is added to the context then it is impossible to account for cases in which the *if*-clause has some presupposition. She then proposes that the protasis should be added to a context $C'$ which is a *revision* of the context set $C$. $C'$ is formed by dropping a number of assumptions valid in the current common ground but maintaining the presuppositions of the protasis.

The main difference between our proposal and Heim's consists in the fact that the revision we propose affects the ordering source.

87. We did not discuss the fact that in counterfactual conditionals the only form of the subjunctive that can appear is the so-called imperfect subjunctive (simple or compound) and not the present subjunctive (simple or compound):

(i)    a.  Se Mario *fosse* arrivato in orario, lo avrei incontrato.

           If Mario had(SUBJ IMPF) been on time I would have met him.

    b.  *Se Mario *sia* arrivato in orario, lo avrei incontrato.

           If Mario is(SUBJ PRES) been on time I would have met him.

Notice that in Italian the *consecutio temporum* holds in subordinate contexts, so that the present subjunctive is used in dependence of a present form and the imperfect in dependence of a past:

(ii)    a.  Credo che sia intelligente.

           I think that he is(SUBJ PRES) intelligent.

    b.  Credevo che fosse intelligente.

           I thought that he was(SUBJ IMPF) intelligent.

This observation might be interpreted along the same lines of reasoning suggested in the preceding discussion. The *temporal* value of the subjunctive form is devoid of a real temporal function and is interpreted as a mark of modality.

# 6

# The Double Accessibility
# Reading in Italian and English

In this chapter we briefly consider the properties of the so-called Double Accessibility Reading (DAR), comparing Italian with British English (BEn) and American English (AEn). We will argue that the two varieties of English differ from each other and that, interestingly, BEn has several properties in common with Italian, as opposed to AEn.

In §6.1. we describe the DAR effects, and in §6.2. we investigate the conditions it is possible to find it under in Italian. For this purpose we consider the interpretation of the indicative — in particular, the imperfect — and of the subjunctive in the contexts created by *credere* (believe) and *dire* (say). In §6.3. we compare Italian with English. Interestingly, English has neither the imperfect indicative nor the subjunctive. However, we will show that, in spite of this, Italian and English are actually much more similar to one another than what appears at first glance and that a more sophisticated analysis of the feature mechanisms can account for the properties of these constructions in both languages.

## 6.1. The Double Accessibility Reading

The DAR belongs to the more general class of Sequence of Tense (SOT) phenomena, which will not be discussed at length in this book. In this chapter we will only consider some facts which seem to interact with our account of the subordinate verbal forms such as the imperfect indicative (see chapter 4) and the subjunctive (see chapter 5). In English the temporal and modal systems include neither an imperfect as opposed to a simple past, nor a subjunctive as opposed to an indicative. However, we will see that in BEn *believe* contexts exhibit some properties which are very similar to those we find in the same environments in Italian.[1]

Let us briefly illustrate the main properties of the DAR. Abusch (1991) discusses the following two sentences:[2]

(1)    a.  John believed that Mary is pregnant. (From Abusch, exx. 1–2)
        b.  John said that his son lives in Chelsea.

The Double Accessibility Reading is an effect concerning the temporal interpretation (SOT) of the embedded clause with respect to the tense of the matrix one. Abusch claims that the predicate of the subordinate, by virtue of being a present tense, is temporally interpreted as holding *now,* which is the normal (non-habitual) interpretation of the present tense in isolation. In addition to this, however, the embedded present predicate must be interpreted as holding *also* at the past time identified by the main predicate — that is, as simultaneous also with the time of the believing and the time of the saying. For instance, in (1a) the pregnancy of Mary must hold both *now* and at the time of the believing; analogously, in (1b), the living in Chelsea must be interpreted as holding both *now* and at the time of the saying. As we will discuss in a while, it can be observed that in some languages (1a) might exhibit different properties than (1b), whereas Abusch does not distinguish between the two. To better characterise the nature of the DAR effect, consider the following contrast:

(2)    a.  John told me that M. is pregnant. But I discovered that she only put on weight.

        b.  John told me that M. is pregnant. But he discovered that she only put on weight.

Sentence (2b) is odd, in the sense that the first assertion does not fit with the second one, clearly contrasting with (2a). As Abusch (1991) points out, this contrast shows that the speaker, *John,* is committed to repeating his assertion at the present time, whereas the same does not hold for the utterer — that is, for the person reporting the speaker's opinion. In other words, we can say that the speaker (*John*) is assumed to assume the truth of his assertions. If the embedded sentence must hold now for independent reasons, the speaker is assumed to assume its truth now, and not only at the time of the saying. The same commitment does not hold for the utterer. This consideration explains why (2b) does not seem to be a coherent discourse, whereas (2a) does.

The goal of this chapter is to show that an integrated analysis of temporal and aspectual phenomena might contribute to an understanding of these facts. We will show that the view developed in chapter 4 on the interpretation of the embedded verbal form with respect to the speech act appearing in the superordinate clause can explain the pattern found in DAR phenomena. Notice that in this way we are strongly arguing in favour of a morphosyntactic view of such an interpretive effect. The DAR in fact will be shown to be due not only to semantic factors but also to the special morphosyntactic properties of the verbal forms.

As we stated above, we will show that examples such as (1a), where a verb of believing appears in the matrix, typically do not exhibit the DAR in Italian and in BEn, whereas examples such as (1b), where a verb of saying appears, do. In AEn, on the other hand, both seem to require the DAR, even if for several speakers (1a) can be worse than (1b) . To account for these properties we propose a (rather radical) revision of Abusch's approach. Our proposal has the advantage of also explaining the characteristics of the temporal relations emerging in other cases which will be shown to exhibit the same pattern as the "traditional" DAR effects of sentences such as (1). We will consider examples which do not contain a present tense embedded under a past form, but nevertheless show a *double accessibility* effect.

From a formal point of view, according to the theory we developed in chapter 4, the DAR is a double mapping of the subordinate predicate onto the speech event on the one hand, and onto the superordinate speech act on the other. We will show that in Italian the DAR is not limited to the present tense and that the same phenomenon occurs with other tenses of the indicative as well.

## 6.2. The Italian data

In this section we consider the distribution of the DAR in Italian.[3] As we discussed in chapter 5 §5.1., in Italian, saying contexts only admit the indicative, whereas believing contexts require the subjunctive but can also admit, more or less marginally, the indicative.[4] Consider the Italian equivalents of the examples given above:

(3)     Ieri Gianni ha detto che Maria è incinta.
        Yesterday Gianni said that Maria is pregnant.

(4)     (*)Gianni credeva che Maria è incinta.
        Gianni believed that Maria is pregnant.

(5)     Gianni credeva che Maria fosse incinta.
        Gianni believed that Maria was(SUBJ-PAST) pregnant.

(6)     *Gianni credeva che Maria sia incinta.
        Gianni believed that Maria is(SUBJ-PRES) pregnant.

Sentence (3) is interpreted with the DAR, whereas (4) is, and must be, interpreted in this way only by those speakers who accept the indicative under a past verb of believing. In other words, as far as a present indicative is acceptable in the context created by *credere* (believe), the DAR is required. The subjunctive forms in (5) and (6) do not exhibit any DAR effect. In fact in (5), the subordinate clause is interpreted as simultaneous with the matrix. Moreover, (6) is ungrammatical due to a violation of the *consecutio temporum*. That is, under a past verbal form such as *credeva* (believed) a subjunctive past form is required, and a present one is ruled out. One might wonder whether the sentence in (6), if acceptable, would have the DAR. It is not clear to us what an answer could be. In any case it seems that the contrast with the indicative is quite sharp, showing that the subjunctive by itself has a strong tendency to be interpreted only with respect to the matrix verb and is not directly mapped onto $S$ — that is, *now*. Finally, no subjunctive is admitted in Italian with *verba dicendi* (see §6.1.).

To conclude, if a past verb of saying appears in the matrix and a present indicative appears in the subordinate clause, the embedded predicate is interpreted as simultaneous both with the time of utterance and with the time of the saying; that is, it has the DAR. With believing contexts the DAR is required only insofar as the indicative is an acceptable option; the subjunctive never admits such a reading.

Let us consider now the distribution of the imperfect indicative. In the previous chapter (§5.2.5.), we discussed the data concerning the central Italian varieties which admit the imperfect indicative in the contexts created by *credere* (believe) instead of a subjunctive.[5] We have shown that in these cases, the subordinate predicate is temporally dependent upon the matrix one but does not exhibit the pattern we attributed to the presence of the feature *mood*. The imperfect in fact does not license CD and does not seem to raise to check this extra feature. Accordingly, it does not license non-D-linked adjunct extraction.

The imperfect indicative does not give rise to DAR effects, as shown by the following examples:

(7)    Gianni mi ha detto che Maria era incinta.
       Gianni told me that Maria was(IMPF) pregnant.

(8)    (#) Gianni credeva che Maria era incinta
       Gianni believed that Maria was(IMPF) pregnant

Let us stress again that sentence (8) is fully grammatical only for the speakers who accept this special type of *consecutio modorum*. In these cases, the subordinate imperfect is understood as simultaneous with the superordinate predicate, in this respect patterning together with the subjunctive.

It might be said, however, that the examples in (5) and (6) are not relevant to the study of the DAR effect, because the imperfect is a past form and past forms do not give rise to the DAR (only present ones do). As an answer to this objection, we are going to argue that the DAR is not a property of the present tense but rather a consequence of a general strategy for a temporal interpretation of the subordinate clauses. We will argue that DAR effects are also detected with embedded pasts. In other words, the DAR is a general property of tense interpretation in natural languages, and not just a property of the (indicative) present tense in certain contexts. Consider the following sentences:

(9)    Ieri Gianni ha detto che Maria è partita.
       Yesterday Gianni said that Maria has left.

(10)   Ieri Gianni ha detto che Maria partirà presto.
       Yesterday Gianni said that Maria will leave early.

In (9) the embedded clause is interpreted as past with respect to *now* and with respect to the time of the saying. It is impossible to locate the leaving between the saying and *now*. That is, the temporal location must be computed *also* with respect to the time of the superordinate event. Notice that the opposite is true for (10). The time of the embedded event cannot be future only with respect to the saying, but must be future *also* with respect to *now*. These data show that in order to obtain the correct interpretation in both cases, both the time of the utterance and the time of the matrix speech act must be taken into account, and the embedded event must be located with respect to both. This emerges clearly by comparing (9) and (10).

To show that this is the case, let us consider what would happen were this *not* the case. Let us claim that a subordinate event must be temporally located *only* with respect to the superordinate one. If so, the interpretation of (9) would correctly follow: the leaving would be prior to the saying and therefore also to *now*. The interpretation of (10), however, would not follow: the embedded future, if it is interpreted only with respect to the saying, could be located between the saying and *now*, contrary to fact. Such a temporal configuration, in which the embedded event can be located between the time of the utterance and the time of the superordinate saying, can be obtained by means of a special form — namely, a conditional:

(11)    Ieri Gianni ha detto che Maria sarebbe partita presto.
          Yesterday Gianni said that Maria would have left early.

In this case a complex conditional, *sarebbe partita* (would have left), appears and the temporal location of the embedded event can be located between the saying and *now*.

Notice also that the interpretation in which the embedded event is temporally located between the saying and *now* is not an obligatory reading, because (11) is also compatible with a reading in which the leaving has not taken place yet. On the contrary, the interpretation of (9) and (10) previously discussed is the only one available. Consider that in order to account for the interpretation of (9) and (10), we could not say that the subordinate event is interpreted only with respect to *now*, because in this case (10) would be accounted for, but not (9). It would be predicted that the reading according to which the leaving takes place between the saying and *now* would be possible, again contrary to fact.

In the light of these data we are led to the conclusion that in (9) and (10) we are dealing with the same property which determines the interpretation of (3). In other words, in order to be interpreted the embedded indicative predicate must be temporally located *both* with respect to *now* and with respect to the matrix predicate. Moreover, this does not follow from an *a priori* given necessity, as shown by the availability in Italian of (11) — that is, of a sentence where the embedded predicate is not doubly evaluated.[6]

Concluding, we can state the following generalisation:

(12)    An embedded (non-imperfect) indicative must be temporally interpreted both with respect to *now* and with respect to the superordinate speech act.

Why does a generalisation such as (12) hold? On the one hand, it might be said that it is a property of certain indicative verbal forms and, presumably, of the temporal features they are connected with. Stowell (1992) proposes that the DAR is obtained because the sentence must be scoped out of its basic position and is therefore temporally interpreted twice: once with respect to the matrix predicate, and then, in the scoped-out position, with respect to $S$. We will not offer a better proposal here, nor will we further discuss Stowell's proposal. Let us just stress that the double interpretation must not be taken to be a property only of the present tense but more generally of the tenses of the indicative, excluding the imperfect, which, as we have already seen in chapter 4, has special interpretive properties.

On the other hand, it must also be said that the DAR is sensitive to the context defined by the matrix predicate. Even an indicative does not exhibit the DAR when embedded under a future tense. Consider the following examples:

(13)    Gianni dirà che Maria partirà presto.
        Gianni will say that Maria will leave early.

(14)    Prima o poi Gianni dirà che Maria è partita.
        Sooner or later Gianni will say that Maria has left.

In (13) a future is embedded under another one, and the temporal location of the embedded event is in the future with respect to *now* and with respect to the saying. Example (14) shows that if there is a past in the subordinate clause, it is possible to have a reading in which the embedded event is past *only* with respect to the saying and not with respect to *now*. That is, there is a reading according to which the leaving of Maria is located before the saying but after *now*. Consider also the following sentence:

(15)    Gianni ti dirà che è ora di andare al cinema (*DAR).
        Gianni will tell you that it is time to go to the movie.

This example shows that it is possible to obtain an interpretation of the present tense according to which the embedded predicate is simultaneous only with the saying and not with *now*. To conclude, the future does not permit the embedded predicate to be evaluated with respect to *now*: the embedded event is dependent only on the temporal location of the superordinate event.[7]

## 6.3. The English data

In this section we compare the data of British and American English with the Italian data illustrated above. The subordinate clauses under the verbs of saying exhibit the same behaviour in both varieties of English:

(16)    John said that Mary is pregnant (DAR).

(17)    John said that Mary was happy (SIMUL; PAST).

(18)    John said that Mary left (*SIMUL; PAST).

(19)    John said that Mary will leave (after NOW and after the saying).

As we saw in the first section, the present tense in sentence (16) exhibits the DAR. The past tense of a stative predicate (to be happy) can be interpreted either as simultaneous or as past with respect to the saying. As we discussed in chapter 4, in Italian the simultaneous reading can only be obtained by means of the imperfect, whereas the non-imperfect simple past does not yield this reading.

Since in English the past tense can have both functions — that is, English does not distinguish two different past forms — the embedded clause in (17) can be interpreted either way.

We also noted in the same chapter that only stative predicates can be interpreted simultaneously, because of the intrinsic properties of the English verbs. Consequently, the embedded predicate in (18) is interpreted as past with respect to the saying. It could not be interpreted as simultaneous with the matrix event, because *leave* is not a stative predicate and therefore cannot be mapped directly onto the matrix speech act. As we have already discussed in chapter 4, this behaviour of the non-stative predicate in English is analogous to the behaviour of the Italian non-imperfect (past) verbal forms: an eventive past predicate in English is interpreted as a simple past, or a present perfect in Italian, and cannot be interpreted as an imperfect — that is, as simultaneous with the matrix predicate.

Again, as in Italian, an embedded future is interpreted as future with respect to the saying and with respect to *now*. Concluding, it can be said that the DAR is obligatory in these contexts in English, too.

Moreover, in English, too, the future blocks this possibility, as we can observe in the following cases:

(20)    John will say that Mary left.

(21)    John will say that Mary will leave.

(22)    John will say that Mary is happy.

The leaving in (20) is obligatorily past only with respect to the saying, but not necessarily with respect to *now*. In (21) the embedded future is obviously future with respect to both. In (22) the happiness of Mary is obligatorily simultaneous only with the saying and can have arisen after *now*.

Let us now consider the believing contexts — that is, the contexts in which Italian selects the subjunctive. In English, there is no (productive) form that is marked as a subjunctive, as opposed to an indicative. Therefore, corresponding to the three past forms admitted in Italian in subordinate contexts (the imperfect, the non-imperfect indicative, and the subjunctive), we always find the same form in English: the indicative simple past.

Now consider the contexts created by believing verbs in BEn and AEn:

(23)    John believed that Mary is pregnant (*BEn; AEn).

Interestingly, this sentence is considered ungrammatical by BEn speakers (and even some AEn speakers consider it quite marginal). As far as it is acceptable, it obligatorily has the DAR. The sentence in (23) contrasts with the following one:

(24)    John believed that Mary was pregnant.
        BEn: SIMUL; *SHIFTED
        AEn: SIMUL; SHIFTED

In (24) the pregnancy is simultaneous to the saying. Note that for British speakers this is the *only* interpretation available for this sentence, as opposed to saying contexts, where a stative predicate could have both a simultaneous interpretation and a shifted one. For AEn speakers there is no contrast — that is, both interpretations are admitted.

Now consider an eventive predicate in the same context:

(25)    John believed that Mary left (*BEn; AEn: SHIFTED).

Example (25) is ungrammatical in BEn, and has only the shifted interpretation in AEn. As we saw in the preceding discussion, in English, independently of the variety, non-stative verbs cannot be interpreted as simultaneous with the superordinate predicate. The judgements in (25) fit in this view, because in BEn the embedded predicate in this context can only be interpreted as simultaneous with the matrix predicate. Consequently, if this option is independently ruled out, the structure becomes ungrammatical. In AEn, on the other hand, both options are in principle available. Therefore, in (25), at least the shifted interpretation is still possible, and the string is grammatical.

Now consider the following examples:

(26)    John believed that Mary has left (*BEn; AEn).
(27)    John believed that Mary had left (BEn; AEn).

*Has left* is unacceptable for British speakers, as expected, whereas (27) is acceptable for both American and British, obviously with the past reading. Again, this pattern is the one expected, given the evidence discussed above.

Let us now consider an embedded future:

(28)    John believed that Mary will leave (*BEn; AEn).
(29)    John believed that Mary would leave (BEn; AEn).

Analogously to the pair given above, (28) is acceptable only in AEn, whereas (29) is grammatical in both varieties. The temporal interpretation given to these sentences in AEn is the same as that given to saying verbs, which shows that the DAR is a general interpretive strategy and not just a characteristic of the present tense, as we have argued with respect to Italian.

In conclusion, it can be said that (a) AEn does not distinguish the contexts of believing from the contexts of saying, whereas BEn does, and (b) the DAR in AEn and BEn has the same properties it exhibits in Italian — that is, it is blocked by a matrix future and is never optional.

We are left at this point with the problems concerning BEn. Let us propose the following explanation for the pattern we have seen above. We discussed in chapter 5 §5.1. that languages which have the subjunctive in their tense inventory do not necessarily select it in believing contexts. Recall that, among Romance languages, Italian and Portuguese select the subjunctive, with the imperfect variant in central Italian varieties; French, Romanian, Spanish, and Catalan select the indicative.[8] Therefore, the choice of mood in these cases is dependent upon considerations which might vary from one language to another.

We would like to claim that the difference between AEn and BEn is similar to the one between Italian and Portuguese on the one hand, and the other Romance languages, such as French, Spanish, and the like, on the other. In other words, BEn selects in these contexts a marked form, namely, the *-ed* form of the verb. This is like Italian (and Portuguese), in which the form, appearing in these contexts — namely, the subjunctive — is marked with respect to the indicative one. In English the *-ed* form is the only marked choice, given that the morphological system is very poor, yielding no other possible alternatives.[9]

This hypothesis successfully predicts the pattern observed above. Example (23) is ungrammatical in BEn, because in this language belief contexts select a marked form, the equivalent of the subjunctive. Therefore, the unmarked *is* is not admitted, exactly as in Italian, where the (non-imperfect) indicative is (at least) marginal. If for some speakers *is* is admitted, it must exhibit the DAR, as in Italian with the (non-imperfect) indicative, which, as far as it is acceptable, has the DAR. In AEn, belief contexts do not differ from saying ones, and do not select a special verbal form. Therefore the DAR is always obligatory. With respect to (24) (John believed that Mary was pregnant), the difference between the two English varieties, as we said above, consists in the absence of the shifted interpretation for the BEn sentence. Again, this fact can be explained by means of our hypothesis. Recall that the only possible interpretation for a subjunctive, as opposed to an indicative, is the simultaneous reading. Example (26) (John believed that Mary has left) is not acceptable in BEn, because *has* does not bear any mark, and as such it cannot appear in a context selecting it. Following the same reasoning, (27) (John believed that Mary had left) is correctly predicted to be acceptable in both languages. The sentences in (28) (John believed that Mary will leave) and (29) (John believed that Mary would leave) represent the mirror image with respect to the future. *Would* is marked with respect to *will* and therefore can be used in these contexts even in BEn.

This hypothesis goes in the same direction as the one discussed in chapter 3 §3.1.1.3. and §3.1.4. concerning modals such as *could*. The mark *-ed* can express different features. That is, it is the lexical realisation at Spell-Out of various features which can be associated with it at a pre-Spell-Out level. Let us also stress that the analysis we gave here constitutes additional evidence in favour of our hypothesis concerning the impossibility of an interpretation of eventive predicates in English as simultaneous with the superordinate verb, proposed in chapter 4. The pattern observed in BEn in fact, can easily be reduced to this property.

Note that, as we discussed in chapter 5 §5.2.5., in Italian, believing contexts select either the imperfect indicative or the subjunctive, depending upon regional variety. We also argued there that the dialects exhibiting an imperfect instead of a subjunctive have different properties with respect to extraction phenomena. We suggested that the imperfect in these contexts has the same properties as the subjunctive as far as the temporal interpretation is concerned, but it does not have the feature *mood* which enables non-D-linked adjunct extraction. One might wonder whether the kind of dependency we find in BEn is subjunctive-like or imperfect-like. The answer to this question cannot be easily given. We argued, in fact, that the two contexts are crucially different with respect to extraction phenomena. Such judgements in English, both in the American and in the British variety, are not clear at all. That is, it is not clear enough whether the extraction of non-D-linked adjuncts from believing contexts patterns with the Italian subjunctive or with the Italian imperfect indicative. Therefore, we think that the question should be considered more closely by linguists who have native judgements. On the other hand, something can be said from the point of view of acquisition. The reasonable proposal seems to be that in English the child does not have enough positive evidence for learning the existence of a +*mood* value on verbal agreement, and consequently the verbal forms are not partitioned according to such a distinction. In English, in other words, there is no positive evidence in favour of the existence of a feature *mood*. As we suggested in the first chapter, the inventory of features from which the child selects those relevant in her language is universal. However, the features are selected and instantiated in the grammar of a certain language only if they can be learned on the basis of positive evidence. Given that such evidence is not available in English, the feature should not be instantiated. *Believe* contexts, however, in BEn require a special temporal dependency to be established with the embedded predicate. That is, they require it to be interpreted as simultaneous with the matrix one. This might be accomplished by the -*ed* form, which behaves like the Italian imperfect.

## 6.4. Conclusions

We think that the study of the DAR provides interesting cases of mutual dependency between semantics, on the one hand, and morphosyntax, on the other. *Verba dicendi,* as far as they select a (non-imperfect) indicative, require the embedded predicate to be interpreted both with respect to *now* and with respect to the speech act instantiated by the superordinate verb, giving rise to the DAR effect. *Believe* contexts, which select an imperfect or a subjunctive, do not. However, not every verb appearing in subordinate contexts with the (non-imperfect) indicative morphology necessarily exhibits the DAR effect. If the matrix predicate appears in the future, the DAR is blocked. It can be said, therefore, that the obligatoriness, or the lack thereof, of the DAR stems from the interaction of the morphosyntactic properties of the subordinate verb and the context defined by the superordinate verb — that is, a present or a past verbal form, as opposed to a future one.

We have also shown that in spite of the fact that English verbal morphology does not distinguish an imperfect from a simple past, or a subjunctive from an indicative, at least in BEn we find a pattern of DAR which closely resembles that of Italian. We accounted for these data by proposing that in BEn the morphological ending -*ed* can express the feature values corresponding to an Italian imperfect indicative.

To conclude, only a comparative approach has proved to be able to shed light on empirical observations such as the lack of DAR in BEn, which otherwise would remain unaccounted for. Languages such as Italian and English, in fact, could at first sight seem too different from one another with respect to the subordinate verbal forms, but a closer analysis shows they both instantiate the same general phenomena.

## Notes

1. In *Standard* Italian *credere* (believe) selects a subjunctive, whereas in some dialectal varieties even an imperfect indicative is accepted. See chapter 5, §5.1. and §5.2.5.

2. Enç (1987) discussed for the first time the special reading attributed to a present embedded under a past tense in English, which she called the *inclusive reading*. Notice that, interestingly, the DAR seems to be limited to times *not too far away*. In other words, speakers find a contrast between the two following sentences:

(i)     a.  #Two months ago, John said that his son lives in Chelsea

        b.  Two hours ago, John said that his son lives in Chelsea

Sentence (i)a is perceived as odd. It is not clear how the existence of such a constraint can be accounted for. In what follows we will not investigate this question further.

3. Brugger & D'Angelo (1994) argue that in Italian there is no DAR *tout court*, rejecting as completely ungrammatical sentences such as the following ones, which we, on the other hand, find grammatical:

(i)     Gino per molto tempo ha detto che Pina è incinta.
        Gino for a long time has said that Pina is pregnant.

(ii)    Ieri Gino ha detto che Pina è incinta.
        Yesterday Gino said that Pina is pregnant.

(iii)   Gino disse che Pina è incinta.
        Gino said that Mary is pregnant.

(iv)    Gino diceva che Pina è incinta.
        Gino said(IMPF) that Pina is pregnant.

To make sense of the different judgements, we suspected dialectal variation and tested these sentences with speakers from different regions of Italy (Piemonte, Lombardia, Trentino, Veneto, Emilia-Romagna, Lazio, Umbria, Campania, Sicily). We have not been able to detect any systematic variation. Note that DAR phenomena can be detected in other Romance languages as well, such as French, Spanish, Catalan, and Portuguese. Given that the DAR exists for a consistent group of Italian and Romance speakers, we are led to the conclusion that it is a phenomenon worth investigating, in spite of the differences which might exist among speakers. We will keep in mind that the evidence might not be clear.

4. Let us briefly recall the data discussed in chapter 5. We pointed out that if the matrix *credere* is in the present tense, the embedded verbal form can be a

(non-imperfect) indicative, even though, especially for Northern Italian speakers, it might be more marginal than a subjunctive:

(i)     Mario crede che sia/ (?) è partita.
        Mario believes that she has (SUBJ/ IND) left.

If the matrix verb is a past form, the (non-imperfect) indicative is quite marginal:

(ii)    Mario credeva che Luisa ?*è/ fosse partita.
        Mario believed that Luisa has (IND/ SUBJ) left.

Finally, for some speakers from Central Italy, the imperfect indicative is acceptable:

(iii)   #Mario credeva che Luisa era partita.
        Mario believed that Luisa had(IMP) left.

5.    We saw in §6.2.5. that this can happen in the subordinate contexts selected by *credere* (believe), but not in the contexts selected by *volere* (want). This question, however, will be put aside in this chapter.

6.    Interestingly, the form in (11) — that is, the conditional — has many properties in common with the subjunctive, as argued in chapter 5 §5.1. We will not further investigate here the properties of conditionals, since their study would lead us too far away from our main topic.

7.    This characteristic of the future looks similar to that of predicates such as *dream* (see chapter 5 §5.1.), which do not select the subjunctive but block an independent evaluation of the embedded predicate on *now*. According to Stowell's (1992) proposal, one is led to the conclusion that the future does not permit the embedded clause to be scoped out and thus receive a temporal interpretation directly dependent on $S$. The question will not be further pursued here. In any case it seems to us that the problem of *what* triggers the scoping out of the indicative clause is still left open and that further investigation is needed.

8.    We also observed (chapter 4 §4.1.) that languages such as French adopt the subjunctive in the same contexts under negation, or in interrogative structures. In believing contexts, the subjunctive is possible in German and obligatory in Icelandic (see chapter 5 §5.1.). However, here we are not comparing English with these Germanic languages. Given that they also select the subjunctive in saying contexts, as discussed in chapter 5, this presumably means that they classify predicates along different dimensions.

9.    We discussed in chapter 3 §3.1.1.3. another case in which the morpheme *-ed* exhibits a double value; that is, it is *ambiguous,* namely, *could*, where *-ed* can either be interpreted as a past form or as a conditional.

# References

Abusch, D., 1990. The Present under Past as a De Re Interpretation. In *Proceedings of WCCFL* (Stanford) 9: 1–12.

Ambrosini, R., 1987. *Tra morfologia e sintassi di lingue classiche*. Giardini, Pisa.

Aronoff, M., 1994. *Morphology by Itself*. MIT Press, Cambridge, Mass.

Bach, E., 1981. On Time, Tense and Aspect: An Essay in English Metaphysics. In R. Cole (ed.), *Radical Pragmatics*. Academic Press, New York.

Bach, E., 1986. The Algebra of Events. In *Linguistics and Philosophy* 9: 5–16.

Belletti, A., 1988. The Case of Unaccusatives. In *Linguistic Inquiry* 19: 1–34.

Belletti, A., 1990. *Generalised Verb Movement*. Rosenberg & Sellier, Turin.

Belletti, A., & L. Rizzi, 1988. Psych-verbs and Theta-Theory. In *Natural Language and Linguistic Theory* 6: 291–352.

Benincà, P., 1994. Agglutination and Inflection. In Northern Italian Dialects. Unpublished manuscript, University of Padua.

Benincà, P., 1995. Complement Clitics in Medioeval Romance: The Tobler-Mussafia Law. In A. Battye, & I. Roberts (eds.), *Clause Structure and Language Change*. Oxford University Press, New York.

Bennett, J., 1988. *Events and Their Names*. Hackett Press, Indianapolis.

Bennett, M. & B.H. Partee, 1972. *Towards the Logic of Tense and Aspect in English*. System Development Corporation, Santa Monica, Ca.

Benthem van, J. F. A. K., 1983. *The Logic of Time. A Model-Theoretic Investigation into the Varieties of Temporal Ontology and Temporal Discourse*. Reidel, Dordrecht.

Bertinetto, P. M., 1986. Intrinsic and Extrinsic Temporal Reference: On Restricting the Notion of Reference Time. In V. Lo Cascio, & C. Vet (eds.), *Temporal Structures in Sentence and Discourse*. Foris, Dordrecht.

Bertinetto, P. M., 1991. Il Verbo. In L. Renzi, & G. Salvi (eds.), *Grande grammatica italiana di consultazione*. Il Mulino, Bologna.

Bianchi, V., M. Squartini, & P. M. Bertinetto, 1995. Perspective Point of Textual Dynamics. In P. M. Bertinetto, V. Bianchi, J. Higginbotham, & M. Squartini (eds.), *Temporal Reference, Aspect and Actionality*. Rosenberg & Sellier, Turin.

Bolinger, D., 1968. Postposed Main Phrases: An English Rule for Romance Subjunctive. In *Canadian Journal of Linguistics* 14: 3–30.

Bonet, E., 1989. Subjects in Catalan. Unpublished manuscript, MIT, Cambridge, Mass.

Bonomi, A., 1995. Aspect and Quantification. In P. M. Bertinetto, V. Bianchi, J. Higginbotham, & M. Squartini (eds.), *Temporal Reference, Aspect and Actionality*. Rosenberg & Sellier, Turin.

Borer, H., 1984. *Parametric Syntax*. Foris, Dordrecht.

Borer, H., 1993. On the Projection of Arguments. In E. Benedicto, & J. Runner (eds.), *Functional Projections*, University of Massachusetts Occasional Paper 17, University of Massachusetts, Amherst, Mass.

Bouchard, D., 1984. Having a Tense Time in Grammar. In *Montreal Working Papers*. Montreal.

Brennan, V., 1993. Root and Epistemic Modal Auxiliary Verbs. *Ph.D. Diss.*, University of Massachussetts, Amherst, Mass.

Brugger, G., & M. D'Angelo, 1994. Aspect and Tense at LF: The Italian Present Perfect. In *Venice Working Papers*, University of Venice.

Burges, J. P., 1984. Basic Tense Logic. In D. Gabbay, & F. Guenthner (eds.), *Handbook of Philosophical Logic*, Vol.2, Reidel, Dordrecht.

Burzio, L., 1986. *Italian Syntax*. Kluwer, Dordrecht.

Campbell, R., 1991. Tense and Agreement in Different Tenses. In *Linguistic Review* 8: 159–183.

Cardinaletti, A., 1994. Subject Positions. In *GenGenP* 1 (2): 64–78.

Cardinaletti, A., 1995. Agreement and Control in Expletive Constructions. Unpublished manuscript, University of Venice.

Cardinaletti, A., & I. Roberts, 1991. Clause Structure and X-second. In W. Chao, & G. Horrocks (eds.), *Levels of Representation*. Foris, Dordrecht.

Carlson, G. N., 1988. Truth-Conditions of Generic Sentences: Two Constrasting Views. In M. Krifka (ed.), *Genericity in Natural Language*, SNS Bericht 88–42. University of Tübingen.

Carlson, G. N., 1989. On the Semantic Composition of English Generic Sentences. In G. Chierchia, B. Partee, & R. Turner (eds.), *Properties, Types and Meaning*, Vol. 2. Kluwer, Dordrecht.

Chierchia, G., 1995a. Individual Level Predicates as Inherent Generics. In G. N. Carlson, & F. J. Pelletier (eds.), *The Generic Book*. University of Chicago Press, Chicago.

Chierchia, G., 1995b. *Dynamics of Meaning. Anaphora, Presupposition, and the Theory of Grammar*. University of Chicago Press, Chicago.

Chisolm, R., 1984. Boundaries as Dependent Particulars. In *Grazer Philosophische Studien* 10: 87–95.

Chisolm, R., 1990. Events without Times. An Essay on Ontology. In *Noûs* 24: 413–428.

Chomsky, N., 1970. Remarks on Nominalization. In R. Jacobs and P. Rosenbaum, (eds.), *Readings in English Transformational Grammar*. Ginn, Waltham, Mass.

Chomsky, N., 1981. *Lectures on Government and Binding*. Foris, Dordrecht.

Chomsky, N., 1986. *The Knowledge of Language*. Praeger, New York.

Chomsky, N., 1991. Some Notes on Economy of Derivation and Representation. In R Freidin (ed.), *Principles and Parameters in Comparative Grammar*. MIT Press, Cambridge, Mass.

Chomsky, N., 1993. A Minimalist Program for Linguistic Theory. In K. Hale, & S. J. Keyser (eds.), *The View from Building 20*, MIT Press, Cambridge, Mass.

Chomsky, N., 1994. Bare Phrase Structure, *MIT Occasional Papers in Linguistics* 5. MIT, Cambridge Mass.

Chomsky, N., 1995. *The Minimalist Program*. MIT Press, Cambridge, Mass.

Cinque, G., 1990. *Types of A'-Dependencies*. MIT Press, Cambridge Mass.

Cinque, G., 1994. Movimento del participio e struttura funzionale della frase. Handout, XX Meeting of Generative Grammar, Padua.

Cinque, G., 1995a. Adverbs and the Universal Hierarchy of Functional Projections. Talk given at the Workshop on Clausal Architecture: Temporal, Aspectual and Verbal Projections. Bergamo.

Cinque, G., 1995b. *Italian Syntax and Universal Grammar*. Cambridge University Press, Cambridge.

Comrie, B., 1976. *Aspect*. Cambridge Universtity Press, Cambridge.

Comrie, B., 1985. *Tense*. Cambridge University Press, Cambridge.

Cresswell, M., & A. von Stechow, 1982. *De Re* Belief Generalized. In *Linguistics and Philosophy* 5(4): 503–535.

Dahl, Ö., 1985. *Tense and Aspect Systems*. Blackwell, Oxford.

Davidson, D., 1967. The Logical Form of Action Sentences. In N. Rescher (ed.), *The Logic of Decision and Action*. University of Pittsburgh Press, Pittsburgh.

Davidson, D., 1970. Events as Particulars. In *Noûs* 4: 25–32.

Declerck, R., 1986. From Reichenbach (1947) to Comrie (1985) and Beyond. In *Lingua* 70: 305–364.

Desclés, J. P., 1989. State, Event, Process and Topology. In *General Linguistics* 29 (3).

Delfitto, D, 1993. How Free is Free Inversion?. Unpublished manuscript, University of Utrecht.

Delfitto, D., & P. M. Bertinetto, 1995a. A Case Study in the Interaction of Aspect and Actionality: the Imperfect in Italian. In P. M. Bertinetto, V. Bianchi, J. Higginbotham, & M. Squartini (eds.), *Temporal Reference, Aspect and Actionality*. Rosenberg & Sellier, Turin.

Delfitto, D., & P. M. Bertinetto, 1995b. Word Order and Quantification over Times. Unpublished manuscript, University of Utrecht & Scuola Normale Superiore, Pisa.

Diesing, M., 1992. *Indefinites*. MIT Press, Cambridge, Mass.

Dikken den, M., 1994. Auxiliaries and Participles. In *Proceedings of NELS 24*. University of Massachusettes, Amherst, Mass.

Does van der, J., 1991. A Generalised Quantifier Logic for Naked Infinitives. In *Linguistics and Philosophy* 14: 241–294.

Dowty, D. R., 1979. *Word Meaning and Montague Grammar. The Semantics of Verbs and Times in Generative Semantics and in Montague's PTQ*. Reidel, Dordrecht.

Dowty, D. R., 1991. Thematic Proto-Roles and Argument Selection. In *Language* 67: 547–619.

Eberle, K., & W. Kasper, 1991. Tense, Aspect and Temporal Structure in French. In H. Kamp (ed.), *Tense and Aspect in English and French*, DYANA deliverable R.2.3.B, University of Edinburgh.

Emonds, J., 1976. *A Transformational Approach to English Syntax*. Academic Press, New York.

Emonds, J., 1978. The Verbal Complex V'-V in French. In *Linguistic Inquiry* 9: 151–175.

Enç, M., 1986. Towards a Referential Analysis of Temporal Expressions. In *Linguistics and Philosophy* 9: 405–426.

Enç, M., 1987. Anchoring Conditions for Tense. In *Linguistic Inquiry* 18: 633-657.

Enç, M., 1991. On the Absence of the Present Tense Morpheme in English. Unpublished manuscript, University of Wisconsin.

Ernout, A., 1953. *Morphologie hystorique du latin*. Klincksieck, Paris.

Ernout, A., & F. Thomas, 1989. *Syntaxe Latine*, Klincksieck, Paris, (first ed., 1951).

Farkas, D. F., 1985. *Intensional Descriptions and the Romance Subjunctive Mood*. Garland, New York.

Farkas, D. F., 1992a. On the Semantics of Subjunctive Complements. In P. Hirschbühler and K. Koerner (eds.), *Romance Languages and Modern Linguistic Theory*. John Benjamins, Amsterdam.

Farkas, D. F., 1992b. Mood in Complement Clause. In I. Kenesei, & C. Pléh (eds.), *Approaches to Hungarian, Vol 4: The Structure of Hungarian*. JATE, Szeged.

Farkas, D. F., & Y. Sugioka, 1983. Restrictive If/When Clauses. In *Linguistics and Philosophy* 6: 225–258.

Fisher. I., 1985. *Latina Dunareana*. Editura Stintifica si Eciclopedica, Bucharest.

Fleischman, S., 1982. *The Future in Language and Thought*. Cambridge University Press, Cambridge.

Friedeman, M. A., 1995. Les Sujets. *Ph.D. Diss.*, University of Geneva.

Galton, A., 1984. *The Logic of Aspect: An Axiomatic Approach*. Clarendon Press, Oxford.

Giannakidou, A., 1994. The Licensing of the (Negative) Polarity Items and the Moderns Greek Subjunctive. Unpublished manuscript, University of Groningen.

Giorgi, A., 1990. *The Italian Anaphoric/Pronominal System*. Unipress, Padua.

Giorgi, A., & F. Pianesi, 1991. Toward a Syntax of Temporal Representations. In *Probus* 2: 187–213.

Graffi, G., 1995. Alcune Riflessioni sugli Imperativi Italiani. Unpublished manuscript, University of Udine.

Graur, A., 1935. Une nouvelle marque de pluriel dans la flexion verbal roumaine. In *Bulletin Linguistique* 3: 178–185.

Guasti, M. T., 1993. *Causative and Perception Verbs*. Rosenberg & Sellier, Turin.

Guasti, M. T., 1994. Acquisition of Italian Interrogatives. Unpublished manuscript, DIPSCO, Milan.

Guasti, M. T., 1995. On the Controversial Status of Romance Interrogatives. Unpublished manuscript, DIPSCO, Milan.

Guéron, J., 1993. Sur la syntaxe du temp. In *Langue Française* 100: 102–122.

Guéron, J., 1995. On the Syntax of Aspect. Talk given at the Workshop on Clausal Architecture: Temporal, Aspectual and Verbal Projections, Bergamo.

Guéron, J., & T. Hoekstra, 1988. T-chains and the Constituent Structure of Auxiliaries. In A. Cardinaletti, G. Cinque, G. Giusti, (eds.), *Constituents Structures*. Foris, Dordrecht.

Hale, K., & S. J. Kayser, 1993. On Argument Structure and the Lexical Expression of Syntactic Relations. In K. Hale, & S. J. Keyser (eds.), *The View from Building 20*. MIT Press, Cambridge, Mass.

Halle, M., 1991. The Russian Declension. Unpublished manuscript, MIT, Cambridge, Mass.

Harris, M., & P. Ramat (eds.), 1987. *Historical Development of Auxiliaries*. Mouton de Gruyter, Berlin.

Heim, I., 1982. The Semantics of Definite and Indefinite Noun Phrases. *Ph.D. Diss.*, University of Massachussetts, Amherst.

Heim, I., 1992. Presupposition Projection and the Semantics of Attitude Verbs. In *Journal of Semantics* 9: 183–221.

Heny, F., 1982. Tense, Aspect and Time Adverbials. Part II. In *Linguistics and Philosophy* 5: 109–154.

Higginbotham, J., 1983. The Logic of Perceptual Reports: An Extensional Alternative to Situation Semantics. In *The Journal of Philosophy* 80: 100–127.

Higginbotham, J., 1985. On Semantics. In *Linguistics Inquiry* 16: 547–593.

Higginbotham, J., 1989. Elucidations of Meaning. In *Linguistics and Philosophy* 12: 465–517.

Higginbotham, J., 1993. Perceptual Reports Revisited, Unpublished manuscript, MIT.

Higginbotham, J., 1994. Events and Aspects. Unpublished manuscript, Somerville College, Oxford.

Higginbotham, J., 1995a. *Sense and Syntax*. Clarendon Press, Oxford.

Higginbotham, J., 1995b. *On the Role of Events in Linguistic Semantics*. Talk given at the Meeting on Facts and Events in the Semantics of Natural Language, Trento.

Hintikka, K. J., 1962. *Knowledge and Belief*. Cornell University Press, Ithaca.

Hoeksema, J., 1984. Categorial Morphology. *Ph.D. Diss.*, University of Groningen.

Hoekstra, E., 1992. On the Parametrization of Functional Projections in CP. Unpublished manuscript, Amsterdam.

Holmberg, A., 1994. Morphological Parameters in Syntax: The Case of Faroese. In *Report 35*, Department of General Linguistics, University of Umeå.

Holmberg, A., & C. Platzack, 1988. On the Role of Inflection in Scandinavian Syntax. In *Working Papers in Scandinavian Syntax 42*.

Hooper, J. B., 1975. On Assertive Predicates. In J. P. Kimball (ed.), *Syntax and Semantics*, Vol. 4. Academic Press, New York.

Hooper, J. B., & T. Terrel, 1974. A Semantically Based Analysis of Mood in Spanish. In *Hispania* 57: 465–497.

Hornstein, N., 1990. *As Time Goes By*. MIT Press, Cambridge, Mass.

Huber, J., 1986 (original ed. 1933). *Grámatica do portugues antigo*. Fundação Calouste Gulbenkian, Lisbon.

Iatridou, S., 1990a. About AGR(P). In *Linguistic Inquiry* 21: 551–577.

Iatridou, S., 1990b. Topics on Conditionals. *Ph.D. Diss.*, MIT, Cambridge, Mass.

Iatridou, S., & D. Embick, 1994. Conditional Inversion. In *Proceedings of NELS 24*, University of Massachussetts, Amherst.

Inclán, S., 1991. Temporal Reference and the Structure of Reference and Event Points. In *Proceedings of ESCOL*, University of Maryland.

Jackendoff, R., 1976. *X-bar Syntax*. MIT Press, Cambridge, Mass.

Jackendoff, R., 1991. Parts and Boundaries. In *Cognition* 41: 47–81.

Jaeggli, O., & K. Safir, 1989. *The Null Subject Parameter*. Kluwer, Dordrecht.

Jespersen, O., 1924. *The Philosophy of Grammar*. Allen & Unwin, London.

Jonas, D., & J. Bobaljik, 1993. Specs for Subjects, the Role of TP in Icelandic. In *MIT Working Papers in Linguistics* 16: 99–148.

Kamp, H., 1968. Tense Logic and the Theory of Linear Order. *Ph.D. Diss.*, UCLA, Los Angeles.

Kamp, H., 1979. Events, Instants and Temporal Reference. In R. Bäuerle, U. Egli, & A. von Stechow (eds.), *Semantics from Different Points of View*. Springer, Berlin.

Kamp, H., 1984. A Theory of Truth and Semantic Representation. In J. Groenendijk, T. Janssen and M. Stokhof (eds.), *Truth, Interpretation and Information*. Foris, Dordrecht.

Kamp, H., & C. Rohrer, 1983. Tense in Texts. In R. Baüerle, C. Schwarze, & A. von Stechow (eds.), *Meaning, Use and Interpretation of Language*. Walter de Gruyter, Berlin.

Kamp, H., & U. Reyle, 1993. *From Discourse to Logic*. Kluwer, Dordrecht.

Kartunnen, L., & S. Peters, 1979. Conventional Implicature. In C. K. Oh, & D. Dinnen (eds.), *Syntax and Semantics 11: Presupposition*. Academic Press, New York.

Katz, G., 1995. States, Events and Representations. Talk given at the Meeting on Facts and Events in the Semantics of Natural Language, Trento.

Kayne, R., 1981. ECP Extensions. In *Linguistic Inquiry* 12: 93–133.

Kayne, R., 1989. Facets of Past Participle Agreement. In P. Benincà (ed.), *Dialectal Variation and the Theory of Grammar*. Foris, Dordrecht.

Kayne, R., 1991. Romance Clitics, Verb Movement and PRO. In *Linguistic Inquiry* 22: 647–686.

Kayne, R., 1993. Toward a Modular Theory of Auxiliary Selection. In *Studia Linguistica* 47: 3–31.

Kayne, R., 1994. *The Antisymmetry of Syntax*. MIT Press, Cambridge, Mass.

Kearns, K. S., 1991. The Semantics of the English Progressive. *Ph.D. Diss.*, MIT, Cambridge, Mass.

Kelley, J., 1955. *General Topology*. Van Nostrand, Princeton.

Kim, J., 1976 Events as Property Exemplifications. In M. Bran, & D. Walton, (eds.) *Action Theory*, Reidel, Dordrecht.

Kiparsky, P., & C. Kiparsky, 1971. Fact. In D. Steinberg, & L. Jakobovits (eds.), *Semantics*. Cambridge University Press, Cambridge.

Klein, W., 1992. The Present Perfect Puzzle. In *Language* 68: 525–552.

Kratzer, A., 1979. Conditional Necessity and Possibility. In R. Bäuerle, U. Egli, & A. von Stechow (eds.), *Semantics from Different Points of View*. Springer, Berlin.

Kratzer, A., 1981. The Notional Category of Modality. In H. J. Hiekmeyer, & H. Rieser (eds.), *Words, Worlds and Contexts: New Approaches to Word Semantics*. Walter de Gruyter, Berlin.

Kratzer, A., 1991a. Modality. In A. von Stechow, & D. Wunderlich (eds.), *Semantik/ Semantics: Ein internationales Handbuch der zeitgenössichen Forschung/An International Handbook of Contemporary Research*. Walter de Gruyter, Berlin.

Kratzer, A., 1991b. The Representation of Focus. In A. von Stechow, & D. Wunderlich (eds.), *Semantik/Semantics: Ein internationales Handbuch der zeitgenössichen Forschung/An International Handbook of Contemporary Research*. Walter de Gruyter, Berlin.

Kratzer, A., 1995. Stage-Level and Individual-Level Predicates. In G. N. Carlson, & F. J. Pelletier (eds.), *The Generic Book*. University of Chicago Press, Chicago.

Krifka, M., 1988. The Relational Theory of Genericity. In M. Krifka (ed.), *Genericity in Natural Language*. SNS Bericht 88–42, University of Tübingen.

Krifka, M., 1989. Nominal Reference, Temporal Constitution and Quantification in Event Domains. In R. Bartsch, J. van Benthem, & P. van Emde Boas (eds.), *Semantics and Contextual Expressions*. Foris, Dordrecht.

Krifka, M., 1990. Polarity Phenomena and Alternative Semantics. In M. Stokhof, & L. Torenvliet (eds.), *Proceedings of the Seventh Amsterdam Colloquium*, ITLI, University of Amsterdam.

Krifka, M., F. J. Pelletier, G. N. Carlson, A. ter Meulen, G. Chierchia, & G. Link, 1995. Genericity: An Introduction. In G. N. Carlson, & F. J. Pelletier (eds.), *The Generic Book*. The University of Chicago Press, Chicago.

Laka, I., 1990. Negation in Syntax: On the Nature of Functional Categories and Projections. *Ph.D. Diss.*, MIT, Cambridge, Mass.

Landman, F., 1989. Group 1. In *Linguistics and Philosophy* 12: 559–605.

Landman, F., 1991. *Structures for Semantics*. Kluwer, Dordrecht.

Landman, F., 1992. The Progressive. In *Natural Language Semantics* 1: 1–32.

Larson, R., 1985. Bare-NP Adverbs. In *Linguistic Inquiry* 16: 595–621.

Larson, R., 1988. On Double Object Constructions. In *Linguistic Inquiry* 19: 335–391.

Larson, R., 1990. Double Object Revisited: Reply to Jackendoff. In *Linguistic Inquiry* 21: 589–632.

Lenci, A., & P. M. Bertinetto, 1995. Aspect, Adverbs and Events: Habituality vs. Perfectivity, talk given at the Meeting on Facts and Events in the Semantics of Natural Language, Trento.

Leuman, M., J. B. Hofman, & A. Szantyr, 1977. *Lateinische Grammatik*, Beck, Munich.

Lewis, D., 1973. *Counterfactuals*. Harvard University Press, Cambridge, Mass.

Lewis, D., 1975. Adverbs of Quantification. In E. L. Keenan (ed.), *Formal Semantics of Natural Language*. Cambridge University Press, Cambridge.

Lewis, D., 1979. Score-Keeping in a Language Game. In R. Bäuerle, U. Egli, & A. von Stechow (eds.), *Semantics from Different Points of View*. Springer, Berlin.

Lindsay, W. M., 1984. *Die Lateinische Sprache*. Georg Olms Verlag, Hildesheim (original edition, 1897, Leipzig).

Link, G., 1983. The Logical Analysis of Plurals and Mass Terms. In R. Bäuerle, C. Schwarze, & A. von Stechow (eds.), *Meaning, Use and Interpretation of Language*. Walter de Gruyter, Berlin.

Link, G., 1987. Algebraic Semantics for Event Structures. In J. Groenendijk, M. Stokhof, & F. Veltman (eds.), *Proceedings of the Sixth Amsterdam Colloquium*, ITLI, University of Amsterdam.

Lombard, A., 1974. *La langue roumaine*. Klincksieck, Paris.

Longobardi, G., 1983. *Connectedness*, complementi circostanziali e soggiacenza. In *Rivista di Grammatica Generativa* 5: 141–185.

Longobardi, G., 1994. Reference and Proper Names: A Theory of N-movement in Syntax and Logical Form. In *Linguistic Inquiry* 25: 609–666.

Madeira, A., 1992. On Clitic Placement in European Portuguese. In H. van de Koot (ed.), *UCL Working Papers in Linguistics*, University College, London.

Manzini, M. R., 1994a. The Subjunctive. In *Paris VIII Working Papers*, Vol. 1, University of Paris VIII.

Manzini, M. R., 1994b. Triggers for Verb-Second: Germanic and Romance. In *The Linguistic Review*. 11: 299–314.

Marouzeau, J., 1953. *L'ordre des mots en latin*. Belles Lettres, Paris.

McCawley, J. D., 1993. *Everything that Linguists Have Always Wanted to Know about Logic*. Chicago University Press.

McCoard, R. W., 1978. *The English Perfect: Tense Choice and Pragmatic Inference*. North-Holland Publishing Company, Amsterdam.

Melvold, J., 1991. Factivity and Definiteness. In L. L. S. Cheng, & H. Demirdash (eds.), *More Papers on Wh-Movement*, MIT Working Papers in Linguistics 15, MIT, Cambridge, Mass.

Moens, M., 1987. Tense, Aspect and Temporal Reference. *Ph.D. Diss.*, University of Edinburgh.

Moens, M., & M. Steadman, 1987. Temporal Ontology in Natural Language. In *Proceedings of the 25th Annual Meeting of the Association for Computational Linguistics*, Stanford University Press.

Moltmann, F., 1997. *Parts and Wholes in Semantics*. Oxford University Press, New York.

Montague, R., 1974. *Formal Philosophy*. In R. H. Thomason, (ed.), *Selected Papers by Richard Montague*. Yale University Press, New York.

Moritz, L., 1989. Aperçu de la syntaxe de la négation en français et en anglais. *Memoire de License*, University of Geneva.

Moro, A., 1988. Per una teoria unificata delle frasi copulari. In *Rivista di Grammatica Generativa* 13: 81–110.

Moro, A., 1992. Analisi sintattica di un primitivo lessicale: il caso degli inaccusativi. Talk given at the XVIII Meeting of Generative Grammar, Ferrara.

Motapanyane, V., 1991. Theoretical Implications of Complementation in Rumanian. *Ph.D. Diss.*, University of Geneva.

Mourelatos, A. P. D., 1978. Events, Processes and States. In *Linguistics and Philosophy* 2: 415–434.

Ouhalla, J., 1988. The Syntax of Head Movement: A Study of Berber. *Ph.D. Diss.*, University College, London.

Ouhalla, J., 1991. *Functional Categories and Parametric Variation*. Routledge, London.

Palmer, F. R., 1986. *Mood and Modality*. Cambridge University Press, Cambridge.

Palmer, L. R., 1977. *La lingua latina*. Einaudi, Turin.

Parsons, T., 1989. The Progressive in English: Events, States and Processes. In *Linguistics and Philosophy* 12: 213–241.

Parsons, T., 1990. *Events in the Semantics of English*. MIT Press, Cambridge, Mass.

Partee, B., 1973. Some Structural Analogies between Tenses and Pronouns in English. In *Journal of Philosophy* 70: 601–609.

Partee, B., 1984. Nominal and Temporal Anaphora. In *Linguistics and Philosophy* 7: 243–286.

Partee, B., 1995. Quantificational Structures and Compositionality. In E. Bach, E. Jelinek, A. Kratzer, & B. Partee (eds.), *Quantification in Natural Languages*. Kluwer, Dordrecht.

Pesetsky, D., 1987. Wh-in-situ: Movement and Unselective Binding. In E. Reuland, & A. ter Meulen (eds.), *The Representation of (In)definetness*. MIT Press, Cambridge Mass.

Peterson, P., 1989. Complex Events. In *Pacific Philosophical Quarterly* 70: 19–41.

Pianesi, F., & A. Varzi, 1996a. Events, Topology and Temporal Relations. In *The Monist* 79: 89–116.

Pianesi, F., & A. Varzi, 1996b. Refining Temporal Reference in Event Structures. In *Notre Dame Journal of Formal Logic* 37: 71–83.

Pisani, V., 1971. *Glottologia indoeuropea*. Rosenberg & Sellier, Turin.

Pisani, V., 1974. *Grammatica latina storica e comparativa*. Rosenberg & Sellier, Turin.

Platzack, C., & A. Holmberg, 1989. The Role of AGR and Finiteness. In *Working Papers in Scandinavian Syntax* 43: 51–76.

Platzack, C., & I. Rosengren, 1994. On the Subject of Imperatives. In *Sprache und Pragmatik. Arbeitsberichte*, 34.

Poletto, C., 1992. The Aspect Projection: An Analysis of the "Passé surcomposé". In E. Fava (ed.), *Proceedings of the XVII Meeting of Generative Grammar*. Rosenberg & Sellier, Turin.

Poletto, C., 1995. Complementizer Deletion and Verb Movement in Italian. In *Working Papers in Linguistics* University of Venice.

Pollock, J. Y., 1989. Verb Movements, Universal Grammar and the Structure of IP. In *Linguistic Inquiry* 20: 365–424.

Pollock, J. Y., 1994. Talk given at Going Romance VIII, Utrecht.

Portner, P., 1994. The Semantics of Mood, Complementation and Conversational Force. Unpublished manuscript, Georgetown University, Washington.

Praetere de, I., 1995. On the Necessity of Distinguishing between (Un)boundedness and (A)telicity. In *Linguistics and Philosophy* 18: 1–19.

Prior, A., 1967. *Past, Present and Future*. Oxford University Press, Oxford.

Raposo, E., 1987. Case Theory and Infl-to-Comp: The Inflected Infinitive in European Portuguese. In *Linguistic Inquiry* 18: 85–109.

Raposo, E., & J. Uriagereka, 1995. Two Types of Small Clauses (Towards a Syntax of Theme/ Rheme Relations). In A. Cardinaletti, & M. T. Guasti (eds.), *Syntax and Semantics 28. Small Clauses*. Academic Press, New York.

Reichenbach, H., 1947. *Elements of Symbolic Logic*. MacMillan, New York.

Richards, B., 1982. Tense, Aspect and Time Adverbials. Part I. In *Linguistics and Philosophy* 5: 59–107.

Rivero, M. L., 1990. The Location of Active Voice in Albanian and Modern Greek. In *Linguistic Inquiry* 21: 135–146.

Rizzi, L., 1982. *Issues in Italian Syntax*. Foris, Dordrecht.

Rizzi, L., 1986. Null Object in Italian and the Theory of *pro*. In *Linguistic Inquiry* 17: 501–557.

Rizzi, L., 1990. *Relativized Minimality*. MIT Press, Cambridge, Mass.

Rizzi, L., 1991. Residual Verb Second and the Wh-Criterion. In *Technical Reports in Formal and Computational Linguistics*, Vol. 2. Faculty of Letters, University of Geneva.

Rizzi, L., 1992. Direct Perception, Government and Thematic Sharing. In *GenGenP 0*, University of Geneva.

Rizzi, L., & I. Roberts, 1989. Complex Inversion in French. In *Probus* 1: 1–30.

Roberts, C., 1989. Modal Subordination and Pronominal Anaphora in Discourse. In *Linguistics and Philosophy* 12: 683–721.

Roberts, I., 1992. A Formal Account of Grammaticalisation in the History of Romance Future. In *Folia Linguistica Historica* 13: 219–258.

Roberts, I., 1993. *Verbs and Diachronic Syntax*. Kluwer, Dordrecht.

Rohlfs, G., 1954. *Grammatica storica della lingua italiana e dei suoi dialetti*. Einaudi, Turin.

Rohrbacher, B. W., 1994. The Germanic VO Languages and the Full Paradigm: A Theory of V to I Raising. *Ph.D. Diss.*, University of Massachusetts, Amherst.

Rooths, M., 1985. Association with Focus. *Ph.D. Diss.*, University of Massachusetts, Amherst.

Rooths, M., 1992. A Theory of Focus Interpretation. In *Natural Language Semantics* 1: 75–116.

Rosetti, A., 1969. *Istoria limbii române*. In Ac. Rep. Soc. Romania, Vol.II.

Roussou, A., 1994. The Syntax of Complementizers. *Ph.D. Diss.*, University College, London.

Runner, J., 1993. A Specific Role for AGR. In E. Benedicto, & J. Runner (eds.), *Functional Projections*. Occasional Paper 17, University of Massachusetts, Amherst, Mass.

Russell, B., 1914. *Our Knowledge of the External World*. Allen & Unwin, London.

Russell, B., 1936. On Order in Time. In *Proceedings of the Cambridge Philosophical Society* 32: 216–228.

Safarewicz, J., 1969. *Historische Lateinische Grammatik*. Max Niemeyer, Halle.

Samek-Lodovici, V., 1994. Structural Focusing and Subject Inversion in Italian. Unpublished manuscript, Rutgers University.

Schmitt, C., 1991. *Ser* and *Estar*: A Matter of Aspect. In *Proceedings of NELS 22*, University of Massachusetts, Amherst.

Schubert, L. K., & F. J. Pelletier, 1987. Problems in the Representation of the Logical Form of Generics, Plurals and Mass Nouns. In E. Le Pore (ed.), *New Directions in Semantics*. Academic Press, London.

Schubert, L. K., & F. J. Pelletier, 1989. Generically Speaking; Or, Using Discourse Representation Theory to Interpret Generics. In G. Chierchia, B. Partee, & R. Turner (eds.), *Properties, Types and Meaning*, vol. 2: *Semantic Issues*. Kluwer, Dordrecht.

Scorretti, M., 1991. Complementizers in Italian and Romance, *Ph.D. Diss.*, University of Amsterdam.

Simons, P., 1987. *Parts: A Study in Ontology*. Clarendon, Oxford.

Smith, C. S., 1991. *The Paramter of Aspect*. Kluwer, Dordrecht.

Solà, J., 1992. Agreement and Subjects. *Ph.D. Diss.*, University of Barcellona.

Souza de, P., 1872. *Grammaire portugaise raisonnée et simplifiée*, Paris.

Stalnaker, R. C., 1978. Assertions. In P. Cole (ed.), *Pragmatics, Syntax and Semantics*, vol. 9, Academic Press, New York.

Stowell, T., 1981. Origins of Phrase Structure. *Ph.D. Diss.*, MIT, Cambridge, Mass.

Stowell, T., 1992. Syntax of Tense. Unpublished manuscript, UCLA.

Stroyk, T., 1990. Adverbs as V-Sisters. In *Linguistic Inquiry* 21: 654–661.

Stump, G., 1985. *The Semantic Variability of Absolute Constructions*. Reidel, Dordrecht.

Suñer, M., 1994. V-movements and the Licensing of Agreement Wh-Phrase in Spanish. In *Natural Language and Linguistic Theory* 12: 335–372.

Taylor, B., 1977. Tense and Continuity. In *Linguistics and Philosophy* 1: 199–220.

Thomas, L., & N. Itzkowitz, 1967. *Elementary Turkish*. Dover, London.

Thráinsson, H., 1990. A Semantic Reflexive in Icelandic. In J. Mailing, & A. Zaenen (eds.), *Syntax and Semantics 24. Modern Icelandic Syntax*. Academic Press, New York.

Thráinsson, H., 1994. On the (Non-)Universality of Functional Categories. Unpublished manuscript, Harvard University.

Tomaselli, A., 1989. La sintassi del verbo finito nelle lingue germaniche. *Ph.D. Diss.*, University of Pavia.

Tsoulas, G., 1994. Indefinite Clauses: Some Notes on the Syntax and Semantics of Subjunctives and Infinitives. In *Proceedings of WCCFL XIII*, University of California, San Diego.

Turano, G., 1995. *Dipendenze sintattiche in Albanese*. Unipress, Padua.

Uriagereka, J., 1994. Aspects of Clitic Placement in Western Romance. In *Linguistic Inquiry* 26: 79–123.

Väänänen, V., 1982. *Introduzione al latino volgare*. Pàtron, Bologna.

Vázquez Cuesta, P., & M. A. Mendes da Luz, 1989. *Grámatica da língua portuguesa*. Edições 70, Lisbon.

Vendler, Z., 1967. *Linguistics in Philosophy*. Cornell University Press. Ithaca.

Verkuyl, H. J., 1993. *A Theory of Aspectuality: The interaction between temporal and atemporal structure*. Cambridge University Press.

Vet, C., 1983. From Tense to Modality. Unpublished manuscript, University of Gröningen.

Vikner, S., 1985. Reichenbach Revisited: One, Two or Three Temporal Relations? *Acta Linguistica Hafniensia* 19: 81–98.

Vikner, S., 1994. Finite Verb in Scandinavian Embedded Clauses. In D. Lightfoot, & N. Hornstein (eds.), *Verb Movement*. Cambridge University Press.

Vikner, S., 1995. *Verb Movement and Expletive Subjects in the Germanic Languages*. Oxford University Press, New York.

Vineis, E., 1993. Latino. In: A. Giacalone, & P. Ramat (eds.), *Le lingue indoeuropee*. Il Mulino, Bologna.

Vlach, F., 1981. The Semantics of the Progressive. In P. J. Tedeschi and A. Zaenen (eds.), *Syntax and Semantics 14; Tense and Aspect*. Academic Press, New York.

Vlach, F., 1993. Temporal Adverbials, Tenses and the Perfect. In *Linguistics and Philosophy* 16: 231–283.

Wexler, K., & R. Manzini, 1988. Parameters and Learnability in Binding Theory. In T. Roeper, & E. Williams (eds.), *Parameter Setting*. Reidel, Dordrecht.

Whitehead, A. N., 1929. *Process and Reality. An Essay in Cosmology* Macmillan, New York.

Zagona, K., 1988. *Verb Phrase Syntax: A Parametric Study of English and Spanish*. Kluwer, Dordrecht.

Zanuttini, R., 1991. Syntactic Properties of Sentential Negation. A Comparative Study of Romance Languages. *Ph.D. Diss.*, University of Pennsylvania.

Zanuttini, R., 1995. Negative Imperatives. Unpublished manuscript, Georgetown University, Washington, D.C.

# Author Index

# Subject Index

308